MIGRATION FROM FINLAND TO NORTH AMERICA IN THE YEARS BETWEEN THE UNITED STATES CIVIL WAR AND THE FIRST WORLD WAR

MIGRATION FROM FINLAND TO NORTH AMERICA IN THE YEARS BETWEEN THE UNITED STATES CIVIL WAR AND THE FIRST WORLD WAR

BY

REINO KERO

*To be presented, with the permission of the Faculty of Humanities
of the University of Turku, for public criticism in
Auditorium I, at 12 noon on March 16, 1974*

VAMMALA 1974

The expenses of the reprint have been covered by the Huhtamäki Company.

Institute of General History
University of Turku

ISBN 951-641-124-X

Vammala 1974. Vammalan Kirjapaino Oy

PREFACE

This study was written at the suggestion of my major professor, Dr. Vilho Niitemaa. During the last ten years he has followed every phase of my research and spared nothing to facilitate its completion. Many errors and oversimplications were removed through his constructive criticism.

I am also indebted to Dr. Eino Jutikkala, the academian, professor of the University of Helsinki, who examined the dissertation in manuscript and offered constructive suggestions and criticism. His help has been of great value.

I also want to thank Dr. John I. Kolehmainen of Tiffin, Ohio, and my other friends in America and in Scandinavian countries. Thanks also go to the members of the post-graduate seminary of general history at the University of Turku. I am very grateful for the help that I have had from them.

I should like to express my gratitude also to the staffs of Library of the University of Turku, Turku Provincial Archives, National Archives of Finland, and to Mr. George Hummasti, who translated the manuscript, to Mr. Jorma Pätynen, who drew the maps and figures, and to Mr. Matti Rantanen, who took care of the ADP handling of the statistical material used in my dissertation.

My research work has been made possible by several grants. The most important of these were those received from Valtion Humanistinen Toimikunta. Grants were also received from Suomi-Seura, Suomen Kulttuurirahaston Satakunnan rahasto, Emil Aaltosen Säätiö, Jänteren rahasto, University of Turku, and ASLA-Fulbright Fund and were of great help. The grant from the last-mentioned made it possible to do research work in the United States.

And last but not least thanks go to my wife, Maija-Leena, my sons Jussi and Markku, and my parents Eeva and Toivo Kero. It is largely due to their understanding that this book has been completed.

Turku, February, 1974

Reino Kero

CONTEST

Introduction

1. The present state of research

In general, the term great emigration, has been taken to mean the stream of emigrants that left Europe in the nineteenth and early twentieth centuries primarily for countries overseas. The major part of this stream flowed to North America, but South America, Australia, New Zealand, South Africa, and Siberia also received their share of it. Some emigrants returned to Europe, but most of them remained in America or in one of these other countries that received immigrants. In their new homelands, the immigrants preserved some cultural traits of the lands from which they departed, but also adopted characteristics of their new environment, thus giving birth to numerous immigrant cultures.

The departure of emigrants interested the newspapers, public officials, and researchers in the countries from which they left. They pondered the question of why millions and millions of people left their homelands and moved to countries overseas. In the overseas lands, the emigrants certainly received just as much attention, although as immigrants, they were examined from a different angle. There, attention has been directed above all to how rapidly or slowly immigrants adapted themselves to the demands of their new environment, and to what sorts of roles they played in the economic life of their new homelands.[1]

Articles on Finnish emigration began to appear in the newspapers at the end of the 1860's. Public officials took an interest in it already in the following decade.[2] Literature dealing with emigration also got its start in this decade.[3] From the beginning, those writing about emigration considered

---

[1] On attitudes towards emigration in different countries see Kälvemark 1972, pp. 15—29. On attitudes towards Finnish emigration see, for example, Tarkkanen 1896, passim; Alanen 1910, passim; Engelberg 1944, pp. 61—110; Kolehmainen—Hill 1951, pp. 7—12; Hoglund 1960, pp. 10—13; Toivonen 1963, pp. 211—244.

[2] On the interest felt by the authorities towards emigration in the 1870's see Kero 1969 II, pp. 77—80; Kero 1967, p. 33.

[3] The first book concerning emigration appeared in 1872. Its author was L. L.

2

it to be at least in part an economic question. Most, however, were unwilling to admit that emigration might be the only means by which some cottager could improve his standard of living or even survive at all. They saw the matter primarily from the standpoint of the state which considered migration from the country to be a heavy economic loss. And since the idea of nationalism was a prevailing idea of this age, emigration was also frequently examined from a patriotic standpoint and seen as treason to one's fatherland. To a large extent, writings concerning emigration preserved this tone until at least the end of the nineteenth century.

Gradually studies directed at the history of emigration also began to appear. The first appraisal of Finnish emigration was a fairly objective study written by Akseli Järnefelt (Rauanheimo). This work, *Suomalaiset Amerikassa* (The Finns in America),[4] which appeared in 1899, and the birth of the official emigration statistics around 1900 [5] were definite signs that emigration was beginning to be seen principally as an economic, rather than a moral, phenomenon. In O. K. Kilpi's 1917 study, *Suomen siirtolaisuus ja 19. vuosisadan kansantalous* (Finnish Emigration and the 19th Century National Economy),[6] the literature of that period reached its peak.

Between the two world wars, abundant literature dealing with emigration was published in Finland.[7] But none of the monographs appearing during this period can be included among the better literature on Finnish emigration. On the other hand, Rafael Engelberg's *Suomi ja Amerikan Suomalaiset* (Finland and the American Finns)[8] published in 1944, and Anna-Leena Toivonen's dissertation *Etelä-Pohjanmaan valtamerentakainen siirtolaisuus, 1867—1930* (Emigration Overseas from Southern Ostrobothnia in 1867—1930),[9] prepared in 1963 certainly belong among the best literature in their field.

The pioneer of research into Finnish emigration done in overseas coun-

Laurén and it appeared in both Swedish and Finnish. Its title was *Warning, mot utflyttning från fosterlandet* or *Waroitus, muuttamisesta pois isänmaasta* (A warning against emigrating from the fatherland).

4 Järnefelt 1899.

5 Passport officials in Oulu and Vaasa Provinces, according to instructions they had received, began drawing up lists of persons emigrating as early as in 1883—84. In the rest of the country the gathering of this information began in 1893. It is only from 1900, however, that those issuing passports began keeping, according to new instructions, detailed lists of individuals receiving passports. On the basis of these lists, the Central Bureau of Statistics in 1905 published the first part of the official emigration statistics.

6 Kilpi 1917.

7 For example, Teijula 1921; Näse 1922.

8 Engelberg 1944.

9 Toivonen 1963.

tries was A l e x L e i n o n e n, who published in 1876 an excellent series of articles dealing with the birth of Finnish settlements in America.[10] Forty years passed after the publication of these articles before another comparable Finnish-American study appeared. In 1919—26, S a l o m o n I l m o n e n published his three-part *Amerikan suomalaisten historia* (A History of the American Finns)[11] and in 1930—31 his two-part *Amerikan suomalaisten sivistyshistoria* (A Cultural History of the American Finns).[12] J o h n W a r- g e l i n's *The Americanization of the Finns* from 1924 [13] and F. J. S y r- j ä l ä's *Historia-aiheita Ameriikan suomalaisesta työväenliikkeestä* (Histori- cal Themes of the Finnish-American Workingmen's Movement) written in the middle of the 1920's [14] are also noteworthy achievements in the field of Finnish-American historical literature. C a r l J. S i l f v e r s t e n's *Finlands- svenskarna i Amerika* (Swedish-speaking Finns in America), which appeared in 1931,[15] was also one of the significant works of this period.

Finnish-American historical writing after the Second World War has produced some rather important achievements. Among the better publica- tions of the first generation of immigrants have been E l i s S u l k a n e n's *Amerikan suomalaisen työväenliikkeen historia* (A History of the Finnish- American Workingmen's Movement) from 1951 [16] and A r m a s K. E. H o l- m i o's *Michiganin suomalaisten historia* (A History of the Finns in Michigan) from 1967.[17] The second-generation students of emigration, J o h n I. K o l e h- m a i n e n and A. W i l l i a m H o g l u n d, have earned credit partly as researchers, and partly for making the results of the research in the history of Finnish emigration known in English.[18]

Although historical literature on Finnish emigration has its »classics», research in this field has generally been of poor quality and the number of research studies written has been rather small compared to some other areas of historical study. In part this undoubtedly results from the state of sources

---

[10] The series of articles appeared in the *Oulun Wiikko-Sanomia*, May 27, June 3, 17, 23, July 8, August 12 and 19 under the title *Suomalaiset Amerikassa* (Finns in America).

[11] I l m o n e n 1919, I l m o n e n 1923 and I l m o n e n 1926.

[12] I l m o n e n 1930 and I l m o n e n 1931.

[13] W a r g e l i n 1924.

[14] S y r j ä l ä 1925.

[15] S i l f v e r s t e n 1931.

[16] S u l k a n e n 1951.

[17] H o l m i o 1967.

[18] The most important studies by J o h n I. K o l e h m a i n e n are a bibliog- raphy of Finnish-American literature, (*The Finns in America. A Bibliographical Guide to their History*), and the history of the Raivaaja (*Sow the Golden Seed. A History of the Fitchburg (Massachusetts) Finnish-American Newspaper. Raivaaja (the Pioneer) 1905—1955*). A. W i l l i a m H o g l u n d's most important work is *Finnish Immigrants in America 1880—1920*.

for emigration history. On the one hand, researchers have so much material available to explain some questions that a »problem of plenty» prevails, and on the other, so few source materials are available for some research problems that no decently documented conclusions can be made.

This study will attempt to center on those problems in Finnish emigration that either have been dealt with very sparingly in research to the present or about which untenable conclusions have been made. Special attention will be paid to the starting process of emigration, to determining the numbers of emigrants, to fluctuations in emigration, and to the composition of emigration. An attempt will also be made to examine more carefully than has been done in previous studies of emigration history published in Finland, how factors outside Finland, e.g. American economic trends, political occurrences, living conditions of emigrants in America, and the competition between transatlantic shipping companies influenced Finnish emigration. We will attempt to look at Finnish emigration as a part of the general migration movement from Europe directed primarily to America. The causes of emigration, on the other hand, will not be stressed, and the phase of emigrant life transpiring in overseas lands will hardly be considered at all. The causes of emigration will not be dealt with extensively because the existing studies explain fairly well why emigration in general occurred and why Finnish emigration in particular centered rather definitely in a given geographical area. The elements of emigrant life in America form such a broad field of study that they deserve to be dealt with more extensively in a special study.

The time period to be studied extends from the Civil War in the United States to the beginning of World War I. Before the outbreak of the American Civil War Finnish migration to America was primarily an immigration of sailors. In 1866, however, emigration got a start at least in the Tornio River Valley and in the area around Kokkola among the ordinary population of the countryside; farmers, crofters, and landless rural laborers. The termination date of this study has been chosen as the outbreak of the First World War, which marked the almost complete cessation of Finnish emigration to America. The statistics used in this study extend to the end of 1914, which merely means that a handful of emigrants leaving after the outbreak of the war are included.

In America, the period under study marked the closing phase of »the winning of the West», but at the same time the United States was also becoming an important industrial country. Since the Finnish migration did not reach its peak until the opening years of the twentieth century, the Finns played only a very modest part in »the winning of the West.» The majority of Finnish immigrants placed themselves in the service of the rapidly growing industries of the United States.

In Finland the beginning of the period of study chances to occur simultaneously with the difficult famine years of the 1860's. If the famine years had any influence on the beginning of emigration, however, it was only indirect.[19] Also, the period of heavy emigration occurred in Finland during the phase when industrial expansion was beginning to influence social development. The rate of industrialization in Finland, however, was much slower than in America. Nonetheless, one result of the growth of industry in Finland was the acceleration of internal migration. And since educational institutions were rapidly developing at the same time, the period of heavy emigration occurred at the very time that the static society was disappearing, when advances and declines from one social class to another were beginning to increase. The period of heavy emigration occurred in Finland also at the same time that many social movements such as the temperance and workers' movements were appearing.

2. The source materials for emigration history

Quantitative information on Finnish emigration has generally been based on the official emigration statistics prepared by the Central Bureau of Statistics from passport lists. These cover Vaasa Province from 1883, Oulu Province from 1884, and the entire country from 1893. The reliability of the statistics collected by the Central Bureau of Statistics will be discussed later in connection with the particular purposes for which they are used. In general the possibilities offered by the official emigration statistics for research work have not been exploited very energetically.

As stated above, the official emigration statistics were based on passport lists. The year 1893 was an important turning point as far as these passport lists are concerned: beginning with this year, all passport lists have been preserved at least in the form of copies prepared for the Central Bureau of Statistics. Most of the lists have also been preserved in the original. On the other hand, some of the passport lists older than 1893 have disappeared. An inventory of passport lists for the period 1865—92 made at the Institute of General History at the University of Turku (IGHUT) has found the following:[1]

[19] Compare J ä r n e f e l t 1899, pp. 21—22; K o l e h m a i n e n — H i l l 1951, pp. 17—18; W a s a s t j e r n a 1957, pp. 43—44. On the influence of the famine years on emigration from Sweden see C a r l s s o n 1967, p. 123. C a r l s s o n says that in Sweden the years of famine most clearly created a mass phenomenon out of emigration in those areas where emigration had already been something of a tradition before the years of famine.

[1] E s a V a i n i o, Vuosien 1865—1892 ulkomaanpassiluetteloiden arvo valtamertentakaisen siirtolaisuuden tutkimuksessa. Unpublished manuscript at the IGHUT.

Passport authority	Existing	Lacking
Passport lists of the Uusimaa provincial government	1865—92	—
»　　»　　»　　» Turku and Pori　　»	1865—92	
»　　»　　»　　» Häme　　»	1865—82	1883—85
	1886—92	
»　　»　　»　　» Viipuri　　»	1865—85	1886—92
»　　»　　»　　» Mikkeli　　»	1883—92	1865—82
»　　»　　»　　» Kuopio　　»	1865—92	—
»　　»　　»　　» Vaasa　　»	1865—92	—
»　　»　　»　　» Oulu　　»	1865—92	—
»　　»　　»　　» Hanko city administration	1877—78	1865—76
	1880—92	1879
»　　»　　»　　» Mariehamn　　»	1882—92	1865—81
»　　»　　»　　» Rauma　　»	1865—77	1878
	1879	1880—92
»　　»　　»　　» Uusikaupunki　　»	1865—81	1882—87
	1888—92	
»　　»　　»　　» Pori　　»	1885—87	1865—84
	1890—92	1888—89
»　　»　　»　　» Kristiinankaupunki　　»	1865—70	1871—79
	1880—92	
»　　»　　»　　» Kaskinen　　»	1874—92	1865—73
»　　»　　»　　» Kokkola　　»	1874—92	1865—73
»　　»　　»　　» Pietarsaari　　»	1865—92	—
»　　»　　»　　» Uusikaarlepyy　　»	1871—74	1875—77
	1878—92	
»　　»　　»　　» Jyväskylä　　»	1868, 1876	1865—67
	1879—92	1869—75
		1877—78
»　　»　　»　　» Raahe　　»	1865—92	—
»　　»　　»　　» Kokkola bailiff (*nimismies*)	1885—92 [2]	—
»　　»　　»　　» sheriff (*kruununvouti*) of the Åland Islands	1865—92	—

The number of passports issued by some passport authorities, such as the Rauma city administration, were so few before 1893 that the loss of these lists is not of great significance. However, a larger gap is caused by the lack of the lists of the city administrations of Kristiinankaupunki and Pori. But generally speaking, we may say that the passport materials offer an excellent basic source for the study of emigration history in Finland.

In the best cases, the passport lists include the passport owner's name, occupation, estate, marital status, the date his passport was issued, country of destination, the period for which his passport is in force, the fees he paid

---

[2] It is probable that the bailiff of Kokkola did not issue passports before the year 1885.

to get his passport, date of birth, place of departure from the country, the number of dependents left at home and his position in the family. The reliability of these entries will be discussed later at those points where each of them is used.

Finnish studies of emigration history have not to date used passenger lists at all. Such lists covering the years 1891—96 and 1899—1914 can be found in the archives of the Finland Steamship Company. The archives of Swedish and Norwegian police departments contain almost similar lists that agents who sold tickets to emigrants turned in to the authorities of the ports from which emigrants departed. The most important of these, the passenger lists of the Gothenburg, Malmö, Stockholm and Trondheim police departments, have been used in this study.[3]

From the passenger lists of the Finland Steamship Company we may discover, among other things, the emigrant's name, his age, knowledge of whether he travelled with a ticket bought in Finland or in America, the shipping line used, the names of the ships on which he travelled from Hanko to England and from England to the country overseas, his destination and the state or province in which it was located, and in the case of prepaid tickets,[4] the agent selling the ticket. The passenger lists in the archives of the Swedish and Norwegian police departments show the emigrant's name, his homeland (also home parish for Swedes and Norwegians), the place and state (or province) of destination, the agent handling the emigrant, the ship on which he travelled from Sweden (or Norway), and its destination and date of departure. The reliability of the information received from these passenger lists will be examined later in different connections.

The archives of Finnish local churches have been employed relatively rarely in studies up to this point. But the parish registers are especially rich in information on the departure and return of emigrants. Employing all these archives would be extremely toilsome because of the large number of parishes, but with their aid we may rather easily map out the strength and structure of emigration from those rather limited areas where passports were not generally used or where the passport lists have disappeared. The precision of the entries in the parish registers varies greatly from parish to parish. In the registers of some parishes the emigrant is described simply with the entry »in America», while in some the date of departure is listed to the day. In uncertain cases, the date of departure can be determined with a certain amount of reliability from records concerning attendance at commu-

---

[3] A rather small number of lists could probably also be found in Denmark and Germany. However, their significance would most likely be very minor. On the reliability of passenger lists of the Swedish police departments see pp. 24—28 below.

[4] On prepaid tickets see pp. 174—195 below.

8

nion. In some parishes there exists also the so-called American book, or the register of parishioners away from home. The value of American books are lessened, however, by the fact that in most cases parishes started keeping the American book only after 1900, for which reason the entries in them made retroactively concerning the oldest emigration are especially untrustworthy.

In general quantitative information on emigration must be based on official emigration statistics, on passport and passenger lists, and on the main registers and emigrant registers of parishes. To a certain extent information from which statistics can be compiled is obtainable also from the archives of Finnish-American parishes, several of which contain carefully kept membership lists. It is also possible to obtain some information about their members from the archives of Finnish-American temperance and working-men's societies. The use of Finnish-American archival material has been made appreciably easier by the fact that a large part of these materials have been microfilmed through the initiative of the IGHUT.

The newspaper is an especially valuable source in emigration history. Papers edited in Finland contain a rich amount of letters from America, editorials concerning emigration, advertisements of emigration agents, and various items about emigration. There are two valuable types of source material in Finnish-American newspapers; first, the tens of thousands of local letters published in them and, second, the death notices that normally included abundant information on the life of the immigrant.

In the 1960's it was still quite easy to gather information by interviewing emigrants and former emigrants. Thus the author interviewed for this study a total of 254 persons in 1964 and 1966—67, of which the majority were interviewed in America and a smaller portion in northern Satakunta. These latter were emigrants who had returned to Finland. When emigration that occurred before the First World War is in question, however, it is now beginning to be quite difficult to find people left to interview.

In addition, a great number of questionnaires are available at the IGHUT from which it is possible to obtain personal information on both emigrants who remained in America and those who have returned to Finland. The American letters collected by this institute also provide a valuable source material for certain research problems.

Generally speaking, we may say that researchers in emigration history have a very large body of source material at hand, a large part of which can be worked up as statistics. Passport lists compose the core of these source materials, but the information obtained from them can be augmented and controlled with the aid of other sources.

3. The application of Automatic Data Processing (ADP) techniques to the study of emigration history

Since the study of emigration history is to a great extent built upon statistical material and interpretations of it, this area of research demands highly developed statistical methods. For this reason the employment of ADP techniques is almost a necessity in the investigation of certain problems. Three of the most important sources for emigration history, the passport lists, the passenger lists of the Finland Steamship Company and the passenger lists of the Swedish and Norwegian police departments, are well suited for ADP handling, because they list systematically certain important facts about emigrants.

If we want to treat the information from these lists with an ADP method in such a manner that each punchcard contains information from only one of these sources, the punching of information on the cards can be performed quite rapidly. But if information from both the passport and passenger lists is punched on the same card, the work is appreciably slower, since information on each emigrant taken from one source must be matched with corresponding information from the other source.

Information on emigrants from 1873, 1882, and 1905 has been collected by the IGHUT for this study. All these years were peak years in emigration and each represent a different phase in Finnish emigration. Emigration for 1873 represents the phase when emigration had gained a foothold on a few coastal areas. The year 1882 represents the phase when emigration already had established a firm foothold in most communes of Oulu and Vaasa Provinces and was in its beginning stage in northern Satakunta and in the Aland Islands. In 1905 emigration was at its broadest and occurred from almost the entire country.

Information about each emigrant has been punched on a single card, in which case information from both the passport and the passenger lists can be cross-referenced. From the passport lists [1] have been taken the name of the emigrant as written there, the date the passport was issued, the issuer of the passport, the emigrant's sex, occupation, home province, home commune, year of birth, and marital status. For emigrants of 1873 and 1882 the destination as marked in the passport lists and the number of those from the same commune taking out passports on the same day have also been punched on the cards. From the passenger lists [2] have been taken the method of payment for the ticket (prepaid, cash, paid in Sweden or Norway,

---

[1] All the passport lists that have been preserved were used in this study.

[2] In this study the passenger lists of the police departments of Gothenburg, Stockholm, Malmö, and Trondheim, and the passenger lists of the Finland Steamship Company, have been used.

and unknown), the agent selling the ticket, the emigrant's age as marked in the passenger lists, the place of departure for the voyage, the port of departure, the destination (locality and state or province), the name of the ship sailed on, the shipping line, the date of the ship's departure, the passenger list used, and information on whether the emigrant travelled alone or with his family.[3]

Since the numbers of emigrants were still rather small in 1873 and 1882, but quite large in 1905, two different methods of matching emigrants from the passport and from the passenger lists have been used. First copies were made of the passenger lists for 1873 and 1882. Then base cards were prepared for those persons who appear in the passport lists of the Oulu and Vaasa provincial governments and who were considered to be emigrants, and these were compared with the names of Finns occurring in the passenger lists. For the rather small number of emigrants appearing in other passport lists, a corresponding name was sought in the passenger lists by comparing the originals of these passport lists to the copies of the passenger lists. In this manner, 528 emigrants were discovered for 1873 on whom there was information in both the passport and the passenger lists. In addition there were in the passenger lists for this year 418 persons for whom corresponding information was not found in the passport lists. For 1882, 1,696 emigrants were discovered on whom there was information in both the passport and the passenger lists and 1,982 emigrants for whom information existed only in the passenger lists. In the following, mainly the statistics which include emigrants on whom information is available from both passport and passenger lists have been used.

Since the number of emigrants for 1905 was very great, the matching of information on them from the passport lists to that from the passenger lists was done in another manner. Here the procedure was to first compile a set of base cards from the passport lists. These included all persons taking out passports who might have been emigrants. Then these cards prepared from the passport lists were divided into alphabetically arranged groups of those individuals who received passports during each month of the year. In the next stage the names occurring in the passenger lists were compared to the names on the base cards. When a »mate» for a name in the passenger lists was found among the base cards, the information from the passenger lists was punched on this base card. In this manner, all the names of emigrants appearing in the passenger lists were checked against the base cards.

Since it was known that more than one Matti Mäkelä, for example, emigrated in 1905, the association of names in the passport and passenger lists progressed in stages so that a Matti Mäkelä found in the passenger lists

---

[3] On the conceptions of family and individual emigration see pp. 119—130 below.

would be matched with the correct Matti Mäkelä from the passport lists. In the first stage, the more common names were matched only in those cases where the passport had been issued immediately before the date of departure given in the passenger list or where other conditions showed indisputably that the names appearing in the passport and the passenger lists represented the same person. When a counterpart for a person listed in the passenger lists was in this manner found in the base cards, the case was marked as matched on the copy of the passenger list.

In the second phase, the hyphenated surnames (for example, Mäkinen—Stenfors) in the base cards taken from passport lists were arranged alphabetically according to the second name. The names in the passenger lists that were still not matched were compared to these second names. In this manner, those cases in which only the latter of two names appearing in the passport lists was entered in the passenger lists, were matched.

In the third phase, advantage was taken of the fact that some travellers appear in groups in the passport lists and in the passenger lists. When, for example, one of a group of four listed in the passenger lists as going to Salt Lake City, Utah, had not been matched, the point in the passport lists where these four were listed was sought. When there was a four-person group in the passport lists of which three had the same surname as in the passenger lists and the fourth had the same given name as the fourth person named in the passenger list, it was assumed that either the fourth emigrant had two surnames, or that in one list his father's name was used instead of his own surname. This procedure was most successful in matching the names of Swedish-speaking emigrants leaving from Ostrobothnia. It seems to have been quite common among them that the name in the passport list was, for example, Matts Björk and that in the passenger list Matts Johansson.

In the fourth phase, the remaining punchcards based on passport lists were arranged in alphabetical order for the year as a whole, and again compared to the remaining names from the passenger lists. In this phase, those cases in which the passport was issued much earlier than the departure on the trip happened were matched. It was discovered that while the passport was normally issued a few days before departure, there were cases in which the emigrant took out his passport as much as ten months before he left.

When the groups of emigrants appearing in the passport lists and in the passenger lists were compared, it was discovered that now and then such a person as Juho Pekka Taavitsainen, for example, appeared in one list as Juho Taavitsainen and in the other as Pekka Taavitsainen. For this reason, it was seen justifiable in the fifth phase to associate those cases where, though the given names were different, a corresponding surname for one of the remaining names in the passenger list was found among the remaining names from the passport lists, provided that the passport was issued less than two months before departure and that the sex was the same and the age mentioned in both lists pointed to the same person. Then (sixth phase) the cases of families were picked out from the remaining names in both the passport and the passenger lists and they were matched in those cases where the first names of the family members were the same in the passport lists as in the passenger lists, though the surname was different.

Finally cards were punched for the unmatched cases in the passenger lists. Those of these unmatched cases who left in the first two months of 1905 were then arranged alphabetically and compared with the names of persons obtaining passports at the end of 1904. This method was succesful in matching the majority of those persons who took out passports at the end of 1904 but who did not travel until after the beginning of the next year. In the same way the cases of those taking out passports in 1905 that remained unmatched were compared with names found in the passenger lists for the first two months of 1906, by which procedure those cases who were issued passports in 1905 but emigrated only in 1906 were matched up. At this point, the comparison was ended.

From the passenger lists from 1905 were found 15,837 names, for which corresponding names were located in the passport lists by the procedure explained above. Of these 249 had taken out passports at the end of 1904 and 15,588 during 1905, while 150 of those taking out passports in 1905 were found to have travelled in 1906. In the following, the last-mentioned group has not been included among emigrants for 1905. There remained among the base cards prepared from the passport lists 3,477 persons, for whom no corresponding name was found in the passenger lists, while the passenger lists contained 2,573 persons who could not be matched up with names in the passport lists. If the two last-mentioned groups of cards are used in the following statistics, it will be specially noted.

The cases that remained unmatched in the comparison of the passport and passenger lists were born primarily of the following causes:

1. The name in the passenger and/or passport list was spelled incorrectly to such an extent that the emigrant's real name could not be made out.

2. The use of two surnames common at the beginning of this century sometimes made it difficult to find among the passenger lists a person listed in the passport lists if the first name was very common.

3. The passenger lists contain the names of persons that do not appear in the passport lists at all. Among these were newly-born babies who were travelling with their mothers. Often only the mother's name was entered in the passport lists. Apparently in some cases the passport of the father of a family sufficed as clearance for departure for the entire family.[4] Among

---

[4] Let us take as an example the August Blomqvist family from Snappertuna.

the travellers were also a rather small group of American citizens — former emigrants visiting Finland — who did not need passports at all. In addition, the passenger lists of the Gothenburg Police Department contain the names of a rather large number of persons, apparently from northern Finland, who began their lives as emigrants by slipping over the Tornio River without a passport.

4. Some of those receiving passports abandoned their voyage shortly after taking out their passport because, for example, they were not able to raise money for the voyage in the manner planned.

5. Some of those intending to go to America were turned back at Hanko because of illness. In these cases the people intending to emigrate had already obtained passports that then remained unused. If he had received his ticket from America, it was at least sometimes noted in the passenger lists that this-and-this-named person did not travel because of illness.[5] But if the ticket was procured in Finland, usually nothing was noted in the passenger lists.

6. Some other person than that marked on the ticket may have travelled with tickets sent from America. The emigrant would in this case have taken out the passport in his own name, but the name of the other person mentioned on the ticket would have been entered in the passenger lists.

4. The choice of samples

When the departure of over 300,000 emigrants from Finland to overseas lands is in question, it is not possible to study the factors connected with the leaving of each emigrant separately. If, then, we want to examine a certain question in detail, we must rely on a sampling. In this study two

---

August Blomqvist took out a passport from the Uusimaa provincial government on June 10, 1905, and left Hanko on June 21 on the ship *Arcturus* for America with a ticket for the Cunard Line. August Blomqvist's name alone appears in the passport lists, but the passenger lists show that he had his wife and two children with him. The passport lists of the Uusimaa provincial government for 1905. Suomen Valtionarkisto (SVA). (Suomen Valtionarkisto = National Archives of Finland); the passenger lists of the Finland Steamship Company for 1905. TYYH:s:m:7:11 (TYYH = IGHUT).

[5] Let us take as an example Maria Juntunen-Tauriainen, who took out a passport from Oulu provincial government on January 9, 1905. In the passenger lists of the Finland Steamship Company this person, who had received a prepaid ticket from America, appears as Maria Tauriainen. However, the name in the passenger list had been crossed out and beside it was written the entry: »Maria did not travel due to an illness of the eyes». The passport lists of the Oulu provincial government for 1905. Oulun Maakunta-arkisto; the passenger lists of the Finland Steamship Company for 1905. TYYH:s:m:7:11.

14

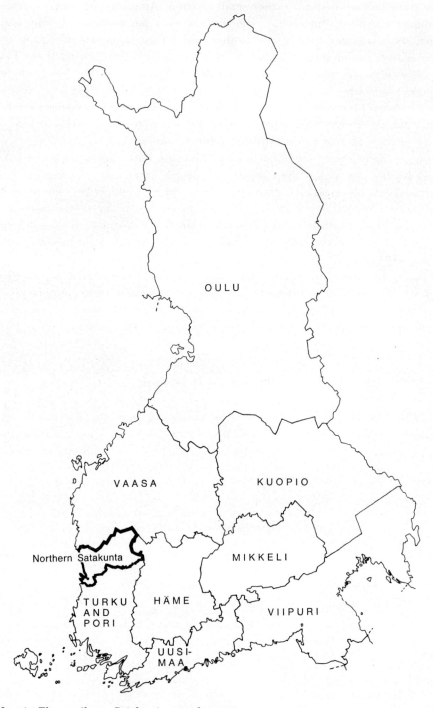

Map 1. *The northern Satakunta sample area.*

major samplings are used. One of these is the emigrant groups of 1873, 1882, and 1905 explained above.

The other sample includes 14 communes in northern Satakunta. This sample area was chosen in an attempt to represent a miniature replica of Finland as far as emigration was concerned. The rural communes of the sample area are Parkano,[1] Ikaalinen,[2] Jämijärvi, Karvia, Honkajoki, Kankaanpää, Merikarvia, Siikainen, Ahlainen, Pomarkku, Noormarkku, Ulvila and Pori. In addition to them the area covers the town of Pori. Many circumstances testify on behalf of the validity of this sample area. The relation between urban and rural emigration in this area was much the same as it was for the country as a whole. In the sample area, about 14 % of the emigrants left from town (Pori) and 86 % from rural areas — in Finland as a whole the corresponding figures were about 12 % and 88 %. The area includes the coast and the interior, poor and rich agricultural areas, industrial communes and those dependent entirely on agriculture and forestry. In some of these communes the crofter population was abundant, in others farmers or landless workers. Some of the communes were in the first elections through universal and equal suffrage politically predominated by the left, some by the right. Emigration was very strong from some of these communes and weak from some others. The number of emigrants leaving the sample area composed 5—6 % of total Finnish emigration.

In addition to the above-mentioned samples (years and communes), several smaller samplings have been made. Among others these include a group of 254 persons who were interviewed. These people had emigrated from northern Satakunta before the First World War. Part of those interviewed were living in America when interviewed, a part — returned emigrants — in northern Satakunta. The former were interviewed in 1966—67, the latter in 1964 and 1966—67.

---

[1] The present Kihniö belonged to Parkano at the beginning of the twentieth century.

[2] In this study the small Ikaalinen village (*kauppala*) has not been distinguished from Ikaalinen commune.

I The Beginnings of Migration Overseas

Numerous studies have been made about the beginnings of Finnish migration to America.[1] In general, these have shown that the lure of emigration
to America spread to Finland partly from northern Norway, partly from
Sweden, and partly by means of Finnish sailors who had begun migrating
to California at the time of the Gold Rush or shortly thereafter. The overall
picture of the beginning phases of Finnish migration to America has, however, remained rather vague due especially to the fact that no one has yet
investigated when emigration actually began from the different areas of Finland.

It is known that at the time of the California gold fever around 1850
Finnish sailors occasionally deserted ships sailing in American coastal waters,
and that a part of these remained in America.[2] It is not at all clear, however, how many Finnish sailors had settled in America already earlier.
I l m o n e n has been able to gather information concerning some Finnish
sailors who were living, at least temporarily, in America as early as the first
half of the nineteenth century.[3] By this time there were certainly Finns also
living permanently in America. For example, according to J ä r n e f e l t,
a Finnish farmer named William Lundell had settled in Massachusetts
around 1830.[4] It is also known that a Finnish sailor by the name Carl Sjödahl (Charles Linn) arrived in America in 1833 and settled shortly thereafter
in Alabama. Since Sjödahl, who was perhaps the most successful Finnish
emigrant of all times, has until quite recently remained almost completely
unknown to students of immigration history,[5] there is reason to assume that

---

[1] For example, J ä r n e f e l t 1899, pp. 19—22; D u r c h m a n 1901, p. 6;
G r o u n d s t r o e m 1901, pp. 93—95; I l m o n e n 1912, pp. 7—11; K i l p i 1917,
pp. 23—26; W a r g e l i n 1924, pp. 52—56; E n g e l b e r g 1944, pp. 21—27; H o g-
l u n d 1960, p. 7: T o i v o n e n 1963, pp. 18—21.

[2] I l m o n e n 1919, pp. 88, 92, 128; K e r o 1969 I, pp. 171—174.

[3] I l m o n e n 1919, pp. 122, 128, 166.

[4] J ä r n e f e l t 1899, p. 21; T o l o n e n 1919, p. 78.

[5] For further information on Carl Sjödahl see K e r o 1971 I, pp. 156—161; K e r o
1971 II, pp. 7, 30. It is rather surprising that I l m o n e n, who had obtained a little
information on the emigrants brought to Alabama by Sjödahl in 1869 (I l m o n e n
1926, p. 279), knew nothing of Sjödahl himself.

many other less successful immigrants who arrived in America in the first half of the nineteenth century have been forgotten.

Even if the deserting from ships and the beginnings of immigration among Finnish sailors were more general in the first half of the 19th century than is presently assumed, there is no reason to doubt that the California Gold Rush appreciably increased emigration among this group. Regarding emigration of the 1850's, we can say that no longer did all sailors come to America by deserting ships, but a number of these applied already at the time they sailed from Finland for passports to America and thus entered the United States legally. One of the first sailors to take out a passport to America was Edvard Kohn of Turku. He may have left for America already in 1849, but it seems more likely that he sailed in 1850.[6] In the 1850's dozens followed Kohn. The center of this Gold Rush induced emigration among sailors was Turku, but some left also from other southern Finnish towns.[7]

By the beginning of the 1860's there were very likely several hundred Finnish sailors in America, the majority of whom probably deserted their ships in American harbor towns. A number of these deserters returned to Finland and doubtlessly spread news about America there, especially in the coastal regions.[8] Finnish sailors also began to settle in Australia in the 1850's and 1860's.[9]

By the 1860's connections with America no longer depended solely upon sailors. For example, in 1873, the governor of Vaasa Province stated that a number of individuals from Vaasa Province had in the last ten or twelve years applied for passports to America, although emigration to America in groups had appeared only since 1871.[10] Emigration was also quite general as early as in the 1860's among the Finns living in Finnmarken, Norway.[11] The urge to emigrate apparently spread from there to the Tornio River Valley, for the parish archives there list persons who had left for America as early as the 1860's, particularly in 1866.[12] Although hardly any persons taking out passports for America appear in the Vaasa Province passport lists in the 1860's,[13] the parish registers show that the provincial governor's state-

---

6 Edvard Kohn took out passports to America in both 1849 and 1850. This may indicate that Kohn did not realize his first decision to leave for America. For more on »gold fever» in Turku see K e r o 1969 I, pp. 167—170.

7 K e r o 1969 I, pp. 169—170.

8 K e r o 1969 I, pp. 172—174.

9 K o i v u k a n g a s 1972 I, p. 38.

10 K e r o 1969 II, p. 83 (The report of the Vaasa Governor in 1873).

11 K o l e h m a i n e n 1946, pp. 20—21, 29.

12 According to the church registers 5 persons (a family) left Utsjoki in 1861, 1 person Kemijärvi in 1866, and 1 in 1868, 1 person Alatornio in 1860, 3 persons Karunki in 1866, 2 in 1868, and 3 in 1869, 16 persons Ylitornio in 1866, and 1 in 1868, 1 person Kuusamo in 1864, and 1 person Pudasjärvi in 1869 for America.

13 The destination is generally listed only as »abroad».

2

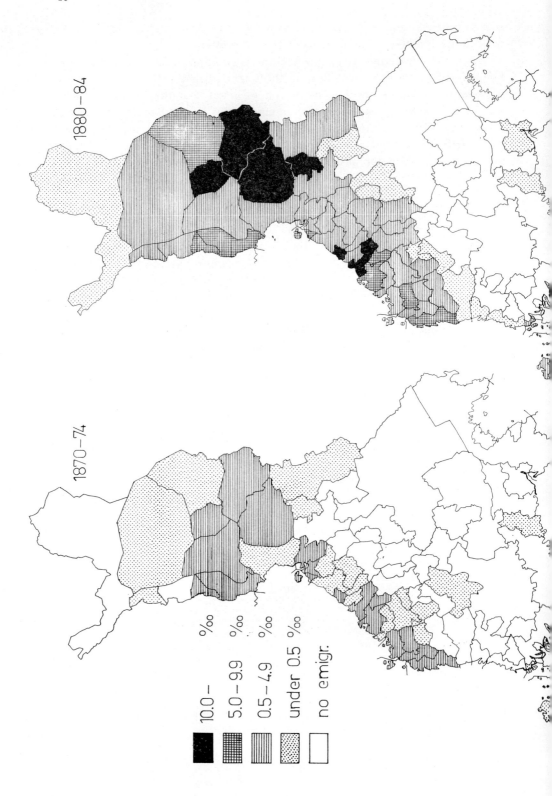

1880—84

1870—74

10.0 — ‰

5.0 — 9.9 ‰

0.5 — 4.9 ‰

under 0.5 ‰

no emigr.

19

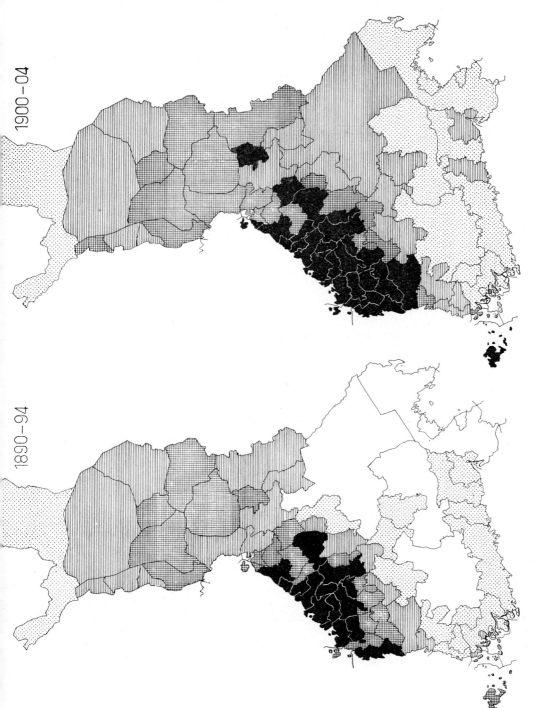

Map 2. The strength of emigration from Finland in 1870—74, 1880—84, 1890—94 and 1900—04. The map has been made on the basis of passport lists, official emigration statistics and parish registers.

ment about the beginning of emigration in the province for the most part holds true. Here again the year 1866 seems to have been the year when mass emigration began.[14] Emigration from the western coastal regions of Uusimaa Province began in 1869 when the above-mentioned Carl Sjödahl brought 53 emigrants mainly from this area to Alabama.[15]

By the beginning of the 1870's, emigration from several areas of Oulu and Vaasa Provinces had grown to truly mass proportions. The information preserved in the passenger lists of the Gothenburg Police Department and in the parish archives of the above provinces indicates that the Tornio River Valley, Kalajoki, the Kokkola district and the areas surrounding the towns of Vaasa and Kristiinankaupunki were at this time the most active »hot-beds» of emigration. Already during this decade, emigration spread to the internal regions of these provinces, although the movement there remained weak. (See Map 2). In southern Finland, emigration to America occurred primarily from towns, Turku still remaining the most important. Emigration touched the rural districts here only in exceptional cases.[16] Emigration among southern Finnish sailors was already by this time, however, rather wide-spread, as is demonstrated in the research done by K o i v u k a n g a s in Australia.[17]

During the 1880's emigration became a mass phenomenon almost everywhere in Oulu and Vaasa Provinces, and was also quite strong in the northern parts of Turku and Pori Province and in the Åland Islands. To a certain extent, emigration also began to occur at this time from the coastal regions between Turku and Pori, although those leaving from here were still only the pioneers of this area's emigration (See Map 2). In addition to this,

---

[14] According to the church registers of the Kokkola rural parish 1 person in 1846, 1 in 1860, 1 in 1864, 7 in 1866, 11 in 1867, and 14 in 1869 left for America. According to the church register of Lohtaja 4 persons in 1867, and 1 in 1868 left for America.

[15] K e r o 1971 I, p. 160; K e r o 1971 II, pp. 7, 30.

[16] The passenger lists of the Swedish police departments only now and then include the locality from which a Finnish emigrant left. In the passenger lists accumulated at the Gothenburg Police Department during 1873—80, 37 emigrants were found for whom a home parish in southern Finland is entered in the lists. Of those 21 came from Turku, 5 from Helsinki, 2 from Tammisaari, 1 from Hanko, 1 from Porvoo, 1 from Loviisa, 1 from Viipuri, 1 from Pori, 2 from Tampere, 1 from Ruovesi and 1 from Orivesi. It is within the realm of possibility that when the home of an emigrant was listed as Turku, the notation indicated the province where the emigrant's home was. The same may hold true for the one emigrant listed as coming from Viipuri. It is more likely, however, that those emigrants listed as having left from Turku, did in fact leave from the town of Turku. One emigrant leaving from Pori is found in the Stockholm Police Department passenger lists. This was in 1869. In the passenger lists of Malmö and Trondheim police departments, Finnish emigrants are listed as being merely from »Finland».

[17] K o i v u k a n g a s 1972 I, table 2.

emigration was continually occurring from Turku and Helsinki, but it would be extremely difficult to define its extensiveness at this stage because of unclear entries in the passport lists. Not many emigrants left yet for America from the internal regions of Turku and Pori Province, or from Häme, Mikkeli, Kuopio, and Uusimaa Provinces. And this situation probably also prevailed in Viipuri Province, except for the environs of Kotka, Säkkijärvi, and the town of Viipuri.[18]

By the beginning of the 1890's emigration began to spread inland elsewhere than in merely Oulu and Vaasa Provinces. The phenomenon, however, had a mass character only in Oulu and Vaasa Provinces and in a rather limited area of northern Turku and Pori Province and the Åland Islands (See Map 2). This spread came to a halt in 1893 when a period of depression began in the United States. Official emigration statistics indicate that only around 1900 did emigration begin to occur from all areas of Turku and Pori, Häme, Uusimaa, Mikkeli, Kuopio and Viipuri Provinces.[19]

It seems that the broadening of the area in Finland from which emigrants left occurred intermittently in tempo with economic trends in America. Roughly speaking there were three general features in this growing of the area of departure. At least in the opening phases, emigration spread from the north southward and from the coast to the interior. In southern Finland — the area south of the line from Pori to Jyväskylä — this broadening occurred most frequently from towns to rural districts, which at the same time generally meant also expansion from the coast inland.

Sailors, the contacts the inhabitants of northern Finland and Vaasa Province maintained with Sweden and Norway, and several emigration recruiters [20] seemed to have played a central role in the beginnings of emigration, but newspaper articles also were of some influence. Information in newspapers about America and immigration thereto spread above all to newspaper-reading circles of the population. America began to interest the Finnish educated class around the middle of the 19th century when at least a portion of the intellectuals considered it as a kind of ideal land of liberalism. The contemporary S. G. Elmgren, the librarian of Helsinki Uni-

---

[18] Either entries concerning destinations are lacking entirely from the passport lists or the destination is listed simply as »abroad». Since there were already by the 1880's a large number of people other than emigrants who took out passports in Helsinki and Turku, the separating of emigrants is possible only by comparing the names in the passport lists with the names of Finnish emigrants appearing in the passenger lists of the Swedish police departments. And this comparison is especially difficult among other reasons, because the Swedes very often spelled Finnish names wrong in their lists.

[19] Suomen Virallinen Tilasto (SVT) XXVIII: 1, Table IX. Suomen Virallinen Tilasto = Official Statistics for Finland.

[20] For further information on emigration recruiters see below pp. 160—169.

versity, defined America in 1853 as »the land to which all eyes are now turning.»[21] The intellectuals also spoke of America's refreshing social spirit and of the land of the future, where social conditions were the opposite of the degenerating society of Europe.[22]

The admiration of America that had its beginning among the intellectual class spread, perhaps by means of newspapers, to other social groups of the country as early as the 1860's and 1870's. In any case, they too began to speak of America as the ideal land of freedom, equality, and democracy, though they thought of these in more concrete terms than the intellectuals did.[23] It is impossible to say how much such symbolization of America increased emigration, but it is certain that it, also, paved the way for the beginnings of emigration and for its growth into a mass phenomenon.

At the end of the 1880's and the beginning of the 1890's, agents selling travel tickets may have spread knowledge of America and immigration thereto into areas where emigration was not yet occurring. Generally, however, it must be said of these agents, that they were active primarily in those areas where emigration had already obtained a foothold; that is, in Oulu and Vaasa Provinces, in northern Turku and Pori Province, and in the coastal towns.[24] There were, however, exceptions. For example in 1888, Iwar Kianstén worked as an agent for the Anchor Line in Mikkeli.[25] Since at this time practically speaking no emigrants had left Mikkeli Province for America, it would be natural that his activities in Mikkeli would have been regarded curious. But whatever it was that Kianstén did there, his results proved very modest.

European emigration to America has been divided, mainly on the basis of the emigrants' land of departure and of the timing of the emigration, into old and new. The former contains above all the English, Irish, German, Norwegian, Swedish and Danish immigrants who came to America in great numbers around the middle of the 19th century. The new emigration includes the movement from a group of southern European countries such as Italy and Greece and from eastern European countries such as Poland, Austria-Hungary and Russia.[26] Finland, which then belonged to Russia as an autonomous state, is usually considered to be one of the »new immigration» countries. This new immigration did not occur in force until the end of the 19th century.

---

[21] *Litteraturblad för allmän medborgerlig bildning 1853*, p. 75.
[22] K e r o 1967, pp. 12—23.
[23] K e r o 1967, pp. 35—41.
[24] See below pp. 135—152.
[25] For example, *Mikkelin Sanomat*, January 14, 1888; *Waasan Lehti*, March 14, 1888.
[26] For example, R o b e r t s 1912, especially pp. 1—17; F a i r c h i l d 1914. pp. 106, 128—133; H r d l i c k a 1925, passim; D a v i e 1936, pp. 96—97.

Scholars have recently begun to consider the division of American immigration into old and new to be completely artificial.[27] If, however, the terms old and new immigration signify merely a chronological division of immigration or a shift of the center of gravity of immigration from western Europe to southern and eastern Europe, perhaps the use of these terms is justified. But, from this point of view Finland does not seem to belong to the old any more than the new immigration group. Emigration from Oulu and Vaasa Provinces began already in the 1860's and 1870's, and can scarcely be distinguished from Swedish and Norwegian emigration — the Tornio River can hardly be considered a dividing line between the old and new emigration. On the other hand, emigration from the other areas of Finland, with the exception of a few towns, began in the 1880's and 1890's, that is the same time that the new emigration in general began.

[27] M a l d w y n A l l e n J o n e s, for example, does not approve of this division and uses the term »new» in quotation marks (for example, J o n e s 1960, p. 4). See also E r i c k s o n 1957, p. 77; E i s e m a n 1970, pp. 78, 86, 108; G r e e n l e a f 1970, pp. 170—181; L o p r e a t o 1970, pp. 10—12; P r p i c 1971, pp. 220—221; W a r d 1971, pp. 52—57.

II The Extent of Finnish Emigration before the First World War

1. Emigration before 1887

Starting in 1893 official emigration statistics contain yearly information about people who migrated overseas. For earlier periods there exist only vague estimates and calculations of the number of these emigrants. For example, O s k a r G r o u n d s t r o e m estimated that the number of emigrants leaving in the period 1870—79 was about 10,000 to 15,000,[1] O. K. K i l p i assessed the number of emigrants for the years 1865—82 to be about 12,000,[2] and T o i v o n e n on the basis of passport lists and church registers of Lapland computed the number for the period 1866—82 to be 7,265 but thinks that the real number of emigrants could have been around 10,000.[3]

The Central Bureau of Statistics has made computations on the basis of passport lists concerning emigration from Vaasa Province from the year 1883 on, and from Oulu Province from the year 1884, and according to these computations 4,268 emigrants left Vaasa and Oulu Provinces in the period 1883—86.[4] T o i v o n e n, also on the basis of the passport lists, has placed the number of emigrants from the whole of Finland for the years 1883—86 at 4,524.[5]

The passenger lists of Swedish [5a] and Norwegian police departments and of the Finland Steamship Company contain reasonably trustworthy information on Finnish emigrants after about 1870 and give a good overall picture of the volume of Finnish overseas emigration in the period 1870—87. For earlier periods, these lists are of not much aid, so the extent of emigration occurring before 1870 must be calculated by other means. It would be extremely difficult to determine the extent of early emigration on the basis

---

[1] G r o u n d s t r o e m 1901, p. 95.

[2] K i l p i 1910, p. 696.

[3] T o i v o n e n 1963, Table 1 and p. 259. See also K i l p i 1917, pp. 25—26; W a r g e l i n 1924, p. 56.

[4] SVT XXVIII: 1, p. 10.

[5] T o i v o n e n 1963, Table 1.

[5a] For further information on the Swedish passenger lists see B r a t t n e 1973, pp. 95—98; Å k e r m a n 1973, p. 19.

of the passport lists, because in these lists, those who migrated overseas cannot be easily distinguished from other users of passports. The value of the
passport lists as sources in this connection is further decreased by the fact
that most emigrants in the 1860's were still sailors, who did not take out
passports at all. T o i v o n e n has estimated on the basis of passport lists
that 219 emigrants left Finland in the years 1866—69.[6] This estimate is,
however, too small, at least in regards to the year 1869, in which, according
to T o i v o n e n, there were 31 applicants for passports. On the basis
of newspaper reports, however, it is known that in September 1869 one group
of 53 emigrants left Finland.[7] Since the leader of this group is known from
these newspaper articles, we may trace the course of his »company» in the
passport lists of the Uusimaa provincial government and show that the
members of the group used the proper passports and that the majority of
them came from either Helsinki or western Uusimaa.[8]

Since the majority of overseas emigrants from Finland before 1870 were
sailors, who deserted their ships, we must content to say as an estimate of
the extent of emigration in its early stages that there were probably several
hundred emigrants who took out passports and that the number of sailors
who emigrated was probably much greater than this. In theory, it would be
possible to compile a more exact estimate on the basis of the lists of arriving immigrants kept by the United States immigration authorities, but in
practice this too would be almost impossible because Finns are lost as a tiny
drop in the overwhelming ocean of European immigrants.

As has already been mentioned, the passenger lists of the Swedish and
Norwegian harbor towns contain reliable information on the number of
Finnish emigrants since 1870. However, the Trondheim lists contain the
names of quite a number of Finns who are listed as leaving Norway, though
they were perhaps born in Finland, and in many cases had been in Norway
only a very short time. The following table shows the number of emigrants
leaving by way of Gothenburg, Malmö and Trondheim during the period
1870—79. During this period, all Finnish emigrants, so far as is now known,
travelling through Stockholm went on to Gothenburg or Malmö and are
thus registered in either the Gothenburg or the Malmö police departments'
passenger lists.

According to computations based on these passenger lists, the number of
Finnish emigrants in the years 1870—79 was 2,848. As has been mentioned,
more Finnish emigrants migrated by way of northern Norway than can be
identified from the passenger lists by a reasonable amount of work. Their
homes were somewhere in northern Finland, but in the passenger lists some

6 T o i v o n e n 1963, Table 1.
7 K e r o 1971 I, p. 160; K e r o 1971 II, p. 30.
8 The passport lists of the Uusimaa provincial government for 1869. SVA.

26

Table 1. *Finnish emigrants travelling through Gothenburg, Malmö and Trondheim, 1870—79.*

	Gothenburg	Malmö	Trondheim	Total
1870	32	—	13	45
1871	101	—	14	115
1872	596	—	2	598
1873	945	—	35	980
1874	101	—	—	101
1875	93	—	—	93
1876	116	—	12	128
1877	145	—	—	145
1878	137	—	—	137
1879	501	5	—	506
Total	2,767	5	76	2,848

northern Norwegian locality is listed as their residence. Neither can it be determined with certainty in every case, whether emigrants from the Tornio River Valley had their homes on the Swedish or Finnish side of the river. An estimate of the number of Finnish emigrants for the years 1870 —79 set at about 3,000 is probably quite close to the truth. In addition to this, there were perhaps a few hundred Finnish sailors who, after being at sea for some time, settled in America during this period.

The number of emigrants for the years 1880—86 can be computed quite accurately from the passenger lists of the Gothenburg, Malmö, Stockholm, and Trondheim police departments. In accordance with these it was as follows:

Table 2. *Finnish emigrants travelling through Gothenburg, Malmö, Stockholm and Trondheim, 1880—86.*

	Gothenburg	Malmö	Stockholm	Trondheim	Total
1880	1,727	54	48	52	1,881
1881	2,383	361	136	34	2,914
1882	3,113	333	170	118	3,734
1883	2,259	301	112	63	2,735
1884	1,514	41	205	15	1,775
1885	991	—	83	3	1,077
1886	2,950	2	358	14	3,324
Total	14,937	1,092	1,112	299	17,440

According to the table the number of emigrants for the period 1880—86 was 17,440. Again this may be increased by several hundred Finnish sailors who emigrated overseas by deserting ship. An estimate of 18,000 Finnish emigrants during the period 1880—86 is probably very near the truth. Thus about 21,000 Finns migrated overseas before 1887. It merits mentioning here that T o i v o n e n's computation of the number of emigrants for the period 1866—86 was according to her table 11,789. On the other hand it must also be mentioned that T o i v o n e n knew that the number of emigrants contained in her table was too small.[9]

2. Emigration during 1887—92

It is more difficult to determine the extent of Finnish overseas emigration during the period 1887—92 than it is in any preceding or following period. This difficulty is due to the fact that passenger lists for this period list only a portion of the Finnish emigrants.

On the basis of passport lists, T o i v o n e n has set the number of emigrants during this period at 19,354. The Central Bureau of Statistics puts the number of emigrants for this period at 32,133. The substantial difference between these two figures is due, according to T o i v o n e n, to the fact that in the preparation of the official statistics

»the concept of overseas emigration [was] taken very broadly, while in the preparation of these statistics [T o i v o n e n's] all those about whose emigration there is some doubt have been excluded.»[1]

T o i v o n e n also argues that »there are appreciable errors in calculation» contained in the Central Bureau of Statistics' number of emigrants for 1892.[2] The number of emigrants calculated by the Central Bureau of Statistics for this year is 6,620,[3] while T o i v o n e n, on the basis of passport lists, came up with 3,922 emigrants.[4] T o i v o n e n does not explain exactly what the error of Central Bureau of Statistics was, but it is evident that she considers the number of emigrants computed by them to be entirely too large.

In any case, the passenger lists preserved in the archives of the Gothen-

[9] T o i v o n e n 1963, Table 1 and pp. 259—260. In 1885, the *Yhdyswaltain Sanomat* (December 1, 1885) made mention of the body of 30,000 Finns, that had by that time reached America. However, the number of Finns could hardly have been so large, even if the Finnish-speaking emigrants arriving from Norway, which the author of this estimate probably included, are counted. Perhaps several thousands of Norwegian Finns arrived in America. On the Finns born in Norway and Sweden see also W a r g e l i n 1924, pp. 66—68; K o l e h m a i n e n 1946, pp. 51—52.
[1] T o i v o n e n 1963, Table 1 and pp. 259—260. Compare SVT XXVIII: 1, p. 10
[2] T o i v o n e n 1963, pp. 259—260.
[3] SVT XXVIII: 1, p. 10.
[4] T o i v o n e n 1963, Table 1.

burg, Stockholm, Malmö and Trondheim police departments can be used as a point of departure in estimating the extent of emigration. For the end of 1891 and for 1892, tables preserved in the archives of the Finland Steamship Company contain information on emigrants leaving as passengers on the company's various ships. On the basis of these sources, the number of Finnish emigrants during the period 1887—92 was as follows:

Table 3. *The number of Finnish emigrants travelling by various routes, 1887—92.*

	Gothen-burg	Malmö	Stockholm	Trond-heim	Hanko [5]	Total
1887	6,074	—	1,713	70	—	7,857
1888	4,123	2	580	157	—	4,862
1889	4,642	—	493	67	—	5,204
1890	4,447	—	271	15	—	4,733
1891	3,482	—	104	47	14	3,647
1892	1,008	—	67	40	3,177	4,292
Total	23,776	2	3,228	396	3,191	30,595

The passenger lists which have been preserved thus show that at least 30,594 persons emigrated. This is about 58 % larger than the number of emigrants T o i v o n e n got on the basis of passport lists, but still about 5 % smaller than the number of emigrants included in the official statistics for this period. The number of emigrants included in the official statistics is a bit larger than that of Table 3 because a part of the emigrants were not included in the passenger lists which form the basis for the table.

In the first place, the number of Finnish emigrants must be increased to include those who journeyed overseas on ships of the German shipping firms, Norddeutscher Lloyd and HAPAG, and who therefore have not left traces as emigrants in the Swedish (or Norwegian) police department archives. Secondly, it must be estimated how many Finnish emigrants left from Copenhagen on ships of Scandinavian shipping companies. Thirdly, it must also be counted how many emigrants the Finland Steamship Company transported to England before the fall of 1891. Materials from various newspapers shed light on these questions.

It seems to be the case that during 1887—89 Finnish emigrants travelling on Norddeutscher Lloyd and HAPAG ships were still registered in the passenger lists of the Swedish police departments. When, however, Norddeutscher Lloyd established its own agent in Finland in the fall of 1889, the

---

[5] Only those transported by the ships of the Finland Steamship Company from Hanko to England according to the lists preserved in the archives of the Finland Steamship Company.

situation changed completely. Part of the emigrants the line transported now travelled from Hanko to Copenhagen and from there to Germany, part from Hanko straight to Lübeck, and part as before through Sweden, but these, since they were under the responsibility of the agent in Finland, were not included in the passenger lists of Swedish police departments.[6] Thus the emigrants transported by the Norddeutscher Lloyd line by way of Sweden during 1890—92 are in so far as source materials are concerned identic with emigrants who did not go through Sweden. Also, the majority of passengers on the HAPAG line went from Hanko to Copenhagen and thence to Germany. In many cases, those who sailed overseas from Copenhagen had probably begun their voyage in Hanko, too.

The best source of information on the number of emigrants who by-passed Sweden is the newspaper *Hangö*, which from the time of its founding in the spring of 1890 published information on the quantity of freight goods and passengers shipped out of Hanko. To a certain extent, the *Vestra Nyland* also published this information. On the basis of this information, we can calculate quite precisely, at least for the winter months, the number of Finnish emigrants who journeyed overseas by way of Copenhagen and Germany. The information in these sources makes no distinction between travellers on the Norddeutscher Lloyd, the HAPAG, and Scandinavian shipping lines, but we know from other sources that the only one of these that was a really significant carrier of Finnish emigrants was at this time Norddeutscher Lloyd.[7]

Information published in the *Vestra Nyland* and the *Hangö* reveals that at least 60 Finnish emigrants travelled to Copenhagen in February, 1890, and at least 172 in March. Eleven of the latter, however, were St. Petersburg Finns. The number for April was at least 275.[8] Emigration for 1890 crested, however, in May and June, when Norddeutscher Lloyd carried most of its passengers by way of Stockholm. However, the number of emigrants leaving Hanko for Copenhagen before the emigration »season» began was at least 500, on which basis a cautious estimate would place the number of

---

[6] The exclusion of emigrants transported through Stockholm by Norddeutscher Lloyd from the passenger lists of the Swedish police departments comes to light from an announcement published in the newspaper, *Hangö*. In this announcement, 17 Finnish emigrants who had used the transportation facilities of Norddeutscher Lloyd announced that they had left Vaasa for Stockholm on June 6, 1890 (*Hangö*, December 28, 1890). The names of at least some of the persons mentioned in the announcement are found in the passport lists, so we can assume the information to be reliable. Nevertheless, the names of these persons are not to be found in the passenger lists of the police departments in Swedish port towns.

[7] In his study appearing in 1899, J ä r n e f e l t estimates vaguely that »formely» Finnish emigrants »for the most part» used Bremen Line (J ä r n e f e l t 1899, p. 36). Finnish emigrants generally knew Norddeutscher Lloyd by this name. For more on the »Finnish conquest» by Norddeutscher Lloyd, see below pp. 135—152.

[8] *Vestra Nyland* and *Hangö* in the winter and spring, 1890.

emigrants sailing on Norddeutscher Lloyd ships in the first half of 1890 at over 1,000.

In the fall of 1890 the *Hangö* published weekly reports on Finnish emigrants prepared, apparently in Germany, by Norddeutscher Lloyd. Since the names of individuals in these reports can also normally be found in the passport lists, we may be certain that these names were not merely invented for propaganda purposes. The first report concerned a vessel which left Bremerhaven on September 6, 1890 and the reports continued until March, 1891. It is not completely certain whether these reports contained the names of all the emigrants carried by Norddeutscher Lloyd in the fall of 1890, so the number of Finns identified from these reports represents the minimum number of Finns travelling on the Norddeutscher Lloyd line. The reports list 790 individuals, if three people are counted in the cases, man »with family» and »mother with children». For some reason, however, 65 persons were listed twice, which means that in the last four months of 1890 Norddeutscher Lloyd carried a minimum of 725 Finnish emigrants.[9] Since it has already been estimated that the number of emigrants carried by Norddeutscher Lloyd in the first part of 1890 was probably over 1,000 and for September to December at least 725, the number of emigrants for the year was over 1,700 without counting the months of July and August. The number of emigrants leaving in these two months was quite probably large enough to make the transportation of at least 2,000 emigrants by way of Copenhagen and Germany during the year highly probable.

A statement has been preserved from the fall of 1890 which supports the above estimate on the number of emigrants travelling through Copenhagen and Germany. According to the *Folkvännen,* over 6,000 Finnish emigrants journeyed by way of Sweden in 1890 from the beginning of January to the end of September. At least 3,000, the article estimated, travelled by other routes.[10] This newspaper article exaggerates somewhat for only about 4,100 names of Finns can be found in the Swedish police department passenger lists for January — September 1890, and it is highly unlikely that the over 6,000 Finns mentioned by the article as travelling through Sweden included any of the emigrants who were carried by the Norddeutscher Lloyd line by way of Stockholm, and who were thus unknown to the Swedish authorities. Assuming that the number of those travelling through Sweden and the number of emigrants using other routes have been exaggerated to approximately the same extent, the true figure for those going by other routes would be about 2,000, precisely the same as has been estimated on the basis of information appearing in the *Hangö* and the *Vestra Nyland.* About 6,700 emigrants thus left Finland in 1890.

---

9 *Hangö,* September—December, 1890.
10 *Folkvännen,* November 11, 1890.

According to reports appearing in the *Hangö,* about 1,000 Finnish emigrants left Hanko for Copenhagen and Germany in the first four months of
1891. Even in May, when traffic was already moving primarily by way of
Sweden, there were about 300 such emigrants. These news items, which
mention the numbers of emigrants by ship, also affirm that about 70 Finns
travelled to Copenhagen through Hanko in December. The Gothenburg and
Stockholm police department passenger lists contain the names of only 824
Finns for the first four months of 1891, although connections from Hanko
with Stockholm were just as good as those with Copenhagen. Only 26
Finns appear for December in the lists kept by the Swedish authorities.[11]
Thus, the number of Finns going by way of Copenhagen to Germany and
from there overseas was greater in January—April and December, 1891,
than the number of those emigrating through Sweden to England and then
on to countries overseas.

The picture given by a travel narrative about emigrants' use of the
shipping lines also indicates that 1891 was the golden year of Norddeutscher Lloyd in Finland. Specifically, this narrative says that there were
over 200 passengers on the steamship *Norra Finland* when it left Vaasa on
May 25, of whom 151 were Norddeutscher Lloyd customers. When the
journey continued from Bremen, about three hundred Finns were aboard
the ship *Elbe.*[12]

The passenger lists of the Gothenburg and Stockholm police departments
contain nearly 3,600 Finns for the year 1891. In other words, the number
travelling by way of Sweden decreased from the preceding year. Since
Swedish, Norwegian, and Danish emigration all increased in 1891,[13] it would
be natural to assume that the same occurred in Finland. The drop in the

---

[11] *Hangö,* 1891; the passenger lists of the Gothenburg and Stockholm police
departments. TYYH:s:m:4:20—21 and m:3:1. Norddeutscher Lloyd lists of Finnish
emigrants travelling in January and February published in the *Hangö* also give a
picture compatible with the numbers published in the *Hangö* of emigrants transported
by each ship. According to Norddeutscher Lloyd passenger lists, 219 Finns emigrated
in January and February (the last ship leaving Germany on February 14). News
reports concerning each ship leaving Hanko include information on the departure of
about 150 travellers, but nothing is mentioned in the paper about the number of
passengers leaving on one ship. On departure from Hanko the group of travellers
however usually included a rather small number of non-emigrants.

[12] *Työmies,* July 29, 1891.

[13] *International Migrations II,* pp. 667, 748, 756. According to Finland's
official emigration statistics, the number of emigrants for 1890 was 5,982 and for
1891 it was 4,869. These numbers, however, cover only Oulu and Vaasa Provinces.
Since by this stage emigration was spreading to new areas, also beyond Oulu and
Vaasa Provinces, the picture of the development of the total number of emigrants
given by the official emigration statistics cannot be held as very trustworthy for this
period.

number of emigrants going through Sweden may, therefore, indicate that Norddeutscher Lloyd gained a larger share of the trade of Finnish emigrants from the Swedish agents. Since the numbers of those going by way of Copenhagen were probably greater than the numbers travelling through Sweden, it seems quite likely that at least 4,000 Finns emigrated overseas by way of Copenhagen and Germany. The Finland Steamship Company also transported in the winter and spring 1891 about 300 emigrants.[14] The total number of emigrants for 1891, then, was perhaps about 7,800.

A particularly large amount of different source materials dealing with Finnish emigration through Copenhagen and Germany in 1892 has been preserved. On the basis of material appearing in the newspaper, *Hangö*, it can be estimated that about 1,525 Finns emigrated along this route during the first four months of the year. From May to August, about 670 emigrants travelled by way of Copenhagen. This year's emigration (carried by Norddeutscher Lloyd) through Stockholm was probably very small. On the other hand, the number of Finnish emigrants carried by German shipping companies in the last four months of 1892 was completely insignificant, for a cholera epidemic almost halted emigrant traffic through Germany. But on the basis of the *Hangö*, we can be almost certain that in 1892 about 2,200 Finnish emigrants left Hanko for Copenhagen and Germany.[15]

In addition to news items in the *Hangö*, a report furnished Finnish newspapers by Norddeutscher Lloyd also contain information on the number of emigrants carried by that company's ships. According to this source, Norddeutscher Lloyd transported 2,112 Finns from the beginning of May to the beginning of October. For the first nine months of the year the number of these Finns was 3,429,[16] thus there were 1,317 emigrants from the beginning of January to the end of April. Since news items in the *Hangö* set this number at about 1,525 emigrants, there is a difference of a little over 200 between these two sources. However, these 200 could well have been customers of HAPAG or Scandinavian shipping lines. As has been mentioned, emigration was very small at the end of the year due to cholera. Thus it seems likely that the number of Finnish emigrants carried by Norddeutscher Lloyd in 1892 was about 3,500. For the same year, the Finland Steamship Company transported a total of 3,177 emigrants.[17] In addition, the names of 1,115 Finnish emigrants can be found in the passenger lists of Swedish and Norwegian police departments,[18] so that we can be certain, on the basis of these sources, that at least 7,800 emigrants left Finland during the year.

---

[14] See below p. 33.

[15] *Hangö*, 1892.

[16] *Nya Pressen*, October 12, 1892.

[17] Statistics in the archives of the Finland Steamship Company. TYYH:s:m:7:17.

[18] The passenger lists of the Gothenburg, Stockholm and Trondheim police departments. TYYH:s:m:4:21—22; m:3:1; m:6:3.

According to the *Hangö,* 7,599 persons emigrated overseas through Hanko in 1892.[19]   Since in the winter, voyages to Sweden left from Hanko, a part of the emigrants going by way of Sweden left from this port. However, in 1892, most emigration by way of Sweden occurred in the summer months, when emigrants from Ostrobothnia no longer travelled through Hanko. It is thus within the realm of possibility that the number of emigrants for the year 1892 was over 8,000.

As alluded to above, T o i v o n e n observed that the Central Bureau of Statistics made substantial errors in calculating the number of emigrants for 1892.   T o i v o n e n's observation can hardly have been due to any other cause than the fact that she was not aware of all the passport lists upon which the Central Bureau of Statistics prepared their calculation of the number of emigrants for 1892.   In any case, the number of emigrants for 1892 is much more incorrect in T o i v o n e n's statistics than it is in the official emigration statistics.

The Hanko figures in Table 3 are based on the statistics on the number of emigrants carried by the Finland Steamship Company that have been preserved in that company's archives.   The earliest entries in this material are from the end of 1891 when the Finland Steamship Company began regular transport of emigrants from Hanko to Hull. But the Finland Steamship Company had carried emigrants already before this.   Lars Krogius, one of the Finland Steamship Company's key people had announced already in 1887 that he was selling tickets to departing emigrants;[20] thus the company, from this year onward, had at least something to do with emigrants.   However, there is nothing to indicate that the Finland Steamship Company carried any appreciable numbers of emigrants before 1891.   As mentioned above in the winter and spring of 1891, the company's ships carried about 300 emigrants.   The *Capella,* which sailed the Hanko—Copenhagen—Hull route, carried about 120 emigrants from Hanko to either Copenhagen or Hull. The ship *Regulus,* which also sailed the Hanko—Copenhagen—Hull route, transported about 175 emigrants.[21] The number of known voyages is not great, but on the other hand, the preservation of information concerning these irregular voyages is so haphazard, so that for the years 1887—91 travel from Finland direct to Hull was probably somewhat more extensive than newspaper reports indicate.

---

19 *Hangö,* June 6, 1893.

20 For example, *Waasan Lehti,* September 7, 1887.

21 *Hangö,* January 4, February 5, March 1, 29, April 26, 1891.   The *Hangö* did not mention, if the emigrants travelled through Germany or England.   In the January 1 issue of the *Hangö* it is said that after new ships were set on the line Hanko—-Copenhagen—Hull a portion of Finland's emigration stream would probably go directly from Hanko to England.

3

34

Since winter sea travel was difficult, some emigration agents also sent Finns by way of St. Petersburg to Libau, whence they were then able to continue their journey by ship. Travel by way of St. Petersburg was advertised in the newspapers already in 1888,[22] but very little information about the actual use of this route has been preserved. In the winter of 1889, a news item in the *Vestra Nyland* mentioned that about fifty emigrants who had been waiting departure from Hanko travelled instead through Hyvinkää to St. Petersburg and Libau, and that more emigrants possibly joined the group at Hyvinkää.[23] Also it is known that in March, 1892, ten persons journeyed through St. Petersburg, because ice prevented the departure of ships from Hanko.[24] On the basis of sources available, however, it seems unlikely that more than a few hundred went to America by way of St. Petersburg. The places of these people on ships sailing from Finland were filled by a number of St. Petersburg Finns, whose emigration was noted by the *Hangö* as early as the fall of 1890.[25] The Finns from St. Petersburg cannot be distinguished in the passenger lists from Finns from Finland. Those who travelled by way of St. Petersburg and Libau may have sometimes been listed in the passenger lists of the Gothenburg Police Department or in the reports published by Norddeutscher Lloyd, but usually this small group of emigrants does not appear in these statistics.

As seen above, it is clear that the number of Finnish emigrants for the years 1887—92 cannot be exactly computed. By using a variety of source materials, it is possible however to make a fairly accurate estimate of the extent of emigration. On the basis of passenger lists of the Swedish and Norwegian police departments and the statistics of the Finland Steamship Company we know for certain of the departure of 30,594 emigrants. Another 9,500—10,000 emigrants probably travelled by the Norddeutscher Lloyd, HAPAG, and various Scandinavian shipping lines. To this may be added several hundred people who travelled by out-of-the-ordinary routes and means, plus perhaps several hundred Finnish sailors. Thus the total number of Finnish emigrants for the period 1887—92 was something over 40,000. The number of emigrants is thus much greater than previous calculations and studies have indicated; more, for example, than T o i v o n e n calculated from the passport lists.[26]

---

22 For example, *Wasabladet,* April 7, 1888.
23 *Vestra Nyland,* February 12, 1889.
24 *Hangö,* March 8, 1892.
25 *Hangö,* November 2, 1890.
26 T o i v o n e n 1963, Table 1. See also SVT XXVIII: 1, p. 10.

3. Emigration during 1893—1914

In addition to official emigration statistics based on passport lists, information for the period 1893—1914 is also available from the lists of emigrants transported by shipping companies, especially the Finland Steamship Company. Statistics for the years 1894—1914 based mainly on information provided by the Finland Steamship Company have been published in *Suomen Tilastollinen Vuosikirja* (Finland's Statistical Yearbook). The following table shows the official number of emigrants based on passport lists as taken from official emigration statistics,[1] and information given by shipping companies on the number of emigrants they carried, as taken from *Suomen Tilastollinen Vuosikirja*.[2] In addition, the figures are augmented, for 1893, by information found in the Finland Steamship Company's archives, and for the entire period, by computations on the numbers of emigrants listed in Swedish and Norwegian[3] police department archives.

A comparison of the official statistics for 1893—1914 to the information contained in the various passenger lists shows that the former lists had a total of 253,016 emigrants and the latter, 264,358. In the years 1893—95 and 1914, the number of emigrants contained in the official statistics is larger than the number in the various passenger lists, while for the years 1896—1913 the passenger lists show slightly larger numbers of emigrants than the official statistics do.

Statistics based both on passport lists and passenger lists contain certain errors which must be taken into account when attempting to estimate the number of Finnish emigrants for the years 1893—1914. In the first place, the fact that not all emigrants used passports lessens the reliability of the passport lists. This practice was probably most general in the opening

---

[1] SVT XXVIII: 1, p. 10; XXVIII: 8, p. 2; XXVIII: 11, p. 2.

[2] *Suomen Tilastollinen Vuosikirja* (STV) 1915, pp. 114—115. It is mentioned in *Suomen Tilastollinen Vuosikirja* that information was received primarily from the Finland Steamship Company, but from 1906 on information from the Helsinki Steamship Company is also included. STV 1915, p. 114 note 1. However, when information on the number of emigrants carried by shipping companies in *Suomen Tilastollinen Vuosikirja* is compared to the number of emigrants carried by the Finland Steamship Company according to the Finland Steamship Company's archives, it appears that the Helsinki Steamship Company did not carry emigrants at all.

[3] From Norway only the lists of the Trondheim Police Department for 1893—1900 have been available. It is highly unlikely that, except in exceptional cases, names of emigrants would be found in the archives of other Norwegian police departments. Moreover, the number of Finns travelling by way of Trondheim around 1900 was so small that the passenger lists of the Trondheim Police Department at this stage no longer have any practical significance as a source for study of Finnish emigration.

36

Table 4. The number of Finnish emigrants according to official statistics and passenger lists of the shipping lines, 1893—1914.

	1	2 Finland Steamship Company and other Finnish companies	3 Passenger lists of Gothen-burg	4 Passenger lists of Stockholm	5 Passenger lists of Trondheim	2 + 3 + 4 + 5
	Official emigration statistics					
1893	9,117	5,231	789	37	631	6,688
1894	1,380	1,075	199	1	9	1,284
1895	4,020	2,981	302	1	12	3,296
1896	5,185	4,942	360	12	15	5,329
1897	1,916	2,557	209	2	4	2,772
1898	3,467	3,667	214	—	5	3,886
1899	12,075	12,357	631	1	4	12,993
1900	10,397	10,642	653	—	21	11,316
1901	12,561	12,659	546	—	..	13,205
1902	23,152	21,753	1,554	4	..	23,311
1903	16,964	16,087	2,129	—	..	18,216
1904	10,952	10,351	918	—	..	11,269
1905	17,427	17,545	1,209	—	..	18,754
1906	17,517	16,466	1,090	—	..	17,556
1907	16,296	16,056	874	—	..	16,930
1908	5,812	6,248	185	—	..	6,433
1909	19,144	20,283	726	—	..	21,009
1910	19,007	19,571	714	—	..	20,285
1911	9,372	9,945	306	—	..	10,251
1912	10,724	11,447	348	—	..	11,795
1913	20,057	21,370	485	—	..	21,855
1914	6,474	5,786	139	—	..	5,925
Total	253,016	249,019	14,580	58	701	264,358

phases of emigration, that is before 1893, but in 1893—1914 emigrating without a passport was still quite common in some parts of Oulu Province.[4]

Emigrants leaving without passports usually show up in the Swedish and Norwegian police departments' passenger lists, but discovering which of the emigrants listed there were those leaving without passports would be so great

[4] Emigrating without passports was most common in the Tornio River Valley, from which it was very easy to get to Sweden. Apparently emigrants sometimes saw the requirement of obtaining a passport as an attempt of the authorities to irritate them. Something of this sort is alluded to in the comment published in the *Amerikan Suometar,* May 1, 1889, which stated that it was not at all strange that someone would come from Finland without a passport: »The passport is for no other purpose than that through it they can take still a few marks from the wallet of the one leaving».

a task as to put it beyond the realm of possibility.[5] Those emigrating without passports probably made up, in the opening phases of emigration, about fifty percent of the total emigrants; by 1893—1914, however, they composed probably only a few percent.

Another reason for errors of official statistics is that not every one who took out a passport actually used it. It is completely impossible to determine systematically which persons applied for passports but did not emigrate. There are, however, numerous indications that passports remained unused. Thus of 30 people who appeared in the register of the Ikaalinen bailiff as emigrants leaving in 1893, three still were living in their home communes at the beginning of 1894, though they had all applied for permission to emigrate to America in the first half of the preceding year. The bailiff's list also says, that one of the persons in the register had »returned from his journey» without reaching America.[6] The Central Bureau of Statistics used the Ikaalinen bailiff's lists in compiling the official statistics and indiscriminately included all those listed as having left for America.[7] In the same year, the emigrant list of the Kankaanpää bailiff contains the names of 15 who took out permits for travel to America, but never left. At least five of these had even reached the stage of applying for passports from the Turku and Pori provincial government.[8] The total number in the copy of Kankaanpää bailiff's emigrant list was 116. This list was also used in compiling the official emigration statistics.

There were many reasons for leaving passports unused. On occasion the hinderance was that the person did not succeed in collecting the total sum

---

[5] A portion of those travelling by way of Sweden also used passports, for which reason computing the number of those leaving without passports would presuppose a comparison of all the names appearing in the passport lists with those found in the Swedish passenger lists. The great number of passports taken out would in itself make this work extremely difficult. And additional difficulties are caused by the fact that some of the Finns listed in the Swedish passenger lists have received »new» names in Sweden, sometimes spelled completely incorrectly.

[6] The Ikaalinen bailiff's register of emigrants leaving Ikaalinen and Jämijärvi in 1893. Archives of the Central Bureau of Statistics. SVA.

[7] SVT XXVIII: 1, Table IX. Compare the Ikaalinen bailiff's register of emigrants leaving Ikaalinen and Jämijärvi in 1893.

[8] The Kankaanpää bailiff's register of emigrants leaving Kankaanpää, Karvia and Honkajoki in 1893. The archives of Kankaanpää bailiff. Turun Maakunta-arkisto (TMA); the copies of the Kankaanpää bailiff's register of emigrants leaving Kankaanpää, Karvia and Honkajoki in 1893. The archives of the Central Bureau of Statistics. SVA; the passport lists of the Turku and Pori provincial government in 1893. TMA. If the Kankaanpää bailiff's register of 1893 emigrants is compared to the number of emigrants for the above communes listed in the official statistics, it can be seen that the information contained in the register was accepted as it into the official statistics. In addition to the 15 persons who did not use their passports, 3 persons took passports and gave them to somebody else who used them.

needed for the journey.[9] At times the cause was perhaps a sudden illness, or that the emigrant was turned back at Hanko because of trachoma.[10] Sometimes, news arriving from America may have postponed the trip for so long that the passport expired. Except for the year 1893, however, unused passports probably had little effect on official statistics. However, the existence of this kind of passport owner makes the preparation of accurate statistics more difficult.

»Limping» cooperation between the Central Bureau of Statistics and the passport officials also caused errors in the emigration statistics. In compiling the official emigration statistics for 1893, the Central Bureau of Statistics counted emigrants from a section of Turku and Pori Province twice, causing errors particularly in the numbers of emigrants from northern Satakunta communes. These errors occurred because the lists containing official statistical materials were compiled in a different manner in Turku and Pori Province than in the rest of the country. In Turku and Pori Province the bailiffs and city administrations that were not necessarily passport authorities collected the statistical material on emigrants, while in the rest of the country these statistics were based on lists kept by passport officials. Since a portion of emigrants leaving from Turku and Pori Province took out passports in other provinces, they appeared in the Central Bureau of Statistics' compilations twice: first on the basis of Turku and Pori Province's bailiffs' and city administrations' lists and then on the basis of passport officials' lists from the provinces where the passports were issued.[11]

On the other hand, the carelessness of passport officials also led to a situation where the numbers of emigrants in statistics based on passport lists was smaller than the number based on the various passenger lists. This is true at least of the Turku and Pori provincial government's and the Uusimaa provincial government's lists. In 1900, the Turku and Pori provincial government sent the Central Bureau of Statistics lists which contained the names of numerous individuals about whom information was incomplete.

---

[9] T o i v o n e n mentions that a man who could not be trusted was not able to get money for travel anywhere (T o i v o n e n 1963, p. 58).

[10] For example the passenger lists for 1905 contain entries on persons who were turned back at Hanko because of illness.

[11] The copies of the registers of emigrants leaving sent to the Central Bureau of Statistics. The archives of the Central Bureau of Statistics. SVA. Compare SVT XXVIII: 1, Table IX. For example, Aleksander Gammelgård from Merikarvia appears in the copies of Merikarvia bailiff's and Kristiinankaupunki city administration's emigrant lists and has been counted twice. According to official statistics 46 emigrants left from Merikarvia in 1893. The copies of Merikarvia bailiff's emigrant lists in the archives of the Central Bureau of Statistics, however, contain only 40 emigrants. The 6 »extra» are those who had received their passports from the Kristiinankaupunki city administration.

Because of this, the Central Bureau of Statistics ran into difficulties when it tried to determine which of those receiving passports actually went to America and which used the passport for different purposes. The Central Bureau of Statistics proceeded in such a manner that »only those individuals whose birth date is listed are counted in the yearly statistics as having left for America, the rest have been excluded.»[12]

The Uusimaa provincial administrators seem to have been especially careless, for, while they were required to mark in the passport lists the place to which the passport applicant desired to emigrate, they in many cases failed to include this destination. Then, in sending the Central Bureau of Statistics the lists of passport applicants who intended to emigrate, the provincial government excluded the names of those without a destination listed. A group at the IGHUT has attempted to determine how many of these »forgotten» individuals there were, by comparing the names of all persons appearing in the Uusimaa provincial government's passport lists for 1905 with the names appearing in the Finland Steamship Company's passenger lists and the passenger lists of the Gothenburg Police Department. The names of 673 people from Uusimaa Province appeared in both the Uusimaa provincial government's passport lists and the passenger lists. Since the number of emigrants from Uusimaa Province listed in the official emigration statistics is 434,[13] it appears that the carelessness of provincial officials produced omissions which caused the number of the province's emigrants appearing in the official statistics to be about 35 % smaller than it in truth was. Of the Uusimaa Province communes, Helsinki contributed the greatest number of these omissions: according to official statistics 255 emigrated from the commune, but on the basis of the comparison of the passport lists to the passenger lists, the departure of 384 emigrants can be verified. In relative terms, the omissions were even greater in Hanko, from which the official statistics list five emigrants leaving in 1905, but from which the departure of 20 persons was confirmed by the above comparison.[14]

The number of emigrants listed in the official statistics for provinces other than Uusimaa Province is larger than the number discovered by the comparison made at the University of Turku. In addition to Uusimaa Province, there are only a few communes in Turku and Pori Province for which the picture of the extent of emigration derived from the official statistics is too slight.[15]

---

[12] Such a notice was written in pencil in the emigrant register sent to the Central Bureau of Statistics by the Turku and Pori provincial government, which included the names of those persons who had received their passports from this government. The archives of the Central Bureau of Statistics. SVA.

[13] SVT XXVIII: 3, Table X.

[14] Ibid.

[15] A comparison of the passport and passenger lists for different provinces shows

40

The comparison of passport lists to passenger lists also uncovered two cases in which the Central Bureau of Statistics has computed the number of emigrants from a certain commune completely incorrectly, without, however, causing errors in the total number of Finnish emigrants. According to the official statistics no emigrants left Ähtävä in 1905, and 29 left Loppi.[16] The above-mentioned comparison revealed that at least 46 individuals left Ähtävä, while probably only three emigrated from Loppi. In the case of Ähtävä, the explanation is that the Bureau of Statistics listed Ähtävänians as Ähtärians, that is, the compiler of the statistics confused the place Ähtävä with Ähtäri. On the other hand, in the calculation of Loppi's emigrants it appears that part of the emigrants from Lappi (Turku and Pori Province) are listed by the Central Bureau of Statistics as Loppians.[17]

It also appears that some passport officials, at least at the beginning of the present century, intentionally excluded from the lists sent to the Central Bureau of Statistics the names of those persons, who because they were approaching draft age would not have been able to receive the passports which remained in force for several years as were usually given to emigrants. For example, the Pori city administration passport lists contain the names of some individuals who had received passports lasting for two months but who were not mentioned at all in the copies of the lists sent the Central Bureau of Statistics. On the basis of passenger lists, however, it can be shown that at least some of these persons receiving short-term

---

that at least the following numbers of individuals were listed in both the passport and passenger lists. This same table also includes information on the number of emigrants from each province according to official statistics for 1905.

Province	In both the passport and the passenger lists	In official statistics
Uusimaa	673	434
Turku and Pori	3,052	3,281
Häme	525	581
Viipuri	818	944
Mikkeli	288	341
Kuopio	594	678
Vaasa	7,452	8,453
Oulu	2,435	2,715
Total	15,837	17,427

16 SVT XXVIII: 3, Table X.

17 The number of emigrants from Ähtäri for 1905 in the official emigration statistics comes to 151. In a comparison of the passports and passenger lists, however, only 87 cases of a person from Ähtäri taking out a passport were found in the passenger lists. The official emigration statistics list 51 emigrants from Lappi (Turku and Pori Province). However, in a comparison of the passport and passenger lists 85 persons from Lappi (Turku and Pori Province) who took out passports were found in the passenger lists.

passports went to America. As an example, let us cite a group of four emigrants from Merikarvia, to whom the Pori city administration gave passports on November 21, 1901. Three members of the group received passports which remained in force for two years. The passport of the fourth was for only one year. The passport list includes the birth dates of all four, which indicate that the members of the group would be facing military conscription within one or two years. The lists do not mention their country of destination.[18] There is no sign of this group in the lists the Pori city administrators sent to the Central Bureau of Statistics,[19] so this group from Merikarvia could not have been included in the official statistics. Passenger lists of the Finland Steamship Company show, however, that four men of draft age left Merikarvia for America. The destination of two of these was Biwabik, Minn., the third, Crystal Falls, Mich., and the fourth, Iron Belt, Wisc.[20]

It would not be possible in practice to compile accurately the number of individuals in each year who did not use their passports once they had received them. It would probably be equally difficult to calculate the number of those who circumvented the regulations required for passport applications, or whose names, for some other reason, did not appear in those materials which the Central Bureau of Statistics used in compiling emigration statistics. The evidence that has come forward during the preparation of this study, however, indicates that the number of emigrants who were excluded from the Central Bureau of Statistics' lists, because they left without passport or because of some other reason, was appreciably larger than the number of those who did not use their passports once they received them, and thus were included in the official statistics, even though they did not emigrate. To a large extent this explains why the number of emigrants for the period 1896—1913 was somewhat smaller according to official statistics than it was according to passenger lists.

Table 4 contains information taken from *Suomen Tilastollinen Vuosikirja* (Finland's Statistical Yearbook) concerning the number of emigrants carried by shipping companies; for the years 1894—1909, 1911 and 1913—14 these figures include only Finland Steamship Company passengers. There were several minor errors and omissions in the figures which the shipping companies supplied to the Central Bureau of Statistics. In the first place, materials preserved in the archives of the Finland Steamship Company show that the number of emigrants for 1905 given to the Central Bureau of

---

18 The Pori city administration passport lists for 1901. TMA.

19 The register of emigrants in 1901 sent to the Central Bureau of Statistics by the Pori city administration. The archives of the Central Bureau of Statistics. SVA.

20 The passenger lists of the Finland Steamship Company for 1901. TYYH:s:m:7:1. The four emigrants left Hanko on November 22, 1901.

Statistics contained 796 Russians, so that the correct number of emigrants is 17,545 instead of 18,341. Nor can we be absolutely certain of the number of emigrants for 1907. *Suomen Tilastollinen Vuosikirja* places the number of emigrants at 16,056, but the Finland Steamship Company archives show that the company transported a total of 32,313 emigrants in 1907 of which 16,257 were Russians. When the number of Russians is subtracted from the total number of emigrants, we get exactly the 16,056 emigrants found in *Suomen Tilastollinen Vuosikirja*. However, the Finland Steamship Company's archives also indicate that, in addition to the above-mentioned 32,313, the company also carried 1,247 people to either Denmark or England. Some of these possessed tickets on transatlantic lines, some not.[21] The records show that only a small percentage of these were Finns, the rest being Russians.[22]

Suomen Tilastollinen Vuosikirja sets the number of emigrants for 1910 at 19,571;[23] while according to a compilation preserved in the archives of the Finland Steamship Company, the company transported 19,462 emigrants this year.[24] In 1912, the number of emigrants according to *Suomen Tilastollinen Vuosikirja* was 11,447;[25] according to the compilation in the Finland Steamship Company's archives, it was 11,358.[26] It seems apparent on the basis of these figures, that some other company besides the Finland Steamship Company transported emigrants in 1910 and 1912. On the other hand, it is also possible that all of the emigrants included in the figures of *Suomen Tilastollinen Vuosikirja* were Finland Steamship Company passengers, and that the differences are due merely to incomplete preservation of source materials.

The reliability of the Finland Steamship Company passenger lists can to a certain extent be tested by comparing the figures on the number of emigrants carried by the company according to its tables on each ship with information published in the newspaper *Hangö*. The following table contains information concerning several ships for the years 1893—95 based both on Finland Steamship Company statistics and on news items in the *Hangö*.

According to articles published in the *Hangö* more emigrants left on Finland Steamship Company vessels than statistics kept by the company concerning third-class passengers reveal. The reason for this difference cannot be known for certain. It is possible that the *Hangö* was given an exaggerated number for propaganda purposes. It seems more likely, however,

---

21 Tickets either for the Pacific, Union-Castle or R.M.S.P. lines. TYYH:s:m:7:17.
22 The passenger lists of the Finland Steamship Company. TYYH:s:m:7:4.
23 STV 1915, p. 115.
24 The collections of the Finland Steamship Company. TYYH:s:m:7:17.
25 STV 1915, p. 115.
26 The collections of the Finland Steamship Company. TYYH:s:m:7:17.

Table 5. The number of emigrants leaving on certain Finland Steamship Company's ships according to passenger lists and to information appearing in the Hangö.

Ship	Date of departure	Number of emigrants according to Finland Steamship Company material	Number of travellers and emigrants according to the *Hangö*	
			Travellers	Emigrants among travellers
Urania	18. 4. 1893	473	506	492
Astraea	25. 4. 1893	330	370	344
Urania	15. 5. 1893	223	250	237
Urania	15. 7. 1893	129	156	130
Astraea	12. 5. 1894	31	48	32
Urania	20. 4. 1895	117	153	124

that first-class or saloon passengers and second-class passengers included a small number of emigrants. It is also within the realm of possibility that a small portion of the emigrants purchased their tickets for the Atlantic crossing only after arriving in England. Knowledge exists of this type of emigrants at least for the year 1899, when the Queensland government paid the way of Finnish emigrants from London to Australia. Thus, when Matti Kurikka left for Australia on the ship *Astraea,* the *Hangö* wrote that there were 62 emigrants and several saloon passengers aboard.[27] But figures preserved in the Finland Steamship Company's archives show that only 16 of the people aboard had purchased tickets for the trip across the Atlantic.[28] Thus there were 46 emigrants aboard the *Astraea* who were not included in the emigration statistics drawn up by the Finland Steamship Company.

In the case of a few years, lists containing the names of Finland Steamship Company passengers who did not possess tickets for transatlantic shipping lines when they left Hanko have been preserved. Most of these persons were of other than Finnish origin, but the group also included a rather small number of Finns, who were probably emigrants.[29]

The 1905 passenger lists, at least, contain several notices mentioning that an individual is an American [30] despite the fact that his name is Finnish as it appears on the list. The majority of these persons were probably Finnish emigrants who had already previously acquired United States' citizenship.[31]

---

27 *Hangö,* August 10, 1899. The ship left on August 9, 1899.

28 The collections of the Finland Steamship Company. TYYH:s:m:7:17. On the departure of Matti Kurikka's group see more N i i t e m a a 1971, pp. 173—175.

29 The passenger lists of the Finland Steamship Company. TYYH:s:m:7:4.

30 Let us take as an example Kalle Waara, who left Gothenburg on September 27, 1905. His home was listed »Amerika» in the passenger lists of Gothenburg for 1905. TYYH:s:m:4:35.

31 It was very easy to get citizen rights in the nineteenth century in the United

These individuals are included in the Finland Steamship Company's statistics, but their number was probably quite small. It should be noted that these differed only in legal terms from those emigrants who had earlier resided in an overseas country long enough to have been eligible to apply for citizenship in that country. United States citizens not only augmented statistics based on passenger lists, but it also sometimes occurred that an individual who had probably received the rights of citizenship in the United States took out a Finnish passport on leaving Finland [32] and thus was also counted in the official emigration statistics.

Although the emigration statistics prepared by the Finland Steamship Company contain some omissions and errors, they may be considered as giving quite a trustworthy picture of their own transportation of emigrants. The figures which the Finland Steamship Company furnished for *Suomen Tilastollinen Vuosikirja* were more often too small than too large. Fairly reliable information about emigrants travelling by way of Sweden and Norway can also be obtained by counting the number of Finnish emigrants in the passenger lists of the Gothenburg, Stockholm and Trondheim police departments.[33] According to Table 4 these totalled 15,339 during the period 1893—1914. Adding to this the 249,019 emigrants carried by the Finland Steamship Company,[34] we arrive at 264,358 as the minimum number of emigrants leaving Finland during 1893—1914. To this, however, must still be added those emigrants who went neither by way of Sweden nor on ships of the Finland Steamship Company.

According to the official emigration statistics based on passport lists, 9,117 emigrants left Finland in 1893. On the basis of information from passenger lists, the departure of 6,688 is certain. Thus the two figures differ by 2,429. These 2,429 emigrants, therefore, travelled with shipping lines whose passenger lists are not available. In making any estimates it should be noted

---

States. Usually Finns were not, however, very eager to become United States citizens.

[32] One such person may have been Anna Granlund, who left Gothenburg on September 27, 1905, and whose home is entered in the passenger lists as »America». However, the passport lists of the Vaasa provincial government show that this person, who it appears was originally from Kvevlax took out a passport to America on September 12, 1905. Entries concerning age indicate that it is the same person who appears in both lists.

[33] As mentioned above the lists of the Trondheim Police Department have been available only to the end of 1900. However, with the exception of 1893, the numbers of Finns appearing in them are in the size class of only a few emigrants. The Stockholm Police Department has lists only to the end of 1904. But the number of Finnish emigrants leaving from Stockholm at the turn of the century was already quite insignificant.

[34] From this number has been subtracted 796 Russians, who were included in the number of emigrants for 1905 by *Suomen Tilastollinen Vuosikirja*.

that leaving passports unused was quite general, particularly in 1893, but that, on the other hand, not everyone whose names appear on the passenger lists had a passport. It is likely that in 1893 the number of emigrants carried by German and Scandinavian shipping lines was still rather large. According to information published by the *Hangö*, nearly 2,400 emigrants left Finland for Copenhagen, and apparently onward from there to Germany and America.[35] Since, in addition, a rather small number of emigrants left by way of St. Petersburg,[36] it appears that the number of emigrants published in the official emigration statistics is very nearly correct. After 1893, however, travel by way of Copenhagen apparently declined decisively. In 1894 under 300 emigrants went by this route, and in 1895 perhaps a little over 300.[37] Random samplings made of the period 1896—1900 indicate that travel by emigrants through Copenhagen continued to be much the same during this time.[38] From 1901 travellers leaving Copenhagen on the Scandinavian—American Line were included in the Finland Steamship Company statistics. It seems likely also, that after 1900 emigrant traffic through Copenhagen not included in the Finland Steamship Company's statistics was minimal if it existed at all. The total number of travellers by way of Copenhagen during the years 1893—1900 was apparently four to five thousand.

The Steamship Company Nord, founded in 1903 as a competitor to the Finland Steamship Company was also transporting emigrants to England in 1903—04.[39] On the basis of information published in the *Hangö* it can be estimated that this line transported something over 800 emigrants in 1903 and something under 900 in 1904,[40] thus making a total of about 1,700 emigrants. The total number of emigrants carried by Norddeutscher Lloyd, HAPAG, and the Skandia, Thingvalla and Scandinavian—American Lines during 1893—1904 was thus 5,500 to 6,500. Since the number of emigrants known for the period on the basis of passenger lists was 264,358, it is highly likely that about 270,000 emigrants left Finland during the years 1893—1914. And since the number of Finns emigrating before 1893 was about 61,000, the total extent of emigration before the First World War was apparently something over 330,000. The official statistics contain information concerning 289,417 people who emigrated before World War I, so that the picture of

---

[35] *Hangö*, 1893.

[36] *Hangö*, February 16, 1893.

[37] On the basis of information published in the *Hangö*, (February 24, 1895), the Finland Steamship Company carried in 1894 the 1,075 emigrants appearing in Table 4. Norddeutscher Lloyd, HAPAG, Skandia, Hansa, Thingvalla and others carried 520 emigrants.

[38] *Hangö*, 1894—1900.

[39] On the founding of the Steamship Company Nord see below pp. 154—155.

[40] *Hangö*, 1903—04.

Finnish emigration given by the official statistics must be considered somewhat incomplete.

Before attempting to determine the extent of emigration for long periods of time — in this case for the whole period before the First World War — on the basis of passenger lists, it should be noted that some of the emigrants appear both in the passport and the passenger lists more than once. How large was this group and how much did they affect the calculation made above on the basis of passenger lists, which placed the number emigrating from Finland before World War I at something over 330,000? In order to determine the effect of emigrants who left Finland two or more times, the following table shows how many emigrants from the sample area of northern Satakunta detailed above took out passports in the years 1881—1914, how many individuals there were in different communes who received passports two, three, four, five, or six times, and how large the number of different people receiving passports in reality was. A corresponding study of passenger lists is in practice impossible, because they do not mention the place from which the emigrant left.

About 7 % of the emigrants leaving northern Satakunta managed to take out passports twice before World War I, and 0.6 % of all emigrants took out passports three times. Those taking out passports more than three times were so few that they have very little significance as »confusers of statis-

Table 6. The number of people from northern Satakunta taking out passports, 1881—1914.

	Passports issued	Persons who have taken the passport					The real number of emigrants	Difference between passports issued and the real number of emigrants
		twice	3 times	4	5	6		
Parkano	1,618	100	4	1	—	—	1,507	111
Ikaalinen	2,134	162	15	—	—	—	1,942	192
Jämijärvi	756	71	9	—	—	—	667	89
Karvia	947	60	8	2	—	—	865	82
Honkajoki	621	30	1	—	—	—	589	32
Kankaanpää	2,063	121	3	—	—	—	1,936	127
Siikainen	1,434	99	8	2	—	—	1,313	121
Merikarvia	1,842	137	13	—	—	1	1,674	168
Pomarkku	681	42	5	—	—	—	629	52
Noormarkku	706	35	1	—	—	—	669	37
Ahlainen	271	8	—	—	—	—	263	8
Pori rural commune	798	46	6	—	—	—	740	58
Ulvila	704	32	1	—	—	—	670	34
Pori town	2,403	133	13	—	—	—	2,244	159
	16,978	1,076	87	5	—	1	15,708	1,270

tics.» Thus, because the people who took out passports more than once were
listed more than once in the statistics for northern Satakunta, the number
of persons from this area taking out passports before the First World War
was in actuality 1,270 smaller than the number of passports issued. The
proportion of each commune's emigrants which received a passport more
than once varies in the different sections of the sample-area, but in each
of the communes included in the sample this proportion was large enough
to cause rather substantial errors in the statistics based on passport materials.
In exactly the same manner, such errors also appear in statistics based on
the passenger lists.

How well does the sample area in northern Satakunta represent Finnish
emigration in general in the matter of issuing passports? Emigration from
the sample-area began slightly later than from Ostrobothnia, but, on the
other hand, quite a bit earlier than from most places in southern Finland.
In regards to the »age» of emigration, which was probably the decisive factor
influencing the number of persons taking out passports more than once,
northern Satakunta was, thus a middle ground between the older and the
newer emigration in Finland. As such, it can be assumed to represent the
whole of Finland fairly well.

Above, it was estimated that somewhat over 330,000 emigrants left Finland before the First World War. Since, in this calculation, 7—8 % of the
emigrants were counted two or more times, this number must be reduced
by about 25,000, thus making the actual number of Finnish emigrants before
the First World War something over 300,000.

Looking at the corresponding figures for the other Nordic countries, we
see that before the First World War about 1,100,000 emigrants left Sweden,
about 750,000 left Norway, and a little over 300,000 left Denmark. Thus
the number of emigrants leaving Denmark and Finland was almost the
same. Denmark and Finland also fall into last place on the basis of the
amount of emigration before World War I relative to total population. But
this comparison must be qualified by mentioning that, beginning in the last
half of the 1890's, Finland's emigration was greater in relative terms than
Denmark's and Sweden's. If, for the period between the middle of the 1890's
and the beginning of the First World War, Finnish emigration is compared
to emigration from other European lands, it becomes clear that emigration
in relative terms was stronger from the British Isles, Italy, Spain and Portu-
gal and weaker from, for example, Belgium and Germany.[41] Thus, during
the twenty years immediately preceding the First World War, Finland
belonged to that group of European countries in which emigration was very
strong.

---

[41] S v a l e s t u e n 1971, pp. 11—16.

III The Extent of Emigration from Different Areas of Finland

O. K. K i l p i, in the first important study dealing with Finnish emigration, which was published in 1917, saw emigration as particularly an Ostrobothnian problem. He does not in his study pose the question of where the boundary between strong and weak emigration ran, or if such a boundary existed at all.[1] After the Second World War A n n a - L e e n a T o i v o - n e n in her dissertation also examined th local distribution of emigration. She attempted to explain what developments have led to the situation in which Southern Ostrobothnia became the major province of emigration.[2] In defining the area of her study, she felt that

> »the determination of the area of study presents no problems in the South and South-east. The border follows the natural and long recognized provincial boundary between Satakunta and Ostrobothnia formed by the Suomenselkä watershed.»

The drawing of the northern border of her area of study provided her with more problems, for as she affirms, one cannot draw a boundary in the north in such a manner that on one side of it would be those communes from which emigration was weak and on the other side those communes from which emigration was strong. Since this criterion could not be depended upon, the border was laid in an attempt to create »an economical geographical area as unified as possible.»[3]

In this study the commune has been used as the basis unit in determining the regional strength of emigration. The numbers of emigrants from Uusimaa and Viipuri Provinces are computed solely on the basis of information available from official statistics for 1893—1914. Doubtlessly, a very small number of emigrants left these provinces for overseas lands before this period, but since the discovery of these emigrants in the passport lists could

---

[1] K i l p i 1917, pp. 135—162.

[2] T o i v o n e n 1963, p. 8.

[3] T o i v o n e n 1963, pp. 15—18. See also J u t i k k a l a 1959, p. 3.

be made only by comparing names in the passport lists with names in passenger lists [4] emigrants leaving these provinces before 1893 are not taken
into account here. The starting point for information on the other provinces
has also been the official emigration statistics for 1893—1914. To this information, however, are added those persons taking out passports during 1870—
92 who, according to passport lists seem likely to have left as emigrants. Such
individuals appeared primarily in Oulu, Vaasa, and Turku and Pori Provinces. This information from the passport lists is available in the statistics
prepared at the IGHUT concerning persons who took out passports during
1865—92.[5] These statistics have been supplemented by adding the emigrants
listed in the copies of the passport lists of the Kokkola bailiff, of Kaskinen
city administration, Pietarsaari city administration and Pori city administration.[6]

Appendix A shows how many emigrants left each commune in the period
1870—1914 (for Uusimaa and Viipuri Provinces in 1893—1914), how many
emigrants on the average left each commune annually, and what the average
yearly emigration was per thousand average population in the years 1870,
1880, 1890, 1900 and 1910. Since some of the passport lists have disappeared
and since some emigrants left without passports, the appendix also
shows the number of emigrants from some communes on the basis of
church registers. This additional information has been considered desirable
in primarily Oulu Province. Especially in the Tornio River Valley, it was
common for emigrants to leave without passports. For this reason the information in the official emigration statistics on the number of emigrants
leaving the communes of Oulu Province is here controlled with information
prepared at the IGHUT on the basis of church registers in Puolanka, Pudasjärvi, Kuusamo, Kuolajärvi (Salla), Kemijärvi, Tervola, Alatornio, Karunki,
Ylitornio, Turtola, Kolari, Muonionniska (Muonio), Enontekiö, Kittilä, Sodankylä, Inari and Utsjoki.[7] The results of this new research on the basis of
church registers which appear in Appendix A, show that the information in
the passport lists and official emigration statistics is extremely unreliable
particularly in regards to the Tornio River Valley. The actual strength of
emigration from those communes of Oulu Province for which calculations
on the basis of church registers have not been made, are estimated on the

---

[4] The preparation of a careful explication using such means would surely
demand several years' time of one man.

[5] The statistics have been prepared primarily by E s a V a i n i o and T a r u -
T e r h i k k i T u o m i n e n.

[6] For further information on the available passport lists see above pp. 5—7.

[7] The materials have been collected and the statistics prepared primarily by
J o r m a P ä t y n e n at the IGHUT.

4

basis of compilations made for neighboring communes and of official emigration statistics (see map 3).[8]

In determining the strength of emigration from the Åland Islands, aid is available from a study by F r a n k B l o m f e l t.[9] Calculations made by computer at the IGHUT on emigrants leaving in 1873, 1882, and 1905, can be used in judging the reliability of the above statistics over the entire country.

An accurate calculation of the number of emigrants from any given commune would be almost impossible because of gaps in the sources. On the other hand, it is possible on the basis of passport lists and church registers to get a sufficiently accurate picture of the number of emigrants to determine with reliability the differences existing in the strength of emigration from different areas. Thus the compilations contained in Appendix A can be seen as giving a quite trustworthy picture of the regional distribution of Finnish emigration.

As mentioned above, information concerning the populations of communes is available from population statistics based on church registers. Because of the merging and dividing of communes, it is not always possible to calculate the average population on the basis of the population figures for all the above-mentioned years, so that in some cases we must be satisfied with the figures for average population for, for example, only the years 1890, 1900, and 1910. The statistics concerning the distribution of population are not completely accurate,[10] but they are reliable to the extent that they do not significantly distort the picture received of the regional distribution of emigration.

Map 3, drawn on the basis of Appendix A, is separated into areas where the average emigration of the years 1870—1914 was under 1.0, 1.0—2.9, 3.0—4.9, 5.0—9.9, and at least 10.0 ‰ of the average population. The appendix and the map indicate that it would be extremely difficult to draw a boundary between areas which differ substantially from each other in regards to emigration, since only in rare cases do neighboring communes differ from each other to a great extent. If, however, we want to separate some sort of Emigration Finland from the rest of Finland, it would perhaps be best to define the area belonging to it as follows: Emigration Finland included the entire coastal region of the Gulf of Bothnia from the Pori rural commune to at least Liminka. The boundary extended inland in such a way as to include also the Pori rural commune, and Ulvila, Noormarkku, Kankaanpää, Ikaalinen, Parkano, Virrat, Ähtäri, Pylkönmäki, Saarijärvi, Uurainen, Viitasaari,

---

8 I have proceeded from the fact that in most cases errors in the official emigration statistics in the numbers of emigrants from neighboring communes have been approximately the same in percentual terms.

9 B l o m f e l t 1968, pp. 77—79, 87—91.

10 L e n t o 1951, pp. 13—22.

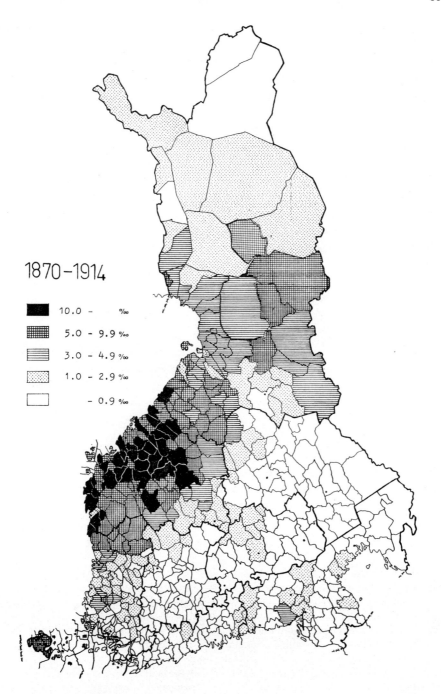

1870–1914

■	10.0 – ‰
▦	5.0 – 9.9 ‰
☰	3.0 – 4.9 ‰
⋯	1.0 – 2.9 ‰
☐	– 0.9 ‰

Map 3. The strength of emigration from Finland, by commune, 1870—1914. The map has been made on the basis of Appendix A.

Pihtipudas, Pyhäjärvi (Oulu Province), Kiuruvesi, Pyhäntä, Kestilä, Rantsila, Liminka, Tyrnävä, Lumijoki, and Hailuoto communes.[11] According to the appendix, 199,600 emigrants left from this area in 1870—1914, which composed 65.9 % of total Finnish emigration. In reality, the number of emigrants was probably somewhat larger, but in terms of percentage, Emigration Finland's proportion of total Finnish emigration was probably quite close to 65 %. According to the appendix, 103,182 emigrants composing 34.1 % of total emigration left from the rest of Finland. For every thousand inhabitants of Emigration Finland, 8.2 emigrated yearly, while for the rest of Finland only 1.2, and for the whole of Finland, 2.8 did, so that the difference between Emigration Finland and the rest of Finland was also extremely great in relative terms.[12]

There can be distinguished in Map 3 a rather well unified area in which the extent of emigration was yearly over 10.0 ‰. The northernmost commune in this area is Lohtaja, the southernmost Laihia, and the easternmost Karstula, in other words parts of both Southern and Central Ostrobothnia were included. This then appears to be the core area of Finnish emigration.

The core area of emigration shaped on the map is not at all sharply distinguished from the surrounding area, but rather spreading south, east, and north of the core area the strength of emigration weakens by degrees. In addition, there is a group of separated communes outside this core area the strength of whose emigration is approximately the same as the central area itself. These are Kalajoki, Petolax, Korsnäs, Övermark, Närpes, Lappfjärd, Sideby, and Karijoki on the coast and Alavus inland.

There are several areas outside of Emigration Finland whose emigration was stronger than the area around them. The first of these areas included the Tornio River Valley and coastal area between Oulu and Tornio, to which area may be added from the inland, Pudasjärvi, Utajärvi, Muhos, Puolanka, Hyrynsalmi, Suomussalmi, Taivalkoski, Kuusamo, and Kemijärvi. The difference between this area and Emigration Finland is very indefinite.

Emigration from the Åland Islands was also noticeably extensive.[13] To

---

11 The drawing of the boundary in Oulu Province between Emigration Finland and the rest of Finland could also be done in such a manner that after Pyhäntä would also be included Säräisniemi, Puolanka, Hyrynsalmi, Suomussalmi, Kuusamo, Kemijärvi, Rovaniemi, Turtola, and the communes remaining to the west of them. Since, however, it appears that there was a thin zone of weak emigration along the Oulu River Valley, the northern boundary in this study has been drawn along the Kestilä—Rantsila—Liminka—Lumijoki—Hailuoto line.

12 In computing the average population of Finland as a whole, and of Emigration Finland, population figures for the years 1880, 1890, 1900, and 1910 according to church registers have been used.

13 For further information on the strength of emigration from the Åland Islands see Appendix A and B l o m f e l t 1968, pp. 77—79, 90—92.

the area of extensive emigration beginning with the Åland Islands, can be added a part of archipelago of Finland Proper, the Kustavi region and the neighborhood of Rauma. Directly to the east of this area is a region where emigration had no significance at all. The boundary to the north, however, is less definite. It could even be argued that, this area should be included in the Emigration Finland sketched above.

There is also a group of communes at the mouth of the Kymi River from which emigration was clearly more extensive than it was from Uusimaa and Viipuri Provinces in general. Another such area is located in the vicinity of the Gulf of Viipuri, where emigration from Säkkijärvi in particular was very extensive. It appears also that emigration from the vicinities of the rapidly growing industrial towns, Helsinki, Tampere, and Turku was clearly more extensive than that from the rural areas surrounding them.

A large part of Turku and Pori, Häme, Uusimaa, Mikkeli, Kuopio, and Viipuri Provinces formed an area where emigration overseas had no significance. Communes can be found in these provinces from which, according to official emigration statistics, less than 10 emigrants left before the First World War. The northernmost part of Lapland appears to have been the same kind of area.

Of emigration from Southern Ostrobothnia T o i v o n e n has said that it was stronger in relative terms from rural areas than from towns. The latter, according to T o i v o n e n, did not differ greatly from each other.[14] T o i v o n e n's compilation is for the period 1866—1930, and it is not therefore fully comparable to the compilation in Appendix A. But on the basis of Appendix A it appears that, for the period 1870—1914, emigration from towns of Vaasa Province was somewhat stronger than from the rural districts. Since, however, it is likely that emigrants from e.g. the Kokkola rural commune are listed in the passport lists as having left merely from Kokkola,[15] it appears that emigration from the towns of Vaasa Province did not differ appreciably in strength from emigration from the province's rural districts. In Oulu Province, on the other hand, emigration from the towns does appear to have been clearly stronger than from rural districts. The same can be said of emigration from the towns and rural districts of southern Finland: here also emigration from the towns was generally stronger than from the rural districts.[16] Thus, for the country as a whole, while 2,8 emi-

---

14 T o i v o n e n 1963, pp. 30—35.

15 Such was the year 1872 when according to passport lists 163 persons from Kokkola obtained passports while none from Kokkola rural commune did. On the other hand, 111 emigrants are listed in the register of Kokkola's rural parish for this year and only two in the parish register of the town of Kokkola. However, it should be stressed that there is nothing to indicate that this mix-up might have occurred to the same extent in other years.

16 In Sweden, scholars have observed the same kind of phenomenon, as can be

grants left rural districts yearly for each one thousand inhabitants, 3.1 emigrants per thousand inhabitants left from towns. Some sleepy, little towns such as Naantali do not seem to have differed much from the surrounding countryside, but emigration from the larger towns such as Helsinki, Tampere, Turku, and the somewhat smaller towns of Pori, Porvoo and Hanko, was definitely stronger than from the areas surrounding them. Thus, for example, according to Appendix A, the strength of emigration from Helsinki was 2.6 ‰, while the strength of emigration from most of the rural communes of Uusimaa Province was under 1.0 ‰.

On the basis of the above, it appears that one of the characteristics of the rapidly growing industrial towns and the rural districts closely connected to them was a rather extensive emigration. However, an extremely large part of the emigrants from these towns apparently were so-called etape emigrants, e.i. emigrants who were born in the country, but had moved to the towns, from which they continued their journey to countries overseas.

In Scandinavian countries scholars have debated whether these etape emigrants should be seen primarily as urban or as rural emigrants.[17] Since this question merits a rather extensive special study for Finland also, it will not be considered very broadly here. Some kind of picture of the extensiveness of etape emigration can easily be obtained, however, from the membership list of the Finnish church in New York's Harlem, where there were numerous emigrants from Helsinki. In addition to the place from which they emigrated, the place of the emigrant's birth is also contained with some regularity in this list. On the basis of this membership list, the composition of emigration from Helsinki was as follows:

Table 7. The number of emigrants from Helsinki born in Helsinki and outside of Helsinki, according to the membership list of the Finnish church in Harlem, N.Y.[18]

Born in	Helsinki			3
»	»	Uusimaa Province		2
»	»	Turku and Pori	»	1
»	»	Häme	»	2
»	»	Viipuri	»	1
»	»	Mikkeli	»	4
»	»	Kuopio	»	6
»	»	Vaasa	»	2
		Total		21

discovered in southern Finland. See C a r l s s o n 1966—67, p. 55; T e d e b r a n d 1972, pp. 144—145.

17 S e m m i n g s e n 1950, pp. 233—236; N i l s s o n 1970, pp. 61—90.

18 The membership lists of the Finnish church in Harlem, N.Y., for about 1900—10. TYYH:s:m:8:28.

The number of emigrants included in the table is so small, that we cannot really make any generalizations merely on the basis of it. The table indicates, however, that it is quite possible that the majority of emigrants from a city like Helsinki were etape emigrants. The passport lists of the Uusimaa provincial government, which quite often mention the name and home of the closest relative of the person taking out a passport, point to the same assumption. These notations show that very often the nearest relative lived in the country, which in most cases probably meant that the person emigrating was also from the country.[19] Thus the membership list of the Harlem church and the passport lists of Uusimaa Province indicate that Helsinki's emigration may have been of much the same character as Stockholm's three-fourths of whose emigrants, at least for several years during the 1880's, had been born outside the city.[20]

Thus, we can say that emigration from Helsinki and other growing industrial towns was clearly stronger than from the surrounding countryside only if we assume that the etape emigrants are to be categorized mainly as emigrants from the town of departure, not from the region of their birth. According to Appendix A, a total of 37,347 emigrants left from towns during 1893—1914, while a total of 265,435 left from rural areas, that is to say that 12.3 % of all emigrants were listed as emigrants leaving from towns. Of these, however, only a very small percent were actually born in the towns from which they emigrated.

As stated above,[21] Finnish overseas emigration has been considered in earlier studies to be either an »Ostrobothnian» or a »Southern Ostrobothnian problem». On the basis of the above examination, it appears that the viewing of emigration as a solely Southern Ostrobothnian problem provides an entirely incorrect starting point for such studies. It would be closer to the truth to look at emigration as a problem that touched the whole of Ostrobothnia in particular. The connection of emigration solely with Ostrobothnia is, however, also a generalization that must be made only with many reservations. And the mere fact that such reservations must be made means that searching for causes of emigration in the exceptional standing of Southern Ostrobothnian women,[22] saying that »the nature of the Southern Ostrobothnian people forces them to emigrate»[23] or connecting emigration with »the Ostrobothnian superman»[24] appear as anything but unsuccessful attempts to explain the reasons for emigration.

---

[19] The passport lists of the Uusimaa provincial government for 1900—14. SVA.

[20] N i l s s o n 1970, p. 64.

[21] See above p. 48.

[22] T o i v o n e n 1963, p. 162.

[23] T o i v o n e n 1963, p. 163.

[24] K i l p i 1917, p. 152.

IV The Causes of Emigration

1. General causes

Already by the 1870's more mature investigators had discovered that emigration, from an individual as well as a social standpoint, was above all economic question, that the most important reasons of emigration were economic.[1] Since the beginning of this century the causes of emigration have also held great interest for Finnish national economists.[2] And in general at the same time that the center of treatment of questions concerning emigration moved from the columns of newspapers to the statistical investigators of the Central Bureau of Statistics, this discussion gained a much more objective tone. The reasons of emigration began to interest students of history in the 1940's and 1950's, when great overseas emigration could already be considered a historical phenomenon.[3]

O. K. K i l p i was a national economist. On the basis of his study that appeared in 1917 he may also be called an economic historian. K i l p i held that emigration was a transitional phenomenon in the transformation of an agricultural society to an industrial society. The most important cause of emigration was the relative overpopulation which developed in Europe during this transitional phase. This relative overpopulation occurred in Finland partly because of legislation designed to encourage the growth of population and partly because of the lessening of wars and famine years, the development of health care, and the progress in agricultural techniques. Very important background factors in the growth of emigration were also the birth of a landless rural proletariat and the fact that farms were normally left to only one heir, so that the other children of the family were predestined to form a new proletariat. Also with a significance of their own are the

---

[1] K e r o 1969 II, p. 79.

[2] The studies of O s k a r G r o u n d s t r o e m (G r o u n s t r o e m 1901), E d v a r d G y l l i n g (G y l l i n g 1906, and G y l l i n g 1910) and A u g u s t H j e l t (H j e l t 1905) should especially be mentioned.

[3] The studies of R a f a e l E n g e l b e r g (E n g e l b e r g 1944), E i n o J u t i k- k a l a (J u t i k k a l a 1959) and A n n a - L e e n a T o i v o n e n (T o i v o n e n 1963) should especially be mentioned.

facts that the demands of the population for a better standard of living were increasing and that social and economic fatalism was disappearing.[4]

As mentioned above,[5] K i l p i considered emigration to be an »Ostrobothnian problem.» The concentration of emigration in Ostrobothnia was in his mind due partly to the fact that the inhabitants of Ostrobothnia had more contact than the population of the rest of Finland with Sweden, where a strong movement to America had appeared before this migration spread to Finland. Thus K i l p i here stressed the importance of the timing of emigration. Another very important factor was that the population of Ostrobothnia grew at a faster rate in the nineteenth century than that of the rest of Finland. Then the »Ostrobothnian nature» played its own role. According to K i l p i »these very characteristics, a strong social selfassurance, self-confidence and love of freedom showed forth in very large measure in the temperament of Ostrobothnian people».[6] Also the facts that the risk to farmers of hard frosts was greater and that agricultural earnings were of a more seasonal nature in Ostrobothnia than in the rest of Finland were important. In conclusion, K i l p i said of his examination of the causes of Ostrobothnian emigration that the thoughts he presented were not »final explanations, they are rather only hypotheses.»[7]

As mentioned above, emigration was to T o i v o n e n particularly a Southern Ostrobothnian problem.[8] In examining why emigration from Southern Ostrobothnia was so strong, she felt, as did K i l p i, that one reason was the extremely rapid growth of population that occurred in Southern Ostrobothnia. This created greater population reserves in Southern Ostrobothnia than in the rest of Finland.[9]

In addition to rapid population growth, economic factors were to T o i v o n e n's mind of fundamental importance in making Southern Ostrobothnia an important area of emigration. She feels that the agriculture of Southern Ostrobothnia did not provide sufficient means of living for its population.[10] She conjectures that the lessening of earnings derived from tar distilling, from the building of sailing ships and in part from seafaring shortly after the middle of the nineteenth century was also an important background factor in the growth of emigration. And since Southern Ostrobothnian forests were of poor quality because of the destructive effects of tar distilling, its forests did not contain in the same degree as the rest of Finland wood that

---

4 K i l p i 1917, pp. 48—135.
5 See above p. 48.
6 K i l p i 1917, pp. 135—152. See also W a r g e l i n 1924, p. 45.
7 K i l p i 1917, pp. 160—162.
8 See above p. 48.
9 T o i v o n e n 1963, pp. 76—79.
10 T o i v o n e n 1963, pp. 80—83.

58

could be sold to meet the needs of the lumbering industry. Therefore, very little profits from the selling of forests went to Southern Ostrobothnia. And »industry did not find a home in Southern Ostrobothnia». Of the relationship between internal migration and emigration she writes, that

> »internal movement has been strongest from those provinces, from which emigration has been least important, particularly from Mikkeli and Kuopio Provinces. And, on the contrary, movement to other parts of Finland has been weakest from Vaasa Province and above all from Southern Ostrobothnia where the strength of emigration was quite high.»

Having once stated this, T o i v o n e n does not deliberate on how this kind of difference between internal migration and emigration was born.[11]

T o i v o n e n stressed, in addition to factors connected with the population growth and the economy, the significance of the fact that people of Southern Ostrobothnia were accustomed to moving from place to place because of seafaring. Regulations connected with military service also had a significance, if indeed they were felt only at given times. Of permanent significance was the drawing power of countries overseas, which was made up of a variety of different factors such as higher incomes and finer clothes and customs. T o i v o n e n also feels that Southern Ostrobothnia was »the moulder of mental preconditions for emigration».[12]

Comparing K i l p i's and T o i v o n e n's studies, the most fundamental difference can be perhaps said to be that K i l p i examines especially those factors that pushed emigrants from Finland. T o i v o n e n examines, in addition to this push, the appeal of countries overseas. Otherwise, T o i v o n e n's study is very much reminiscent of K i l p i's.

To what extent can the explanations of K i l p i and T o i v o n e n be accepted and to what extent are they untenable? The view that the rapid growth of the population was an extremely decisive factor especially seems to strike home. Also the stressing of the significance of the fact that Ostrobothnia remained on the economic periphery can be approved. When speaking of Ostrobothnia being on periphery, however, there is reason to remember that there were many other areas in Finland where »industry had not found a home». And in appraising the significance of the agricultural conditions in Southern Ostrobothnia and Ostrobothnia, there is also reason to remember that there were other areas in Finland where agriculture was almost completely unproductive and perhaps even more liable to risk than in Ostrobothnia.

A people's centuries-old tradition of mobility would of course have been

11 T o i v o n e n 1963, pp. 83—84, 93—104, 111—120.
12 T o i v o n e n 1963, pp. 122—132, 140—165.

of some influence, but the inhabitants of northern Satakunta, for example, did not have a long tradition of mobility, and the experiences of the population of Alavus with seafaring were hardly very strong. Yet emigration both from northern Satakunta and from Alavus was appreciably extensive.

Connections with the outside world, the significance of which K i l p i stresses,[13] were without doubt important factors in the beginning of emigration. They determined primarily in which order different areas would come into contact with emigration. It is quite natural that through sailors the contacts of a coastal population with other countries would be such that emigration would gain its first footholds there.

The inhabitants of Ostrobothnia doubtlessly took a more negative stand on regulations governing military service than did those of the rest of Finland.[14] But this negative stand and the generality of strikes against the draft are not in themselves sufficient proof that the men of Ostrobothnia fled military service by emigrating overseas more frequently than others did.

The attempts of both T o i v o n e n and K i l p i to find in the Ostrobothnian people characteristics which fostered emigration appear rather mysterious. While the author takes a very doubtful attitude towards K i l p i's speaking of an »Ostrobothnian superman» and T o i v o n e n's analyzing of Ostrobothnian women, he will not attempt to dispute the point of whether the economic and social structure and the historical development of a given area might be able over a time to generate certain habits of reaction that might differ decisively from those of the inhabitants of another area. The examination of the character traits of emigrants simply has not thus far produced any results worth mentioning.

Both K i l p i and T o i v o n e n have almost completely overlooked the significance of the system of transporting emigrants. This can be justified because the transportation system did not create the need to emigrate in scarcely any area, but grew up instead to serve the transportation needs of a mass phenomenon that had already emerged. But, on the other hand, only the existence of an energetic transportation system made it possible for hundreds of thousands of individuals to migrate easily from one part of the world to another. Since very little has been done to explain the significance that this transportation system held for Finnish emigration, this will be dealt with in more detail later in this study.[15]

As has earlier been shown, Emigration Finland was in reality larger than K i l p i's and T o i v o n e n's Ostrobothnia. For this reason, the question appears why emigration from Ostrobothnia and from certain areas joined

[13] K i l p i 1917, p. 136.
[14] For more on the attitudes of the inhabitants of Southern Ostrobothnia on the conscription question see T o i v o n e n 1963, pp. 122—132.
[15] See below pp. 131—204.

to it was exceptionally extensive. In searching for reasons, we can to a considerable degree concur with what K i l p i and T o i v o n e n have said in explaining why emigration from Ostrobothnia was so extensive. In the author's opinion, however, three circumstances in particular should be stressed. In the first place it should be emphasized that the birth rate was especially high [16] in approximately the same area from which emigration was strongest. For this reason Emigration Finland had an especially large relative overpopulation from which emigration received its raw material. The second important circumstance is that emigration areas contained no industrial centers to attract their populations. These two very important factors are mentioned frequently in T o i v o n e n's study and also to some degree in K i l p i's. T o i v o n e n recognized also a third factor — which this author believes to be the most important — the interaction of internal migration and emigration. She leaves unanswered, however, the question of why internal migration obtained such a strong foothold in eastern Finland and emigration, on the coast of the Gulf of Bothnia.[17]

R o s e n b e r g has shown that in the 1870's very little internal migration occurred.[18] By this time emigration to America had already obtained a foothold in parts of Oulu and Vaasa Provinces. Even in the 1880's, when emigration had become a mass phenomenon in Ostrobothnia and northern Satakunta, internal migration was comparatively insignificant, although it was already on the increase. Thus it can be said, that even before internal migration gained appreciable strength, emigration had become a tradition in Ostrobothnia and northern Satakunta.

Emigration began from most parts of southern Finland only around 1900. Since internal migration had become a very significant phenomenon already in the 1880's and 1890's, it emerged in these areas before overseas emigration obtained a foothold. Migration to Helsinki, Viipuri, and St. Petersburg also became something of a tradition.[19] Thus at the beginning of the twentieth century the inhabitants of Savo, for example, often had relatives or friends in these towns who could be of aid in finding work and in helping in all the difficulties that might befall one newly arrived in the city from the countryside. The high wages in America did not attract them, for there were no relatives or friends in America — going there would mean a jump into the unknown. But the relatives and friends of the people of Ostrobothnia, northern Satakunta and perhaps also the Åland Islands were in America,

---

[16] J u t i k k a l a 1934, pp. 121—123.

[17] On the interaction of internal migration and emigration see W a r i s 1932, pp. 74—79.

[18] R o s e n b e r g 1966, pp. 101—103, 170—171.

[19] L e n t o 1951, pp. 55—57. Compare N o r m a n 1973, pp. 99—102.

so that it was easier to migrate there than to the unfamiliar towns that geographically were closer.

If we assume that migration to overseas lands and to towns in the homeland became traditions which greatly influenced the inhabitants of given regions, it still remains to be explained why emigration or internal migration began earlier in some areas than in others. Geographical factors, the significance of which K i l p i stressed, probably offer the best explanation. Because of sailors and seafaring, coastal areas had much more contact with foreign nations than did the interior. Thus the population of these coastal areas had early contacts also with emigration to America. In looking at the regional distribution of emigration, we see that it was generally stronger from coastal areas than from the interior. That the area of strong emigration actually composed only a part of the Gulf of Bothnia coast can perhaps be explained by the fact that the coastal regions south of Pori and east of Turku were within the area of influence of the large, growing towns, St. Petersburg, Viipuri, Helsinki, and Turku.

At the same time that the significance of the point when emigration began is stressed, it must also be emphasized that the departure of an isolated group of emigrants was not in itself sufficient, but that emigration had to become in fact a tradition. This can be clearly illustrated in Uusimaa. In 1869 a group of 53 emigrants left Uusimaa for Alabama, which means that in this year perhaps more emigrants left from this province than from northern Finland. Passport lists [20] indicate, however, that a tradition of emigration did not grow out of the departure of this group, but that regular emigration from Uusimaa began only around 1900. — And the »late arrival» of emigration in Uusimaa Province meant that internal migration became the dominant form of population movement, a tradition that the attractions of America were not able to break down.

In stressing the significance of the traditions of emigration and of internal migration, it must be kept in mind that the normal situation at the beginning of this century was that internal migration and emigration were occurring simultaneously in most localities in Finland, though in places one of these was very rare. Thus it is possible that emigration might over a period of years have »conquered» certain areas from internal migration and internal migration certain areas from emigration. Something of this sort did indeed occur in the district of the Kankaanpää bailiff, the work permits issued by whom give an especially good picture of the employment-seeking trips of the district's inhabitants. The work permits were given those who left to work outside their home district, either in the homeland or abroad. According to the register of permits kept by the bailiff, permits to work outside the home district were given as follows:

---

[20] The passport lists of the Uusimaa provincial government for 1870—1900. SVA.

Table 8. The number of work permits issued by the Kankaanpää bailiff to Pori, to the rest of Finland, and to America in 1890, 1895, 1900 and 1905.[21]

	1890	1895	1900	1905
To Pori	102	125	344	40
To the rest of Finland	65	67	66	62
To America	28	15	169	299
Total	195	207	579	401

The number of work permits issued by the Kankaanpää bailiff to Pori thus declined at the same time that emigration from the district to America increased. The number of work permits to the rest of Finland remained at the same level throughout the period. It is not completely certain that this decline was solely due to a decline in the number of people leaving the district for Pori. It is possible that the habit of leaving for work without a permit from the bailiff might have become more common. There is nothing, however, to indicate that this change was not in fact real. This being the case, it appears that, since in the latter part of the 1880's and in the 1890's trips to seek employment both in some areas of Finland and in America were quite common in Kankaanpää district, emigration to America to a large extent replaced trips seeking employment in the homeland after the turn of the century. T o i v o n e n has shown that after immigration quotas came into effect in the 1920's the inhabitants of Ostrobothnia were attracted much more than before to towns of the homeland.[22] In this case internal migration »conquered» Ostrobothnia from emigration.

T o i v o n e n deals very extensively with the mobility of a people as a background factor in emigration. She feels that the heritage of mobility among the people of Ostrobothnia went back at least as far as the Middle Ages. She examines, in addition to the ancient, medieval migrations, how the people of Southern Ostrobothnia began in the nimeteenth century to seek employment in southern Finland and in neighboring nations.[23] T o i v o- n e n, however, gives no attention to the fact, extremely important from the standpoint of emigration, that the mobility of Finnish people in general was increasing continually at the end of the nineteenth century and in the twentieth century.[24] This increase of mobility was an important background

---

[21] The lists of work permits issued by the Kankaanpää bailiff in 1890, 1895, 1900 and 1905. TMA.

[22] T o i v o n e n 1963, p. 119.

[23] T o i v o n e n 1963, pp. 114—121, 156—159.

[24] L e n t o 1951, pp. 55—59. In Sweden, B i r g i t t a O d é n in particular has stressed that the increase of social mobility of a population was a very important background factor of emigration (O d é n 1963, p. 261).

factor of emigration, too, although this increase was not typical only to Finland's emigration areas.

Emigration from Finland thus grew to extensive proportions at just the time that the mobility of the society in general was recovering from the »low point» of the 1870's. This increase in mobility, which apparently was due to changes occurring in industrial life, is also reflected in the figures of Table 8. According to these, the number of those seeking employment outside their home district increased significantly in the 1890's when internal migration was growing very strong.[25]

The significance of mobility as a background factor in emigration can be seen quite clearly in the material the author has collected from interviews. Thus, of 254 people interviewed, 52, or about 20 % had been employed outside their home district before they left for America. To the interviewed, all of whom were from northern Satakunta, Pori and Tampere, in particular, were the places where employment could be sought and obtained. They had worked in the factories in both of these towns, and in Pori also in sawmills and on the docks. Some also had worked as farm hands in the vicinity of Pori. The majority of those finding work in Pori and Tampere were men, but there were also several women in the group. Some of those interviewed had sought work in more distant towns such as Helsinki and Oulu.[26] Thus a very large portion of the emigrants had made shorter trips in search of employment before leaving for America, and had already partially broken the ties they felt toward their home district. It appears that in the eyes of these people emigration to America was basically an employment-seeking trip that was longer than usual.

In addition to the most important background factors sketched above — the rapid growth of population, changes in the economic structure, increasing mobility among the population, and internal migration — we can also list a number of other factors existing in Finland that affected the increase of emigration. One such factor was the regulations concerning military service and russification in general. T o i v o n e n has dealt extensively with these questions.[27] It can also be argued that, in certain areas, religious bigotry was a factor which made emigration an attractive alternative.[28] We will

---

[25] On the increase of internal migration see L e n t o 1951, pp. 54—76.

[26] For example, Oskari Laine, Vihtori Åkerlund and Herman Vesterviik from Ahlainen, Eli Kivistö, Verner Sippola, Verner Siro and Kalle Törmä from Ikaalinen, Hilma Laitinen from Merikarvia and Emil Juhola from Kankaanpää. Interviews in 1964, 1966—67. TYYH:s:ä:tapes 10, 14, 15, 33, 39, 79—81, 107—109, 113—115; notes of the author.

[27] T o i v o n e n 1963, pp. 122—132. See also D u r c h m a n 1901, p. 3; W a r g e- lin 1924, pp. 41—42; E n g e l b e r g 1944, p. 34; K o l e h m a i n e n—H i l l 1951, pp. 20—21; G r e e n l e a f 1970, pp. 131—132.

[28] J u t i k k a l a 1963, pp. 331—332.

consider later the system of transporting emigrants and the attraction of overseas lands, both of which were also important factors in the emigration process.

When an emigrant leaving at the beginning of the twentieth century explains his departure for America by some lack in the local surroundings, his explanation always contains the assumption that at least some thing is better in America than in Finland. This real or imagined superiority of America can be called the »pull» of America. In examining the general causes of emigration, the attraction of America can be said to have been caused primarily by the fact that in the nineteenth and early twentieth centuries the economic expansion of America was much more rapid than that of Europe, for which reason well-paying jobs were being offered in America. To the average emigrant leaving at the beginning of the twentieth century, the most essential feature in America was just this high wage, of which letters from America and returning emigrants had spread information. But American food, American clothing and customs, and images of »American freedom» also were included in the picture which the attraction of America formed in the eyes of average emigrants. The attraction of America hardly remained the same from decade to decade. In the 1880's, some Finnish emigrants perhaps left on their journey with the idea of obtaining a farm in America — by the beginning of the twentieth century, however, the dominating feature in the attraction of America was undoubtedly the possibilities for employment offered by its industry.

2. Individual reasons for emigrating

Emigration historians may in their studies talk about the general causes of emigration such as growth of population and economic development; but each emigrant also had his own reasons for leaving. In some cases these personal reasons were of the same kind as the general causes, but the point of view of the individual emigrants was different from that of the researcher who examines emigration at a later time. Someone may well have emigrated because his family contained too many children for all of them to obtain a means of living at home, but he would hardly believe that he left because of a growth in the population of the home district.

Most emigrants probably had some conception of why emigrating was necessary or at least better than remaining at home. On the other hand, the motives of emigrants were so vague that it is not possible with the aid of interviews any more than with other sources, to determine, for example, exactly how great a number of emigrants left for economic reasons and how many for political reasons. But on the basis of information from interviews and certain other sources, it is possible to determine to some extent the kinds of reasons emigrants and former emigrants felt caused them to leave overseas, and the kind of reasons their neighbors imagined to have caused their leaving.

Toivonen has interviewed numerous individuals who said they left for America in order to avoid being conscripted into the Russian army.[1] This was certainly one ground on which emigrants based their leaving. Apparently the majority of emigrants, however, explained their leaving on economic grounds. Toivonen came to this conclusion after interviewing emigrants from Southern Ostrobothnia.[2] Also a great number of those interviewed by the author said that they emigrated for economic reasons. Some of these reasons were rather indefinite. One said that he left because he »could not get started [economically in Finland] at all».[3] Another claimed »hunger» as his reason for leaving.[4] Emigrants doubtlessly gave such reasons already at the time of their departure. These grounds were undoubtedly based on the real situation in the case of some people, but as vague generalizations they were suited as well for presentation when a person planning to emigrate had no more concrete reason to offer for his departure.

Some of those interviewed said that they left for America to earn money to redeem their tenant farm[5] or to pay off debts on it.[6] This kind of concrete reason for leaving may have of course sometimes been fabricated, the real reason having been perhaps only an indefinite desire to get to America, where so many others were going. But in most cases, the people who grounded their decision in these kinds of concrete reasons had deliberated the matter thoroughly before leaving and had concluded that the trip to America was the best solution for difficulties experienced in Finland.

Several of those interviewed claimed that they left for America because of a gloomy atmosphere or the emergence of differences of opinion at home.[7] These sorts of reasons were not perhaps extremely rare, even though they came forth in the interviews much less frequently than those based on economic factors.

A number of those interviewed told of how they left for »adventure» or »to see the world»,[8] and some said nothing at all about the causes of their departure. Some of these probably had a very concrete reason for leaving,

---

1 Toivonen 1963, pp. 122—132.
2 Toivonen 1963, p. 72. See also Hoglund 1960, pp. 15—16.
3 Interview with Emil Juhola in 1967. TYYH:s:ä:tape 33.
4 Interview with Jaakko Niemi in 1967. TYYH:s:ä:tape 105.
5 Interview with Eli Kivistö in 1967. TYYH:s:ä:tapes 79—81.
6 Interview with Juho Havunen in 1966. Notes of the author.
7 Interview with Matti Heikkilä in 1967. TYYH:s:ä:tape 104.
8 Interview with Väinö Vähätalo in 1966. Notes of the author. Interview with Frank Törmä in 1967. TYYH:s:ä:tape 44.

which in the passage of years had been forgotten, had changed, or which the person interviewed wanted to keep secret. The decision of most such people to emigrate, however, was based merely on an indefinite desire to do the same as relatives and friends, whose experiences in America sounded appealing.

When examining in the light of interview materials, what causes for leaving for countries overseas those intending to emigrate considered compelling, it appears that economic factors played an overwhelmingly central role in the decision-making process. On the part of many emigrants it seems also that the departure was seen as merely a longer than usual employment-seeking trip lasting several years. Instead for most emigrants this trip became in practice the beginning of a life-long sojourn as an immigrant in America. There is also reason to believe that around the turn of the century emigration could have been the solution for any problem whatever.

Clergymen were supposed to draw up yearly for the Central Bureau of Statistics, a list of the individuals from their parish who had moved to a foreign nation, and to include in this list, their reasons for leaving. These lists provide a good comparison to the statements given by emigrants themselves. Most clergymen seemed to be of the opinion that emigrants went to America above all to earn money.[9] Some clergymen felt, however, that emigrants also had political motives. Thus in Ikaalinen in 1899 the cause of departure of more than the usual number of people was seen to be »easterly winds of state».[10]

Clergymen in general rarely looked adversely on those who left for America to earn money or who left the country fleeing conscription into the Russian army. Several clergymen, however, had a propensity to view the motives of emigrants in a negative light, in which cases »working for wages» might be replaced with the words »lust for money».[11] And some clergymen were of the opinion that people left because of »laziness», »wildness», or »a desire for adventure». One emigrant even received beside his name in the list the entry »lazy and a dastard».[12] Some clergymen seem to have been very familiar with family matters in their parishes, since in some cases the reason for departure was noted with the following entries: »family complications», »stratagem for breaking an engagement», »fleeing his wife»,

---

[9] For example the lists of emigrants for 1893 sent by the pastors of Siikainen and Merikarvia to the Central Bureau of Statistics. SVA.

[10] The list of emigrants for 1899 sent by the pastor of Ikaalinen to the Central Bureau of Statistics. SVA.

[11] For example, the list of emigrants for 1893 sent by the pastor of Ikaalinen to the Central Bureau of Statistics. SVA.

[12] The lists of emigrants for 1893 sent by the pastor of Noormarkku and for 1902 and 1903 sent by the chaplain of Honkajoki to the Central Bureau of Statistics. SVA.

»escape from his mistresses», and »forbidden love».[13]   And different kinds
of small crimes were also seen as reasons for emigrating. Thus one clergyman
knew a certain man from Pomarkku who left »in order to avoid the debts
of bankruptcy».[14]

Generally the views of clergymen on why their parishioners emigrated
seem to have been much the same as the conceptions of the emigrants themselves: that is, that while the motives for leaving were most often economic,
emigration might be the solution to any problem whatsoever.

---

[13] The lists of emigrants for 1892 sent by the chaplain of Honkajoki, and for
1895 sent by the pastors of Pomarkku and Merikarvia to the Central Bureau of
Statistics. SVA.

[14] The list of emigrants for 1893 sent by the pastor of Pomarkku to the Central
Bureau of Statistics. SVA.

V Cyclical Phases in Emigration

1. Seasonal fluctuations in the strength of emigration

Emigration movements have perhaps always possessed the character that their strength has fluctuated noticeably. It can also be shown at least as far as great emigration is concerned, that these fluctuations have been quite regular. There are at least three different kinds of these regular cycles:

1) seasonal cycles
2) cycles connected to short-term economic trends
3) and cycles influenced by long-term trends.

In order to ascertain the nature of the seasonal fluctuations in the strength of emigration, information on emigrants leaving Finland during the period 1869—1914 has been collected for this study. Statistics for the years 1869—91 are based upon figures compiled from the passenger lists of the Gothenburg and Stockholm police departments.[1] Statistics for the years 1892—1902 have been collected from lists preserved in the archives of the Finland Steamship Company, which show, with a few exceptions, the number of emigrants who left on each ship. Statistics for the year 1893 have been excluded, because figures are available only for the first part of the year. The lists of the Finland Steamship Company for the years after 1902 are so incomplete as to be of no aid. For the years from 1904 on, however, there are official statistics available, which tell how many emigrants applied for passports each month. Since passports were generally taken out only a few days before departure, statistics based on these passport lists are comparable to statistics taken on the day of a ship's departure.

The following figure and Appendix G show how many emigrants left Finland in each month during the four periods 1869—79, 1880—91, 1892—1902, and 1904—14. The division into four periods is such that the statistics for each period are taken from only one source. For the years 1869—91, figures taken from the same source are divided into two periods in order that we may make comparisons between the various phases of Finnish emigration.

---

[1] The material available on the emigrants who travelled by way of Malmö only reveals the year of departure of the emigrants.

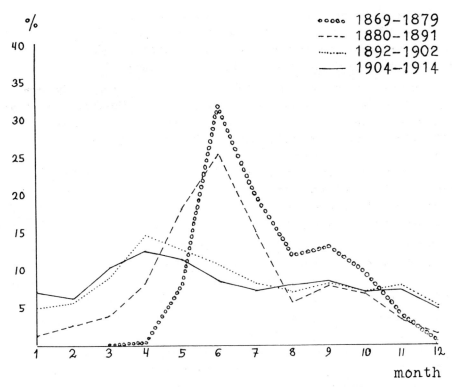

Figure 1. The strength of emigration from Finland, by month, 1869—1914.

Figure 1 and Appendix G show that emigration in the 1870's was clearly concentrated in June and July. On the average, over half of the emigrants each year left the country during these two months. The pattern becomes noticeably more balanced in the period 1880—91, and this trend continues into the next period.

In examining the fluctuations in this emigration, it can be seen that in the first period the peak of emigration came in June. In the period 1880—91 the situation is the same, but in the periods 1892—1902 and 1904—14, emigration crested a couple of months earlier, that is, in April. The compiler of the official statistics, in an observation made on the eve of World War I, characterized Finnish emigration for the years 1892—1914 quite accurately when he wrote:

> »The normal state of affairs seems to be that emigration reaches a crest in the spring, that is in March, April and May, declines during June and July, shows a tendency to rise in August and September, and declines again thereafter, reaching its lowest point in December.»[2]

2 SVT XXVIII: 10, p. 27.

The most distinct exceptions from this »normal» pattern are the years 1904 and 1908, when emigration reached a peak in December. In looking at these two years, the compiler of the official statistics concluded that their division into monthly periods »creates curious patterns».[3]

Emigration in the 1870's and 1880's crested in June doubtlessly because emigrants travelled almost without exception by way of Sweden, and because winter sea voyages were then still only in their beginning stages. In the 1870's it was almost a rule that the first ships bringing Finnish emigrants arrived in Sweden sometime after the middle of May and that Finns were not among the emigrants leaving from Gothenburg until the last days of the month. In the 1880's some Finnish emigrants did go in small groups by way of Sweden in the winter months also, but again emigration reached its peak in June, when connections with Sweden were good.

When the Finland Steamship Company began to arrange the transit of emigrants at the beginning of the 1890's, the peak of emigration shifted to early spring, and when winter navigation slowly developed beyond its infancy emigration changed to an almost year-round phenomenon. In addition to the maintenance of shipping connections between Hanko and England in the winter months, the development of a railroad network that made movement from one part of Finland to another easy at any time of the year, is also of great importance here. For from the middle of the 1880's, Ostrobothnian emigrants were due to the completion of a railway from Tampere to Seinäjoki and Oulu no longer tied in the beginning stage of their journey, to the sailings of coastal vessels.[4] For quite some time, the journey of Ostrobothnian emigrants had begun on some coastal vessel leaving one of the Ostrobothnian harbor towns.

In addition to transportation connections, fluctuations in overseas economic trends and the seasonal nature of employment offered to emigrants also substantially affected the number of emigrants leaving during each month. A number of the mines in which Finns were employed always opened in the spring and closed in the fall.[5] The same was doubtlessly true of many of the construction sites and of the harbors where Finns worked as longshoremen. These conditions led to a situation where job opportunities for arriving immigrants were best in the spring, a fact that letters arriving from America and returning emigrants made known in Finland. As an

[3] SVT XXVIII: 10, pp. 26—27.

[4] Castrén 1935, pp. 11—12.

[5] This is told by many emigrants who worked in northern Minnesota in the beginning of the twentieth century. Interview with, for example, Ville Niemistö in 1967. TYYH:s:ä:tape 91. See also Syrjälä 1925, p. 70.

example of a letter which explained the work opportunities available in America, let us quote from a letter which arrived in Karvia in the spring of 1890, in which it was written that

> »there are now again good times here in the summertime, but no one should come during the winter or his skin would soon wither and cling to his backbone».[6]

As far as Finnish emigration is concerned, it is important also to note that work in lumber camps generally began in the fall and that a very large portion of Finnish emigrants sought their first jobs in just these lumber camps. The fact that logging began in the fall may explain why emigration was generally more extensive in September than in July or August.

The most important of the factors balancing these fluctuations in emigration was probably that employment offered to women was not so seasonal as that offered to men. It is also possible that the direction of immigration, by the end of the 1880's, toward industrial towns such as Waukegan, Ill., was in part responsible for the noticeable lessening of the seasonal character of emigration as time progressed.

We can further demonstrate the fact that emigrants, in their leaving, took the seasonal nature of work available into consideration by looking at emigration directed toward South Africa, Australia and New Zealand. This movement occurred mainly in the period between July and November, when it was spring in the Southern Hemisphere.[7]

It is possible that the seasonal nature of the work available in Finland also influenced to a certain extent the rather regular cycles in the strength of emigration which occurred during the course of the year. In particular, the closing of lumber work in the spring may have given a push to emigration in the spring months. It seems unlikely, however, that seasonal fluctuations in the demands for an agricultural work force influenced cyclical movements in emigration.[8]

---

6 Nikolai Nieminen, March 1890, to Svante Peltoniemi. TYYH:s:m:Satakunta: KAR:VII:1.

7 See Appendix F.

8 In volume 2 of the official emigration statistics it is mentioned that »in relative terms, the flood of emigrants thus reaches its greatest strength just after the completing of spring work and after the end of fall work». (SVT XXVIII: 2, p. 21). On the eve of the First World War, the appraisal was appreciably more guarded, for the compiler of official statistics stated then merely that »the increase and decline of emigration in different months apparently depends upon constantly active causes» and does not enumerate these »constant causes» at all. SVT XXVIII: 10, pp. 26—27.

2. Cycles connected to short-term economic trends

The dependence of the strength of Finnish emigration on economic trends was already an axiom at the Central Bureau of Statistics by the beginning of this century, although research into economic trends was then still in its infancy.   Studies into the relationship between economic trends and the strength of emigration movements became a mode in the 1920's when the American H a r r y J e r o m e published his study, »*Migration and Business Cycles.*»[1] J e r o m e in this work compared quantitative fluctuations in certain fields of production, such as the preparation of pig iron, with quantitative fluctuations in emigration from Europe to America.   The major purposes of this study are; first, to determine whether European or American economic development had a greater effect on fluctuations in immigration movements, and, secondly, to show how rapidly changes in the economic life of the United States were reflected in the numbers of immigrants arriving in and of emigrants leaving the country.   In this study, J e r o m e concludes that

> The above study of the international aspects of cyclical fluctuations in the current of migration, particularly of the immigration movement into the United States, reveals that this movement is on the whole dominated by conditions in the United States.   The »pull» is stronger than the »push».[2]

On the existence of a dependent relationship between economic development and the strength of migration movements, J e r o m e writes that

> Frequently the turns in the migration movement lag behind the corresponding change in employment, indicating that the passage of some time is required before the full effect of a change in employment is felt upon migration.   The extent of this lag varies in different cycles, and is also frequently found to vary on the downturn and the upturn of the same cycle.»[3]

After J e r o m e, numerous scholars of various nationalities have made similar comparisons. A n n a - L e e n a T o i v o n e n has written such a study dealing with Finnish emigration,[4] in which she came to approximately the same conclusions as J e r o m e.[5]   She also shows that fluctuations in the economic life of the United States clearly influenced the ebb and flow of emigration: boom periods in America meant an increase in the number of Finnish immigrants arriving there; periods of slump, on the other hand meant a decrease in migration to and an increase in migration from America.

---

[1] J e r o m e 1926.

[2] J e r o m e 1926, p. 208.

[3] J e r o m e 1926, p. 240.

[4] T o i v o n e n 1963, pp. 140—144.

[5] In Norway A r n e S k a u g and in Sweden D o r o t h y S w a i n e T h o m a s have made this kind of study (S k a u g 1937 and T h o m a s 1941).

The results of J e r o m e's study on the cycles of American immigration in general, and of T o i v o n e n's study of one part of this immigration — that coming from Finland — can, in the main, be considered trustworthy. But on a few points, these works need to be supplemented. For example, the Dane K r i s t i a n H v i d t has recently placed special emphasis on the significance of the transportation system and of prepaid tickets in explaining the character of emigration.[6] As regards Finland, there are excellent prospects for studying the effect of prepaid tickets on fluctuations in emigration. This question, however, can be more profitably considered in the chapter dealing with the transportation system. Another question that has been little studied is that of how emigrants' beliefs about American economic development affected the ebb and flow of emigration. While J e r o m e examined the problem of how great a time lag occurred between American economic developments and cycles in migration movements, we can also ask, did emigrants ever make »false starts» in the light of economic situations in the United States, and, if so, why.

There are two years in Finnish emigration that are extremely interesting in regards to fluctuations of emigration. These were 1904 and 1908 when emigration, diverging from the normal »model», crested at the year's end. To a certain extent this growth in emigration at the end of the year was natural, because in both these years economic troughs had at that time passed into a period of boom. But since similar rises did not occur at the end of the year in other periods of economic boom, the question arises whether other factors than the possible knowledge that work was available for immigrants in the United States can be connected to the increase of emigration. It seems evident that in 1904 and 1908 a sort of »false start» occurred, which was related to the results of the American presidential elections.

Emigrants knew from their own experiences that in America the intervals between »good» and »bad» times were quite regular. These »good» and »bad» times were always to a certain extent connected to the results of the American presidential elections. Evidence that Finns believed that the employment situation depended on the results of presidential elections and on the party in power can be found as early as 1885. Sometime after a Democrat was elected president in 1884, the most important Finnish-American newspaper appraised the matter thus:

> »Although the times are not the product of the government, nonetheless the passage of power into untrustworthy hands has considerably retarded the progress of this land for several years, for new and large enterprises will not be attempted while political affairs are unstable.»[7]

[6] H v i d t 1971, pp. 347—480. See also Å k e r m a n 1973, p. 39.
[7] *Amerikan Suomalainen Lehti,* June 5, 1885.

In addition to newspapers, letters written by immigrants also contain evidence that the employment situation was supposed to have depended upon the timing of the presidential elections and also, at times, upon their results. These letters reveal above all what the »ordinary» immigrant thought about the significance of the presidential elections, and what kind of information about them he transmitted to Finland. Already in 1888 a letter arrived in Merikarvia in which the following was written:

> »There is sure a lot of talk now that times are bad because the presidential elections are coming in the spring. But it is thought that good times will then come ... they will probably elect the same chief they have had before, then good times might come.»[8]

Another letter which arrived in Finland contained this comment on the 1892 presidential elections:

> »I can't really say what kind of times are now coming, since a new president is coming into office.»[9]

The 1904 elections caused Viktor Myllymäki from Siikainen to write in August, 1904, that

> »the elections will be soon, and it is not known whether the times will improve or decline.»[10]

A number of comments on the 1908 elections have been preserved in letters sent to Finland. A woman from Ikaalinen wrote to her parents immediately after the elections that

> »there were presidential elections here yesterday. And now good times have come and now, for sure, money will start coming to you.»[11]

Another letter arriving in Siikainen, said that

> »there were here in the United States of America presidential elections again on the third of the month, and those golden Republican times are again here for four years ... You wrote that Kalle intends to come here. If he really means to come, it seems to me that it would be best to come in the spring, since work will begin to improve in the spring, and times will probably otherwise improve for a couple of years.»[12]

---

[8] Frans Heinonen, August 5, 1888, to his wife. TYYH:s:m:Satakunta:MER:I:11.

[9] Viljam Mäki, February 27, 1893, to Emilia Hautala. TYYH:s:m:Satakunta:KAR: XI:1.

[10] Viktor Myllymäki, August 31, 1904, to Heikki Myllymäki. TYYH:s:m:Satakunta:SIIK:LXXVIII:2.

[11] Ellen Luoma, November 10, 1907, to her mother. TYYH:s:m:Satakunta:IKA: LVII:3. Instead of the year 1907, given in the letter, the year must have been 1908.

[12] Viktor Myllymäki, November 25, 1908, to his relatives. TYYH:s:m:Satakunta: SIIK:LXVIII:8.

In a similar manner, an emigrant from Kankaanpää asked his relatives:

>How old is your oldest boy, Eino? Has he already gone to confirmation school? I would like to send a ticket to him in the spring, so that he could come here this spring, since there were presidential elections here, and the better party won. Thus it looks like next spring and summer work will be going at full swing.»[13]

A comment has been preserved on Wilson's election to the presidency in 1912. A letter arriving in Karvia read, that

>it would be nice to be there [Finland] for at least a few summers, since here that Democratic party has now won, although you don't really know whether times will stay the same as before.»[14]

Thus, both before and after presidential elections in the United States letters came to Finland which stressed the decisive significance of the elections on the employment situation. Quite often emigrants apparently thought that the election of the Republican candidate produced good times, while that of the Democratic candidate meant bad times. The cresting of emigration at the end of the year in 1904 and 1908 can thus perhaps be explained by the fact that a Republican victory in the presidential elections was seen as a sign of arrival of »better times», and on this basis people decided to emigrate. This assumption is strengthened by the fact that, when a Democrat won in the elections of 1912, Finns did not, apparently on the basis of instructions from America, see any hurry to emigrate: emigration began to increase only in the spring of 1913.

In addition to the economic trends and seasonal influences which caused somewhat regular fluctuations in emigration, it is possible that there were other chance factors that caused small and local oscillations in the stream of emigration. One such factor was cholera: in order to prevent its spreading, the United States put limitations on immigration at the end of 1892.[15] Labor struggles may also have been of influence. For Finnish immigrants the most important of these were the strike of Minnesota iron mines in the summer of 1907 and the strike which prevailed in the northern Michigan copper-mining district in 1913—14.[16] Those unemployed by strikes naturally did not want to be troubled with relatives arriving from Finland, and these relatives leaving for America depended in many cases on a ticket sent from

---

[13] K. A. Hemiä, December 12, 1908, to Johan Riihimäki. TYYH:s:m:Satakunta:KAN:XII:3.

[14] Anselm Hulkko, January 12, 1913 (in the letter 1912), to Oskari Hulkko. TYYH:s:m:Satakunta:KAR:XLI:1.

[15] See below pp. 149—150.

[16] Further information on these strikes, see Syrjälä 1925, pp. 69—72, and Holmio 1967, pp. 393—403.

America. During times of large labor struggles many probably sent letters
to Finland similar to this one:

> »You wrote that Kalle wants to come to this country. I would cer-
> tainly send him a ticket, but it wouldn't work now, if I have to leave
> here myself if this strike lasts a long time ... If we win our strike, I'll
> send Kalle a ticket right away.»[17]

The desire among the population of a given area to leave for America
was influenced also by how old a phenomenon emigration was in the area.
This fact becomes clear when we compare northern Satakunta to the Tyrvää
district. Emigration had begun from northern Satakunta already in the
1880's, or at the latest by the beginning of the 1890's. On the other hand,
signs of emigration could be seen in the Tyrvää district only at the beginning
of the 1890's, and it was only around 1900 that emigrants began leaving from
most villages in the district. In 1902 a vigorous period of boom was in progress in America, and it was quickly reflected in the northern parts of Satakunta, from which hundreds had already emigrated to America. Letters
came telling of »good times» in America. When in the following year job
opportunities in America declined, hundreds of letters arrived in northern
Satakunta saying that it did not pay to come to America at this time, and
immediately the stream of emigration began to slow up. The influence of
the 1902 »fever» also extended to the Tyrvää district, but the arrival of the
period of economic decline in America was not felt so quickly in this area
as it was a little further north. Thus emigration from the Tyrvää district
was stronger in 1903 than in the preceding year. This was probably due
to the fact that communications with America were much weaker in the Tyrvää district than in the area to the north. American letters arrived here in
much smaller numbers than in northern Satakunta. And the character of
these letters could have been a little different; only in rare cases had emigrants from the Tyrvää district experienced periods of economic decline in
America, thus there is reason to assume that letters sent by emigrants from
Tyrvää had a more optimistic air than those sent by northern Satakunta emigrants. These latter had already had the chance to experience what both
»good» and »bad» times were in America, and they knew that the lot of the
unemployed in America was by no means easy. When, by 1909, emigration
had become a common feature in the Tyrvää district, this district in no way
differed from northern Satakunta. The expansion and decline of job opportunities in America were now also reflected immediately in the numbers
of emigrants leaving this district. In order to clear up this question emigration from Ikaalinen and Tyrvää sheriff districts is illustrated in Figure 2.

---

[17] Viktor Myllymäki, August 5, 1907, to his relatives. TYYH:s:m:Satakunta:
SIIK:LXXVIII:5.

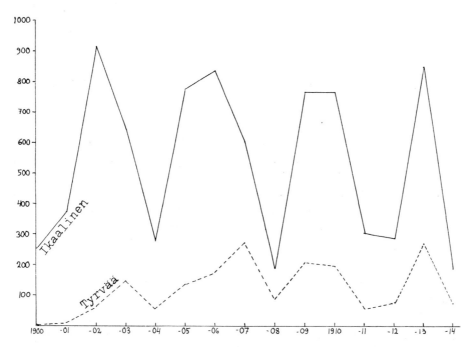

Figure 2. Emigration from Ikaalinen and Tyrvää sheriff districts, 1900—14.[18]

Economic events in the area of departure may also have caused the ebb and flow of emigration from at least some districts to diverge, for short periods of time, from the »normal» pattern, or have strengthened or weakened »normal» development. T o i v o n e n in her study argues that

> »internal industrial-mercantile trends did not promote any more than they prevented emigration. The results of the country's harvest may have had slightly more influence. Small yields from ones own field might ripen the desire to leave, or a good harvest might check it — that is if other factors, especially the economic conditions in the given overseas country, were such that they induced the same decision as did the harvest results in the homeland.»[19]

T o i v o n e n's appraisal, which has reference mainly to Southern Ostrobothnia, can perhaps be extended to cover all of Finland. At least, evidence supporting T o i v o n e n can be found in source materials from northern Satakunta. Thus the sheriff of Ikaalinen surmised, in an explanation of the causes of emigration sent to the governor of Turku and Pori Province in 1900, that the difficult economic conditions of the years 1892, 1893 and 1896

---

[18] SVT XXVIII:6 and 11, Tables X.
[19] T o i v o n e n 1963, pp. 139—140.

were one reason why emigration from the area increased noticeably.[20]   And
the sheriff of Ulvila believed that emigration had increased from the Noormarkku bailiff's district in 1899, because, among other reasons,

> »in recent years, food and dwelling costs have risen so rapidly in rela-
> tion to local wage increases.»[21]

However, not even rough numerical estimates of the effects of local economic
life on temporary oscillations in emigration are possible.

If the flow of economic trends in the United States is compared to factors
existing in Finland that might have influenced fluctuations in emigration, it
seems that the significance of the United States was much greater than that
of Finland.   Events in America caused the numbers of emigrants to grow
and decline much more forcibly and regularly than conditions in Finland did.

3. Long-term trends as regulators of emigration

Since the Second World War, scholars have shown extreme interest in
long-term trends perceivable in both economic life and emigration.   One of
the first scholars to examine emigration from this point of view was B r i n-
l e y T h o m a s whose work, »*Migration and Economic Growth*», appeared
in 1954. T h o m a s sees emigration as a part of the economic growth of the
»Atlantic community», in which cycles of about 20 years are discernible.
Emigration itself to a certain extent influenced the movement of these cycles,
but for the most part other factors determined their course.[1] The first such
cycle in Finnish emigration extended from about 1874 to about 1894, both
of which years were clearly trough years in emigration.   Another long-term
cycle in Finnish emigration extended from about 1894 to approximately the
beginning of the First World War.   Following the appearance of T h o m a s's
study, long term trends in emigration have become a popular field of study.[2]

In the period 1874—93 almost 70,000 emigrants left Finland for overseas
lands.   For the period 1894—1913 the number of these emigrants was about

---

[20] The sheriff of Ikaalinen, July 20, 1900, to the governor of Turku and Pori
Province.   An appendix to the letter from the governor to the Senate.   The collections of the Central Bureau of Statistics. SVA. The letters are among the copies of
passport lists for 1900.

[21] The sheriff of Ulvila, November 7, 1900, to the governor of Turku and Pori
Province.   An appendix to the letter from the governor to the Senate.   The collections of the Central Bureau of Statistics. SVA. The letters are among the copies of
passport lists for 1900.

[1] T h o m a s 1954, pp. 83—94.

[2] As an example A l l e n C. K e l l e y's article »*International Migration and
Economic Growth: Australia, 1865—1935*» might be mentioned (K e l l e y 1965).

260,000. Comparing Finland to the other Nordic countries, we discover, that the pattern of emigration from other Nordic countries during these two periods differs from that in Finland in that more emigrants left from these countries during the first period than during the second.[3]

Again, according to T h o m a s long-term cycles in emigration are a consequence of the course of economic life. He argues that at least until the middle of the 19th century conditions in Europe were the determining factor in these long-term economic cycles, but that in later years economic fluctuations in the United States had a dominating influence.[4] T h o m a s's conception is probably in general terms correct, although there are some gaps in the documentation of his study.[5] In applying this theory to Finnish emigration in particular, we can as a starting point affirm with certainty that the development of world-wide economic trends determined the beginning of an emigration cycle, the fluctuations in the strength within the cycle, and the cycle's finishing point. On the other hand, conditions in Finland seem to have determined how large the number of emigrants within each long-term cycle grew.

What factors in Finland caused the number of emigrants leaving during the period 1894—1914 to be so much larger than that of the preceding 20-year period, despite the fact that just the opposite occurred in the other Nordic countries? One important explanation seems to be that overseas emigration from Finland began rather late when compared to Scandinavia. In the 1880's most of Finland was still an area from which overseas emigration had not occurred at all. Connections between Finland and America were thus still rather weak in the 1880's when emigration from Scandinavia was cresting. Returnees from America were still very scarce — at least in absolute terms. The transportation system was still in its infancy. A network of emigration agents developed only at the end of the 1880's. Only in the oldest

---

[3] *International Migrations* I, pp. 667—668, 748, 756. The following numbers of persons emigrated from Sweden, Norway and Denmark to overseas countries in 1874—93 and 1894—1913:

	1874—93	1894—1913
Sweden	512,306	370,148
Norway	284,490	276,524
Denmark	132,170	126,960

[4] T h o m a s 1954, pp. 94—96, 116. But the dependence of size of emigration on basically European conditions at the beginning of the nineteenth century had already been demonstrated a quarter of a century before. See *International Migrations* I, p. 83.

[5] As an example, we may mention that he uses figures obtained from Swedish emigration rather uncritically as examples. However, the reliability of the emigration figures in Swedish official emigration statistics varies appreciably from one year to another.

emigration area — mainly in the area around Kokkola and in Lapland [6] — did emigration »overcome» the factors which were limiting its growth, and possibly reach a peak already in the 1880's.

Although the above-mentioned factors certainly fostered the late cresting of emigration in Finland, the deciding factor here was probably population growth. The age group which was born during the famine years of the 1860's was exceptionally small. Thus the population of Finland grew in the period 1861—70 by only a little over 1 %, while population growth in the other Nordic countries was 7—10 %. In the 1870's and 1880's, however, the growth of Finland's population was the largest in the Nordic countries. In both decades the population in Finland grew by about 15 %, in other Nordic countries, by 4—10 %.[7] Changes in the birth rate and the growth of population signified that in Finland in the 1880's the age group most inclined to emigrate (16—25 years old) was exceptionally small, much smaller in relative terms, than in Scandinavia. Since the age groups born in Finland in the 1870's and 1880's were exceptionally large, the number of those reaching in the 1890's and 1900's the stage in their lives when they would be inclined to migrate was very great. The long depression which had arrived in the United States around the middle of the 1890's checked the bursting of this pressure at that time, but the new period of boom that began in the United States around the turn of the century made it possible for the overly-large age groups dammed up in Finland to gush out in an avalanche-like stream to countries overseas.

---

[6] On the basis of studies made in the archives of parishes by the IGHUT and on the basis of the passport lists, it is known that, in Kokkola rural commune, Kronoby, Lohtaja, Turtola, Sodankylä, Kuolajärvi (Salla) and Kittilä at least, emigration reached its peak in absolute terms in the 1880's.

[7] Kero 1971 III, p. 126; Svalestuen 1971, pp. 9—11.

VI The Composition of Finnish Emigration

1. The occupational-social composition of emigration

It is possible, based on Finnish official statistics, to determine the social and occupational composition of Finnish emigration for the years 1893 to 1914. The official statistics concern the entire country. Thus, if one wants to know which elements composed the emigration from some smaller region, it is necessary to collect statistics based on passport lists.

In the official statistics, emigrants are divided into 28 different groups, of which however only a few are really important. The most noteworthy groups are »farmers» (talolliset), »farmers' children», »crofters» (torpparit), »crofters' children», »dependent lodgers and cottagers» (loiset ja mäkitupalai-set), »workers and landless rural proletariat» (työväki ja irtain väki) and »hired help» (palvelusväki). The terms in the statistics indicate partly the emigrant's occupation, partly his social standing. In this study, the 28 groups of the official statistics have been combined into 7 groups, so that a better general picture of the occupational and social composition of Finnish emigration may be obtained. The seven groups are: farmers, farmers' children, crofters, crofters' children, cottagers, workers, and others. The following sections discuss how, according to official statistics, emigrants were divided into the above groups.[1]

It is important to emphasize that the terms used to indicate occupation and social standings for the period 1893—1914 are rather imprecise. First, it must be noted that the terms changed as the society industrialized and

---

[1] In the first group are included both landowning farmers and a very small group of tenant farmers (lampuodit), former farmers and their wives, and pensioners, who usually were former farmers. This group corresponds to groups 1—2 in the official emigration statistics. In the second group, farmers' sons- and daughters-in-law are also listed. This group corresponds to group 3 in the official emigration statistics. The third group (group 4 in the official statistics) also includes the wives of crofters and former crofters and their wives. The fourth group (group 5 in the official statistics) includes also the sons- and daughters-in-law of crofters. The fifth group corresponds to group 6 in the official statistics. The sixth group corresponds to groups 22—24 and the seventh group to groups 7—21 and 25—28 in the official statistics.

6

82

Table 9. The occupational-social composition of emigration, 1893—1914 (according to official emigration statistics).

Farmers	13,433	5.3 %
Farmers' children	61,422	24.3 %
Crofters	6,857	2.7 %
Crofters' children	24,634	9.7 %
Cottagers	67,915	26.8 %
Workers	49,536	19.6 %
Others	29,219	11.5 %
Total	253,016	100.0 %

economic life became more complex. Secondly, a term signifying a social or occupational station might have a completely different meaning in different areas of the country. The changes that have occured in the terminology used in the passport lists become clearly apparent in those many cases in which it is possible to compare the terms used to categorize a particular emigrant as he departed a first, second, and third time. Let us take as examples emigrants who left from Karvia. Of those who emigrated from this parish, 69 departed more than once and were issued a passport more than once. In 21 of these cases, the term used to indicate social standing or occupation changed as the emigrant received a second or third passport.[2] The nature and number of these changes is shown in the following chart. In the chart, an arrow indicates the direction of the change; a simple dash indicates a station that remained unchanged in those cases in which a passport was issued for a second or a third time.

Change	Number of cases
Farmer's son → farmer	3
Farmer's son → worker	1
Farmer's son → rural proletarian (itsellinen)	1
Farmer's daughter → rural proletarian	1
Wife of farmer's son → wife of rural proletarian	1
Farmer's daughter → maiden (neito)	1
Farmer's grandson → rural proletarian's son	2
Crofter's son → farmer	1
Crofter's son → farmer's son	1
Crofter's son → rural proletarian — rural proletarian	1
Crown land crofter → rural proletarian	1

[2] Some of these had been in America for many years and when they took their second passport they were perhaps only visiting Finland. But in some cases the person had been in America for a very short time and after his return to Finland many years went before he took his second passport.

Crofter's son → rural proletarian's son	1
Crofter's son-in-law — crofter's son-in-law → farmer	1
Crofter's son → former crofter's son → rural proletarian	1
Crofter's daughter → wife of rural proletarian	1
Crofter's daughter → rural proletarian → servant	1
Rural proletarian → crofter — crofter	1
Lower rank professional's (vaccinating officer) son → rural proletarian	1
Total	21

Nearly a third of the Karvia emigrants who received passports for a second or third time are categorized in the official statistics in at least two social groups. Doubtlessly, this is partly due to the fact that the social standing of the passport owner actually changed, as for example in such a case as that of farmer's son becoming a farmer. However, some changes, such as that of a farmer's daughter to maiden and that of a crofter's son to a rural proletarian's son, point to the fact that the criteria by which the standing of the passport owner was defined, was not clear. Regardless of whether changes in terms indicating social position were due to an actual change in the position in question or to an ambiguity in the terms themselves, it remains true that the changes were many. This means that while statistics based on passport lists may give a dependable picture of the social-occupational station of an emigrant at the time of his departure, no particularly reliable conclusions can be drawn about the social class from which the emigrant originated.

In the statistics that cover the whole country, the group »crofters», for example, also includes somewhat different elements. As G e b h a r d has confirmed

>»such terms as, for example, 'crofter' [torppari], 'cottager' [mäkitupa-lainen], 'rural proletarian' [itsellinen], 'rural worker' [maatyömies], 'truck servant' [muonamies] and 'dependent lodger' [loinen] often have entirely different meanings in different parts of the country.»[3]

On the other hand, although the size and tenure of lands cultivated by a crofter have changed noticeably, the term »crofter» has in a given locality probably defined rather precisely the »step» on the local occupational and social ladder on which the person in question belonged.

While statistics based on the passport lists have their limitations, the information they contain concerning which of the social groups emigrants belonged to on their departure can be viewed as generally dependable. If farmers and farmers' children are combined they form the largest emigrant group: 29.6 % of all emigrants. The bulk of emigration coming from inde-

---

[3] G e b h a r d 1913, p. 87. See also L e n t o 1951, pp. 23—24.

pendent farms came from the younger group, that of farmers' children. Since another 12.4 % of the emigrants were either crofters or their children — in other words, people who made their living from agriculture in a legally dependent station — a total of 42.0 % of Finnish emigrants were from various kinds of farms.

Different kinds of cottagers made up 26.8 % of Finnish emigration. This group was evidently quite motley in its occupational composition. The major portion, it seems, made its living from the opportunities for work offered either by farming or forestry. In coastal areas this group probably included some who actually made a living fishing or seafaring. Cottagers who lived in the vicinity of towns, doubtlessly worked also at different jobs available in these towns. Somewhat the same types of people belonged to the group »worker» as to »cottager». This group, which formed 19.6 % of Finnish emigration, included hired hands, maids, factory workers, and in some politically »awakened» localities, cottagers, who had begun to use the title »worker».

The group »others» made up 11.5 % of Finnish emigration. This group consisted of a great variety of different types, for example, sailors, fishermen, artisans, merchants, and lower-ranking professionals.

Did the occupational and social composition of Finnish emigration change in the years between the opening phases of large-scale emigration,[4] which began in the early 1870's, and the eve of the First World War? The following table shows the occupational and social composition of emigration for the years 1873, 1882, 1893, 1902 and 1913, all of which were peak years for emigration. The figures for the first two years come from the studies done at the IGHUT,[5] those for the latter three, from official emigration statistics.[6]

The same weaknesses exist in Table 10 as in the previous table, but there is good reason to conclude that the information given in this table gives at least an indication of how the social-occupational composition of emigration changed. The table may not give a completely comprehensive picture, also because the social-occupational composition of emigration in the through years perhaps diverged to a certain extent from that of the peak years shown in the table.

On the basis of the table, it seems that the social composition of emigration changed to a very large extent between the beginning of the 1870's and the outbreak of World War I. In the opening phases of large-scale emigration over half of the emigrants seem to have been farmers or their children; the

---

4 In the 1850's and 1860's a majority of emigrants were sailors, so at this stage the occupational composition of emigration of course differed from latter periods.

5 These figures include only those cases in which the person taking out a passport has also been found in the passenger lists.

6 SVT XXVIII:1, Table VIII (pp. 72—73); 10, Table VI (p. 21).

Table 10. The occupational-social composition of emigration in the years 1873, 1882, 1893, 1902, and 1913.

	1873		1882		1893		1902		1913	
Farmers	83	15.7 %	257	15.2 %	863	9.5 %	1,324	5.7 %	808	4.0 %
Children of farmers	200	37.9 %	557	32.8 %	2,263	24.8 %	5,245	22.7 %	4,887	24.4 %
Crofters	30	5.7 %	75	4.4 %	567	6.2 %	711	3.1 %	312	1.6 %
Children of crofters	29	5.5 %	96	5.7 %	723	7.9 %	2,433	10.5 %	1,855	9.2 %
Cottagers	77	14.6 %	418	24.6 %	2,642	29.0 %	5,849	25.3 %	4,712	23.5 %
Workers	46	8.7 %	149	8.8 %	1,047	11.5 %	4,578	19.8 %	4,805	24.0 %
Others	63	11.9 %	144	8.5 %	1,012	11.1 %	3,012	13.0 %	2,678	13.4 %
Total	528	100.0 %	1,696	100.0 %	9,117	100.0 %	23,152	100.0 %	20,057	100.0 %

former making up almost 16 %, the latter, almost 38 % of the total group. At the beginning of the 1880's these groups still seem to have composed almost half of the total emigration. In 1893 they composed only a little over 34 % and, in the first decade of the twentieth century, already under 30 % of total emigration, so that the reduction of their percentage was indeed appreciable in the periods following the opening phases of emigration. The reduction of the percentage of farmers was especially large: in 1873 they made up 15.7 % of the emigration, but in 1913 their proportion was only 4.0 %. During the same time the proportion of farmers' children dropped from 37.9 % to 24.4 %.

The percentage of crofters and their children among the emigrants remained much the same throughout the period. Their proportion seems to have been at its largest in 1893 and 1902, when these groups composed about 14 % of total Finnish emigration. The proportion of these seems to have been smaller in the opening phases of emigration and in the period just before the First World War. Within these two groups a large change seems to have occurred: in 1873 there were more crofters than their children among the emigrants (5.7 % and 5.5 % respectively of the total emigration), but the crofters' percentage fell noticeably during the period as that of crofters' children grew. In 1913 only 1.6 % of Finnish emigrants still belonged to the former group, while the proportion of the latter group was 9.2 %. The development within these two groups was much the same as that within the farmers and farmers' children groups.

In 1873 the cottagers composed 14.6 % of total Finnish emigration. In 1882 the group's proportion had already grown to 24.6 % and in 1893 it was 29.0 %, after which it seems to have declined slowly. In 1913, however, the group still made up 23.5 % of total Finnish emigration. The proportion of

»workers» was in the beginning of both the 1870's and the 1880's a little under 9 %, after which it grew so that in 1893 it was 11.5 %, in 1902, 19.8 % and in 1913, 24.0 % of total Finnish emigration. The group »others», in the beginning of the 1870's, the 1880's and the 1890's, made up about 10 % of total emigration, and at the beginning of the twentieth century, about 13 %.

The structural changes in emigration sketched above were in part actual, but in part only apparent. The social-occupational composition of emigration changed because of at least three factors. These were: the price of tickets for travel, the spreading of emigration from the Oulu and Vaasa Provinces to include also southern and eastern Finland, and the changes which occurred in the structure of Finnish population in general between the beginning of the 1870's and the opening of the First World War.

During the opening phases of emigration; that is, during the 1870's and early 1880's, the price of a ticket was higher than in later periods (see below pp. 169—174). It seems quite likely also that in the opening phases of emigration a relatively small proportion of those who sailed received a prepaid ticket from America. Borrowing money to meet the needs of the journey was probably more difficult at this time than later — there was then still no certain assurance that the traveller to America would be able to repay the money loaned. This signifies that, the ability to procure tickets for travel extended primarily to farmers, their children, and some of the more well-to-do crofters, while it was extremely difficult for crofters' children, cottagers, hired hands, and serving maids to collect the money required for tickets. Already by the end of the 1880's the trip to America was evidently within the reach of a noticeably broader segment of the social structure (especially in Oulu and Vaasa Provinces), because the sending of prepaid tickets from America had probably by this time become a general practice, and perhaps, to a certain extent, because returning emigrants brought money to areas from which emigration was occurring and were ready to loan it to persons desiring to go to America. Also, successful returnees from America doubtlessly served as evidence to the community that the borrowers of money for the voyage would very likely be able to repay their loans.

In the 1870's and 1880's emigration occurred mainly from Oulu and Vaasa Provinces. Especially in Oulu Province, the proportion of the total population living on small independent farms was greater than that in the country as a whole. The population structure of these central areas of emigration was an important reason why about one half of the emigration of the 1870's and 1880's was from among Ostrobothnian farmer families. As the pattern of emigration spread in the 1890's and the beginning of the twentieth century to southern and eastern Finland, it also spread to the areas, where crofters and cottagers predominated and as emigration became a mass phenomenon in southern Finnish towns, urban workers also joined these movements. Then the percentage of farmers and their children among the emigrants declined while that of workers and other segments of the population rose. The relative and absolute growth within Finnish population of urban elements and others not making a living directly from agriculture also played an important role in the changes which occurred in the social-occupational composition of emigration.

The structural changes sketched in Table 10 are in part only apparent, in other words, are due to the fact that new terms began to be applied to some groups in the social structure. Specifically, the wider application of the term »worker» around 1900 was probably a cause of the relative decline in the table of cottagers at the same time that »workers» were growing in number. It is quite evident that many cottagers began at this time to call themselves »workers», although neither their social standing nor occupation had changed.

If we wish to compare the social standings and occupations of emigrants leaving from different parts of Finland, we must compile statistics based on the passport lists. Since there are regions in Finland where, for example, the crofter population, or some other segment, was relatively very large, it would be interesting to see how clearly the social and occupational composition of the population of a given region is reflected in the composition of the emigrant group leaving that region. In order to clarify this problem, Table 11 shows, by province, how many of the group of emigrants leaving each province in 1905 were farmers, farmers' children, crofters, crofters' children, cottagers, workers and »others».

The occupational-social composition of emigration for the year 1905 is very much the same as it was for the entire period 1893—1914 (compare Tables 9 and 11). Thus the year 1905 can be used as a representative year for the period. The trustworthiness of the table is most suspect in that the same term may be used to indicate a person in a somewhat different station in, for example, eastern Finland than in western Finland. The information given by the table may, however, be considered as at least an approximation.

It becomes clear from the table that there were noticeable local differences in the occupational-social composition of emigration. There were 687 farmers among the emigrants of 1905, which composed 4.3 % of the year's total. The majority of this group came from Vaasa Province, but in relative terms the farmers' proportion of emigration was a little greater in Oulu, Viipuri, and Mikkeli Provinces, than in Vaasa. In Uusimaa, Häme, and Turku and Pori Provinces the proportion of this group was extremely small.

There were 3,983 farmers' children among the 1905 emigrants, making up 25.1 % of the total. The largest percentage of this group came from

Table 11. The occupational-social composition of emigration, by Finnish provinces, 1905

	Farmers		Children of farmers		Crofters		Children of crofters		Cottagers		Workers		Others		Total
Uusimaa	5	0.7 %	45	6.7 %	1	0.1 %	19	2.8 %	21	3.1 %	353	52.5 %	229	34.0 %	673
Turku and Pori	66	2.2 %	444	14.5 %	157	5.1 %	589	19.3 %	598	19.6 %	712	23.3 %	486	15.9 %	3,052
Häme	6	1.1 %	70	13.3 %	6	1.0 %	49	9.3 %	79	15.0 %	213	40.6 %	102	19.4 %	525
Viipuri	48	5.9 %	263	32.2 %	—	—	11	1.3 %	159	19.4 %	256	31.3 %	81	9.9 %	818
Mikkeli	15	5.2 %	93	32.3 %	10	3.5 %	25	8.7 %	85	29.5 %	44	15.3 %	16	5.6 %	288
Kuopio	25	4.2 %	148	24.9 %	6	1.0 %	29	4.9 %	230	38.7 %	97	16.3 %	59	9.9 %	594
Vaasa	378	5.1 %	2,139	28.7 %	279	3.7 %	990	13.3 %	2,318	31.1 %	747	10.0 %	601	8.1 %	7,452
Oulu	144	5.9 %	781	32.1 %	42	1.7 %	198	8.1 %	725	29.8 %	380	15.6 %	165	6.8 %	2,435
Total	687	4.3 %	3,983	25.1 %	501	3.2 %	1,910	12.1 %	4,215	26.6 %	2,802	17.7 %	1,739	11.0 %	15,837

Mikkeli, Viipuri and Oulu Provinces, while its smallest percentages occurred in Uusimaa, Häme, and Turku and Pori Provinces.

Altogether, 501 people who were called »crofters» in the passport lists left Finland in 1905, composing 3.2 % of total Finnish emigration. Relatively the largest share of crofters seems to have left from Turku and Pori Province, where they composed 5.1 % of the emigration. Particularly in Viipuri, Uusimaa, Kuopio, and Häme Provinces, the percentage of this group was extremely small.

1,910 crofters' children left as emigrants in 1905, making up 12.1 % of that year's emigration. In relative terms, the largest proportion of this group came from Turku and Pori Province — especially its northern part.[7] 589 or 19.3 % of this province's emigrants were crofters' children. The percentage of this group was extremely small in Viipuri, Uusimaa, and Kuopio Provinces.

The number of cottagers among the emigrants was 4,215, thus composing 26.6 % of the emigrants leaving Finland in 1905. Relatively, this group was greatest in Kuopio and Vaasa Provinces. In Uusimaa Province only 3.1 % of the total emigration belonged to this group.

There were in 1905, 2,802 different kinds of »workers» among the group of Finnish emigrants, making up thus 17.7 % of the total. In Uusimaa Province over half of all emigrants belonged to this group. The percentage of this group was also noticeably greater than the average for the whole country in Viipuri and Häme Provinces. The proportion of this group was smallest in Vaasa Province, where it made up only 10.0 % of the emigrants.

In 1905, there were 1,739 emigrants who fell into the group »others», which thus composed 11.0 % of total Finnish emigration. The percentage of this group was greatest in Uusimaa Province: 34.0 %. The group was relatively smallest in Mikkeli Province where only 5.6 % of the emigrants can be considered as belonging to it. As indicated earlier, this group consisted of a great variety of different kinds of people.

The social and occupational composition of the stream of emigration coming from different parts of Finland thus seems to have varied to a rather large extent. It seems evident, that the population structure of the province left is clearly reflected in the composition of the emigration. Farmers and farmers' children composed the greatest percentage of emigration in just those areas where these groups formed a larger than average proportion of the population[8]. Crofters and their children among the emigrants came from those areas where this system of land use was prevalent, in other words,

---

[7] For further information on the occupational structure of emigration from northern Satakunta see Kero 1970, pp. 86—87.

[8] Jutikkala 1963, p. 331.

the northern part of Turku and Pori Province.[9] Cottagers came in relatively greatest numbers from Savo's cottage areas, while workers in greatest numbers from Uusimaa, particularly Helsinki. The »others» also came in relatively greatest numbers from Uusimaa Province, where the economic structure (particularly because of Helsinki) was clearly more complex than elsewhere in Finland.

Comparisons of the occupational composition of emigration from different countries cannot reliably and accurately be made, because the comparability and reliability of the statistics are poor. In a comparison between Finnish emigration and emigration from other Nordic countries, it can be said, however, that Finnish emigration came more definitely than that of other Nordic countries from the agricultural sphere. And if the examination is extended to the whole of Europe, it appears that, in its occupational composition, Finnish emigration more resembles emigration from eastern and southern Europe than from western Europe. That is, a very large portion of emigration from eastern and southern Europe was from the agricultural sectors, while, on the contrary, an appreciable portion of the emigration from western Europe came from the industrial working population.[10]

2. The sex composition of emigration

In the intensive research done in recent years emigration historians have paid much attention to the structure of the population taking part in emigration movements. In this research, scholars have debated, among others, the question of why the great emigration, considered as a whole, has been so heavily male-dominated.

Quite trustworthy official statistics are available for Finnish emigration for the years between 1893 and 1914, from which we can determine how many of the emigrants were men and how many were women.[1] In addition to these published statistics, the writer has gathered corresponding informa-

---

[9] For further information on the proportion of crofter population in different parts of the country see R a s i l a 1961, pp. 21—33. In the northern parts of Turku and Pori Province there were communes, where almost half of the emigrants came from the group of crofters and their children (K e r o 1970, pp. 85—86).

[10] For further information on the occupational composition of emigration from different countries see *International Migrations* I, pp. 215—223; S v a l e s t u e n 1971, pp. 47—50; H v i d t 1971, pp. 210—245.

[1] In addition, corresponding statistics for Oulu and Vaasa Provinces are available for 1883—92. A more reliable picture is derived from the use of the passenger lists because, these contain, practically speaking, all emigrants leaving Finland during 1883—86. In 1887—92, a part of the emigrants did not travel through Sweden and Norway and are thus not found in the passenger lists of police departments of these

tion for the years 1869—92 from the passenger lists found in the Gothenburg,
Malmö, Stockholm and Trondheim police department archives.[2] For the
year 1892, information may also be obtained from passenger lists preserved
in the archives of the Finland Steamship Company.[3] In the light of these
statistical materials, the sex composition of Finnish emigration for the years
1869—1914 was as follows:

Table 12. The sex composition of Finnish emigration, 1869—1914.

	Men		Women		Unknown		Total
1869	11	73.3 %	4	26.7 %	—	—	15
1870	30	66.7 %	15	33.3 %	—	—	45
1871	65	56.5 %	50	43.5 %	—	—	115
1872	572	95.7 %	26	4.3 %	—	—	598
1873	808	82.4 %	172	17.6 %	—	—	980
1874	45	44.6 %	56	55.4 %	—	—	101
1869—74	1,531	82.6 %	323	17.4 %	—	—	1,854
1875	60	64.5 %	33	35.5 %	—	—	93
1876	72	56.3 %	56	43.8 %	—	—	128
1877	81	55.9 %	64	44.1 %	—	—	145
1878	92	67.2 %	45	32.8 %	—	—	137
1879	416	82.2 %	89	17.6 %	1	0.2 %	506
1875—79	721	71.5 %	287	28.4 %	1	0.1 %	1,009
1880	1,376	73.2 %	484	25.7 %	21	1.1 %	1,881
1881	2,166	74.3 %	635	21.8 %	113	3.9 %	2,914
1882	2,791	74.7 %	832	22.3 %	111	3.0 %	3,734
1883	2,025	74.0 %	658	24.1 %	52	1.9 %	2,735
1884	1,246	70.2 %	508	28.6 %	21	1.2 %	1,775
1880—84	9,604	73.7 %	3,117	23.9 %	318	2.4 %	13,039

countries' port towns, but for this period also, the information on the composition
of emigration in these passenger lists is probably at least as reliable as the figures
based on passport lists appearing in official statistics.

[2] The passenger lists of the Gothenburg, Stockholm and Trondheim police
departments have been used for the whole period (1869—92), the passenger lists of
Malmö for the years 1874—88.

[3] Statistics preserved in the archives of the Finland Steamship Company reveal
that in 1892 the Finland Steamship Company carried 3,177 emigrants from Finland to
England. For several shipping companies, however, information concerning individual emigrants is lacking in the passenger lists that were kept separately for each
shipping line by the Finland Steamship Company, so that the field of study is limited
to 1,041 emigrants. Of these, 29 are such that their sex cannot be determined because
of a deficiency or lack of clarity in their names. Thus the sex of the emigrant is
known in 1,012 cases. At the end of 1891, the Finland Steamship Company transported only 14 emigrants to England. Information as to their sex has not been
preserved.

1885	626	58.1 %	429	39.8 %	22	2.0 %	1,077
1886	2,589	77.9 %	687	20.7 %	48	1.4 %	3,324
1887	6,427	81.8 %	1,379	17.6 %	50	0.6 %	7,856
1888	3,533	72.7 %	1,295	26.6 %	34	0.7 %	4,862
1889	3,704	71.2 %	1,490	28.6 %	10	0.2 %	5,204
1885—89	16,879	75.6 %	5,280	23.7 %	164	0.7 %	22,323
1890	3,300	69.7 %	1,417	29.9 %	17	0.4 %	4,734
1891	2,417	66.5 %	1,217	33.5 %	—	—	3,634
1892	1,501	69.6 %	628	29.1 %	29	1.3 %	2,158
1893	6,277	68.8 %	2,840	31.2 %	—	—	9,117
1894	637	46.2 %	743	53.8 %	—	—	1,380
1890—94	14,132	67.2 %	6,845	32.6 %	46	0.2 %	21,023
1895	2,063	51.3 %	1,957	48.7 %	—	—	4,020
1896	3,078	59.4 %	2,107	40.6 %	—	—	5,185
1897	866	45.2 %	1,050	54.8 %	—	—	1,916
1898	2,001	57.7 %	1,466	42.3 %	—	—	3,467
1899	7,599	62.9 %	4,476	37.1 %	—	—	12,075
1895—99	15,607	58.5 %	11,056	41.5 %	—	—	26,663
1900	6,265	60.3 %	4,132	39.7 %	—	—	10,397
1901	8,237	65.6 %	4,324	34.4 %	—	—	12,561
1902	16,075	69.4 %	7,077	30.6 %	—	—	23,152
1903	10,449	61.6 %	6,515	38.4 %	—	—	16,964
1904	6,158	56.2 %	4,794	43.8 %	—	—	10,952
1900—04	47,184	63.7 %	26,842	36.3 %	—	—	74,026
1905	12,001	68.9 %	5,426	31.1 %	—	—	17,427
1906	11,921	68.1 %	5,596	31.9 %	—	—	17,517
1907	10,470	64.2 %	5,826	35.8 %	—	—	16,296
1908	3,313	57.0 %	2,499	43.0 %	—	—	5,812
1909	12,509	65.3 %	6,635	34.7 %	—	—	19,144
1905—09	50,214	65.9 %	25,982	34.1 %	—	—	76,196
1910	12,444	65.5 %	6,563	34.5 %	—	—	19,007
1911	4,821	51.4 %	4,551	48.6 %	—	—	9,372
1912	5,652	52.7 %	5,072	47.3 %	—	—	10,724
1913	12,919	64.4 %	7,138	35.6 %	—	—	20,057
1914	3,651	56.4 %	2,823	43.6 %	—	—	6,474
1910—14	39,487	60.2 %	26,147	39.8 %	—	—	65,634
1869—1914	195,359	64.7 %	105,379	35.1 %	529	0.2 %	301,767

The information given in the official statistics on the numbers of men and women emigrants can be considered to be quite accurate. The same may be said of the passenger lists, for it is normally very easy to confirm whether the traveller was male or female. The fact that several of these lists are missing reduces somewhat the trustworthiness of the picture obtained from the passenger lists. By the period 1887—92, Finnish emigration was no longer moving wholly through Sweden and Norway. In this connection, the number of emigrants carried by Norddeutscher Lloyd Line in the years 1890—92 was particularly noticeable. And, in addition to it, a number of other shipping lines, for which passenger lists are lacking, carried Finnish emigrants who are not registered in the passenger lists preserved in the Swedish or Norwegian police archives. Also part of the Finland Steamship Company's lists for 1892 have disappeared. There are thus certain gaps in the evidence, but the lack of certain passenger lists will not distort, at least not to a significant degree, the picture obtained of the sex composition of Finnish emigration.

According to the passenger lists of the Scandinavian police departments and the Finland Steamship Company, and official emigration statistics, 301,767 emigrants left Finland during the years 1869—1914. Of these, 195,359 were men and 105,879 women; in 529 cases the sex of the emigrant cannot be determined from the information available. Thus, according to the statistics, 64.7 % of emigrants leaving Finland between 1869 and 1914 were men, 35.1 % were women, and in 0.2 % of the cases the sex is not determinable. The sex composition of Finnish emigration as it appears in the official statistics for the years between 1883 and 1914 matches to a large extent that of the total emigration from Finland before the First World War.[4]

If the sex composition of Finnish emigration is compared with that of the other Nordic countries, it becomes clear that Finnish emigration is the most male-dominated. While 64.7 % of Finnish emigrants were male, the corresponding figure for Denmark was 61.1 %, for Norway 59.1 %, and for Sweden 54.6 %. Compared to that of some southern and eastern European countries, however, the sex composition of Finnish emigration was rather well-balanced. Thus, in 1907, for example, when immigration to the United States was the most heavily male-dominated of all times, 69.5 % of Finnish emigrants were (according to American statistics) male, while, for example, 96.5 % of Greek emigrants were.[5]

The reasons for the differences in these figures have been much discussed in recent years at the various conventions of Nordic emigration historians. It could be argued that the proportion of men and women among a given

4 According to official emigration statistics 186,403 men and 103,014 women left Finland in 1883—1914. Thus, 64,4 % of emigrants were men.

5 *International Migrations* I, pp. 667—668, 748, 757—758. For information on the sex composition of eastern and southern European emigration see *International Migrations* I, pp. 214—215, II, pp. 111—112; F o e r s t e r 1924, pp. 327—328; F o x 1922, p. 60.

94

country's emigrants depends upon how industrialized the country was, upon how strong internal migration was, and upon how large a proportion of the emigrants left from towns. The most persuasive argument behind these assumptions is that in both internal migrations and urban population women were in general clearly in the majority. It is, then, natural that emigration would be extremely male-dominated in those industrializing countries in which a strong internal migration brought noticeably more women than men from rural districts to the cities — provided that emigration from the cities was not very extensive. If a country's emigration was largely urban, we may assume that the opposite would be true, that is, that the percentage of women emigrants would be noticeably larger. It is very difficult, however, to verify these theories because of factors compensating each other.[6] Let us take as examples Denmark and Finland. About half of Danish emigration came from towns,[7] while Finnish emigration for the years 1870—1914 was only about 12 %/o urban.[8] The urban character of Danish emigration explains in part, why there was a greater percentage of women among Danish than among Finnish emigrants. But on the other hand, industrialization had advanced further in Denmark than in Finland and we can assume that Danish towns had brought noticeably more women from Danish countryside than Finnish towns in Finland did. Thus the »women reserves» of the Finnish countryside ought to have been larger than the Danish countryside's reserves were. These reserves to a certain extent may have compensated the fact that urban emigration from Finland was minor. So it seems impossible to make any »rules» governing the relationship between the industrialization of the country and the percentage of female emigration, although it would be natural that both the industrialization and internal movements would have had influence on the sex composition of emigration.

In addition to industrialization, internal migrations and urbanization there were other factors influencing the sex composition, such as a country's agricultural structure, its customs, the quantitative relationship between the emigration of families and of individuals, migration to neighboring lands, and the differences in the roles of men and women within the social structure.

There were only three years in the entire period 1869—1914 when women outnumbered men among Finnish emigrants: 1874, 1894, and 1897. The

---

[6] The inadequacy of this explanation has been pointed out by, among others, Andres Svalestuen. See Svalestuen 1971, pp. 39—41.

[7] H v i d t 1971, p. 112. During 1870—1900, 44 %/o of Danish emigration was urban and during 1900—14, 52.3 %/o was.

[8] According to official statistics, during 1893—1914 33,171 Finnish emigrants came from towns and 219,476 from rural districts. SVT XXVIII:1, p. 12, and SVT XXVIII:11, p. 2. If only those who were born in towns were counted as urban emigrants, the proportion from towns would be still much smaller.

women's proportion of total emigration was largest in 1874 when their share was 55.4 %. However, Finnish emigration was particularly meager that year; according to passenger lists only 101 emigrants left the country. In all years other than the above-mentioned three, the majority of emigrants were men. The largest proportion of men occurred in 1872, when of 598 emigrants, 572 or 95.7 % were male.

The percentage of male emigrants seems to have been regularly greatest in those years when emigration was growing or at a peak. The women's percentage was correspondingly largest in those years when the number of emigrants was declining or at a low point. This generalization holds true for the entire period from the end of the 1860's to the First World War. On the other hand, this does not mean that fluctuations in the strength of female emigration were qualitatively different than those of male emigration — these fluctuations were merely sharper in the case of men than of women. As early as at the beginning of this century it was argued that this was true because changes in economic trends affected much more forcibly those fields of work where men were employed than those employing women.[9]

If we examine the proportions of male and female emigrants in five-year periods, we get a good picture of changes in sex composition as emigration developed through the years. Such an examination shows that in the first five-year period of emigration, the proportion of men was 82.6 % and that in the last five-year period it was 60.2 %. Thus, it seems to be true that the sex composition of Finnish emigration became much more balanced as the phenomenon of emigration became more established. The percentage of men, however, did not decline in a straight line; in the last half of the 1870's the percentage of men was smaller than in the 1880's and in the last half of the 1890's it was smaller than during any later five-year period.

If the development of Finnish emigration is compared to the corresponding development of the other Nordic countries, we find that the changes which occurred in the sex composition of Finnish emigration deviated somewhat from those of the Scandinavian countries. The percentage of men among Finnish emigrants declined more than that of Scandinavian countries as the phenomenon of emigration became more established; in Denmark and Sweden the decline of the proportion of male emigrants was quite small and in Norway there was not any clear decline at all.[10]

Official statistics, which are available for Finnish emigration since 1900, reveal how many men and women left, on the one hand, from rural districts and, on the other, from towns. In addition to these, emigration statistics for the years 1873 and 1882 have been compiled at the IGHUT. According to

9 SVT XXVIII:11, pp. 6—7.

10 For further information on the sex composition of emigration from Scandinavian countries see S v a l e s t u e n 1971, pp. 39—41.

this compilation, in 1873, 381 men and 17 women left from rural areas; that is, 95.7 % of these emigrants were men. 101 men and 12 women left from towns, thus 89.4 % of these emigrants were male.[11] In 1882, 1,265 men and 254 women left from the rural areas: men composing 83.3 % of rural emigrants. 49 men and 45 women left from the towns: in other words 52.1 % of urban emigrants were men.[12] According to official statistics 121,448 men and 64,170 women left from rural areas in the period 1900—14; therefore, 65.4 % of the rural emigrants of this period were men. During the same time, 15,437 men and 14,801 women left from towns; thus 51.1 % of these emigrants were male. Men composed a clear majority of the emigrants from rural areas in every year of the period 1900—14; urban emigration was on the other hand female-dominated in the years 1900, 1904, 1908, 1911, 1912 and 1914.[13] The above figures reveal that rural emigration was heavily male-dominated, while the number of men and women among emigrants leaving from towns was approximately equal apparently from the beginning of the 1880's. The same difference in the composition of rural and urban emigration also existed in Denmark.[14]

Official emigration statistics also contain information, for the years beginning with 1900, on the sex composition of the emigrants from each of the Finnish provinces. For the years 1873 and 1882 the compilations done at the IGHUT are also available. The following table, based on these sources, shows the sex distribution of rural and urban emigration from each province for the years 1873, 1882 and 1900—14.[15]

During the years 1873 and 1882 emigration occurred primarily from Oulu and Vaasa Provinces. In 1873, 91 men and 6 women left from the rural areas

---

[11] The number of emigrants leaving from towns in 1873 was probably in reality appreciably smaller than 113, since the Kokkola city administration had apparently listed emigrants who left from Kokkola's rural commune as leaving from the town of Kokkola. In addition to the 511 persons leaving from towns and rural areas, 14 men and 3 women left from communes, the names of which, for one reason or another, are not clear in the passport lists.

[12] In addition, 54 men, 23 women and 6 persons whose sex is unknown left Finland in 1882. These emigrants can be found in both the passport and passenger lists but their home communes (or sex) are unknown.

[13] SVT XXVIII:1—11, Tables IV.

[14] Hvidt 1971, p. 178.

[15] SVT XXVIII:1—11, Tables IV.

[16] In addition, 14 men and 3 women whose names are found in both the passport and passenger lists, left from Oulu Province in 1873, but their home commune cannot be determined.

[17] In addition, 43 men and 20 women left from Oulu Province, 5 men and 2 women from Turku and Pori Province, 7 men and 1 woman from Häme Province, whose names are found in both the passport and passenger lists, but their home commune cannot be determined. And also 5 persons whose sex is unknown left from Vaasa Province.

Table 13. *The sex composition of emigration, by province, 1873, 1882, 1900—14.*

	Towns				Rural areas				Total			
	Men	%	Women	%	Men	%	Women	%	Men	%	Women	%
1873												
Turku and Pori	12	70.6	5	29.4	—	—	1	100.0	12	66.7	6	33.3
Häme	—	—	—	—	1	100.0	—	—	1	100.0	—	—
Vaasa	83	92.2	7	7.8	289	96.7	10	3.3	372	95.6	17	4.4
Oulu 16	6	100.0	—	—	91	93.8	6	6.2	97	94.2	6	5.8
Total	101	89.4	12	10.6	381	95.7	17	4.3	482	94.3	29	5.7
1882												
Uusimaa	5	100.0	—	—	1	100.0	—	—	6	100.0	—	—
Turku and Pori	—	—	—	—	11	84.6	2	15.4	11	84.6	2	15.4
Viipuri	—	—	2	100.0	1	100.0	—	—	1	33.3	2	66.7
Vaasa	33	50.8	32	49.2	992	84.6	180	15.4	1,025	82.9	212	17.1
Oulu	11	50.0	11	50.0	260	78.3	72	21.7	271	76.6	83	23.4
Total 17	49	52.1	45	47.9	1,265	83.3	254	16.7	1,314	81.5	299	18.5
1900—14												
Uusimaa	4,121	48.2	4,422	51.8	2,319	64.8	1,261	35.2	6,440	53.1	5,683	46.9
Turku and Pori	2,548	52.8	2,277	47.2	21,729	68.0	10,246	32.0	24,277	66.0	12,523	34.0
Häme	1,461	49.1	1,517	50.9	3,874	70.4	1,627	29.6	5,335	62.9	3,144	37.1
Viipuri	981	49.9	983	50.1	9,238	67.4	4,472	32.6	10,219	65.2	5,455	34.8
Mikkeli	252	71.8	99	28.2	3,458	76.9	1,038	23.1	3,710	76.5	1,137	23.5
Kuopio	659	59.0	458	41.0	5,928	72.1	2,293	27.9	6,587	70.5	2,751	29.5
Vaasa	3,997	54.9	3,289	45.1	57,903	63.9	32,708	36.1	61,900	63.2	35,997	36.8
Oulu	1,418	44.8	1,756	55.3	16,999	61.8	10,525	38.2	18,417	60.0	12,281	40.0
Total	15,437	51.1	14,801	48.9	121,448	65.4	64,170	34.6	136,885	63.4	78,971	36.6

of Oulu Province: in other words 93.8 % of these emigrants were men. In the same year 289 men and 10 women left from Vaasa Province: thus 96.7 % of this province's emigrants were male. Emigration without passports was such a general phenomenon in 1873, particularly in Oulu Province, that trustworthy conclusions cannot be derived by comparing this year's statistics for Oulu and Vaasa Provinces.[18] The statistical sources for the year 1882 are already to a certain degree more trustworthy, even for Oulu Province. At this time 260 or 78.3 % of Oulu Province's rural emigrants were men. At the same time 992 or 84.6 % of Vaasa Province's rural emigrants were men. On this basis emigration from Oulu Province seems to have been more balanced between the sexes than that from Vaasa Province.

According to official statistics, 121,448 men and 64,170 women left from rural districts of Finland during the period 1900—14.[19] Thus on the average, 65.4 % of the emigrants were male. Men composed a larger than average majority of rural emigration from Mikkeli, Kuopio and Häme Provinces, where over 70 % of the emigrants were male. The smallest proportions of male emigrants left from Oulu and Vaasa Provinces: 61.8 % of the former's emigrants and 63.9 % of the latter's were men. The same relationship still dominated between Oulu and Vaasa Provinces as in the years 1873 and 1882, so that it seems quite clear that emigration from Oulu Province was throughout the entire period more balanced between the sexes than that from Vaasa Province.

Why were there noticeable local differences in the sex composition of Finnish emigration? The explanation lies in part in the fact that emigration from Oulu and Vaasa Provinces was in the period 1900—14 already a common-place event which had been occurring for decades. On the other hand, emigration was an entirely new phenomenon in Mikkeli, Kuopio and Häme Provinces. Since it seems that emigration to a certain degree lost its male-domination as it became more common-place, it is natural that the sex composition of emigration at the beginning of the twentieth century was most balanced in the older emigration areas, that is in Oulu and Vaasa Provinces. It is also possible that internal migrations to some extent affected the sex composition of emigration. Internal migrations touched the populations of Oulu and Vaasa Provinces the least, so that fewer women from these provinces migrated to Finnish towns than from the other parts of Finland.[20]

According to official statistics 30,332 emigrants left Finnish towns in the period 1900—14, of which 15,437 or 51.1 % were men. Over half of the urban emigrants from Oulu, Häme, Uusimaa, and Viipuri Provinces during this

[18] Compare the numbers of men and women for 1873 in Table 13 with the numbers of men and women in Table 12.

[19] SVT XXVIII:1, Table I; 11, Table 8,a.

[20] Lento 1951, p. 58.

period were women. The smallest percentage of women among urban emigrants came from Mikkeli Province. On the basis of figures compiled from
1905 emigration statistics at the IGHUT, we know that in this year more men
than women left for countries overseas from the towns of Pori, Turku,
Rauma, Naantali, Jyväskylä, Kaskinen, Pietarsaari, Uusikaarlepyy, Kemi,
Kuopio, Joensuu, Hämeenlinna, Mikkeli, Savonlinna, Kotka, Viipuri, Hamina,
Käkisalmi, Lappeenranta, Porvoo, Loviisa and Tammisaari. On the other
hand more women than men left from Uusikaupunki, Vaasa, Kokkola, Kristiinankaupunki, Oulu, Tornio, Kajaani, Raahe, Iisalmi, Tampere, Helsinki
and Hanko.[21] The numbers of urban emigrants for the year 1882 were still
so modest that no conclusions can be drawn on the basis of the distribution
for this year. While, at this stage of research no far-reaching conclusions
can be made, it seems quite probable, on the basis of statistical sources collected by the IGHUT and of official statistics on the provinces, that more
than half of the emigrants from the towns of Vaasa, Helsinki, Tampere, and
Oulu were normally women. It also seems likely that emigration from Pori
and Turku was continually male-dominated.

In the above consideration of the sex composition of urban emigration,
the author has used primarily the computations about emigration for the
year 1905 compiled by communes at the IGHUT. The materials for the years
1873 and 1882 are scarce. These statistical computations for 1905 are also of
value in determining whether there were rural areas in Finland in which
the sex composition of emigration diverged noticeably from the normal pattern. It is impossible on the basis of materials covering only one year to
estimate to what extent chance happenings influenced the composition of
emigration from a given commune. Moreover, it should be mentioned that
in using 1905 as a representative year we get a picture of Finnish emigration
that is somewhat overly »male-dominated». According to official statistics,
there were 12,001 men and 5,426 women among the emigrants of 1905; that
is 68.9 % of these emigrants were male. However, men composed 64.7 % of
total Finnish emigration before the First World War. In order to test the
reliability of the compilations for 1905, the following comparison is made
between the picture of the sex composition of emigration from northern
Satakunta communes which has been derived from them and the corresponding picture based on the passport lists for the period 1881—1914.

The communes used in this comparison have been divided into four groups
in such a manner that the upper groups include those seven communes in
which the percentage of male emigrants according to 1905 or 1881—1914
materials is larger, the lower groups those seven in which this percentage
is smaller. An examination of the table reveals that ten communes remained

---

[21] The same number of women as men left from Heinola and Mariehamn. Not
one person emigrated overseas from Sortavala in 1905.

100

Table 14. The sex composition of emigration from northern Satakunta according to the materials for 1905 and passport lists for 1881—1914.

	1905				1881—1914			
	Men		Women			Men		Women	
Ahlainen	22	88.0 %	3	12.0 %	Ahlainen	218	80.4 %	53	19.6 %
Ikaalinen	146	86.4 %	23	13.6 %	Ikaalinen	1,680	78.7 %	454	21.3 %
Parkano	153	82.7 %	32	17.3 %	Jämijärvi	590	78.0 %	166	22.0 %
Jämijärvi	57	81.4 %	13	18.6 %	Parkano	1,238	76.5 %	380	23.5 %
Karvia	66	80.5 %	16	19.5 %	Pomarkku	499	73.3 %	182	26.7 %
Noormarkku	46	79.3 %	12	20.7 %	Karvia	692	73.1 %	255	26.9 %
Merikarvia	155	76.0 %	49	24.0 %	Pori rural	563	70.6 %	235	29.4 %
Pomarkku	55	73.3 %	20	26.7 %	Merikarvia	1,287	69.9 %	555	30.1 %
Kankaanpää	103	70.1 %	44	29.9 %	Noormarkku	490	69.4 %	216	30.6 %
Siikainen	104	68.4 %	48	31.6 %	Siikainen	950	66.2 %	484	33.8 %
Pori rural	42	67.7 %	20	32.3 %	Honkajoki	404	65.1 %	217	34.9 %
Ulvila	39	67.2 %	19	32.8 %	Ulvila	454	64.5 %	250	35.5 %
Pori town	80	57.6 %	59	42.4 %	Kankaanpää	1,301	63.1 %	762	36.9 %
Honkajoki	27	51.9 %	25	48.1 %	Pori town	1,458	60.7 %	945	39.3 %

continually in the same horizontal group regardless from which source material is used, while four communes »changed» groups. Since, even in the case of these four communes, the information in the statistics is not particularly contradictory, the comparison indicates that it is possible on the basis of figures for 1905 emigration to sketch in some degree the composition of emigration from the various districts of Finland.

Table 13 indicates that in the period 1900—14, 68.0 % of the emigrants from the rural districts of Turku and Pori Province were men. In comparison to the country as a whole, emigration from the rural districts of this province was therefore particularly male-dominated. In two separate areas however the proportion of women emigrants was exceptionally large. The first of these comprised the Åland Islands, the islands of Finland Proper, and some of the coastal communes of Finland Proper.[22] In the communes of this area, the proportion of male and female emigrants seems to have been approximately equal. The second of these areas was situated in northern Satakunta and consisted primarily of Honkajoki and Kankaanpää communes.[23]

---

[22] Esa Vainio is at present engaged at the IGHUT in a study of emigration from Kustavi, Taivassalo, Velkua, Rymättylä, Merimasku, Iniö and Houtskär, and has convinced the author that the larger than normal percentage of women among the emigrants can be generalized to cover the whole period of emigration.

[23] The difference is quite clear when these communes are compared to the communes east of them, and somewhat less clear when compared to the communes to the west.

Rural emigration from Vaasa Province was not quite so male-dominated as that from Turku and Pori Province; 63.9 % of its emigrants being men. Emigration from the Jyväskylä area for the year 1905 seems to have been extremely male-dominated as was that from the southernmost part of Ostrobothnia. Emigration was somewhat more male-dominated from Swedish-speaking than from Finnish-speaking areas of the province,[24] a difference that was already evident in 1882.[25] In 1905, the neighboring communes of Laihia, Vähäkyrö, Isokyrö and Ylistaro diverged clearly from the general pattern in Vaasa Province: 38—47 % of these communes' emigrants were women, while in the surrounding communes women formed only 20—30 % of the emigrants. In addition there was a group of more widely-scattered communes, including Toholampi, Kronoby, Veteli, Evijärvi and Lappajärvi, in which the proportion of women emigrants was around 40 %. In the scattered communes of Alahärmä, Peräseinäjoki, Kivijärvi and Karstula the number of male emigrants was also relatively small and that of women, relatively large in 1905. The statistical material available for 1882 indicates only that at this time neither the commune-group Laihia, Vähäkyrö, Isokyrö and Ylistaro nor the communes of Toholampi, Kronoby, Veteli, Evijärvi and Lappajärvi diverged greatly from the surrounding communes.[26]

The rural districts of Oulu Province, taken as a whole, formed an area in which the majority of male emigrants was smaller than any other corresponding area of the country. It seems, however, from the statistics for 1905 that such was not the situation in the entire province. Emigration from the province's southern portion was heavily male-dominated: 70—80 % of the emigrants were men. On the other hand, the proportion of women emigrants seems to have been comparatively large in the communes Pudasjärvi, Taivalkoski, Kuusamo and Utajärvi, where 36—49 % of the emigrants

24 Listed as rural Swedish-speaking communes are Sideby, Lappfjärd, Kristiinankaupunki rural commune, Närpes, Övermark, Korsnäs, Pörtom, Petolax, Bergö, Malax, Solv, Korsholm, Replot, Kvevlax, Maxmo, Vörå, Oravais, Munsala, Uusikaarlepyy rural commune, Jeppo, Pedersöre, Purmo, Esse, Terjärv, Kronoby, Larsmo, Kokkola rural commune and Nedervetil. Of emigrants from these, 1,207 were men and 490 women (3 unknown). 3,717 men and 1,639 women (10 unknown) left from rural Finnish-speaking communes. 193 men and 183 women left from towns. In addition 10 emigrants are found in both the passport and passenger lists, who were probably from Vaasa Province but whose home commune cannot be determined.

25 In 1882 556 men and 90 women (5 unknown) left from Swedish-speaking rural communes. Thus 85.4 % of emigrants were men. 436 men and 90 women left from Finnish-speaking rural communes. Thus, 82.9 % of these emigrants were men. 33 men and 32 women left from towns.

26 In 1882 84.6 % of emigrants from Vaasa Province's rural districts were men. Among the 97 emigrants from the group of communes Laihia, Vähäkyrö, Isokyrö and Ylistaro, 81 (83.5 %) were men. Among the 97 emigrants from Toholampi, Kronoby, Veteli, Evijärvi and Lappajärvi 79 (81.4 %) were men.

Table 15. Men among population and emigration in northern Satakunta.

	Men among population in 1910		Men among emigration in 1881—1914	
Ahlainen	2,214	50.3 %	218	80.4 %
Ikaalinen	6,341	51.2 %	1,680	78.7 %
Parkano	4,164	52.1 %	1,238	76.5 %
Jämijärvi	1,898	51.4 %	590	78.0 %
Karvia	2,170	51.4 %	692	73.1 %
Noormarkku	2,164	49.5 %	490	69.4 %
Merikarvia	4,145	50.5 %	1,287	69.9 %
Pomarkku	2,830	51.1 %	499	73.3 %
Kankaanpää	4,429	50.2 %	1,301	63.1 %
Siikainen	2,550	50.0 %	950	66.2 %
Pori rural commune	3,684	50.2 %	563	70.6 %
Ulvila	3,710	50.2 %	454	64.5 %
Honkajoki	1,787	49.1 %	404	65.1 %
Rural communes	42,086	50.9 %	10,366	71.1 %
Pori town	7,994	47.2 %	1,458	60.7 %
Total	50,080	50.3 %	11,824	69.6 %

were female. This area diverged similarly from the rest of the province already in 1882, for in that year, while 259 or 79.2 % of the emigrants from Oulu Province's rural districts were men, emigration from the above-named communes contained 13 men (56.5 %). However, the small number of emigrants leaving in 1882 somewhat reduces the value of statistics for this year. The numbers of emigrants leaving from the northern communes of Oulu Province are so small in all the available statistical sources, that no conclusions can be drawn from them.

Emigration from the rural areas of Häme, Mikkeli, Kuopio, Uusimaa and Viipuri Provinces was heavily male-dominated. A rather large number of the communes in these provinces were such that over 80 % of the emigrants leaving them in 1905 were male. Since so small a number of emigrants left from each of these communes, it is impossible on the basis of statistics for one year to conclude whether or not there were areas within these provinces in which the sex composition of emigration diverged sharply from that in surrounding districts.

When we compared the sex composition of the emigrant streams from different countries, we found that perceptible differences were due to a variety of different causes. The same is perhaps true when we seek the reasons for the noticeable differences existing between the different areas within Finland. One factor would be the structure of the population of the various areas. It is only natural that the proportion of men among emigrants would be larger than average in those areas in which the male proportion of the population was at the turn of the century larger than average. Table 15 (p. 102) attempts to illustrate, with the aid of statistics for northern Satakunta, the extent to which a given locality's exceptionally male-dominated emigration (or its comparatively large number of women emigrants) was due to the population structure of the locality.[27]

In 1910, 50.9 % of the population of the rural communes of northern Satakunta were men, while in 1881—1914 71.1 % of the emigrants from these communes were men. Using these numbers as a basis for comparison, the proportion of men among both the population and the emigration was larger than average in Parkano, Karvia, Ikaalinen, Jämijärvi and Pomarkku communes. The male proportion of the population of these communes ranged from 51.1 % to 52.1 %, and the percentage of men among the emigrants from these communes from 73.1 % to 78.7 %. In all other communes except Ahlainen the male proportion of the population was under 50.9 % and that of emigration under 71.1 %. Thus the only commune in which there was a disparity between the structure of the population and the structure of emigration was Ahlainen.

Thus sex composition of emigration from northern Satakunta seems to have depended at least in part on the population structure; if a larger than average percentage of a locality's population were men, emigration from that locality was correspondingly more male-dominated. The existence of this correlation does not mean, however, that variations in the proportion of male (and female) emigrants depended only on the population structure. This becomes quite clear when we compare the composition of the population and emigration of Kankaanpää commune to that of Pori rural commune. In both communes, 50.2 % of the population were men. However, 63.1 % of the emigrants from Kankaanpää were male, while men composed 70.6 % of Pori rural commune's emigration.

It has been stated that internal migration was one factor which affected the sex composition of overseas emigration. In addition to internal migration and the structure of the population, the attitudes of people toward emigration very likely influenced to a certain extent the manner in which emigration was divided between the sexes. It is quite possible (but cannot be documented) that in some localities people looked upon emigration by women with strong disfavor, while they considered male emigration to be an every-day and quite acceptable occurrence. It is also possible that the amount of employment available for men and women in each locality had an influence in this matter. The amount of employment, again, depended to a large extent on the local agricultural structure and the stage of the locality's economic development.

---

[27] STV 1914, Table 10. In question is the population listed in the parish records on December 31, 1910.

Thus the conditions which existed in each area from which emigrants left definitely influenced the sex composition of local emigration. In addition, it is quite probable that the place to which the largest portion of each locality's emigrants migrated influenced this sex composition. Let us take as an example northern Satakunta. Here there were three rural communes — Kankaanpää, Honkajoki and Ulvila — and one town (Pori) from which emigrants left for the east coast of the United States, especially New York City and the industrial areas of Massachusetts, in noticeably greater numbers than from the other communes in the area. In all four of these communes, the percentage of women among emigrants was perceptibly larger than in neighboring areas, from which migration was directed primarily toward the Great Lakes region of the United States, and whose migration was more heavily male-dominated than the norm.[28] It should also be noted that emigration from the islands and coastal areas of Finland Proper was directed mainly toward New York and that more women than men left from some of these communes. Again, the most important goal of overseas migration from Peräseinäjoki, was New York, at least in 1905, and the proportion of women emigrants from this commune was larger than from the surrounding area.[29]

Since the available statistical sources covering the destination and the sex composition of migration from areas smaller than the provinces are at present quite scanty, it is still impossible to make far-reaching conclusions concerning the correlation between destination and the sex composition in

[28] The following tabulation shows how many immigrants from group I (Kankaanpää, Honkajoki, Ulvila and Pori) and group II (Ikaalinen, Merikarvia, Parkano, Siikainen, Jämijärvi, Karvia, Noormarkku, Pomarkku, and Pori rural commune) went to New York and Massachusetts and how many to other parts of North America, and also how many of the immigrants from these groups were men.

	Migration to New York and Massachusetts		Migration to other states and provinces		Men among the emigrants from the area	
I	212	53.5 %	184	46.5 %	249	62.9 %
II	208	19.7 %	849	80.3 %	824	78.0 %

[29] The assumption presented above holds true particularly for Taivassalo and Kustavi. In 1905 a total of 35 emigrants left these communes, of whom 32 went to New York. 14 of the emigrants were men. On the other hand there are two communes in the same area that do not support the above-made assumption as far as emigration for 1905 is concerned. For in 1905, a total of 63 emigrants left from Houtskär and Rymättylä, of whom 55 went to New York or Massachusetts. Of the 63 emigrants, 53 were men. Of the emigrants from Peräseinäjoki, 44 (42.7 %) went to New York and Massachusetts and 59 (57.3 %) elsewhere in North America. This commune's emigration included 62 (60.2 %) men. Of emigrants from Peräseinäjoki's neighboring commune, Jalasjärvi, 71 (26.4 %) went to New York or Massachusetts while 198 (73.6 %) went to other places in North America. This commune's emigration included 208 (77.3 %) men.

these smaller areas. It seems to be the case, however, that emigration to the east coast of the United States occurred, above all, from those communes in which the proportion of female emigrants was larger than average. Migration to the mid-western states came to a large extent from those communes in which the percentage of male emigrants was larger than average. The pattern sketched on the basis of these sparse examples also seems quite natural because, around the turn of the century, employment for women was readily available in the eastern states, while the mid-western states offered excellent opportunities for men.

Although the existence of a correlation between the destination and the sex composition of overseas migration could be undeniably established, it is still by no means clear what kind of correlation it is. It is possible that communities in the eastern portion of the United States established by emigrants from a given locality such as Kankaanpää more readily attracted women as emigrants than communities established in the mid-western states. This would have increased the proportion of that locality's (Kankaanpää's) female emigrants. On the other hand, it is also quite possible that some localities in Finland »pushed» either men or women away from them. These men or women would then be attracted to the area in America which offered them the best opportunities for work. If those »pushed» to America were primarily men, they would have migrated mainly to the mid-western states. If they were primarily women, the stream of emigration would be directed mainly toward the eastern portions of the United States.

A greater proportion of men who left Finland as emigrants returned to their homeland than women.[30] Because of this fact, the Finnish population of an immigrant community in America was not as male-dominated as the stream of emigration itself. From the beginning of the migration to its final phases, however, men always formed a majority of the Finnish population living in overseas countries. The differences between the various immigrant communities were surely quite large. The »best» balance probably occurred in the United States and Canada. The Finnish immigrant-population in South Africa was probably the most male-dominated[31] and the male majority among Finns in Australia was not far behind this.[32] There were, however, also in the United States and Canada areas where the immigrant population, at least at times, consisted primarily of men. Most of the newly-

---

[30] K e r o 1972, pp. 24—25.

[31] For example, in 1905 all Finns, who left Finland for South Africa, were according to passenger lists men.

[32] K o i v u k a n g a s 1972 II, pp. 31—32; N i i t e m a a 1971, pp. 254—260.

founded mining and lumbering areas were of such a type. On the other hand, there were places, such as New York City, where the number of Finnish women was perhaps greater at times than that of Finnish men.[33]

3. The age distribution of emigrants

Only T o i v o n e n 's dissertation of almost all the studies dealing with Finnish emigration examines questions concerning the ages of emigrants. The nucleus of the results of her study is included in the statement that people of prime working age composed from decade to decade 80—90 % of all emigrants.[1] In part, T o i v o n e n has used the official emigration statistics as source material, and in part she herself has gathered information from the passport lists. In the other Nordic countries, problems concerning the age distribution of emigrants have been dealt with much more. Especially noteworthy is K r i s t i a n H v i d t 's dissertation in which he statistically examines changes in the age distribution of emigration through time, the differences in the age distribution of male and female emigration, differences between towns and rural districts and between different parts of Denmark.[2]

Official emigration statistics that include information on the ages of emigrants are available for studying the age distribution of Finnish emigrants from 1893 onward. However, the principles behind the compiling of the official statistics have changed somewhat, so that it is not possible to get an accurate picture of all the changes that occurred in the age distribution of emigrants between 1893 and 1914. In addition to official statistics, compilations concerning the ages of emigrants prepared at the IGHUT, were also available for this study. These compilations concern the emigrants of 1873, 1882, and 1905. Information for the first of these years was taken solely from passenger lists, since at that time the year of birth was not yet listed in the passport lists. Information for the years 1882 and 1905 is, on the other hand, based on both passport and passenger lists.

The age of an emigrant in the statistics prepared from passport lists at the IGHUT is calculated in such a manner that, for example, a child born in 1904 and leaving in 1905 is considered to be one year old. Since it is possible that a child born in December, 1904, for example, might have emi-

---

[33] At the end of the nineteenth and the beginning of the twentieth centuries, the majority of the membership in Finnish churches in New York was composed of women. This does not, of course, necessarily mean that the composition of Finnish population as a whole was the same, but does indicate that the role of women in the area of parish activities was exceptionally large.

[1] T o i v o n e n 1963, pp. 48—49.

[2] H v i d t 1971, pp. 148—174.

grated with his parents already in January, 1905, but is nonetheless listed as one year of age, these compilations from passport lists make emigrants a little older than they actually were. But this principle applied in interpreting the passport lists should not to any great extent affect the form of an age pyramid.

Whereas the year of birth is mentioned in the passport lists, the passenger lists give the age of emigrants. In comparisons of the average age of emigrants for 1882 and for 1905 on the basis first of passport lists, then of passenger lists, reveal the precise differences that would be expected. In 1882, the average age according to passport lists was 27.4 years and according to passenger lists 26.8 years, while in 1905 the average age was 24.1 years according to the passport lists and 23.5 years according to the passenger lists.[3] Thus it may be assumed that both the passport and passenger lists present a consistent picture of the age distribution of emigrants. If the distribution of emigrants' ages for 1905 is pictured with age pyramids based on first passport and then passenger lists, the structure of both pyramids is, as expected, pretty much the same. There are, however, several differences in the pyramids which raise the question of how accurate information based on passport and passenger lists really is.

Figure 3 shows that the number of under one-year old children was much greater according to the passenger lists than according to the passport lists. This is due part to the fact that children born in 1904 and leaving in 1905 have been punched according to the passport lists as one-year old although a number of them were doubtlessly the younger children entered in the passenger lists as »infants». But the difference could also have been due to the fact that children under one year could travel almost free, for example, in 1905, from Hanko to New York on the Anchor Line for 22 marks.[4] For this reason, children of one year or older may have been represented as under one year when tickets were purchased.

---

[3] In calculating the average age, those persons whose age is not known are, of course, not included. The percentage figures in the age pyramids were calculated from the total number of emigrants on whom information is available in both the passport and the passenger lists. Among them are a number of persons whose age is not given, or who are listed only as adults or children. In the figures for 1882, there are included from the passenger lists one person (0.1 %) who is known only to be a child and 25 persons (1.5 %) whose ages are completely unknown. Likewise the figures include 305 (18.0 %) whose years of birth are not listed in the passport lists. The figures for 1905 contain 22 children and 707 adults whose exact ages are not known on the basis of passenger lists and 1,496 persons about whose ages nothing at all is known. From the passport lists are included 471 persons whose years of birth are not mentioned in the lists.

[4] The passenger lists of the Finland Steamship Company for 1905. TYYH:s:m: 7: 3.

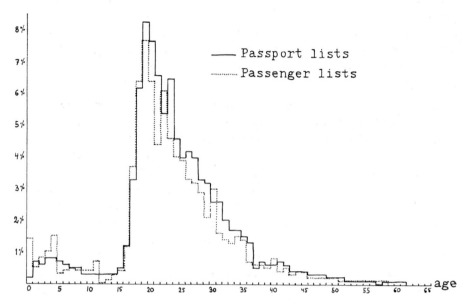

Figure 3. The age structure of emigration in 1905 according to passport lists and passenger lists.

Another clear difference in the pyramids occurs in regards to 4 and 5-year olds. According to the passenger lists, the former were much more numerous than the latter, while the passport lists show the number of each age to be about the same. Exactly the same kind of difference occurs in regards to 11-, 12-, and 13-year olds: according to the passenger lists the 11-year olds were more numerous than 12- and 13-year olds, while according to the passport lists each of these age groups contain approximately the same number of emigrants. Again it appears that incorrect ages were given when purchasing tickets because of regulations governing the price of tickets. For children from one to eleven years of age could travel on ships for half price, while those under five years travelled free on the American railroads.[5] It appears that for this reason five-year olds were often represented as four and twelve- and thirteen-year olds, as eleven.

Both passport and passenger lists give very much the same picture of the numbers of 14—19-year old emigrants. On the other hand the columns of 20- to 26-year olds differ from each other to a surprising degree. The most amazing difference is that according to passenger lists there were

---

[5] Pricing policy is revealed both in the directives received by the Finland Steamship Company from the joint organs of the transatlantic shipping companies (TYYH:s:m:7:18), and in entries in the passenger lists concerning the price of tickets. On the number of emigrants in each age group see Appendix B.

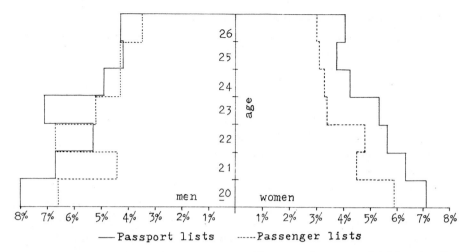

Figure 4. The percentage of 20- to 26-year old men and women of total emigration in 1905 according to passport lists and passenger lists.

700 21-year olds who thus composed 4.4 % of all emigrants named in these lists, while according to passport lists there were 1,045 or 6.6 % of the emigrants named in these lists. 22-year olds comprise, in the passenger lists 962 emigrants or 6.1 % of all emigrants, in the passport lists, 851 or 5.4 %, while 23-year olds comprise 730 or 4.6 % in the passenger lists and 1,036 or 6.5 % in the passport lists.[6]

It is possible, especially in the age pyramid based on passenger lists, that those whose ages were unknown were the cause of the inconsistencies found in the pyramids. However, we must then ask the question why these deviations occurred in just certain, succeeding age groups. In order to clear up this question, separate age pyramids for 20- to 26-year old men and women are illustrated in Figure 4.

Figure 4 and Appendix B show that the sections of the age pyramids for 20- to 26-year olds are much more inconsistent for men than for women. Relatively more 20- and 21-year old men appear in the passport lists than in the passenger lists, while 22-year old men appear relatively more frequently in passenger lists than in the passport lists. The percentage of 23- and 24-year olds is also greater in the passport lists than in the passenger lists. 25-year old men appear somewhat more frequently in passenger lists than in passport lists. But in regards to 26-year olds the situation is again just the opposite.

In the women's age pyramids, we see that in the passenger lists 22-year

---

[6] See Appendix B.

olds appear somewhat more frequently than 21-year olds (4.8 % and 4.5 % of total emigration respectively), while in the passport lists 21-year olds appear somewhat more frequently than 22-year olds (6.3 % and 5.6 % of total emigration, respectively). This inconsistency is however very minor when compared to the inconsistencies appearing in the male age pyramids.

The fact that the inconsistencies in the age pyramids of 20—26-year-old men are greater than those for women of the same age probably indicates that the ages of men were more often misrepresented in either the passport or the passenger lists (or in both) than are the ages of women. Apparently men misrepresented their ages either because of laws regarding military duty or because of the fear of being forced to fight in the Russo—Japanese War.[7] However, since there are also conflicts in the pyramids of women, matters concerning military service cannot have been the only reason. It is also possible that parish pastors would have on occasion given clergymen's certificates in which an incorrect age was given for the emigrant. Another possibility is that passport officials marked a more »appropriate» age for an emigrant in the passport list than his actual age was.

In principle it would be possible to discover whether passport lists or passenger lists are the more reliable source by comparing the entries concerning the ages of 20- to 26-year olds in these lists with information found in parish registers. In practice, however, the completion of such a comparison would be almost impossible, for it would involve the collecting of information from hundreds of parish archives. But, although the information on 20- to 26-year olds given by different sources is inconsistent, it should be emphasized that the mistakes in the sources are probably a matter of no more than one or two years.

In the remainder of the age pyramid based on passenger lists there are two peculiar platforms: first at the 30-year old, and then at the 40-year old column. These ages hardly would have differed in actuality from the ages just above and below them in the manner shown in the pyramid, but this must have been a case of rounding off the ages 29 and 31, for example, to 30. The pyramid based on the passport lists doubtlessly gives a more reliable representation in these cases.

As mentioned above, information on the ages of emigrants for 1873 is available on the basis only of passenger lists. Both passport and passenger lists are available for 1882, however, though the comparison between information presented in them was made on the basis of a much smaller sampling for this year than for 1905. As far as 1882 is concerned the inconsistency between the ages of one-year and under one year does not appear. In this year, on the other hand, five-year olds were apparently listed

---

7 In 1905 rumors circulated that Finns would be sent to fight in the Russo—Japanese War. Interview with Artturi Tuorila (Stark) in 1966. Notes of the author.

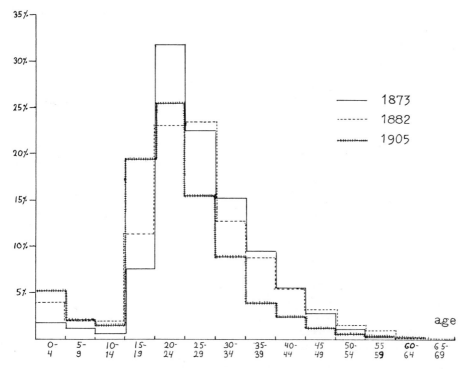

Figure 5. The age distribution of emigrants, 1873, 1882, and 1905.

as four-year olds, and 12- and 13-year olds as 11-year olds. No inconsist-encies are to be found in the adult age groups except that the numbers of 30- and 40-year olds are apparently exaggerated in the passenger lists. It is also possible that, at this time, those whose ages were near 25, 35, and 45 were listed in these age groups.[8]

A comparison between the passport and passenger lists of 1882 and 1905 indicates that information concerning the ages of emigrants is equally reliable in both these sources. Both sources contain a number of minor errors, but the general picture given by both is probably correct. Information on the ages of emigrants in the 1870's is available only from passenger lists, so that their reliability could be tested only by comparing the infor-mation in these lists to information found in parish archives. Since, however, passenger lists for the 1870's do not seem to have differed appreciably from passenger lists in the 1880's, it appears that the picture of the age distribu-tion of emigrants taken from them for the 1870's is relatively accurate.

8 See Appendix B.
9 See above p. 106.

As mentioned above, studies dealing with the age distribution of emigrants have been especially concerned with the question of whether this distribution changed or remained the same over a period of decades.[9] Figure 5 illuminates this question in terms of Finnish emigration with information based on passenger lists for 1873, 1882, and 1905. In this figure, emigrants have been grouped in age groups covering five years, so that the first group includes 0- to 4-year olds, the second, 5- to 9-year olds, the third, 10- to 14-year olds, etc.

Figure 5 and Appendix B reveal that in general outline the age pyramids of all three years appear much the same. Several differences can be found however. The 0—4-year old group was at its smallest, in relative terms, in 1873 and at its largest in 1905. The number of children travelling with emigrants thus seems to have grown continually in relative terms. The same holds true of the 5—9-year old group, whose numbers, however, seem to have been smaller than those of the younger group. This was undoubtedly due in part to the fact that in many cases five-year olds were listed in the passenger lists as four-year olds, but information from passport lists also indicates that the percentage of the 0—4-year old group among emigrants was in fact larger than that of the 5—9-year old group.[10]

In all three sample years the percentage of the 10—14-year old group was smaller than that of the two younger age groups. This could be an indication that only rather young fathers and mothers generally emigrated. Of course the sizes of these three youngest age groups might also indicate that parents attempted to take younger children along with them more often than 10—14-year olds, who perhaps were left to the care of grandparents or were found jobs as »little farmhands» or »little maids».

The percentage of 15—19-year old emigrants clearly increased as the phenomenon of emigration aged. Thus their proportion in 1873 was only 7.6 %, in 1882 it was 11.5 %, and by 1905 it was already 22.5 %. The percentage of the 20—24-year old group was at its largest in 1873, when 31.9 % of all emigrants belonged to this group. In 1882, this group's proportion was 23.5 %, but it was again noticeably larger in 1905, when 29.6 % of all emigrants were 20—24-year olds. With the exception of the year 1882, this was the largest age group.[11]

The proportions of emigrants belonging to the 25—29; 30—34; 35—39; 40—44; 45—49; 50—54; and 55—59-year old age groups were all smaller in 1905 than in 1873 and 1882. There were, however, no substantial differences between 1873 and 1882. 25—29-year olds composed 22.6 % of all emigrants in 1873, 23.8 % in 1882 and 18.0 % in 1905. The size of the 30—34-year old group was also rather appreciable: in 1873, 15.2 % of all emi-

---

10 See Appendix B.
11 See Appendix B.

grants belonged to this group, in 1882, 12.9 % and in 1905, 10.2 %. But the age groups older than this were already rather small, especially in 1905. There were no 60-year olds or older at all included in the 1873 emigration, and, in 1882 and 1905, this group made up only 0.2 % of the emigration.[12]

On the basis of the sources included in this sampling it appears that through the years a definite change occurred in the age distribution of Finnish emigrants; the proportion of emigrants who were rather young, but already of working age grew at the expense of those who were somewhat older, but still of working age. This change in distribution perhaps occurred as early as the 1880's, that is at the time when overseas migration had already become a tradition in the strong emigration areas of Oulu and Vaasa Provinces. The official emigration statistics thus reveal that the proportion of 16—20-year old men within total emigration remained approximately the same through the period, 1893—1907. Their percentages for these years ranged from 23.6 % to 33.8 % of total male emigration. After 1907 this group's proportion decreased: it ranged from 19.4 % to 23.4 % of total male emigration in the period, 1908—14. On the other hand, the proportion of 16—20-year old women remained pretty much the same for the entire period, 1893—1914; fluctuating irregularly between 19.0 % and 30.6 % of total female emigration.[13]

This »turn toward youth» in emigration is also evident in the trend indicated by the average age of emigrants. In 1873, this was 26.7 years on the basis of passenger lists, in 1882, it was 26.7 according to passenger lists and 27.4 according to passport lists, while in 1905 it was 23.5 according to passenger lists and 24.1 according to passport lists.[14]

The shift of emigration to a migration especially of the young occurred also in at least Norway and Denmark.[15] Thus, it seems quite possible, on the basis of studies of Nordic countries, that this process of emigrants getting younger was a part of the nature of overseas emigration from all of Europe.

To what is this »turn toward youth» in emigration due? It is, of course, possible that changes in the birth rate were of some influence. It appears more likely, however, that the »turn toward youth» in emigration was caused by emigration itself. One draws this sort of conclusion from the examination of, for example, some Southern Ostrobothnian communes where emigration became a mass phenomenon around 1880.[16] The age group born,

---

[12] See Appendix B.

[13] See Appendix C.

[14] The calculations were made on the basis of the statistics prepared at the IGHUT.

[15] Svalestuen 1971, pp. 41—43.

[16] As an example of the communes where the first emigrants departed in 1880 could be mentioned Jalasjärvi.

for example, in 1855 would be likely to have had its first contact with emigration at the age of 25, while the age group born, for example, in 1870 would have experienced strong contact with emigration from the age of ten. By the time the age group born in 1870 had reached 25 years, emigration had already been reducing their presence for fifteen years. Thus, by around 1895, there would be few of this group remaining who were interested in emigrating. Those disposed to emigrate would have already left at a younger age. Emigrants would come largely from those age groups that were just becoming old enough to migrate.

In addition to this process by which the balance in the age distribution of emigrants shifted to the younger age groups, several regular changes connected to the development of economic trends seem to have been taking place. One of these was that the under-16-year old men's percentage of total male emigration was at its smallest during peak years of emigration during 1893—1914 and at its greatest during trough years.[17] This indicates that during trough years a greater than average portion of emigration consisted of the movement of entire families, in which the percentage of under 16-year old boys would naturally be greater. On the other hand, the same type of regular change did not occur with under 16-year old women. This was probably due to the fact that 14- and 15-year old girls often left for America to work as maids particularly for relatives,[18] while the departure of 14- and 15-year old boys to America to work for wages was very rare.

Another group whose proportion of emigration seems to have depended on the movement of overseas economic trends were 21—25-year old men. In the period 1900—14, their percentage fluctuated between 20.4 % and 34.2 %. The percentage of this group appears to have increased in those years when emigration as a whole was growing and decreased in those years when emigration as a whole was declining. No such regular fluctuation occurred within the 21—25-year old women's group.[19]

No regular changes are discoverable, in regards either to men or to women, in the 16—20-year age group and in the groups older than the 21—25-year old group.[20] This being so, it appears that the emigration of 21—25-year old men depended most distinctly on overseas economic trends. Emigration of families and women continued in a more balanced manner, though the absolute number of women and of those belonging to families was greater during »good» years in America than in »bad» years.

To some extent it has already been shown above that the age distribu-

---

[17] See Appendix C.

[18] On young girls' coming to America, see for example Bruno Kallio, *Elämäni tarina* (Story of my life). A manuscript at the IGHUT, pp. 15—16.

[19] See Appendix C.

[20] See Appendix C.

tion of male and female emigrants were not always exactly the same. In the first place, official emigration statistics show that under 16-year old women almost regularly composed a larger percentage of total female emigration than the corresponding group of men did of total male emigration. Exactly the same holds true for 16—20-year olds in 1905—14. It also appears true among 21—25-year olds during 1900—04, but in the period 1905—14, the situation was exactly the opposite in this age group. But then, the percentage of men in the 26—30-year age group and older age groups among male emigrants is almost regularly greater than the percentage of women in these age groups.[21]

The statistics prepared at the IGHUT give much the same picture of the age distributions of male and female emigrants as the official statistics do. In 1882, 16-year old women and all younger age groups formed a greater percentage of total female emigration than men in the same age groups did of total male emigration. In some of the 17—25-year age groups, women and in some, men formed a greater percentage. Among over 25-year olds, the percentage of men in each age group of total male emigration was almost always larger than the percentage of women in each age group of total female emigration.[22]

In the 1905 emigration, women in the 0—18 age groups composed a greater percentage of all female emigration than men in these groups did of all male emigration. This was also probably true of 21- and 22-year olds. In all other groups, however, the percentage of men among total male emigration was greater than the percentage of women among total female emigration.[23]

A comparison of the sizes of different age groups of men and women clearly indicates that women emigrated younger than men did. The same is revealed by the average ages of male and female emigrants. In 1873 the average age of men leaving as emigrants was, according to passenger lists, 27.5 years, of women, 24.7 years; in 1882 the average age of male emigrants was 27.3 years according to passenger lists, and 28.1 years according to passport lists, while that of female emigrants was 23.6 years according to passenger lists, and 22.9 years according to passport lists. In 1905 the average age of male emigrants was 23.9 years according to passenger lists and 24.8 years according to passport lists, while that of women was 21.0 years or 22.4 years.[24]

Information on the age distribution of emigrants from different parts

---

[21] See Appendix C.

[22] See Appendix D.

[23] See Appendix D.

[24] The calculations were made on the basis of the statistics prepared at the IGHUT.

of Finland is available from 1900 on by province divided into the following age groups: under 16, 16—20, 21—25, 26—30, 31—35, 36—40, 41—45, 46—50, 51—55, 56—60, and over 60. On the basis of these statistics, the largest percentage of under 16-year olds seems to have come from Oulu and Viipuri Provinces. This age group was also somewhat over-represented in Uusimaa and Vaasa Provinces. On the other hand, this group was smaller than average in Turku and Pori, Häme, Mikkeli, and Kuopio Provinces.[25]

According to official statistics the 16—20-year age group was relatively largest in Vaasa Province. This group was relatively smallest in Uusimaa, Viipuri, and Häme Provinces.

The most prominent feature of the 21—25-year age group is that it was relatively small in Vaasa Province for the whole period. In regards to the two following age groups, 26—30-year olds and 31—35-year olds, Vaasa and Oulu Provinces differed from the rest of Finland having relatively few emigrants in these age groups. These two age groups were, on the other hand, relatively large in Uusimaa, Mikkeli, and Viipuri Provinces.

A comparison of the age distribution of emigrants from the different provinces indicates that emigration of families occurred relatively frequently from Oulu Province and perhaps also from Viipuri and Uusimaa Provinces, for which reason the youngest age group is quite heavily represented in this emigration. A special feature of emigrants from Vaasa Province was that more frequently than average they were very young, although already of working age. This was due to the fact that an extensive emigration continuing over a long period of time had already removed from the older groups almost all those who were »disposed» to emigrate. Thus new emigrants could come principally from the age group that was just reaching working age.

Statistical material on the age distribution of urban and rural emigrants is available from official emigration statistics from 1900. On the basis of this material, Table 16 shows how great a proportion of emigrants leaving from towns and from rural areas belonged to the groups, under 16 years, 16—20 years, etc.

The table shows that a clear structural difference existed between urban and rural emigration: under 16-year olds and over 25-year olds composed a relatively larger group among urban emigrants than among rural emigrants, while a greater percentage of rural than urban emigrants belonged to the 16—25-year old groups. This structural difference remained much the same throughout the period, 1900—14.

The largest groups leaving from towns were 21—25-year olds and 26—30-year olds. To these two groups belonged 45.7 %, or nearly half, of the

---

25 SVT XXVIII:1, Table II; 2, Tables 1903 II and 1904 III; 3—11, Tables III.

Table 16. The age distribution of urban and rural emigrants, 1900—14.[26]

	Rural areas		Urban areas	
under 16	19,274	10.4 %	3,875	12.8 %
16—20	49,247	26.5 %	5,296	17.5 %
21—25	52,662	28.4 %	7,728	25.6 %
26—30	30,698	16.5 %	6,095	20.2 %
31—35	15,272	8.2 %	3,275	10.8 %
36—40	7,998	4.3 %	1,672	5.5 %
41—45	4,378	2.4 %	816	2.7 %
46—50	2,394	1.3 %	430	1.4 %
51—55	1,213	0.7 %	236	0.8 %
56—60	747	0.4 %	130	0.4 %
Over 60	606	0.3 %	130	0.4 %
Unknown	1,129	0.6 %	555	1.8 %
Total	185,618		30,238	

urban emigrants. The largest groups of rural emigrants were 16—20-year olds and 21—25-year olds: 54.9 % of all rural emigrants belonged to these groups. Since the major portion of Finnish emigrants left from rural districts, the 16—20-year old and 21—25-year old groups also were the largest groups of emigrants from the entire country. 53.2 % of the emigrants from the entire country were from 16- to 25-years old. A comparison of the average ages of emigrants from urban and rural districts indicates that emigrants left from rural areas at a slightly younger age than from towns. According to passport lists for 1905, the average age of emigrants leaving rural areas was an even 24 years, while that of emigrants leaving from towns was 24.8 years.[27]

Thus emigrants leaving from towns were on the average a little older than those leaving from rural areas. A more fundamental difference in the age structures, however, is that there were rather large numbers of children and middle-aged persons among urban emigrants, while among rural emigrants there were more 16—25-year old emigrants than average. The age distribution indicates, first, that urban emigration was more definitely an emigration of families than rural emigration was. A partial reason may also be that a large portion of urban emigrants were so-called etape emigrants, who had been born in the country and who migrated overseas after living in town for a few years. By then they were somewhat older than those who went directly overseas when they first left home. It is further possible that 16—25-year olds were more in demand as a work force in towns than those over 25-years, in which case employment possibilities may have influenced

---

[26] SVT XXVIII:1, Table II; 2, Tables 1903 II and 1904 III; 3, Tables 1905 III and 1906 III; 4—11, Tables III.

[27] The calculations were made on the basis of the statistics prepared at the IGHUT.

118

the age distribution of emigrants. Also the fact that women appeared more frequently among urban than among rural emigrants may have affected the matter.

A large birth rate is generally considered to be one of the causes of emigration.[28] But no »rules» governing the relationship between it and the number of emigrants can be drawn up. The relationship between births and emigration could be explained to a certain extent, however, if accurate enough statistics on the age distribution of Finnish emigrants from the 1880's to the First World War were prepared. Then, we could probably estimate quite accurately how much the low birth rate of the 1860's and the high birth rate of the 1870's were later reflected in the age distribution of emigrants. On the basis of material available at present, we can say that the low birth rate caused by the famine years of the 1860's can still be seen distinctly in the age distribution of emigrants in 1905. This is made apparent in the following figure:

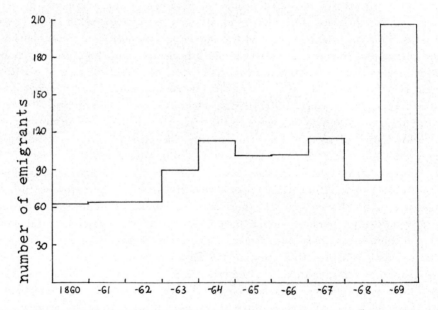

Figure 6. Age groups born in the 1860's among 1905 emigrants according to passport lists.

The figure shows that of the age groups born in the beginning of the 1860's, the later the group was born the more frequently it is represented among emigrants for 1905. This trend stops, however, for those born after

---

28 For example, Toivonen 1963, pp. 76—79.

1864. The effect of the series of famine years in 1865—68 can still be clearly seen in the age distribution of emigrants for 1905: the age group born in 1868 is here smaller than the age group born any year during 1863—67. Since the age groups born at the end of the 1860's were in 1905 already 35- to 40-years old, their percentage of the total emigration was not very significant.

Statistics on the age distribution of emigration have been prepared at the IGHUT for 1882 also. These statistics are of not much benefit, however, since the age groups born in the famine years of the 1860's formed an exceptionally small portion of the emigration for 1882, due in part to the fact that there were normally very few 12—15-year olds among the emigrants. Thus, in 1882, there were only 7 emigrants born in 1868, the worst famine year, who composed 0.4 % of total emigration for 1882. In 1905, there were 46 emigrants of this same age, composing 0.3 % of total emigration for 1905. But, we could assume, on the other hand, that, from the middle of the 1880's to the middle of the 1890's when the age groups born at the end of the 1860's were of »prime migrating age», their effect would have been much greater. And, if decent statistics were available for emigration at this stage, it would perhaps also be possible to discover how the arrival at working age of the large age groups born in the 1870's affected the extent of emigration.

4. Family emigration and individual emigration

Some emigrants travelled overseas in such a manner that the entire family or most of its members made the journey at the same time. Some families also migrated separately, for example, the father went first followed after a couple of years perhaps by the mother with one or two children, and then by the rest of the children accompanied by a relative or a friend. This overseas migration of entire families is called in the following section »family emigration». An individual emigrant was an adult[1] who travelled either entirely alone or with a party of emigrants leaving from his home area.

The problem of family and individual emigration has been studied especially in Sweden and Denmark. Sten Carlsson has published an article on Swedish emigration that examines this question,[2] and Kristian Hvidt has dealt with the same question in Danish emigration in his dissertation.[3] In addition, the Norwegian Andres Svalestuen has compared the numbers of family and individual emigrants in the different Nordic countries.[4] These studies have especially emphasized the conclusions that

[1] 16-year olds and older have been included with adults.
[2] Carlsson 1968, pp. 101—122.
[3] Hvidt 1971, pp. 192—209.
[4] Svalestuen 1971, pp. 43—47.

120

family emigration was most common in the opening phases of emigration and that individual emigration slowly increased as the phenomenon grew older.

There are practically speaking no studies dealing with the question of family and individual emigration from Finland. In her dissertation, T o i- v o n e n, using information from the official emigration statistics, has examined the number of emigrants with different marital status. In this context, T o i v o n e n demonstrates in her study only that the composition of Southern Ostrobothnian emigration did not seem to differ from that of the rest of Finland.[5]

The official emigration statistics contain information on the marital status of emigrants from 1900 on. According to these statistics, the percentage of married people among emigrants between 1900 and 1914 fluctuated irregularly between 19.7 % and 31.5 %. There were no fundamental differences appearing regularly between the peak and trough years of emigration. There was a slightly larger percentage of married people among rural than among urban emigration, but neither was this regular from one year to the next. The highest percentage of married people appeared in emigration from Viipuri and Vaasa Provinces, while the lowest percentages occurred in Kuopio and Mikkeli Provinces.[6]

The information on the marital status of emigrants in the official statistics has been based on passport lists, where there are a rather large amount of errors. It was quite common, for example, for the wife of a landless rural laborer to be listed as being unmarried. Thus it seems quite likely that the proportion of emigrants who were married was somewhat larger than the official statistics indicate.[7] On the other hand, it appears that the picture given by the official statistics which shows no fundamental changes occurring in the composition of emigration during the period 1900—14, is in general correct.

Since information for the years before 1900 is not available in the official emigration statistics, it is not possible on the basis of this material to determine whether the movement from family emigration to individual emigration which occurred in Sweden, Denmark and Norway, also occurred in Finland. Available for use in this study, however, are the statistics on emigration for the years 1873, 1882, and 1905 that were prepared at the IGHUT in 1970—72. In these statistics the distribution of emigrants into the family emigration

[5] T o i v o n e n 1963, pp. 50—51.
[6] SVT XXVIII:1—11, tables IV.
[7] In the archives of the parishes there is material that would make it possible to get exact information on how many of the emigrants of the locality were married and how many unmarried. To use this material would, however, require so much time, that in practice, it would be possible to take only some samples.

and individual emigration categories was made according to the entries in the passenger lists and passport lists. Usually it was possible on the basis of passenger lists to determine whether an emigrant should be listed in the family or the individual emigration category. The passport lists which are somewhat incomplete in the early phases of emigration were used only as a secondary aid when it was difficult to determine on the basis of passenger lists whether an individual was travelling alone or with his family. The following table contains information on the number of family and individual emigrants for 1873, 1882 and 1905. In addition to the emigrants on whom information is available in both the passport and passenger lists, those emigrants on whom information is available only in the passenger lists are included in the table.

Table 17. *The number of family and individual emigrants, 1873, 1882, and 1905.*

	1873		1882		1905	
Family emigrants	228	23.2 %	996	27.1 %	3,274	17.8 %
Individual emigrants	754	76.8 %	2,648	72.0 %	15,136	82.2 %
Uncertain	—	—	34	0.9 %	—	—
Total	982		3,678		18,410	

On the basis of this table it appears that in 1873 23.2 % of emigration was family emigration. In 1882 the proportion of family emigrants increased to 27.1 %. In 1905 the proportion of family emigrants was again smaller than it was for 1882. According to the table, 17.8 % of the emigrants belonged to this group.

According to official statistics 23.5 % of those emigrating in 1905 were married.[8] As has been indicated, however, the proportion of married emigrants listed in the official statistics is probably a bit too small, so that we could perhaps estimate the percentage of married persons to have been in reality about 25 %. Of the 2,736 persons categorized as family emigrants on the basis of passenger lists and who can also be found in the passport lists, 1,431 were children and 1,245 adults, but, according to official emigration statistics 4,092 married emigrants left Finland in 1905, and in reality the number was probably still somewhat larger. This means that about 3,000 married persons [9] left the country without being accompanied by their spouse or their children. It cannot be said with certainty whether these individuals

---

[8] SVT XXVIII:3, p. 9.

[9] Also those married persons who emigrated without a passport are included in this number.

122

can properly be called family emigrants. For example, the fact that the father of a family left for overseas lands did not necessarily mean that the rest of the family followed later. It happened quite often that he returned fairly soon,[10] that he died soon after arriving in the overseas country, or that he merely left his family in Finland to their own resources, in which cases we can no longer speak of family emigration, but only of a trip overseas by one member of the family or of the breaking up of a family.

If family emigration is seen as including those people who were married when they left, children travelling with them and children travelling to join them, the number of family emigrants for 1905 was about 6,300. Since the total number of emigrants for this year was according to passenger lists 18,410, this means that in rough terms we may say that family emigration made up about one third of all emigration, while individual emigration composed two-thirds. A more restrictive calculation (used in the Table 18), however, sets the proportion of family emigration at only about 18 %.

The passport lists for 1873 and 1882 do not contain enough material on the marital status of emigrants to make them useful here. For this reason we can only estimate on the basis of figures for 1905, how great a percentage of these years' emigrants were married persons, children travelling with them, or children going to join parents. Assuming that the relation existing between those who were family emigrants according to the passenger lists and married persons remained the same, about 45 %, instead of 23.2 %, of the 1873 emigrants were family emigrants and about 50 % of the 1882 emigrants, instead of 27.1 %, were.[11] Thus a comparison of the numbers of family and individual emigrants for 1873 and 1882 to the numbers of family and individual emigrants for 1905 indicates that a shift from family emigration to individual emigration occurred.[12]

---

[10] Among the married the percentage of return to Finland was higher than among the unmarried. K e r o 1972, pp. 23—24.

[11] The numbers of family and individual emigrants could also be computed in a slightly different manner than was done above. That is, it can be assumed that, in most cases, a mother emigrating with children was travelling to meet the father already in America. For this reason, we can shift a number of fathers of families, computed originally as individual emigrants, from the number of individual emigrants derived on the basis of the passenger lists, to the family emigrants category equal to the number of mothers travelling with children each year. Using this procedure, the number of family emigrants for 1873 comes to 237 which is 24.1 % of total emigration for the year. The number of family emigrants for 1882 is 1,098 which is 29.9 % of total emigration for the year. The number of family emigrants in 1905 would then come to 3,979 which is 21.6 % of the 1905 emigration.

[12] Of this change, it should be added that in 1873, cases where father, mother, and children travelled together composed 12.3 % of the emigration. In 1882, the percentage was 12.6 %, and in 1905, the percentage of these cases was only 3.3 %. In 1873, 3.5 % of the emigrants were mothers and children, who were apparently travelling to meet the father of the family. In 1882, 8.9 % of total emigration con-

.A comparison between the composition of emigration from different countries in terms of family and individual emigration is quite difficult for several reasons. In the first place, statistics do not generally cover the opening phases of emigration. Secondly, the statistics were not always compiled according to the same principles. Such a comparison is perhaps made most difficult, however, by the fact that the percentage of family emigration generally declined as the phenomenon of emigration grew older. For this reason the decades 1881—1910, for example, represented different stages in Finnish than they did in Swedish emigration. For the period 1881—90, perhaps about 50 % of Finland's emigration overseas was family emigration, while only 36.9 % of Sweden's emigration to the USA was.[13] In the decade 1901—10, 35.4 % of Finland's emigration was, according to S v a l e s t u e n, family emigration. Only 25.9 % of Sweden's emigrants were married persons and their children.[14] Although the differences are quite great, there is still no cause to believe that Finnish emigration was more clearly an emigration of families than Sweden's was, because already by the 1880's the family emigration phase of Sweden's emigration was over,[15] while in Finnish emigration this happened to be just the period when the percentage of family emigration was perhaps at its greatest.

As mentioned above a shift in the structure of Finnish emigration from family to individual emigration occurred as the phenomenon of emigration developed. A comparison between the composition of emigration from different countries is very difficult, but in any case we can argue that the same kind of structural change in emigration occurred in Finland as in the other Nordic countries.

From what did this change result? It seems apparent that changes in the composition of emigration were due to changes in the population structure of the area of departure. Emigration itself had an effect on the changes in this structure, but so did the death and birth rate and internal migration. In Finland it is apparent that the changes were due also to the fact that in the 1870's and 1880's the portion of Oulu Province of total emigration was larger than in the beginning of the twentieth century. The percentage of family emigrants from Oulu Province always seems to have been larger than from perhaps any province in southern parts of Finland.

---

sisted of them, while in 1905 such cases composed 10.7 % of the whole year's emigration. This being so, it can be stated that as time progressed from the 1870's to the beginning of the twentieth century, a change occurred in that, while at the beginning of the 1870's families often emigrated as whole units, it became more common with the passage of time for a family to migrate separately: the father first and the rest of the family some time later.

[13] C a r l s s o n 1968, p. 109.
[14] S v a l e s t u e n 1971, p. 47.
[15] S v a l e s t u e n 1971, pp. 44—47.

On the basis of the emigration statistics prepared at the IGHUT, it is possible to estimate to some extent whether the composition of emigration was the same all over Finland or if local differences existed. The statistics cover the years 1873, 1882 and 1905. In addition to this, official emigration statistics contain information by province on the marital status of emigrants leaving during 1900—14. Since practically speaking emigration in 1873 and 1882 came only from Oulu and Vaasa Provinces, the following table shows how great a percentage of emigration from these two provinces separately, and from the rest of Finland as a whole, was family emigration and how great a percentage was individual emigration.

Table 18. *Family emigration and individual emigration from Oulu and Vaasa Provinces and from the rest of Finland, 1873 and 1882.*

	1873				1882					
	Family		Individual		Family		Individual		Uncertain	
Oulu	16	13.3 %	104	86.7 %	137	32.9 %	276	66.2 %	4	1.0 %
Vaasa	12	3.1 %	377	96.9 %	184	14.8 %	1,032	83.1 %	26	2.1 %
Rest of Finland	11	57.9 %	8	42.1 %	11	29.7 %	26	70.3 %	—	—
Total	39	7.4 %	489	92.6 %	332	19.6 %	1,334	78.7 %	30	1.8 %

Comparing Oulu and Vaasa Provinces we find that in both 1873 and 1882 the percentage of family emigration was greater in Oulu Province than in Vaasa Province. In 1873 the proportion of family emigration was 13.3 % and in 1882, 32.9 % of total emigration from Oulu Province, while in Vaasa Province it was 3.1 % and 14.8 %. The numbers of emigrants leaving from other provinces are so small that a comparison between emigration from these provinces and that from Oulu and Vaasa Provinces would not be of much value.

By 1905 there were already a sufficient number of emigrants to make it possible to consider each province separately. The following table shows the extent of family and individual emigration by province for 1905.

The same difference can be discovered between emigration from Oulu and Vaasa Provinces in 1905 as before, that is, family emigration composed a larger percentage of Oulu Province's emigration than of Vaasa Province. By this time, however, the difference was quite small, since 18.4 % of Oulu Province's emigrants belonged to this group, while 17.7 % of Vaasa Province's did. In any case, since family emigration was relatively more extensive in Oulu Province than in Vaasa Province for all three of the sample years, it appears that the phenomenon of emigration in these two provinces differed structurally from each other to some extent.

Table 19. Family and individual emigration in Finland's different provinces, 1905.

	Family		Individual	
Uusimaa	151	22.4 %	522	77.6 %
Turku and Pori	385	12.6 %	2,667	87.4 %
Häme	65	12.4 %	460	87.6 %
Viipuri	183	22.4 %	635	77.6 %
Mikkeli	35	12.2 %	253	87.8 %
Kuopio	89	15.0 %	505	85.0 %
Vaasa	1,320	17.7 %	6,132	82.3 %
Oulu	448	18.4 %	1,987	81.6 %
Total	2,676	16.9 %	13,161	83.1 %

When emigration from Oulu and Vaasa Provinces is compared to that from other provinces, it will be found that emigration from Mikkeli, Häme, and Turku and Pori Provinces was comparatively more an emigration of individuals, while emigration from Viipuri and Uusimaa Provinces seems to have been more inclined toward family emigration.

As has been stated, official statistics are available covering emigration in the period 1900—14, which show by province the marital status of emigrants. The following table contains a summary by province of this period's emigration.

Table 20. Emigrants of different marital status, by province, according to official emigration statistics, 1900—14.[16]

	Married		Unmarried		Widows, widowers, divorcees and unknown		Total
Uusimaa	2,718	22.4 %	9,173	75.7 %	232	1.9 %	12,123
Turku and Pori	8,173	22.2 %	28,105	76.4 %	522	1.4 %	36,800
Häme	1,744	20.6 %	6,620	78.1 %	115	1.4 %	8,479
Viipuri	4,754	30.3 %	10,712	68.3 %	208	1.3 %	15,674
Mikkeli	874	18.0 %	3,858	79.6 %	115	2.4 %	4,847
Kuopio	1,534	16.4 %	7,640	81.8 %	164	1.8 %	9,338
Vaasa	25,759	26.3 %	70,969	72.5 %	1,169	1.2 %	97,897
Oulu	6,073	19.8 %	23,977	78.1 %	648	2.1 %	30,698
Total	51,629	23.9 %	161,054	74.6 %	3,173	1.5 %	215,856

According to Table 20 the percentage of married people was greatest among emigrants from Viipuri Province. This is in complete harmony with the conclusions made on the basis of the 1905 emigration, which also set Vii-

---

[16] SVT XXVIII:1—11, tables IV.

puri Province as the major region of family emigration in Finland. Since the table shows that the percentage of unmarried emigrants from Kuopio and Mikkeli Provinces was greater than the average for Finland, it is here also in agreement with the information presented in Table 19, according to which individual emigration was more common than average in Kuopio and Mikkeli Provinces than in Finland as a whole. Tables 19 and 20 also give the same picture of the extent of family and individual emigration from Häme, Turku and Pori, and Vaasa Provinces. On the other hand, the tables give contradicting pictures of Uusimaa and Oulu Provinces. Here, according to one source, family emigration was relatively more extensive than in the rest of the country, while the other source indicates that it was less extensive. For Oulu Province the contradiction results in part from the fact that a larger than average portion of its family emigrants were children. In Uusimaa, however, children composed a smaller than average portion of all emigrants.[17] It has been shown that Uusimaa Province's government kept passport lists more carelessly than any other passport authorities,[18] so that this contradiction might also result from the fact that the official emigration statistics for Uusimaa Province were based on less reliable materials than those for the rest of the country. In addition to this, official statistics indicate that there was a larger percentage of married people among Uusimaa Province's emigrants in 1905 than there was during the period 1900—14; the opposite, however, was true of Oulu Province.[19] This perhaps indicates that the figures based on passengers lists exaggerate to some extent the picture of Uusimaa Province's family emigration and give too modest a picture of family emigration from Oulu Province.

Thus, the material now available clearly indicates that there existed local differences in family and individual emigration. For the present, however, source materials are too few to make it possible to determine the extent of these structural differences.

On the basis of the statistics prepared at the IGHUT, it is also possible to answer the question of whether the composition of rural emigration differed from that of urban emigration. The following table shows how great a percentage of urban and rural emigration was family emigration and how great a percentage was individual emigration.

---

[17] In 1905, there were 448 family emigrants in Oulu Province, 251 (56.0 %) of these were children. In Uusimaa Province there were 151 family emigrants, 70 (46.4 %) of which were children. In the entire country there were 3,274 family emigrants, 1,797 (54.9 %) of whom were children.

[18] See above p. 39.

[19] SVT XXVIII:3, table IV. According to official statistics 19.5 % of the emigrants from Oulu Province and 24.2 % of these from Uusimaa Province were in 1905 married.

Table 21. The extent of family and individual emigration from towns and rural areas, 1873, 1882, and 1905.

| | 1873 | | 1882 [20] | | 1905 | |
	Family	Individual	Family	Individual	Family	Individual
Rural areas	20 4.8 %	395 95.2 %	283 18.2 %	1,273 81.8 %	2,294 14.7 %	11,947 83.9 %
Towns	19 16.8 %	94 83.2 %	40 42.6 %	54 57.4 %	382 22.8 %	1,214 76.0 %
Total	39 7.4 %	489 92.6 %	323 19.6 %	1,327 80.4 %	2,676 16.9 %	13,161 83.1 %

According to the table, family emigration was relatively more common from towns than from rural areas in all three of the sample years. It must be remembered, however, that an extremely large number of emigrants leaving from towns were people who had first migrated there from rural areas, for which reason the separating of urban and rural emigration is at least in some cases artificial. If the structural difference outlined above between urban and rural emigration did indeed exist, it may be due to the fact that a family left without the father doubtlessly could manage better economically on a farm than in town.

The following table shows how extensive family and individual emigration were among the Finnish- and Swedish-speaking population of Vaasa Province, the most important province of overseas emigration in Finland.

Table 22. The extent of family and individual emigration in the Finnish-speaking and Swedish-speaking areas of Vaasa Province, 1905.

	Family		Individual		Total
Finnish-speaking	986	18.3 %	4,397	81.7 %	5,383
Swedish-speaking	278	14.8 %	1,599	85.2 %	1,877
Total	1,264	17 4 %	5,996	82.6 %	7,260 [21]

The table shows that of emigration from Finnish-speaking areas in 1905, 18.3 % was family emigration. The corresponding figure for Swedish-speaking areas is 14.8 %, in other words, family emigration was more common in Finnish-speaking than in Swedish-speaking areas. It is likely that

---

[20] In addition to the emigrants mentioned in the table there was a small group of persons whose home commune is unknown, and a small group of persons who could not be included with either individual or family emigrants because of gaps in source material.

[21] There were 192 persons from Vaasa Province, who could be included in neither the Finnish- nor the Swedish-speaking population, because information on the language was not available. 136 or 70.8 % of these were individual and 56 or 29.2 % family emigrants.

128

differences in language districts depended upon the population structure of the area of departure. In part this might have resulted from the fact that emigration from Swedish-speaking areas of Vaasa Province was older than emigration from the Finnish-speaking areas. This being so, it can be argued that by 1905 it was possible for a greater shift from family emigration to individual emigration to have occurred in the Swedish-speaking areas than in the Finnish-speaking areas.

If we look at the destination in North America of individual and family emigrants,[22] we find that both were distributed rather equally in the various areas. In the most important states and provinces from the standpoint of Finnish immigration, — Minnesota, Michigan, Wisconsin, Illinois, New York, California, Washington, Colorado, Maine, Utah, and Ontario — individual immigrants were more common than average. Individual immigrants composed 83.6—89.9 % of these states' total immigrants, while on the average 83.1 % of those immigrating in 1905 were individual immigrants. On the other hand, a somewhat greater proportion than average of immigration to Massachusetts, Ohio, Pennsylvania, Oregon, Montana and Quebec consisted of families: of those coming to these states, 17.2—26.4 % were family immigrants. But these differences are so small, that there is no merit in deliberating on their causes. Moreover, it is quite possible that the distribution for 1905 is exceptional.

But, if the destinations of men and women travelling alone in 1905 are compared to each other, several clear differences can be discovered. While on the average 63.0 % of all emigrants were men travelling alone and 20.1 % women travelling alone, among emigrants travelling to the most mid-western and Rocky Mountain states over 70 % were men who departed alone, while over 40 % of the emigrants to New York were women who departed alone. These differences were due mainly to the fact that such »mining states» as Minnesota and Utah offered work primarily for men, while in such places as New York City excellent employment opportunities were available for women.

South Africa and Australia were quite clearly centers of individual immigration, at least when compared to North America. Thus all emigrants going to South Africa in 1905 were men who departed alone. Immigration to Australia was likewise basically composed of men travelling alone, for, as K o i v u k a n g a s has shown, 1,778 Finnish men and only 25 Finnish women have obtained Australian citizenship during the period 1866—1946.[23]

As stated above, the percentage of married and unmarried persons among emigrants fluctuated irregularly during the period 1900—14 with no

---

[22] The statistics have been prepared at the IGHUT.

[23] K o i v u k a n g a s 1972 I, p. 32.

dependence on changes in the extent of emigration. In other words, it appears that the composition of emigration did not depend on the course of economic life in overseas countries. Although such a dependence cannot be discovered from yearly statistics, it is not absolutely certain that the numerical relation between family and individual emigration was not at all influenced by phases in North-American economic cycles. In a given year, for example in 1910, the course of economic life could be such that the peak of an economic cycle would occur at the beginning of the year and that the latter part of the year would experience a period of decline. In emigration this would be reflected in such a manner that emigration would be quite extensive during the first part of the year, and more insignificant during the latter part. Therefore, in order to determine the correlation between economic cycles and the form taken by emigration, monthly statistics on the composition of emigration are required for several successive years. At present statistics are available only for 1873, 1882 and 1905. For these years the numbers of family emigrants in different months were as follows. Also the emigrants who could be found only in the passenger lists have been included.

Table 23. *The extent of family emigration, by months, 1873, 1882, and 1905.*

	1873		1882 [24]		1905	
January	—	—	—	—	178	9.0 %
February	—	—	—	—	140	9.3 %
March	—	—	20	15.0 %	338	15.2 %
April	—	—	48	21.5 %	268	13.9 %
May	1	0.6 %	104	15.2 %	418	18.0 %
June	116	28.4 %	334	33.4 %	400	25.5 %
July	42	26.9 %	288	44.7 %	311	27.4 %
August	36	33.3 %	52	29.5 %	323	26.6 %
September	24	30.8 %	74	27.0 %	318	24.3 %
October	9	20.0 %	35	20.0 %	255	23.4 %
November	—	—	3	4.7 %	190	16.9 %
December	—	—	......	—	135	15.7 %
Total	228	23.2 %	996	27.4 %	3,274	17.8 %

The distribution of emigrants in the sample diverge markedly from each other because in 1873 and 1882 emigration was very insignificant in the late fall and the winter, while in 1905 emigration occurred the year round. It can be said, however, that in 1873 and 1882 most families migrated in the

[24] In addition to the emigrants mentioned in the table there were (in 1882) 38 family and 127 individual emigrants whose month of departure is not known, and 34 emigrants who could have been included neither family nor individual emigrants because of some gaps in the source material.

summer months and in September. Individual emigration was also at its greatest in the summer months, but there was, however, proportionally more individual emigration in the spring and fall months than family emigration.

In 1905 individual emigration composed more than 90 % of the emigration for January and February. The proportion of family emigration began to grow in the spring and was at its greatest in relative terms from June to October. In absolute figures, however, family emigration crested at the same time as individual emigration, that is, in May.

On the basis of the sample years, it may be said that, although the composition of emigration in different months changed to some extent over the course of decades due to the development of the system of transportation, etc., it was a continuing general feature that family emigration occurred mainly in the summer months, while individual emigration was distributed more equally among the different months of the year, generally being, however, at its greatest in the spring. For this reason the percentage of individual emigration was at its largest in the winter months and in early spring and at its smallest in the summer months.

It can be argued that the changes which occurred in the composition of emigration during 1873, 1882 and 1905 resulted partly from the course of overseas economic developments. The most important causes of these structural changes were however seasonal. It would be natural, for example, that emigrants travelling with children would attempt to time their trip in the summer when travel was most pleasant.

VII Finnish Emigrants as Objects of Competition between Shipping Lines

1. The golden age of Swedish agents in Finland (from the beginning of the 1870's to the latter part of the 1880's)

The competition of shipping companies for the trade of Finnish emigrants, the procuring of tickets, and the travelling of emigrants from Finland to countries overseas have been examined in numerous connections. The studies of J ä r n e f e l t, E n g e l b e r g, and T o i v o n e n can be mentioned as examples. These explain briefly how English and German shipping companies competed for the trade of Finnish emigrants, how the Finland Steamship Company played its role in this transportation, how tickets were procured, and how the trip from the emigrant's home to his destination took place.[1] However, the studies mentioned are based on very scanty source materials, for which reason the results of the research contain many gaps. Because of this, questions concerning the travelling of emigrants from Finland will be examined rather thoroughly in the following section.

In the study of the conditions leading to increase of overseas emigration, much emphasis has been placed on the fact that the birth of regular steamship traffic brought overseas lands much closer to Europe, making emigration easier than it had been before. In the age of sailing vessels exact information on the sailings and arrivals of ships could not be given. After the beginning of steamship traffic, on the other hand, departures and arrivals could be announced quite accurately. In addition, steamships by making the trip quicker greatly decreased the many inconveniences connected with travelling.[2]

By the time overseas emigration from Finland began, steamships were already pushing sailing ships aside as carriers of emigrants. The number of Finns travelling as emigrants on sailing vessels was probably minuscule,

---

[1] J ä r n e f e l t 1899, pp. 24—25, 36—39; E n g e l b e r g 1944, pp. 26—57; T o i v o n e n 1963, pp. 56—71. See also H o g l u n d 1960, pp. 8—9.

[2] On the transcendance of the steamships over the sailing vessels see, for example, E r i c k s o n 1957, p. 77; G u i l l e t 1937, pp. 233—248.

although it was still considered worthwhile to emphasize in the first known advertisement by a shipping line distributed in Finland the advantages steamships offered over sailing vessels. This advertisement for the Allan Line dates from 1871.[3]

When mass overseas emigration began from Finland around 1870, a good number of regular shipping connections existed for transportation of emigrants, especially between Europe and America. The competitors as carriers of emigrants were above all German and English companies. The most important of these were the German Hamburg—Amerikanische Packetfahrt Aktien Gesellschaft, or HAPAG, and Norddeutscher Lloyd, and the English Cunard, Inman, National, Dominion, White Star, Anchor, Allan, State, and Wilson lines.[4] Some of these companies had been established in the age of sailing ships, while some were founded only after the transporting of emigrants had already proved itself profitable. At times these companies had agreements on the prices of tickets and on their fields of activity, while at times free competition prevailed.

The incentive for the beginnings of emigration from Finland came in part from Sweden and Norway, the majority of whose emigrants used English shipping lines in the 1860's and 1870's, and since Finnish emigrants travelled until the end of the 1880's almost without exception through either Sweden or Norway, it is only natural that the stream of emigration coming from Finland was connected with the international transportation system by emigration agents active in Sweden and Norway.

Very few Finns are to be found in the passenger lists of the Trondheim Police Department at the beginning of the 1870's. As has already been shown, Finns appeared instead by the hundreds in the passenger lists of the Gothenburg Police Department, already by the beginning of the 1870's. On the basis of a sample testing for the year 1873, it can be affirmed that the most important agents with Finnish customers at this time were C. W. Hällström, Karl Möllersvärd, John Odell and B. B. Petersson. C. W. Hällström represented the White Star Line, K. Möllersvärd the Allan Line, John Odell the Inman Line, and B. B. Petersson the National Line.[5] Of the 982 Finns travelling by way of Sweden in 1873, the share of these agents was 863, or 87.9 %.[6] Thus, the sale of tickets to Finnish emigrants travelling by way of Sweden seems to have been concentrated in the hands of relatively few agents most of whom probably had ticket-selling sub-agents in both Stock-

---

3 For further information on this advertisement see K e r o 1969 II, pp. 80, 102—109.

4 H v i d t 1971, pp. 358—361.

5 L j u n g m a r k 1971, p. 179.

6 The calculation has been made on the basis of statistics prepared at the IGHUT.

holm and Gothenburg. The operations of these agents in Finland at the beginning of the 1870's will be examined in more detail in the chapter on the recruiting of immigrants.

At the beginning of the 1870's, Finnish authorities took an extremely negative view of emigration propaganda. The confiscation of newspapers that printed articles on emigration [7] indicates that the use of the word »emigration» was almost forbidden. For this reason it must have been extremely difficult to spread written information about America in Finland. None of the propaganda material that might have originated in Sweden at the end of the 1870's and the beginning of 1880's has been preserved. But the fact that, by the beginning of the 1880's, emigration agents in Stockholm had Finnish-speaking assistants who went to the harbor to meet ships bringing in Finns [8] indicates that attention was paid to Finnish emigrants. According to passenger lists the most important agents selling tickets to Finns in 1882 were J. P. Fehrlund, Fredrik Nelson, C. W. Hällström, Chas A. Berglund, John Odell, F. P. Denovan, Leonard Borg and J. E. Sörenson.[9] According to entries in the passenger lists, C. W. Hällström represented the White Star Line, F. P. Denovan the American Line and J. P. Fehrlund the Allan Line. The lines represented by the other important agents are not indicated.

It is known that by the beginning of the 1880's some of the transatlantic lines had Finnish translators.[10] This perhaps indicates that companies dealing with transatlantic transportation also saw Finnish emigration as important enough to be worth competing for.

In the 1870's and the beginning of the 1880's, it was not possible to buy a ticket to countries overseas in Finland, and those wanting to emigrate had to procure their tickets from Sweden or Norway. In addition, Finnish emigrants began at a very early period receiving tickets from America, where transatlantic shipping lines employed people to sell tickets to immigrants. From these employees, immigrants could buy prepaid tickets, which they could send to individuals in Europe who desired to emigrate. In the beginning Finns had to be satisfied with prepaid tickets, which paid for the trip to America only from Stockholm. The first advertisement concerning the sale of tickets that appeared in a Finnish-American newspaper was placed in 1878 by C. K. Henrikson. He offered, in the paper *Swen Tuuwa*, to sell »steamship tickets on the best lines, and promissory notes to Europe».[11] The following year his advertisement in the *Swen Tuuwa* was joined by adver-

---

[7] K e r o 1969 II, p. 77 note 3.

[8] *Sankarin Maine,* October 8, 1880.

[9] The calculation has been made on the basis of statistics prepared at the IGHUT. See also B r a t t n e 1973, pp. 98—100.

[10] *Amerikan Suomalainen Lehti,* February 27, March 31, 1882.

[11] *Swen Tuuwa,* November 22, 1878.

tisements by agents of the National and Allan lines.[12] In 1880, the *Swen Tuuwa*'s successor, the *Sankarin Maine* contained advertisements for the Inman, Allan, National, State and Norddeutscher Lloyd lines.[13] In the same year, Inman, White Star, Allan, and National lines, or their agents advertised in the *Amerikan Suomalainen Lehti*,[14] they were joined the following year by Cunard and Norddeutscher Lloyd,[15] and thereafter by the Danish Thing-valla Line and the State, Stettin, Monarch, and Anchor lines.[16] In 1883 the Dominion line, and in 1884 the American and Swenska lines, entered the picture.[17] On the other hand, the first advertisement for the Guion Line appeared in the *Amerikan Suomalainen Lehti* only in 1887.[18]

At first, probably Scandinavians sold prepaid tickets to Finns, but by the beginning of the 1880's at the latest, the majority of these prepaid ticket sellers were Finnish-American small businessmen. The Finnish-American newspapers of the 1880's contain quite a large amount of information about their activities. On the basis of material preserved, it appears that the above-mentioned *Amerikan Suomalainen Lehti* was the most important newspaper for advertising by the shipping lines and their agents. Indeed, a majority of the advertising in the *Amerikan Suomalainen Lehti* was pur-chased by these shipping lines and their agents. In addition, the number of advertisements was extremely large when compared to those placed in other Finnish-American newspapers preserved from the 1880's. It appears that the paper's editor, Alex Leinonen,[19] actively attempted to work in concord with the shipping lines by publishing guides for those intending to emigrate each spring, when emigration from Finland was beginning.[20] The paper's circulation in Finland was very large. In 1882, it is said to have been cir-culated in 80 localities in Finland, primarily in Oulu and Vaasa Provinces. The greatest number of subscriptions went to Pudasjärvi where 20 copies were distributed. The *Amerikan Suomalainen Lehti* was spread in addition to Finland to several Finnish settlements in Sweden and Norway, and even Germany received one copy.[21]

---

[12] *Swen Tuuwa*, January 3, 31, 1879.

[13] *Sankarin Maine*, January 9, 23, December 17, 1880.

[14] *Amerikan Suomalainen Lehti*, January 23, February 20, 27, March 5, April 2, 30, December 24, 1880.

[15] *Amerikan Suomalainen Lehti*, January 7, April 8, 1881.

[16] *Amerikan Suomalainen Lehti*, March 3, 10, 17, May 19, December 15, 1882.

[17] *Amerikan Suomalainen Lehti*, April 27, 1883, January 4, March 14, 1884.

[18] *Amerikan Suomalainen Lehti*, September 21, 1887.

[19] Alex Leinonen was from Paltamo and had arrived in America in 1869. For more on him see Ilmonen 1923, pp. 92—93; Holmio 1967, pp. 508—509.

[20] For example, *Amerikan Suomalainen Lehti*, February 27, March 5, 1880, March 31, 1882, March 27, 1885, April 24, 1886, February 21, 1890.

[21] *Amerikan Suomalainen Lehti*, September 8, 1882. The subscription sent to

Mainly through the agency of the *Amerikan Suomalainen Lehti*, but also to some extent of other Finnish-American newspapers, the emigration propaganda of shipping lines thus reached individuals in the major emigration areas of Finland who intended to leave for America. Finnish authorities, who at the beginning of the 1870's confiscated issues of Finnish newspapers and the traveller's guides that were spread in some areas, which were quite »innocent» compared to Finnish-American newspapers, hardly realized how systematically the information needed by those desiring to emigrate was continually arriving in Finland.

Agents who sold tickets to primarily American Finns could be discovered in the first half of the 1880's, at least in all the most important Finnish-American settlements such as Hancock, Ishpeming, and Minneapolis.[22]

Starting in 1886, emigrants leaving Finland were able to buy their tickets in Finland. In this year, the Inman Line representative in Sweden appointed Vaasa merchant, K. J. Wahlstein, his sub-agent in Finland. The authorities, who had feared emigration almost hysterically in the 1870's do not seem to have interfered with his activities in any manner, which indicates a clear shift in the position taken by them. Another indication of this »freer atmosphere» was that by 1887 emigration agents were able to advertise in Finnish papers.[23]

2. Norddeutscher Lloyd's conquest and loss of the Finnish emigrant market (c. 1886—1894)

As stated above, the first known person selling tickets to emigrants in Finland was the Vaasa merchant, K. J. Wahlstein. Once this merchant had opened his office in Vaasa, the competition for Finnish emigrants took a new form. The *Wasabladet* wrote later, in 1894, that

> »once the directors of competing Swedish emigration companies took notice of Wahlstein's business operation, they quickly set up their own sub-agents in almost all the harbor towns along the Gulf of Bothnia coast and in Seinäjoki».[1]

As mentioned above, Wahlstein was the Finnish representative of the Inman Line agent in Sweden. The development of a network of agents which accompanied this competition for Finnish emigrants can be easily followed in newspaper advertisements placed by the shipping lines and their agents.

Germany was probably sent to Norddeutscher Lloyd, one of the advertisers in the newspaper.

[22] For example, *Amerikan Suomalainen Lehti*, April 6, 1883, October 17, 1884.

[23] See below p. 136.

[1] *Wasabladet*, May 19, 1894.

In 1887, advertising by emigration agents was still rather scarce. The author has found advertisements by only four different agents. One was the advertisements in the *Wasabladet* placed by E. F. Larsson, the Swedish agent of the Guion Line. Another was placed by S. G. Borin, Swedish agent for Norddeutscher Lloyd, and a third by Oscar Larsson, Swedish agent for the White Star Line. These advertisements appeared in the *Wasabladet* also.[2] The fourth appeared in the *Waasan Lehti* in the fall 1887. According to this advertisement, it was cheapest to travel to America by leaving from Helsinki to Copenhagen, whence the trip »is made on one of the following lines: Inman, Guion, White Star, Red Star, and others.» Lars Krogius & Co. was named as the agent selling tickets.[3] As already mentioned, Lars Krogius was one of the key people at the Finland Steamship Company at the end of the 1880's,[4] so it seems likely that this company was already at this stage planning to begin a regular passenger service consisting primarily of the transportation of emigrants. The founding of Krogius' agency meant that the opportunity opened to Finnish emigrants of travelling overseas without having to depend on Swedish emigration agents.

In 1888, German shipping companies joined the competition in earnest. At this time, HAPAG hired Chr. Rasmussen as its agent in Finland.[5] Rasmussen established his office in Hanko, and he advertised in at least the *Wasabladet*, *Wasa Tidning*, *Waasan Lehti*, *Satakunta*, and *Mikkelin Sanomat*. Rasmussen represented in addition to HAPAG the English Union Line. According to his advertisements, in the winter the first stage of the journey would be made to St.Petersburg and from St.Petersburg to Libau whence the trip could be continued by ship. In the summer the trip was made by ship from Hanko to Hamburg or to England.[6]

The Swedish agent for Norddeutscher Lloyd, S. G. Borin, advertised in the *Wasa Tidning* in 1888,[7] and his propaganda activities in Finland produced good results. The passenger lists of the Stockholm Police Department show that, at the end of the 1880's, the majority of this agent's customers were Finns, and almost all the Finns, whose names appear in the lists, were Norddeutscher Lloyd customers.[8]

---

[2] For example, *Wasabladet*, February 23, July 9, 1887.

[3] For example, *Waasan Lehti*, September 7, 1887.

[4] See above p. 33.

[5] Or Rasmussen succeeded in obtaining the right to represent HAPAG and Union Line.

[6] For example, *Waasan Lehti*, January 28, 1888; *Satakunta*, February 23, 1888; *Wasa Tidning*, February 28, May 1, 1888; *Wasabladet*, September 8, 1888; *Mikkelin Sanomat*, June 9, 1888.

[7] For example, *Wasa Tidning*, April 6, 1888.

[8] The passenger lists of the Stockholm Police Department for 1887—89 (Äldre Poliskammarens arkiv:emigrantlistor). TYYH:s:m:3:1.

In the spring and summer of 1888, the above-mentioned Vaasa merchant, K. J. Wahlstein served as an agent for German and English shipping companies, although Swedish agents still acted as intermediaries. Wahlstein advertised himself as the representative for the White Star Line,[9] but he apparently attempted to sell tickets for other lines as well, for in the fall of 1888 ten agents with offices in Sweden warned potential emigrants against buying tickets from Wahlstein. The Stockholm agents who published this warning stated that Wahlstein had claimed to be the representative for eight English ocean lines to America, and, they continued, since Wahlstein had broken the common rules of all the shipping companies, he no longer had the right to act as representative for any shipping line. The companies that »rebuffed» Wahlstein were Guion, Anchor, White Star, Norddeutscher Lloyd, Allan, Thingvalla, HAPAG, Inman, American, Dominion, National, and Cunard.[10] These apparently were the lines interested in conveying Finnish emigrants in 1888.

In addition to advertisements by Wahlstein and Rasmussen, advertisements by an Iwar Kiansten, who represented the Anchor Line and whose office was in Mikkeli appeared at least in the *Mikkelin Sanomat* and the *Waasan Lehti.*[11] Advertisements by Swedish agents, S. G. Borin, the Norddeutscher Lloyd representative mentioned above, E. F. Larsson, the Guion Line agent, John Wennerström, the White Star Line agent, and a man named Andr. Larsson, who did not mention in his adventisements which company he represented, also appeared in some Ostrobothnian newspapers.[12]

It appears that in 1889 a number of Swedish emigration agents established representatives in Finland. In Vaasa, a man named Laurell represented the Cunard Line.[13] At first the Guion Line had a man named Conrad Freese representing them in Vaasa and, a man named Bruno Wendelin in Kristiinankaupunki, but at the end of the year the company's representative in Vaasa was Selim Stendahl.[14] Cairenius & Co. of Vaasa represented the

---

[9] For example, *Wasa Tidning,* May 13, 1888; *Wasabladet,* May 5, 1888. In addition to this the Swedish agent of the White Star Line, John Wennerström, had his own advertisements in Finnish newspapers. See, for example, *Waasan Lehti,* August 1, 1888.

[10] For example, *Wasabladet,* September 22, 1888.

[11] For example, *Mikkelin Sanomat,* January 28, 1888; *Waasan Lehti,* March 14, 1888. The Swedish agent of the Guion Line had in March 27, 1888 *Wasa Tidning* an advertisement, which stated that the line had not an agent in either Vaasa or Sundsvall. On the other hand the advertisement stated that »reliable agents wanted».

[12] For example, *Wasa Tidning,* April 6, 10, 15, August 10, 1888; *Wasabladet,* March 28, 1888.

[13] For example, *Waasan Lehti,* November 13, 1889; *Wasa Tidning,* November 19, 1889.

[14] For example, *Waasan Lehti,* May 29, October 26, 1889; *Wasabladet,* October 26, 1889.

138

National, Allan, American, and Inman lines, and, at first, also Norddeutscher Lloyd.[15] On the basis of newspaper advertisements, the most active of the agents was, however, the frequently-mentioned K. J. Wahlstein who advertised that he represented the Inman, American and Beaver lines.[16] It seems that he had not really been »rebuffed». An agent for the Inman and American lines was also Oskar Tallus, whose office was »the Kaukola station»[17] (in Ylistaro). It was Sergeef & Co. of Hanko, however, who advertised themselves as the head agent for these two companies. This agency announced that it would transport emigrants by way of Hanko in the summer and by way of St. Petersburg-Libau in the winter.[18] The fact that Sergeef & C:o. advertised itself as the head agent for the Inman and American lines, may indicate that these shipping lines no longer allowed Swedish agents a monopoly in Finland, but were ready to depend also on native businessmen. Sergeef & C:o's advertisements, however, do not show with complete certainty what the true position of this agency actually was.

In 1889, K. J. Wahlstein represented, in addition to the above-mentioned English and American shipping companies, HAPAG, the main agent of which was again Chr. Rasmussen.[19] In August, 1889, Chr. Rasmussen turned over his position in Hanko to an Otto Rohde. J. Sandås became the agent in Vaasa in place of K. J. Wahlstein. J. Forsberg served as an agent in Kristiinankaupunki.[20]

The Swedish agent of the Guion line also advertised at least in the *Wasa Tidning* and the *Wasabladet,* where he urged Finns arriving in Stockholm to come to his office where Finnish-speaking employees were available.[21] In addition to this Guion Line agent, the Swedish agents for the Cunard, Inman, National, American, and Beaver lines also advertised in Finnish newspapers, before they procured their own representatives in Finland. On the other hand, the White Star Line apparently had only a Swedish agent, who attempted to obtain customers in Finland solely by means of newspaper advertising.[22]

The competition for Finnish emigrants developed into a real war in the fall of 1889 when The Scandinavian & Finlanders Emigrant Co. of New York

---

[15] For example, *Waasan Lehti,* October 5, 1889; *Wasa Tidning,* October 6, 1889; *Wasabladet,* October 5, 1889.

[16] For example, *Waasan Lehti,* May 15, 1889; *Wasa Tidning,* October 8, 1889.

[17] For example, *Waasan Lehti,* November 20, 1889.

[18] For example, *Waasan Lehti,* February 23, May 22, 1889; *Wasa Tidning,* February 26, 1889.

[19] For example, *Waasan Lehti,* May 29, 1889; *Wasa Tidning,* May 12, 1889.

[20] For example, *Waasan Lehti,* August 17, 21, October 2, 9, 1889; *Wasa Tidning,* August 18, 22, 1889.

[21] For example, *Wasa Tidning,* June 23, 1889; *Wasabladet,* August 21, 1889.

[22] For example, *Wasa Tidning,* March 10, 1889.

joined forces with Norddeutscher Lloyd. The goal of this alliance was apparently to direct the major portion of Finnish emigration through Germany. The founder of The Scandinavian & Finlanders Emigrant Co. was G. A. Grönlund, who is said to have been the son of a Jewish merchant from Tampere.[23] Grönlund probably came to America in either the late 1870's or at the beginning of the 1880's.[24] Before founding his own company, he worked for a short time as an employee of the American Emigrant Co. Then, in 1887, he established The Scandinavian & Finlanders Emigrant Co.[25]

From the beginning The Scandinavian & Finlanders Emigrant Co. initiated a broad advertising campaign in Finnish-American newspapers. At first, Grönlund sold tickets for many transatlantic lines, and in addition transferred money of immigrants arriving from Finland and possibly from other Nordic countries to their homelands. The currency exchange adopted by Grönlund's company was so advantageous to immigrants that it succeeded in winning at least Finnish immigrants from The American Emigrant Co. As has been stated, the company made an agreement with Norddeutscher Lloyd in the fall of 1889 and began a true conquest of the trade of transporting Finnish emigrants.[26] Preparations had apparently already begun earlier, for already in June the company announced that it was publishing a Finnish-English dictionary with the title *Siirtolaisen Tulkki* (Emigrant's Interpreter) and a Swedish-English dictionary. Ten thousand copies of the former and 26,000 of the latter were printed. It was announced that the dictionaries would be distributed free of charge to anyone coming to the company's New York office.[27]

---

23 *Amerikan Uutiset,* June 7, 1894.

24 According to information taken from the Swedish-American newspaper, the *Nordstjernan,* that appeared in the *Wasabladet* for June 16, 1894, Grönlund was 33-years old when he declared bankruptcy in 1894. This indicates that, if he came to America as an adult, he being born in about 1861, would have had to arrive in either the late 1870's or in the 1880's.

25 The first advertisement of The Scandinavian & Finlanders Emigrant Co. in the *Amerikan Suomalainen Lehti* appeared on June 1, 1887. However, already in 1886, Grönlund advertised in the paper that he sold Finnish books (*Amerikan Suomalainen Lehti,* March 6, 1886) and announced that he was an agent of the *Kansanvalistusseura* (Society for Public Education) in America. Before Grönlund began his activities, the most important company transferring immigrants' money to Finland and also selling tickets was the American Emigrant Co. In addition to the two above-mentioned companies, numerous others offered their services to Finns, but they were of less significance. These dated primarily from the 1890's, when, for example, A. Österholm & Co. (*Työmies,* November 5, 1890) and the Oldenburg—Jasberg Co. were founded (the first advertisement of this company in the *Työmies* was in the December 16, 1892 issue).

26 For example, *Yhdyswaltain Sanomat,* April 5, 1887; *Uusi Kotimaa,* August 4, 1887; *Työmies,* December 4, 1889; *Amerikan Uutiset,* May 31, 1894.

27 For example, *Wasabladet,* June 29, 1889. Of course, it is possible that the

The numbers of dictionaries printed indicate that at this stage of its activity the company intended to direct the main weight of its »conquest operations» toward Swedish-speaking areas, possibly in both Sweden and Finland. However, Finnish-speaking emigrants composed a majority of the company's customers during the period of its existence.[28]

In the fall of 1889, The Scandinavian & Finlanders Emigrant Co. sent as its agent to Finland a man named V. K. Hultin, who according to a newspaper report had been in service to the company in New York for more than two years.[29] In September, 1889, Norddeutscher Lloyd still had only four agents in Finland, situated in Oulu, Kokkola, Tampere, and Hanko.[30] But upon his arrival in Finland, V. K. Hultin rapidly established a network of agents that was much denser than before. Apparently this network of agents was built up until the fall of 1893. In the spring of 1890 the company had already representatives in at least Oulu, Hanko, Helsinki, Seinäjoki, Heinola, Karstula, Vimpeli, Sievi, Raahe, Oulainen, Himanka, Pyhäjoki, Lapua and Kauhava.[31]

---

dictionary had not been printed at the time it was announced, in which case the realisation of the plan must be seen as beginning later. And it is also possible that the dictionary was not printed at all.

[28] The majority of the names appearing in the lists of Finnish emigrants transported by Norddeutscher Lloyd that were published in the newspaper, *Hangö*, in the latter part of 1890 and the first part of 1891 are Finnish. However, Grönlund's objective apparently was to gain a foothold also in Sweden and Norway. This is indicated in the first place by the company's name, by the sizes of the dictionary editions printed, and by the fact that Grönlund had some kind of agreement of co-operation with *Den Norske Credit Bank* in Norway and with the *Skand. Cred. Aktie Bolaget* in Sweden. The banks in Finland with which Grönlund worked in co-operation were the *Vaasan Osakepankki* and the *Yhdyspankki*. The banks working in co-operation with Grönlund are indicated in a letter sent by Grönlund, on the upper border of which are printed, in addition to the company's own name, the names of the above-mentioned banks. G. A. Grönlund, March 29, 1892, to Oskar Heinonen. TYYH:s:m:MER:X:1. The letter was sent to Heinonen after he consulted Grönlund when money he had sent to Finland through Grönlund's agency had not reached its destination.

[29] *Työmies*, December 4, 1889; *Waasan Lehti*, December 28, 1889.

[30] For example, *Hufudstadsbladet*, September 21, 1889. The agents were Wilhelm Juustinen in Oulu, Otto Roden in Kokkola, H. Heerman in Tampere, and Emil Lemcke in Hanko.

[31] *Waasan Lehti*, November 16, 1889, March 5, April 2, 5, July 19, 26, 1890; *Wasabladet*, November 13, 1889, February 1, March 15, April 2, 16, 30, May 7, 1890; *Satakunta*, September 2, 1893. In 1893 there were agents also in Kokkola, Uusikaarlepyy, Kristiinankaupunki, Pietarsaari, Kannus, Kaustinen, Kälviä, Lohtaja, Ylihärmä, Kauhajoki, Jalasjärvi, Tornio, Kemi, Alavieska, Pori, Reposaari, Turku, Merikarvia, Siikainen and Porvoo. In addition to these there was a travelling agent. On the other hand, in 1893 there were not agents in Heinola, Karstula, Vimpeli, Raahe, Pyhäjoki and Lapua.

At the same time that he was creating a network of agents, Hultin began a widespread advertising campaign in the newspapers. Most of his advertisements were in the Vaasa newspapers *Waasan Lehti, Wasa Tidning* and *Wasabladet.* A typical advertisement included, among other things, information on the company's agents in different localities.[32] In addition he published testimonials obtained from emigrants telling of the excellent qualities of his line and of the incompetence of other shipping lines. In all likelihood the first such testimonial was the advertisement appearing in the February 8, 1890 *Wasabladet,* in which Jan Bertell from Maxmo and Matts Nyysti from Laihia announced that they had bought tickets from The Scandinavian & Finlanders Emigrant Co. office on the Bremen Line, which had attended laudably to their return trip to Finland. The advertisement ended with the statement that »we hope that all our country men, who intend to travel to America, will journey along this pleasant and speedy route». As an immediate sequel to this, Hultin paid for advertisements at least in the *Wasabladet,* in which the testimonials of Jan Bertell and Matts Nyysti were joined by those of John Mattsson and I. Backman. These declared how favorable an experience it was travelling on the Bremen Line.[33]

In the fall and winter of 1889—90 The Scandinavian & Finlanders Emigrant Co. arranged publication of newspaper articles favorable to its own interests. So many of these are to be found in the *Waasan Lehti* that it almost seems that V. K. Hultin had by one means or another bought for himself column space in this paper outside the regular advertising section. In the first place, the *Waasan Lehti* borrowed an article entitled »Finnish Emigration Company's Agency in Vaasa» from the paper *Työmies* (Worker), which was published in Ishpeming, Mich.[34] This article praised V. K. Hultin and the undertakings that he directed in Finland. In January 1890, an article entitled »In the Emigration Business» written in the same spirit appeared in the *Waasan Lehti.* This article says,

> »Six Finns... had bought tickets from a certain agent in Vaasa for themselves on the 'National Line' to Orange, Texas, the journey to which took about 50 days, but could have been made in 18 days... Of the Norddeutscher Lloyd company we can speak only with the highest praise... 'The Finlanders Emigrant Company' has also taken the greatest care that their agencies in various localities have been placed in the hands of reliable firms. The head office in Vaasa is directed by Mr. V. K. Hultin, who served in the company's New York

---

[32] For example, *Wasabladet,* February 1, 1890.

[33] For example, *Wasabladet,* April 2, 1890. The Scandinavian & Finlanders Emigrant Co. announced at the same time that Grönlund had resigned his position as director of the company, which position was taken by a man named Geo Brown. Confirmation of this information is not found in Finnish-American newspapers.

[34] *Työmies,* December 4, 1889; *Waasan Lehti,* December 28, 1889.

office for several years, and who, because of his true and upright con-
duct there, has received this large trust...»[35]

In April, 1890, there appeared in the *Waasan Lehti* a letter sent by
»S.V.T.» from Jacobsville, Mich., which is clearly directed at bolstering the
position of Norddeutscher Lloyd employees in Finland. This letter includes
the following:

> »... The emigration business seems to have received laudable improve-
> ments recently. It is especially to the credit of the 'Finlanders Emi-
> grant Company' that one is now able to travel all the way from Finland
> to America protected from all the 'swindlers' who have often cheated
> emigrants... And in conclusion, I would like to kindly advise everyone
> who travels to America in the future to buy their tickets from the
> Vaasa office of the 'Finlanders Emigrant Company'... I have heard
> that everyone travelling the 'Bremen Line' has boasted that the service,
> food, and treatment are good during the whole of the journey on said
> line...»[36]

In addition to glorifying the Bremen Line, the letter contained a dose of
information on the difficulties of travelling by way of Sweden.

In May 1890, the *Waasan Lehti* published a notice entitled »A Warning
to Emigrants» which read as follows:

> »Our paper has been asked to give space for the following warning:
> The undersigned bought their tickets at the Seinäjoki station from the
> Guion Line agent, Mr. H. Sjöblom on March 18... we payed 130 Finnish
> marks. The ticket was in force from Hanko, but without meal service
> of which we partook only from England onward... service and food
> were, in addition, very poor... for which reason we do not want to
> recommend that any of our fellow citizens travel this line.»[37]

The Russian consul in New York certified that the emigrants themselves
signed the article quoted above. There are two points in »A warning» that
indicate that special arrangements were made in order for *Waasan Lehti*
to get the article. The disadvantages that might generally befall emigrants
during their journey are recalled in amazing detail in »A warning». Above
all the fact that »A warning» was certified by the Russian Consul in New
York, however, points to a special arrangement. For this raises the questions
of how a group of Finnish emigrants, just arrived in the United States, knew

---

[35] *Waasan Lehti*, January 25, 1890. In the same issue of the paper is a half-page
advertisement which tells how excellent Norddeutscher Lloyd is.

[36] *Waasan Lehti*, April 2, 1890.

[37] *Waasan Lehti*, May 3, 1890. Also contained in the advertisement is a point
which tells of how those giving the warning were compelled to journey onward
from England on a ship of the American Line, although they had bought tickets for
the Guion Line. The names of the complainers were Frans Oskar Manni, Gustaf
Härmänmaa and Juho Perttula.

how to obtain an audience with the Russian consul in New York to make their »warning» more genuine, and of why the group was so eager that its account be published in the *Waasan Lehti*. The explanation can scarcely be other than that The Scandinavian & Finlanders Emigrant Co. in New York drew up the account, collected persons from New York harbor who were dissatisfied with the voyage, took them to the Russian consul in New York, and then sent the properly certified »warning» to the *Waasan Lehti*.[38]

At the end of 1890, the *Waasan Lehti* repeatedly printed two rather peculiar advertisements by Hultin. One of these told of how the German Kaiser had visited a Norddeutscher Lloyd ship and given it the highest praise.[39] In the second, 17 Finnish travellers on Norddeutscher Lloyd praised the company to the skies in an advertisement under the headline, »How to travel on the Bremen Line». To give this commendation more plausibility endorsements by the Russian consul in New York and by the New York City notary were included in the advertisement.[40]

The Swedish emigration agents and their Finnish sub-agents did not submit before the attack of Norddeutscher Lloyd without a fight. They received support in their activities from the shipping companies transporting emigrants from Finland to Sweden, from the Swedish railroads and from the Wilson Line which carried emigrants from Gothenburg to England. According to information in the newspapers, they offered to Finnish emigrants discounts which totalled 24 marks. Despite these discounts, it apparently still remained more expensive for emigrants to travel by way of Sweden than to go from Finland directly to Denmark, England or Germany and then to America. For, before the discounts, the journey by way of Sweden was reported to have cost 32 marks more than the journey by way of Denmark, England, or Germany.[41]

In the manner of Hultin, the Swedish agents, their sub-agents and the transatlantic shipping lines intensified their networks in Finland. In 1890, the White Star Line was working in common with The American Emigrant Co. Their main representative in Finland was Cairenius & Co., which had its office in Vaasa. In addition to Vaasa they had agents in Kaskinen,

---

[38] It is told that in about 1900 nobody spoke Finnish in the Russian consulate of New York (D u r c h m a n 1901, p. 7). It is probable that the situation was not better in 1890. This raises the question of how the consul could know what the group of Finns wanted. On the basis of this it is apparent (if the warning was not false) that in the group of Finns was somebody who could speak either English or Russian. This could have been the representative of The Scandinavian & Finlanders Emigrant Co.

[39] For example, *Waasan Lehti*, July 23, 1890.

[40] For example, *Waasan Lehti*, November 29, 1890.

[41] For example, *Folkvännen*, January 20, 1890; *Vestra Nyland*, February 28, 1890. See also *Hangö*, July 16, 1893.

Finby,[42] Kauhajoki, Ilmajoki, and Jalasjärvi.[43] Somewhat later there were
agents also in Pietarsaari, Oulu, Hanko, and Uusikaarlepyy.[44] The Guion
Line had agents in Vaasa, Seinäjoki, Kristiinankaupunki, and Hanko, in addition to which the company's advertisements generally also mentioned its
Swedish agent, E. F. Larsson.[45] A. N. Strömberg served in Vaasa as
representative for the Inman, Dominion, and Beaver lines.[46] The representative of the Cunard Line was again Laurell of Vaasa.[47] The Cunard Line had
also a representative in Pori.[48] HAPAG had agents in Helsinki, Vaasa, Kristiinankaupunki, Seinäjoki, Tampere, Pori, Rauma, Turku, Uusikaupunki,
and Mariehamn, while agents served the Danish Thingvalla Line in Vaasa,
Helsinki, Hanko, Turku, Oulu, and Pori.[49] In addition, the Swedish agents
still placed advertisements in at least the Vaasa newspapers.[50]

The competitors to Norddeutscher Lloyd attempted to take advantage
of, in addition to networks of agents, newspaper advertisements. These
attempted to show that travelling by way of Sweden was more pleasant than
by way of Germany. For example, the Guion Line agent declared that
»travellers on this line also avoid the unpleasant and circuitous route through
Germany.»[51] When compared to the amount of advertising paid for by Hultin in 1890, however, the use of newspaper advertisements by the other companies was minor.

On the basis of the number of emigration agents active in Finland at the
beginning of the 1890's, this period can be called the golden age of emigration agents. The competition was so fierce, however, that it was probably
more a matter of a contest for life and death of agents than any golden age.
In the important localities such as Vaasa, Seinäjoki, and Hanko, agents were
numerous. Thus in March, 1890, 12 transatlantic shipping companies that
transported emigrants had agents in Hanko. These lines were Allan, Anchor,

---

[42] On the basis of the advertisement one cannot know where the village named
Finby was. Because the advertisement was in an Ostrobothnian paper and because
other localities mentioned in the advertisement were in Ostrobothnia, we can assume
that the Finby mentioned above was a village somewhere in Ostrobothnia and not
Särkisalo, a commune in Turku and Pori Province, the Swedish name of which was
Finby.

[43] For example, *Waasan Lehti,* March 5, 1890; *Wasabladet,* March 1, 1890.
[44] For example, *Waasan Lehti,* June 11, 1890; *Wasabladet,* June 4, 1890.
[45] For example, *Waasan Lehti,* June 11, 1890; *Wasabladet,* February 15, 1890.
[46] For example, *Wasabladet,* August 23, 1890.
[47] For example, *Wasa Tidning,* June 19, 1890.
[48] For example, *Satakunta,* May 10, 1890.
[49] For example, *Waasan Lehti,* April 2, 1890; *Aamulehti,* June 28, 1890; *Satakunta,*
June 5, 1890; *Rauman Lehti,* June 4, 1890; *Sanomia Turusta,* April 15, 1890; *Uusi
Suometar,* March 27, 1890.
[50] For example, *Waasan Lehti,* February 19, 1890; *Wasa Tidning,* March 20, 1890.
[51] For example, *Waasan Lehti,* June 11, 1890; *Wasabladet,* February 15, 1890.

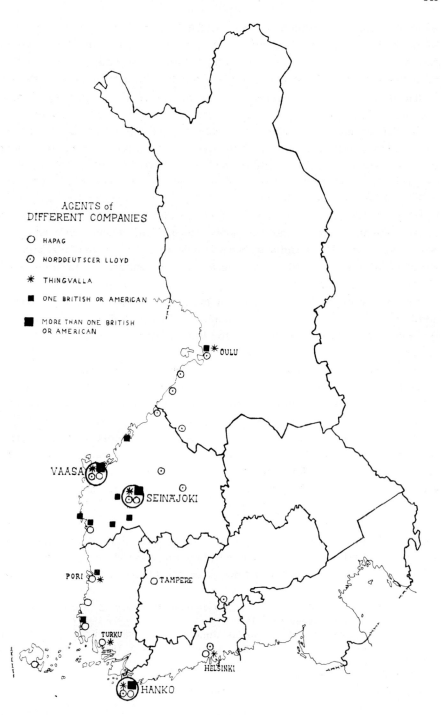

Map 4. The emigrant agents active in Finland in the beginning of 1890.

Beaver, Cunard, Dominion, Guion, HAPAG, Inman, Norddeutscher Lloyd, State, White Star, and Thingvalla.[52] In addition to these the American and National lines were also in the competition for Finnish emigrants,[53] so there were at least 14 shipping lines trying to obtain customers in Finland.

There is one common feature found in the advertising of all these shipping companies: the majority of their advertisements were in newspapers that were distributed in Ostrobothnia. Newspapers published in Vaasa were particularly popular. Apparently the advertisers did not attempt to influence those areas from which emigration had not yet begun and where it did not yet possess the character of a mass movement. The only exception seems to have been HAPAG, which frequently placed advertisements in a large number of newspapers that circulated outside Emigration Finland.[54] The advertisements were aimed primarily toward influencing the emigrants streaming from Ostrobothnia to become customers of a given line, and only secondly, if at all, toward awakening a fever for emigration in areas where it had not yet begun.

In attempting to win over customers to their own line, agents used, in addition to newspaper advertising, handbills which gave information on the types of transportation available on the line, its time-tables and ticket prices. Hultin's emigration office in particular is said to have distributed these in countless numbers.[55] Some agents even peddled their tickets on trains,[56] while a group of agents at the Seinäjoki station fought with one another in enticing the newly-arrived individuals who intended to emigrate to use their line.[57]

With bold and intensive activity, and with the support he received from America, Hultin gained a large share of the trade of Finnish emigrants. Thus, already in 1890, Norddeutscher Lloyd probably carried more Finnish emigrants than any other shipping line, and in 1891 more than all other shipping companies combined.[58]

In the fall of 1890, newspaper advertising by shipping company agents declined in comparison to the beginning of the year, and advertising for the entire year, 1891, was down from the preceding year.[59] It appears that the situation settled down for some time after Norddeutscher Lloyd had gained

---

[52] *Vestra Nyland,* March 21, 1890; *Wasabladet,* February 22, April 12, 1890.

[53] *Vestra Nyland,* August 12, 1890.

[54] For example, *Mikkelin Sanomat,* June 28, 1890; *Sanomia Turusta,* January 2, 1890; *Rauman Lehti,* March 19, 1890; *Aamulehti,* May 3, 1890; *Satakunta,* June 5, 1890; *Uusi Suometar,* March 27, 1890.

[55] *Wasabladet,* May 19, 1894.

[56] *Päivälehti,* November 27, 1891; *Satakunta,* December 1, 1891.

[57] *Wasabladet,* May 19, 1894.

[58] See above pp. 29—32.

[59] See appendix E.

for itself the major portion of the trade in transporting Finnish emigrants.

In the fall of 1891, when the Finland Steamship Company began the regular conveyance of emigrants from Hanko to England and concluded an agreement for collaboration with the companies transporting emigrants overseas from England, the situation in the emigrant market again changed fundamentally. The Scandinavian & Finlanders Emigrant Co. now received a new competitor. However, by then, troubles had already begun for Grönlund's company in America.

It appears that in the beginning G. A. Grönlund's collaboration with Finnish-American newspaper men succeeded quite well. Grönlund was such an important advertiser that newspapers wrestling with economic difficulties were ready to meet him more than half way. In the beginning Grönlund also acted in complete understanding with Finnish-American businessmen. In the summer of 1891, however, Grönlund apparently began to run into difficulties. Relations with the paper, *Työmies,* published in Ishpeming, were broken off — the last advertisement of The Scandinavian & Finlanders Emigrant Co. in this paper appeared in the July 1, 1891 issue. Shortly thereafter the *Työmies* began an attack against Grönlund which lasted many years. The reason for this probably lay in the fact that the company which published the *Työmies* owned a block of shares in a Finnish gold mine in Montana. And Grönlund had begun a violent attack against this mine in the *New Yorkin Lehti,* which he owned, claiming that the venture was a lot of »humbug».[60]

In time Grönlund made enemies of other Finnish-American newspapers besides the *Työmies.* In order to eliminate charges against him, he tried to circulate the *New Yorkin Lehti,* which was edited by his brother among Finnish-Americans and which, probably because it was distributed gratis, had perhaps a larger circulation than any other Finnish-American newspaper.[61]

In the fall of 1891 and in 1892 news articles and travel accounts sharply attacking Grönlund, Norddeutscher Lloyd and The Scandinavian & Finlanders Emigrant Co. began to appear in Finnish-American newspapers.[62]

---

[60] *Työmies,* July 1, September 23, December 23, 1891; *New Yorkin Lehti,* April 15, 29, May 6, 20, July 1, 15, 1891. Grönlund's representative in Michigan, J. H. Jasberg, had advertisements in the *Työmies* after July 1, 1891. — Grönlund perhaps bought the *New Yorkin Lehti* in order to be able through it to increase the effectiveness of his company's operations. Apparently he also owned the newspaper *Svenska Kuriren* for a time. On the procuring of these papers see, for example, *Työmies,* February 25, 1891; *Amerikan Suomalainen,* May 5, 1894; *Wasabladet,* June 16, 1894.

[61] The *Työmies* claimed on November 18, 1891, that the *New Yorkin Lehti* »is sent by bundle every week to Grönlund's agents for distribution».

[62] For example, *Työmies,* November 18, December 23, 1891, March 25, May 27, June 24, 1892.

148

Some of these were sent from Finland. This systematic criticism of Norddeutscher Lloyd, while perhaps grounded on the truth, could hardly have started spontaneously. It seems likely that the representatives of English and American shipping companies had organized the same kind of campaign that Norddeutscher Lloyd had itself organized a few years earlier. Since the Finland Steamship Company had at the very same time opened its regular transit of emigrants, it would not be mere coincidence if this very company were the prime mover in the mud-slinging campaign.

The campaign against Norddeutscher Lloyd attempted to demonstrate that the line's officials served Finnish customers poorly. Another fact, used in the campaign to awaken the mistrust of Finns, was that from Bremerhaven onwards Finnish emigrants would have to travel on the same ships as eastern European emigrants. The fact that Finnish emigrants were carried from Copenhagen to Germany in ships that also carried pigs obviously also had great negative advertising value. For this reason it was proposed that Norddeutscher Lloyd be called »The Pig Line».[63] In its closing phases, the campaign also brought forward the charge that Grönlund was not even a Finn, but the son of an »Israelite» Jewish merchant from Tampere.[64]

As seen above, the Finland Steamship Company was already interested in the transport of emigrants in 1887, and the company was carrying a small number of emigrants to England in 1891.[65] The passenger lists kept by the company reveal that regular transit of emigrants began on October 17, 1891.[66] Before this the Finland Steamship Company had succeeded in negotiating an agreement concerning the transporting of emigrants from Hanko to England with certain English and American shipping companies.[67] Although the initiative was probably taken by the Finland Steamship Company, it should be noted that it was also practical from the viewpoint of the English and American shipping companies to leave out the middle step formed by Swedish agents in the competition for Finnish emigrants: This middle step meant, of course, more expense. Travel from Finland by way of Sweden was unnecessarily complicated, and furthermore the success of Norddeutscher Lloyd in Finland also spoke on behalf of pushing the Swedish agents aside. In any case, the Swedish agents lost their Finnish customers soon after Norddeutscher Lloyd had made its breakthrough in Finland.

The first agreement between the Finland Steamship Company and English and American companies was negotiated in the fall of 1891. A draft of this agreement, found in the Finland Steamship Company's archives shows

63 For example, *Työmies*, May 27, June 24, 1892.
64 *Amerikan Uutiset*, June 7, 1894.
65 See above pp. 33, 136.
66 The passenger lists of the Finland Steamship Company. TYYH:s:m:7:17.
67 *Suomen Höyrylaiva Osakeyhtiö* 1883—1933, pp. 28—29.

that it was in force until June 30, 1892. This draft concerned transportation on the Cunard, Guion, Inman, and White Star Lines.[68] However, the agreement was probably negotiated at the very beginning with other lines than merely those mentioned in the draft, for in a table drawn up for keeping accounts in the fall of 1891, space was immediately reserved for, in addition to the above-mentioned companies, the Allan, American, Anchor, Beaver, Dominion, and State lines.[69]

The tables that the Finland Steamship Company prepared for keeping accounts show quite clearly which companies it was collaborating with. It is not certain how reliable these tables were in the beginning, for in the spring of 1892 the Finland Steamship Company advertised in the newspapers that it represented the Allan, American, Anchor, Beaver, Cunard, Dominion, White Star, National, State, and Warren lines,[70] but the tables concerning the company's conveyances for 1892 lack the National and Warren lines, but include the Guion and Inman lines, that do not appear in the newspaper advertising. Probably the contradictions between the tables and the newspaper advertisements were due primarily to the facts that some lines changed ownership at just this time, while some lines stopped operations completely.[71]

Once the Finland Steamship Company had negotiated this agreement with English and American shipping companies, competition developed between it and Norddeutscher Lloyd's agent in Finland, V. K. Hultin. In America the war was carried on primarily in the Finnish-American newspapers. As stated above, the main theaters of this war in the United States were the *New Yorkin Lehti,* the contents of which were determined by The Scandinavian & Finlanders Emigrant Co., and the *Työmies,* with which the Finland Steamship Company had good relations.[72]

The cholera which raged over Europe in 1892, played an especially decisive role in the war between V. K. Hultin and the Finland Steamship Company. In the spring of 1892 newspapers began to carry information on the cholera which was raging in Russia and which was feared to be spreading to Finland. According to newspaper reports, in the fall the president of the

---

[68] Means of arrangement between Finnish Steam Navigation Co. of Helsingfors, the Cunard, Guion, Inman and White Star Lines. TYYH:s:m:7:18.

[69] The passenger lists of the Finland Steamship Company. TYYH:s:m:7:17.

[70] For example, *Wasa Tidning,* July 19, 1892.

[71] G i b b s 1952, passim.

[72] For example, *New Yorkin Lehti,* September 1, 22, October 6, 20, 27, 1892; *Työmies,* February 26, June 24, 1892, February 24, 1893. In this war the *New Yorkin Uutiset* attacked furiously upon A. Hornborg, the representative of the Finland Steamship Company in America. The *Työmies* again attacked especially upon G. A. Grönlund and made favourable statements about the Finland Steamship Company. And in 1893 the Finland Steamship Company's representative in America had plenty of advertisements in the *Työmies.*

United States had placed a three-week quarantine on all ships arriving in the United States carrying emigrants.[73] For this reason, emigration from Finland to America seems to have ceased altogether for some time. The quarantine apparently touched all ships arriving in the United States, but German shipping companies that carried eastern European emigrants probably suffered the most. Thus, Finnish newspapers reported that

> »in Germany a certain steamship company has refused henceforth to transport emigrants coming from Russia. Since presumably Finland is there [in Germany] considered as a cholera-polluted land, our emigrants will hardly be able to continue their journey forward from Bremen.»[74]

Advertisements of shipping companies revealed that all transport of emigrants ceased for a time in the fall of 1892.[75] Apparently rumors about the restrictions enforced because of cholera had more influence than the restrictions themselves, for the agents both of the Finland Steamship Company and of Norddeutscher Lloyd felt it paid in 1893 to publish an advertisement denying the existence of the quarantine.[76]

It remains unclear whether or not anyone employed the quarantine for their benefit in the mud-slinging that competing agents were recklessly practicing. In any case, the representative of Norddeutscher Lloyd felt it necessary to announce that

> »our worthy competitors have repeatedly tried, even through their agents, to spread the news, on the one hand, that there exists some sort of quarantine against the Bremen Line in America, and on the other hand, that there is cholera in Germany ... such rumors are completely false.»[77]

If the claim of the Norddeutscher Lloyd representative about their competitors spreading rumors is in fact true, there is little reason to doubt that the Finland Steamship Company's network of agents was behind such rumors. In any event it appears that the cholera epidemic was an especially heavy blow to the representative of The Scandinavian & Finlanders Emigrant Co. in Finland, to the company itself, and to the activities of Norddeutscher Lloyd in Finland.

The Finland Steamship Company also tried to secure its conquest of the trade in transporting emigrants with a broad advertising campaign in the newspapers. Especially during 1892—96, the Vaasa newspapers contained

73 *Satakunta*, September 13, 1892.
74 *Päivälehti*, August 28, 1892; *Satakunta*, September 1, 1892.
75 For example, *Hangö*, August 18, September 27, October 2, 27, 1892.
76 For example, *Wasa Tidning*, January 8, 1893; *Wasabladet*, March 15, 29, 1893.
77 *Satakunta*, September 2, 1893.

its advertisements in abundance.[78]   On the other hand, advertising by Norddeutscher Lloyd agents was — due perhaps to a lack of funds — comparatively rare at this time.

The operations of Norddeutscher Lloyd in Finland received a severe blow in the spring of 1894, when The Scandinavian & Finlanders Emigrant Co. went bankrupt.   It is possible that the company's business never rested on a healthy base, and that G. A. Grönlund actually suffered from the delusions of grandeur his opponents claimed and wanted to clear the field of all competitors no matter what the cost.[79]   At any rate, when Grönlund gradually made enemies of the Finnish-American newspapers, of the business men behind them, and through these papers of Finnish-American immigrants, the basis of the company's activities was pulled out from under it.   The depression that began in America in 1893 probably also increased Grönlund's difficulties.   Emigrants did not have money to send to Finland and prepaid tickets were not purchased as in good years.   At the same time, the company's activities in Finland were made more difficult by the ambiguous reputation it had received and the cholera epidemic explained above.

An American banking firm attempted to continue Grönlund's operations after The Scandinavian & Finlanders Emigrant Co. went bankrupt.   The company was given a new name, The Scandinavian & Finlanders Money Exchange and Steamship Co., and it was still advertising in Finnish-American newspapers in the spring of 1896,[80] but thereafter quietly closed its operations. Apparently Norddeutscher Lloyd was no longer trusted after Grönlund's bankruptcy.

In addition to the two »giants», the Finland Steamship Company and Norddeutscher Lloyd, there were several minor participants in the competition during 1892—94 for the trade in transporting Finnish emigrants. One such was HAPAG which in 1892 had agents in Vaasa, Kristiinankaupunki, and Seinäjoki.   In 1894, this company had representatives at least in Vaasa and Hanko, and still in 1895, HAPAG had an agent in Finland, who also represented the Skandia and the Hansa lines.[81]   These last two lines

78 For example, *Waasan Lehti,* December 14, 1892, June 10, 1893; *Wasa Tidning,* March 22, 1892, March 24, 1893, March 17, 1894, March 5, 1895, March 28, 1896; *Wasabladet,* April 16, 1892, March 29, 1893, March 24, 1894, March 7, 1895, March 21, 1896.

79 *Amerikan Uutiset,* May 31, 1894.

80 *Siirtolainen,* May 9, July 25, October 24, December 26, 1894, November 27, 1895, March 11, 1896.   The name »Scandinavian & Finland-American Emigrant Company» was also used.   The last advertisement of the company in the *Siirtolainen* appeared in the April 8, 1896 issue.   The bank »C. B. Richard & Co.», the owner of the Scandinavian & Finland-American Emigrant Company, however, advertised later in the *Siirtolainen* (for example, *Siirtolainen,* September 16, 1896).

81 For example, *Waasan Lehti,* September 14, 1892, April 15, 1893; *Wasa Tidning,* September 20, 1892, June 8, 1893, April 27, 1894, March 7, 1895; *Wasabladet,* February 13, 1892, April 26, 1893.

transported emigrants in the winter of 1893 through St. Petersburg to Libau and thence onward by ship, while in the summer the voyage by ship began already in Hanko. The emigration agency in Vaasa, Cairenius & Co. mentioned above, was also still in the picture. In 1893 it tried to induce emigrants to travel by way of Umeå and Trondheim on the White Star, Allan and Beaver lines.[82] Sigward Aas, agent for the above-mentioned Skandia Line from Trondheim, also tried to enlist emigrants to go by way of Trondheim by using in his newspaper advertisements the enticement that only Finns, Swedes and Norwegians travelled on the ships of this line.[83] Thus advertising attempted to play upon the suspicions Finnish emigrants felt toward eastern Europeans. — The exceptionally large amount of travel by way of Trondheim in 1893 was, however, due to the fact that winter navigation between Hanko and England was blocked by ice for a larger than normal time.

In 1892—93, the »German—Australian Steamship Company» also offered its services,[84] but without very much success. Another »special» of this year was the announcement by the Swede, Nic. Eriksson, that he was leaving for America in May and would take along any who wanted to come. The price of the ticket from Sundsvall to Montreal was, at most, 125 marks. Eriksson claimed that he would also be able to help in finding work and free land.[85] No large group of Finnish emigrants has been found in the passenger lists of the Swedish police departments for May, 1893, however, so it seems likely that Eriksson failed in his venture.

3. The period of the Finland Steamship Company's monopoly (1894—1914)

When Norddeutscher Lloyd ran into difficulties with its Finnish customers, Finland again became the area of operations for English and American shipping companies and, as has been stated, their Finnish representative was the Finland Steamship Company. In the fall of 1891, the Finland Steamship Company was working jointly with at least the Allan, American, Anchor, Beaver, Cunard, Dominion, White Star, State, Guion, and Inman lines.[1] Joint operations with the Inman Line lasted, however, only until the end of 1892 and that with the Guion Line until the end of 1894.[2] The

---

[82] For example, *Wasa Tidning*, March 3, 1893; *Wasabladet*, March 15, 1893.

[83] For example, *Wasa Tidning*, March 17, 1893.

[84] For example, *Wasabladet*, May 25, 1892, June 23, 1893; *Uusi Suometar*, May 27, 1893.

[85] *Wasabladet*, March 11, 15, 1893.

[1] See above p. 149.

[2] The passenger lists of the Finland Steamship Company. TYYH:s:m:7:17.

reason for ceasing co-operation with the former line was that its ships joined »the fleet» of the American Line, while with the latter it occurred because the Guion Line had ceased operations.[3]

From the beginning of 1894, the Finland Steamship Company represented also the Union Line which carried emigrants to South Africa, and the Orient Line carrying emigrants to Australia. In 1895 the Finland Steamship Company received the right to represent also the Castle Line, which like the Union Line transported emigrants to South Africa.[4] The number of emigrants going to Australia and South Africa was so small, however, that the agreements made with Union, Orient, and Castle lines were of little significance.

For a few years after 1894 emigration was very sparse, which situation was not suited for attracting new competitors into the contest for transportation of emigrants. The most serious disturbance of the Finland Steamship Company's monopoly was perhaps the severing of its relationship with the American Line in the spring of 1896. The above-mentioned G. A. Grönlund appears to have attempted to continue at his former trade, and he perhaps had some sort of role in the sequence of events leading to the severing of relations. In any case, the Finland Steamship Company announced in the newspapers that it was ending its agreement for joint work with the American Line, because that company had taken G. A. Grönlund as an agent in Finland.[5] But it is, of course, possible that it was the American Line that cancelled the agreement. The break in the relationship was short, however. It appears that already by the fall of 1896 the American Line had revoked its agreement with Grönlund and had again begun working with the Finland Steamship Company.[6]

After 1896, the advertising by shipping companies in Finnish newspapers was very sparse. Corresponding information is not available for Finnish-American newspapers because so few of them have been preserved from the latter part of the 1890's, much fewer, in fact, than from the 1880's or the first half of the 1890's. This decrease in advertising was probably due in part to the fact that serious competitors no longer existed. Decreased advertising was perhaps also an indication that the Finland Steamship Company did not think that it would be able to increase the number of its customers, at least not fundamentally, by advertising.[7]

Only at the end of the 1890's, when emigration again began to grow, was a kind of competition for the emigrant trade born again, one which was

---

[3] Gibbs 1952, pp. 114, 203.

[4] The passenger lists of the Finland Steamship Company for 1891—95. TYYH: s:m:7:17.

[5] For example, *Wasa Tidning*, May 16, 1896; *Wasabladet*, May 19, 1896.

[6] For example, *Wasa Tidning*, October 7, 1896; *Wasabladet*, October 1, 1896.

[7] On the possibilities of companies to increase the number of their customers by advertising see Rondahl 1972, pp. 190—194.

154

however, quite minor when compared to the beginning of the decade. In 1898—99, the Scandinavian—American Line (formerly Thingvalla) attempted to gain customers in Finland and advertised in the newspapers,[8] but probably with little success. Statistics of the Finland Steamship Company show that from 1901 on this company and the Scandinavian—American Line worked together.[9] Apparently the latter company considered the possibilities of competing with the Finland Steamship Company to be so poor, that an alliance was thought to be a better choice than competition. Nor is there any reason to doubt that the Finland Steamship Company would have been eager to strengthen its monopoly with a new agreement for collaboration.

In 1902, the American millionaire, John Pierpont Morgan, gained control of several companies, such as White Star and Dominion lines, that transported emigrants, and a bitter price war among transatlantic shipping companies followed.[10] The price war that appeared in Finland in 1903—04 can probably be seen as a reflection of this. Already in 1902 Bore Co. of Turku was offering to convey emigrants along the Turku—Stockholm—Gothenburg—Hull—Liverpool route. The advertisement does not mention which transatlantic line Bore Co. represented, if it represented any at all.[11] It seems likely that the company transported emigrants to Stockholm where there were Finnish-speaking agents from which the tickets for transatlantic lines were probably obtained. — The true price war, however, began in the spring of 1903, when the Steamship Company Nord began transit of emigrants. This company announced that it was the Finnish representative of the HAPAG, Norddeutscher Lloyd, and Skandia lines. Bore Co. was also in the picture, being the representative of the new company in Turku. Through the aid of the Steamship Company Nord, the German shipping companies once again received the opportunity to compete for Finnish emigrants. Nord cut the price of tickets drastically, promising to convey emigrants for 100 marks and later for 86 marks. The Finland Steamship Company answered this by dropping the price of a ticket to 79 marks.[12]

But the story of the Steamship Company Nord was not a long one, for in the fall of 1904 the Finland Steamship Company bought Nord's ships.[13] Thus the Finland Steamship Company again gained a monopoly of emigrant

8 For example, *Satakunta,* May 20, 1899.
9 The passenger lists of the Finland Steamship Company for 1901. TYYH:s:m: 7:17.
10 For further information on the price war see H v i d t 1971, pp. 367, 458—459.
11 For example, *Satakunta,* May 10, 1902.
12 For further information on the price war in Finland see for example, *Satakunta,* August 22, 1903, April 16, May 21, 1904; *Waasa,* March 22, 31, April 7, 12, 21, 1904.
13 *Suomen Höyrylaiva Osakeyhtiö 1883—1933,* pp. 44—45.

traffic between Finland and England, and apparently also a major share of the freight transfer, while the German shipping companies suffered their second defeat in the contest for Finnish emigrants.

The Finland Steamship Company thus represented the Scandinavian—American Line from 1901. In the same year Union and Castle, the companies transporting emigrants to Africa seem to have merged, for they appear in the Finland Steamship Company's statistics for 1901 as the Union-Castle Line. The Finland Steamship Company began to represent also the Canadian Pacific Railway Company (C.P.R.) in 1904, and somewhat later the Donald-son, Royal, Pacific, Holland Lloyd and Thomson lines. With the exception of the C.P.R., however, these lines had little significance in the transportation of Finnish emigrants.[14]

Thus, from 1894 onward, the Finland Steamship Company had, practically speaking, a monopoly as a transporter of Finnish emigrants. A few attempts were made to break this monopoly, but they all failed. Emigration by way of Sweden did indeed still continue, but it only exceptionally rose above 10 % of the total number of emigrants in the year. The major proportion of travellers through Sweden were from Oulu Province or the Åland Islands.[15] Beginning in 1892, the Finland Steamship Company represented at least ten transatlantic lines, of which, — as seen above, only several were really important. Appendix H, compiled from statistics in the archives of the Finland Steamship Company, indicates the part played by each of the companies represented by the Finland Steamship Company in 1892, 1895, 1900, 1905, and 1910.[16]

---

[14] The passenger lists of the Finland Steamship Company for 1901—13. There are no statistics for 1914. TYYH:s:m:7:17.

[15] For the most part, the persons travelling by way of Sweden in 1905 who used passports were from the Åland Islands. In addition to this, northern-Ostrobothnian names, for which no corresponding names are found in the passport lists, appear in great abundance in the passenger lists of the Gothenburg Police Department (see above p. 13 and below p. 196).

[16] There are various sets of statistics on emigrants in the archives of the Finland Steamship Company, most of which show how many emigrants used each shipping line. For some years the information is not completely consistent. The following can be said about the years 1892, 1895, 1900, 1905, and 1910 employed in Appendix H. For the years 1892, 1895, 1900, and 1905 there are statistics that show how many emigrants travelled on each of the Finland Steamship Company's ships and for which transatlantic shipping lines they bought tickets. These statistics were probably prepared as the ships left. The tables used also contain returning emigrants — the group »eastbound» — which have been excluded from Appendix H. For 1910 there are no longer tables drawn up by ship. Information concerning the numbers of emigrants carried by the different shipping lines during this year was obtained from statistics in the Finland Steamship Company's archives appearing under the heading, »North Atlantic Passenger Conference. Return of third Class passengers. Forwarded from Finland for the year 1910.»

According to the Appendix in the period between 1892 and 1910 (and also 1911—13) the most important shipping lines were clearly Allan, Cunard, and White Star. The share of the Allan Line was generally about 20 %, that of the Cunard Line regularly over 20 %. White Star transported about 15 % of Finnish emigrants in the 1890's and about 25 % after the turn of the century. These shipping lines, thus, remained significant throughout the entire period under question. In 1892, the number of emigrants transported by the Guion and Inman lines was also noticeably large, but, after a »good start», these companies disappeared altogether from the competition for Finnish emigrants. The American Line had its heyday in Finland around the turn of the century, but its share thereafter fell to under 10 %. Within the group of the most important companies mention must still be made the Dominion Line, which was important around the turn of the century and the C.P.R., which on the eve of World War I was fourth in order of importance behind the White Star, Cunard, and Allan lines. The share of Finnish emigrants carried by the other shipping lines was at most in the neighborhood of only a small percent of the total.

Why did Finnish emigrants use, during the period of the Finland Steamship Company's monopoly, only a few transatlantic lines, although over ten choices were constantly offered them? This was probably in part due to the agreements negotiated between the Finland Steamship Company and the transatlantic lines. It should be noted, however, that those wanting to emigrate could buy tickets on whichever shipping line they wanted, and that the Finland Steamship Company was not in a position to influence in the least which lines the prepaid tickets bought in America were for.

The effect of prepaid tickets on the composition of emigration and on changes occurring in the strength of emigration will be examined later in a separate chapter. However, it appears reasonable to examine already in the

---

Most statistics of the Finland Steamship Company that cover extended time periods list the numbers of emigrants carried by the company for 1892, 1895, 1900, 1905, and 1910 as follows: 1892 — 3,191 emigrants; 1895 — 2,982; 1900 — 10,642; 1905 — 17,536; 1910 — 19,571.

The difference for 1892 between Appendix H and other statistics of the Finland Steamship Company results from the fact that the emigrants the company transported in the fall of 1891 were usually counted as 1892 emigrants. The difference of one emigrant for 1895 is due to an error in addition in the Finland Steamship Company's statistics amounting to one emigrant. The figures for 1900 are in agreement. The disparity for 1905 results from the fact that Appendix H includes 796 Russians, since figures concerning the use of shipping lines purely by Finnish emigrants do not exist for this year. However, on the basis of the regular passenger lists it can be affirmed that the Russian emigrants of this year used principally the Anchor, American, Dominion and State lines when they travelled by way of Finland. The reason for the difference of about 100 emigrants in the 1910 figures is not apparent from the available material.

present connection the kind of role prepaid tickets played as far as the shipping companies were concerned.

Appendix I (p. 243) shows the relationship between the number of customers on different shipping lines and the number of prepaid tickets received by these customers.[17]   According to it, the amount of prepaid ticket users in 1895, 1900, 1905, and 1910 was respectively 27.6 %, 37.7 %, 29.7 %, and 28.8 % of the total number of emigrants.   Almost regularly, a larger than average proportion of passengers on the Allan, Cunard, and White Star lines used prepaid tickets.   In addition, American, Dominion, Scandinavian-American and C.P.R. also at one stage or another transported a rather large number of prepaid ticket users.   Anchor, Beaver, State, Orient, Castle, Union and Union-Castle on the other hand transported only a small number of prepaid ticket users if any. The number of emigrants carried by the other lines included in the table was so small that no conclusions can be made regarding them.

Thus it was the Allan, Cunard and White Star lines whose passengers used prepaid tickets in the greatest numbers.   But these were also the most important lines used by Finnish emigrants.   On this basis, it appears that there existed some sort of relationship between the percentage of prepaid tickets and the popularity of a shipping line: one distinguishing feature of those shipping lines important to Finnish emigrants was a relatively large portion of passengers using prepaid tickets, while a distinguishing feature of a less important line was a relatively small portion of its passengers travelling with prepaid tickets. Thus, when seeking the reasons for the popularity of a given shipping line, it would seem well-grounded to examine what sort of system existed for selling prepaid tickets.

The major portion of the propaganda of enterprisers selling prepaid tickets reached the paying public through newspapers. Since very few Finnish-American newspapers from the end of the 1890's and the beginning of the 1900's have been preserved, it is not possible to discover exactly how much propaganda activity the various sellers of prepaid tickets employed. On the basis of material available, however, it seems that the majority of agents advertising in newspapers did not announce themselves as the representative of any given shipping line, but pledged to sell tickets for all the best transatlantic lines. A portion of the advertisements were placed by the shipping lines themselves: these, of course, advertised only one shipping line.[18]

---

17 The passenger lists of the Finland Steamship Company for 1895, 1900, 1905, and 1910. TYYH:s:m:7:17.

18 For example, *Siirtolainen,* January 9, 30, July 8, December 25, 1900, February 26, March 26, 1901; *Amerikan Suometar,* September 4, 1901, April 2, 1902, March 25, 1903; *Tietokäsikirja Amerikan Suomalaisille* 1912.

158

There were a large number of agents selling prepaid tickets to Finnish immigrants. In 1905, these in fact numbered 246. But most of these agents sold only a small number of prepaid tickets each year. Thus, in 1905, the number of agents selling more than 50 prepaid tickets to Finnish immigrants was only 18. Of the 4,700 prepaid tickets sold to Finns by American agents, 3,253, or 69.2 % were sold by these 18. Two agents, Nielsen & Lundbeck and Hornborg & Co., alone sold 1,435 prepaid tickets, or 30.5 % of all prepaid tickets. Thus although hundreds of agents offered the service the prepaid tickets sold to Finns originated from relatively few places.[19]

The impartial presentation of different shipping lines that appeared in the advertisements placed by agents selling prepaid tickets, is not, of course, a definite proof that a given agent did not, in practice, favor a given shipping line. It could be argued that an appreciable proportion of emigrants buying prepaid tickets would have been willing to buy them for the line which the emigration agent recommended to him in his office. In practice, at any rate, the most important emigration agents seem to have favored given lines. Thus of the 778 prepaid tickets sold by Nielsen & Lundbeck in 1905, 609 or 78.3 % were for travel on the White Star or Cunard lines, while Hornborg & Co., sold 657 prepaid tickets of which the White Star and Cunard lines' portion was 495 or 75.3 %. And an agent named Tavajärvi sold 65 prepaid tickets of which the Cunard and Allan lines' share was 58 or 89.2 %.[20]

Since the sale of prepaid tickets centered on so few agents, it would have probably been very easy to reach an agreement in the contracts between these agents and the shipping companies as to what proportion of the number of tickets sold would go to each line. On the other hand, it is also possible that Finnish emigrants themselves, for one reason or another, might have favored the White Star, Cunard, and Allan lines. This popularity might well be due to the fact that these long-established emigrant lines had over time become familiar to Finnish immigrants who had been using the Allan Line, for example, since the beginning of the 1870's. It may have been so much a habit to trust these old lines that new competitors found it difficult to »drive themselves through».

[19] According to a computation made at the IGHUT on the basis of the passenger lists of the Finland Steamship Company, the agents who sold more than 50 prepaid tickets to Finnish-Americans were Adson (263 tickets), Aironen (127), Carlson (78), Grönroos (77), Hornborg (657), Johnson (99), Kitti (56), Koski (119), Lieberthal (89), Mäki (120), Nielsen & Lundbeck (778), Peterson (62), Perrin (163), P. Sumner (51), Tavajärvi (65), Thompson (118), Waara (249), and Warren (82). The names are written in the form in which they appear most often in the Finland Steamship Company's passenger lists.
[20] Those used as examples appear to have advertised frequently in Finnish-American publications.

Information is also available on how frequently emigrants leaving from different parts of Finland in 1905 travelled on different transatlantic lines.[21] According to Appendix J the shipping lines most frequently used by Finnish emigrants in 1905 were Cunard, White Star, Allan, and American, which transported almost 87 % of all persons travelling overseas from Finland. A comparison reveals that the emigrants from each province were distributed in about the same proportion among the shipping lines. Only the following exceptions appear to be worth noting. First, an exceptionally large number of persons leaving from Turku and Pori Province travelled by way of Sweden. Most of these were from the Åland Islands. Emigrants from Kuopio Province used the Allan Line more frequently than those leaving from other provinces, while Häme Province's emigrants used this line exceptionally rarely. Those leaving from Viipuri Province used the transportation of C.P.R. to an exceptionally large degree, and emigrants from Uusimaa used the White Star Line more often than average, and the Cunard and Allan lines clearly less often. Taken in general, however, the distribution for 1905 indicates that in no province did people have at the beginning of the century a clear tradition of using a given transatlantic line.

The propaganda activities of emigration agents and shipping companies before the First World War can be divided into several periods. At the end of the 1870's and the beginning of the 1880's most of the propaganda reached the public by means of Finnish-American newspapers. The propaganda was directed mainly at Finnish-Americans, but since Finnish-American newspapers were also circulated in Finland, emigration propaganda also reached a rather large audience in Oulu and Vaasa Provinces. At the end of the 1880's and especially at the beginning of the 1890's, the propaganda of emigration agents and shipping companies spread more widely on both sides of the Atlantic than at any time before or since. The reason for this was Norddeutscher Lloyd's attempt to gain customers among Finnish emigrants. Once Norddeutscher Lloyd's attempt failed, the amount of propaganda by emigration agents declined substantially, at least in Finland: the monopoly of the Finland Steamship Company meant that propaganda was not needed. Only for a brief moment in 1903—04 were the Steamship Company Nord and the German shipping companies behind it able to start the propaganda mills grinding again. The contest between emigration agents in North America continued to be more heated, although there, too, a few agents gained mastery over the others. In addition to agents operating in North America, the shipping companies themselves also carried on their own propaganda activities there.

---

21 The statistics have been made by computer at the initiative of the IGHUT.

4. Recruiters of immigrants

In Finland in the nineteenth and beginning of the twentieth centuries, the term emigration agent generally denoted the representatives of shipping companies who sold tickets to departing emigrants. These emigration agents, the sellers of tickets, should be distinguished from actual recruiters of immigrants. In the following, only those persons who are said to have, while in the commission of some company, state (or province) or nation, enticed Finns to emigrate are considered to be recruiters of immigrants, and thus when we speak of recruiters of immigrants it is assumed that the attempt of some nation, state (or province) or company to obtain a work force or residents from Finland was closely associated with the recruiter. How much of this sort of recruiting of immigrants occurred in Finland?

Finns are said to have come into contact with a recruiter of immigrants for the first time in 1864. According to I l m o n e n a man named Christian Taftes from the Tornio River Valley went to northern Norway in 1864 to recruit immigrants to the northern Michigan copper mines for the Quincy Mining Company. According to I l m o n e n Finns were recruited, too.[1] In many presentations of emigration historians, I l m o n e n's statement has been accepted almost without question.[2]

S e m m i n g s e n, in her study of Norwegian migration, has shown that in 1864 a recruiter of immigrants named B. F. Tefft arrived in Sweden with the purpose also of procuring a work force from Norway for northern Michigan copper mines. A year later another recruiter sent from the northern Michigan copper mines, whose name was Christian Taftesen or Taftezon, was operating in northern Norway.[3] It is likely that one of these was the recruiter with whom the beginning of the Finnish migration directed toward northern Michigan is generally linked. It is, of course, possible that both these men had succeeded in recruiting Finns as emigrants. It should be stressed, however, that I l m o n e n's information was probably taken from reminiscenses and, as the confusion of names indicates, is anything but precise in its accuracy. In exact terms, we can hardly be sure of more than the facts that Finns living in northern Norway began to leave as emigrants to the copper mines of northern Michigan at just the time that the above-mentioned recruiters were attempting to gain an influence in northern Norway, and that Finns living in northern Norway had at least heard of the

[1] I l m o n e n 1923, p. 65.

[2] For example, E n g e l b e r g 1944, pp. 23—24; H o g l u n d 1960, p. 9; H o l m i o 1967, pp. 124—125.

[3] S e m m i n g s e n 1950, pp. 104—107. See also K o l e h m a i n e n 1946, pp. 20—21; E r i c k s o n 1957, pp. 43—44.

possibilities for work offered in northern Michigan from one (or both) of these recruiters.

The nature of the recruiting operations practiced among Finns in northern Norway in the 1860's is thus not completely clear. However, the emigration that began from northern Norway apparently had far-reaching consequences regardless of whether or not some recruiters provided the impetus for its beginning. For it appears quite likely that knowledge about opportunities offered in America spread to at least several localities in northern Finland from northern Norway, and that, for example, the movement of emigrants from Kuusamo primarily to the copper mining region of northern Michigan results from the fact that migration from Kuusamo to America received its stimulus by way of people originally from Kuusamo who had migrated to the coast of the Arctic Ocean.[4]

Chronologically, the second or third recruiter of immigrants whose operations reached Finns was probably Charles Linn, who was born in 1814 in Pojo parish and who had arrived in America sometime around 1836. Linn went to Finland in 1869 and returned with 53 Finns the majority of whom were from Helsinki or western Uusimaa.[5]

During the time that Linn was performing his recruiting activities, the *Hufvudstadsbladet* announced that the female immigrants following Linn would be placed at work with families living in Montgomery, Alabama, except for one who would be placed in New Orleans, Louisiana. According to the news item, friends of Linn in America were interested in obtaining maids from Finland. On the other hand, men would be placed at work constructing a railroad in the mountain regions of Alabama. Those leaving would be given a free trip to America and in four years a free return trip as well.[6] It appears that Linn's clients were in part his friends in America, but evidently in addition some railroad company was interested in obtaining a Finnish work force. There is reason to view Linn's recruiting activities also in the light of the immigration policy of the southern states at that time: after the Civil War in the United States several states were attempting to replace negro labor with immigrant labor, for which reason they were actively trying to induce a part of the immigrant stream arriving from Europe to turn toward the southern states.[7] In the case of Linn, the idea of recruiting immigrants thus might have also originated with Alabama's highest-ranking officials.

---

[4] On the destinations in America of emigrants from Kuusamo see P ä t y n e n 1972, pp. 87—107. The early beginnings of emigration from the Tornio River Valley could also indicate that the urge to emigrate could have spread there from Sweden.

[5] K e r o 1971 I, pp. 157—161; K e r o 1971 II, pp. 7, 30.

[6] *Hufvudstadsbladet,* August 25, 1869.

[7] Further information on immigration to Alabama and other southern states see W i t t k e 1967, pp. 106—109.

11

If the migration occurring from northern Norway had very far-reaching consequences, the recruiting done by Linn is an example of just the opposite. For there is no indication that the group of immigrants brought to Alabama by Linn had any followers, who on the basis of the example set by them migrated to the southern portion of the United States.

Josiah Tustin, an American preacher, was apparently the next recruiter whose operations extended into Finland. When he was trying to obtain a position with the Northern Pacific company in 1873, he said that his special area was Finnish immigrants whom he claimed to have been recruiting to Michigan since 1870. In October, 1872, as many as about 60 Finns had arrived in Grand Rapids, Mich., at his instigation. Tustin's client had been the Continental Improvement Company of Michigan.[8]

The Gothenburg passenger lists show that beginning in 1869 there were some Finnish immigrants who had tickets to Grand Rapids. For this reason, we cannot begin with the assumption that all the Finns who bought tickets to Grand Rapids at the beginning of the 1870's were recruited by Tustin. The number of those buying tickets to Grand Rapids before 1872 was, however, very small: in 1869 only one, in 1870, two, and in the following year, none at all. In 1872 the number rose to 211.[9] Thus Tustin's activity seems to have produced results primarily in 1872.

At the beginning of the 1870's, the passenger lists now and then note also the home communities of Finnish immigrants. On the basis of these, it appears that the majority of the immigrants going to Grand Rapids were from Swedish-speaking areas of Ostrobothnia. Therefore Tustin's operations can be assumed to have been directed toward this area.

No information has been preserved on the details of Tustin's operation. It is possible that the Finnish and Swedish language »American guides» (*vägledning för emigranter till Amerika)* that, according to the report of the governor of Vaasa Province for 1873, were distributed in Vaasa, Kokkola and Kristiinankaupunki in the fall of 1872 and the winter following,[10] were a result of Tustin's activities. However, we can only conjecture as to the origin of these guides, since no more information about them, other than the above statement, has been preserved.

---

8 Ljungmark 1971, pp. 174—175.

9 The passenger lists of the Gothenburg Police Department for 1869—72. TYYH: s:m:4:1—4. The number of tickets purchased to other localities in Michigan cannot be computed exactly, because the destinations of some immigrants appear in the passenger lists as Sault Ste Marie, or as some other community of which there are more than one in North America. In addition it is possible that some of those who bought tickets to Chicago, New York or Quebec, for example, were in fact going to Michigan. At any rate, in 1872 Grand Rapids seems clearly to have been the most important destination in Michigan for Finns.

10 Kero 1969 II, p. 82.

Also Hans Mattson, a Swedish-American immigration agent, attempted to recruit Finnish immigrants in 1872. He is known to have printed material intended for Finland in Gothenburg and to have gone to Helsinki and St. Petersburg in the fall of 1872, apparently to explore the possibilities of recruiting immigrants.[11] It is not likely, however, that Mattson's operations directed to Finland in 1872 produced any results. On the other hand, it is within the realm of possibility that the above-mentioned guides that were circulated in Ostrobothnia in the fall of 1872 were the work of Hans Mattson.

The head agents in Sweden for the Allan Line, first David Lyon and later Karl Möllersvärd, were also interested in Finnish immigrants at the beginning of the 1870's. Thus they had an office in Haparanda through which they tried, according to some sources, to recruit Finnish immigrants.[12] The founding of this office, however, does not necessarily mean that they had a particular interest in recruiting activities. They could just as well have established the office in Haparanda with the purpose of making contact before the other Swedish agents with Finnish migrants arriving in Haparanda from Oulu Province. It was perhaps established with the assumption that Finns would buy their tickets from the first office they came upon in the course of their journey.

The best known attempt at recruiting Finnish immigrants, that was organized to obtain immigrants to the United States, occurred in 1873 and was connected with the operations of the above-mentioned Möllersvärd. I l m o n e n has preserved the following information about this recruiting:

> Peter Swanberg (Haapa), an agent for the Allan Line living at Haparanda, was engaged in this gathering up of emigrants. He had made an agreement with a certain Swedish employment agency in Duluth, Minn., to procure several hundred Finns and Swedes for work on the railroad ... He had an assistant Sakari Törmälä from Siikajoki, who had returned after a couple of years in America to get his family ... On June 7 the group of emigrants collected in the above-mentioned manner, or the so-called Swanberg party, left from the Haparanda harbor ... They arrived in Sundswall on the 12th and in Stockholm on the 19th and a week later in Hull ... On the third [of July] they departed on a huge liner for America. The party of Finns, having been joined by our countrymen coming from Norway, had grown by a couple of hundred persons and was estimated to number five hundred. The Finns coming from Norway had bought tickets to Hancock, Mich., those coming from Finland, primarily to Duluth, Minn. ... At the Duluth lakeside Mr. Johnson, the manager of Swedish employment agency met the Finns with the purpose of sending them directly to the

11 Ljungmark 1971, pp. 174—175.
12 Ljungmark 1971, pp. 178—180.

164

railroad being laid by Northern Pacific in the areas around Fargo...
Swanberg remained in America for a couple of months, returning to
Haparanda in the fall of that year...[13]

The American J a m e s B. H e d g e s has also dealt with the »Swanberg
party» in one of his articles. He says that

In the same month [June], the Swedish agent [Möllersvärd]
announced that he had forwarded a colony of 230 adults for the Northern Pacific territory. These people were Finns from the northern part
of Sweden and Finland, and were of the sort who would make excellent settlers... In July, the London office announced that the Swedish
agent had another group of 242 adults and a large number of children
ready to embark for Minnesota. This party, too, was composed of
Finns.[14]

On the basis of the passenger lists of Swedish and Norwegian police
departments and L j u n g m a r k's work it is possible in some degree to
clarify to what extent the information about the »Swanberg party» holds
true. A very large group of Finns, that left Gothenburg on June 27, 1873
can be found in the passenger lists of the Gothenburg Police Department.[15]
Quite probably this was the above-mentioned Swanberg party. However,
Swanberg's name is not found among the group. This does not necessarily
mean that Swanberg was not along on the trip, however, for, as a recruiter
of immigrants he could well have travelled as a second-class passenger, the
names of which were not included in the police department passenger lists.

Swanberg's assistant, Sakari Törmälä, is mentioned first in the list containing the Finnish group leaving on June 27. I l m o n e n's statement that
Törmälä was in Finland to get his family can be at least partly confirmed,
for Törmälä did in fact have his wife and two children along with him. The
fact that Törmälä appears first in the passenger list indicates that he had a
special position in the group; on the basis of this he could even have been
the leader for the whole group. On the other hand, there is reason to note
that Törmälä would be some sort of »frontrunner» in the group for the simple reason that he was apparently making the trip to America for a second
time. The first-timers would naturally try to make him their leader, even
if he had no authority from Swanberg.[16] A peculiar fact about Törmälä is
that he and his family were travelling to Hancock, Mich., not to Duluth,
Minn., where the recruited group is said to have been going. This at least

---

13 I l m o n e n 1923, pp. 32—35.

14 H e d g e s 1926, p. 323.

15 The passenger lists of the Gothenburg Police Department. TYYH:s:m:4:4.

16 On how the »yankees» were some sort of »frontrunners» in the group of first-
timers see, fro example, Hedman 1926, pp. 29—32.

means that it was not Törmälä's task to bring the Swanberg party all the way to Duluth.

According to I l m o n e n's information the »Swanberg party» arrived in Hull on June 26. This cannot be correct since the group left Gothenburg only on June 27. Apparently a rather large number of Finns from northern Norway joined the group in England, as I l m o n e n states. For the passenger lists of the Trondheim Police Department show that on June 26—27, 105 emigrants from Vadsjö, for example, left Trondheim, and that they were travelling on the Allan Line. On the basis of their names, at least some of these were Finns. In addition, emigrants from other localities in northern Norway left Trondheim on the same days,[17] so I l m o n e n's estimate of the number of Finns coming from northern Norway could very well be correct.

According to I l m o n e n the majority of the emigrants coming from Finland had bought tickets to Duluth, Minn., while those coming from Norway were travelling primarily to Hancock, Mich. The Trondheim passenger lists show that most of those leaving northern Norway on June 26—27 did indeed have tickets to Hancock. However, only 103 of those travelling through Gothenburg had procured tickets to Duluth, while 123 were going to Hancock; two, to Quebec; three, to Chicago; ten, to Minneapolis; and one, to Rockford.

The dispersal of the »Swanberg party» to six different localities indicates that the recruiting activity was not as large-scale as I l m o n e n has presented it. Since, in addition, those going to Duluth had bought their tickets themselves, the only thing that we can be sure of besides the number of emigrants presented above, is that information from Duluth which said that work was being offered immigrants in Minnesota was spread in northern Finland through the activities of a Swedish agent.

The information given by H e d g e s appears to be just as uncertain as that presented by I l m o n e n. On the basis of the Gothenburg passenger lists, it can be stated that under no circumstances were two groups of immigrants each containing over 200 persons recruited in Finland. H e d g e s found his information on the first of these groups in a letter sent on June 2 by the Gothenburg agent, Möllersvärd, mentioned above. The second group was mentioned in a letter sent on July 5 by the London agent of the Northern Pacific Railroad. Since relatively few Finnish immigrants travelled through Gothenburg in May and early June 1873, it appears that both of the letters used by H e d g e s in fact mention the same group of emigrants of which I l m o n e n has written.

L j u n g m a r k, in his study concerning the recruiting activity directed to Sweden from Minnesota, has dealt with the background and the various

---

17 The passenger lists of the Trondheim Police Department. TYYH:s:m:6:2.

166

phases of the Swanberg party primarily on the basis of material in letters.
His study states that Karl Möllersvärd, the Gothenburg agent for the Allan
Line and the Northern Pacific Railroad Company, and Peter Swanberg, the
Haparanda agent for the Allan Line, were behind the operation, which was
part of the attempt by the Northern Pacific Company to obtain from northern
Europe a work force for its construction sites and settlers for the broad areas
of land it owned.[18]

Thus on the basis of the studies by I l m o n e n and H e d g e s as well as
by L j u n g m a r k, it appears undeniable that the agents mentioned performed recruiting operations in northern Finland in 1873. On the other hand, it
appears that the recruiting activities were not very extensive, for most of
the members of the Swanberg party had purchased tickets to Hancock, Mich.
Immigrating to northern Michigan was probably by this time a tradition in
some communities in northern Finland so that travelling there did not presuppose any recruiting. L j u n g m a r k's studies indicate that Möllersvärd
and Swanberg took this into account in their operations: they built their
attempt to a very large degree on the possibility that during the journey
from Finland to America some of the travellers to Hancock would agree to
continue their journey to Duluth.[19] The materials available do not tell
whether the number of passengers to Duluth increased after departure from
Gothenburg. However, I l m o n e n's statement that those going to Duluth did
not in the end leave for construction work on the Northern Pacific Railroad
is probably correct.

On the basis of material that has been preserved, it appears that the
recruiting operations performed in Finland at the beginning of the 1870's
were rather limited. However, L j u n g m a r k's studies in particular
uncontestably demonstrate that, in Minnesota and possibly also in Michigan,
Finland was seen at the beginning of the 1870's as an area from which an
immigrant population suited for settlement in the Great Lakes area might
be attracted. However, the economic depression that began in the United
States in 1873 made long-term recruiting of emigrants from Europe to Minnesota unnecessary.

In addition to the recruiting attempts discussed above that were channeled
toward the United States, Finnish immigrants were also recruited to Canada.
The above-mentioned Hans Mattson handled the organization of this
recruiting. For in 1874 the *Uusi Suometar* and the *Sanomia Turusta* published
selections from a Finnish-language book by »Colonel H. Mattson» in which
Canada was praised to the skies.[20] Mattson's reminiscences show that he

[18] L j u n g m a r k 1971, p. 171, 186—189.
[19] L j u n g m a r k 1971, pp. 186—189.
[20] *Uusi Suometar*, July 20, 1874; *Sanomia Turusta*, July 17, 1874.

had attempted to recruit immigrants to Manitoba.[21] However, the names of no Finns going to Canada can be found in the passenger lists for 1874, so it appears that this recruiting attempt was wholly without results.

No large recruiting attempts are known from the 1880's. It is true that in 1882 the newspaper, *Satakunta,* mentioned that »there also appear to be some American 'recruiters' on the move in our district.»[22] However, very little is known about the nature of this recruiting attempt. The item appearing in the newspaper the following year, which placed the blame for the growth in emigration from the neighborhood of Pori on the *Suomalainen Ilmoituslehti* (Finnish Advertising Sheet), was possibly concerned with the »recruiting attempt» of 1882. The *Satakunta* claimed that the *Suomalainen Ilmoituslehti* had promised »so much good and beautiful that if a fifth of it were true, the whole world would probably leave for America». On the circulation of the sheet, the *Satakunta* knew that someone had sent »large bundles to the Pihlava sawmill, among other places».[23] It is possible that the *Suomalainen Ilmoituslehti* only included guides for those intending to emigrate, in which case it would not necessarily have involved actual recruiting.

In the beginning of the 1890's advertisements appeared in the newspapers that offered free trips to Brazil to persons with families who were accustomed to agricultural labor.[24] The government of Rio Grande do Sul was perhaps behind the enterprise.[25] Some accepted the offer, but on the whole the results remained very meagre. Since those leaving for Brazil apparently failed completely,[26] Brazil perhaps received such a bad reputation in Finnish eyes as a result of this recruiting attempt that there was no interest at all in immigrating to Brazil in the 1890's and the first years of the twentieth century.

Two attempts at recruiting are known from the late 1890's. In 1895—99, the Canadian Pacific Railroad tried to lure emigrants from Finland. The company had a Swedish agent named N. D. Ennis, who urged Finns to travel to »sunny Canada and become rich».[27] In 1895 the Finland Steamship Com-

---

[21] Mattson 1890, p. 162.

[22] *Satakunta,* May 27, 1882.

[23] *Satakunta,* January 3, 1883.

[24] *Hufvudstadsbladet,* February 22, March 12, 1890; *Vestra Nyland,* March 11, 1890. The newspapers say that emigration of families was hoped in Brazil, because it was very difficult for families to return, more difficult than for individuals.

[25] Information from O l a v i L ä h t e e n m ä k i.

[26] *Folkvännen* mentions (December 31, 1890) that three Ostrobothnian emigrants had returned from Brazil after having thoroughly failed. See also *Hufvudstadsbladet,* June 11, 1892.

[27] For example, *Wasa Tidning,* January 4, 1895.

168

pany also seems to have been a representative of the C.P.R.[28] Advertisements by N. D. Ennis are also found in newspapers for 1897 and for 1899. Free land that was said to be offered in Canada to men over 18-years old was almost regularly used as the propagandic trump.[29]

Since a delegation from Finland travelled to Canada in the summer of 1899 to find a place for a »New Finland»,[30] it could be that the seeking for the place in Canada was a result of the above propaganda. It seems, however, that the propaganda operations directed from Canada to Finland did not reach the population in Finland that was interested in emigrating.[31]

In 1899 a recruiter of immigrants named John Antell was active in Finland on behalf of the Queensland government. In his recruiting operations, he used newspaper advertisements which labelled Queensland »the garden of Australia» as an allurement.[32] This attempt at recruiting did not remain completely fruitless, for at least 175 Finns took advantage of the free trip from London to Queensland offered by the Queensland government.[33] Queensland's recruiting operations were of no really great significance, however. At least the group that followed Kurikka to Queensland failed rather thoroughly, with the result perhaps that emigration to Australia no longer aroused appreciable interest among Finns in the opening years of the twentieth century.

In 1907 a recruiter of emigrants was sent to Finland from New York state with the purpose of obtaining farmers from Finland for the deserted farms of that state. However, Finnish authorities prevented this attempt from succeeding.[34] Another known attempt at recruiting in the twentieth century occurred in 1913: the province of Victoria at that time tried to get immigrants from Finland because there was »a great shortage of rural labor» in Victoria Province and because there was more land »than can be properly utilised by the present small population.» Those leaving were offered considerable discounts on the prices of tickets and guaranteed work immediately upon arrival in Australia. The Finland Steamship Company acted as agent in Finland.[35] Koivukangas's compilations of the numbers of Finns arri-

[28] For example, *Wasa Tidning,* May 12, 1895.
[29] For example, *Wasa Tidning,* February 2, 1897; *Satakunta,* May 6, 1899.
[30] Niitemaa 1971, pp. 164—165.
[31] There is not any source material which would indicate that the recruiting was successful. The passenger lists of the year 1898 have disappeared, which makes it impossible to count, if more Finns emigrated to Canada in 1899 than in 1898.
[32] For example, *Uusi Suometar,* May 21, 1899.
[33] Koivukangas 1972 II, p. 56. Further information on this group see Niitemaa 1971, pp. 163—187; Koivukangas 1972 I, p. 40; Koivukangas 1972 II, pp. 56—63.
[34] Hoglund 1960, p. 9.
[35] Statement by Mr. E. Rayment, assistant superintendent of immigration for New South Wales & Victoria, in reply to statements in a number of articles which

ving in Australia on the eve of the First World War [36] indicate that the Finnish migration to Australia was at that time noticeably more extensive than it had been during the first decade of the twentieth century. This does not necessarily mean, however, that the recruiting operations practiced by the Victoria government were a fundamental cause of the growth in this migration.

In the above, all the recruiting attempts concerning which the author has found source materials have been dealt with. The small number of known cases indicates that the amount of recruiting activity directed toward Finland was not very large. As far as the United States is concerned such activity seems to have occurred primarily in the 1860's and at the beginning of the 1870's. And the amount of recruiting done at this time was apparently very small. The results of this recruiting activity were possibly quite far-reaching, however, for the very general tendency of Finnish emigration toward northern Michigan may well have been a result of the fact that immigrants coming later followed the example of those leaving in the 1860's for the mines in northern Michigan. Finnish immigrants have also been recruited for Canada, South America, and Australia, but these recruiting operations had been rather fruitless: the number of those leaving as a result of this recruiting has been relatively small and these attempts at recruiting have not led to the bursting forth of new streams of immigrants.

5. The price of tickets

It has already been mentioned that on at least two occasions the representatives of shipping companies in Finland engaged in a price war. Such was the situation in 1889, when Norddeutscher Lloyd began its conquest of the trade in transporting Finnish emigrants. A second price war broke out in 1904 when the Steamship Company Nord and the transatlantic lines behind it attempted to win the emigrant market from the Finland Steamship Company.

Continuous statistics on the prices of tickets have not been published. According to information T o i v o n e n obtained from the Suomi-Seura, a third-class ticket from Hanko to New York cost about 150 marks in 1890, while on the eve of World War I its price was 220—280 marks.[1] The information procured by T o i v o n e n can be augmented by information published

---

appeared in the newspaper »Dagens press» and in a pamphlet issued by the Swedish national association. The archives of the Finland Steamship Company. TYYH:s:m: 7:18.

[36] K o i v u k a n g a s 1972 II, pp. 39—40.

[1] T o i v o n e n 1963, pp. 56—57.

by shipping companies in the newspapers. For the most part, however, information on prices was published only during situations of competition, for which reason it is available only for a brief period around 1890 and for 1904. For the years 1892—95 and 1899—1914, we can also discover from information in the Finland Steamship Company's passenger lists, how much the price of a ticket fluctuated for the trip between Hanko and North America.

When comparing the prices of tickets, it should be noted that the benefits included in the ticket price were not always the same. However, this apparently diminishes the comparability of prices only for the period around 1890, when an especially large number of different travel alternatives were offered.

The earliest information on the price of tickets can be found in the emigration report of the governor of Vaasa Province for 1873 saying that one could get to America for about 270 marks.[2] The next information can be found in newspapers for 1887 when Lars Krogius & Co. announced that it was transporting emigrants from Helsinki to Copenhagen, whence it was possible to continue the trip on a transatlantic line. The price of the ticket was 150 marks, and its destination point was either New York, Montreal, or Philadelphia.[3] Thus the price of the ticket decreased noticeably by the end of the 1880's. Somewhat more material is already available for 1888. In this year, the HAPAG representative, Chr. Rasmussen, advertised that he was selling tickets (Hanko—New York) for the prices of 162, 178 or 180 marks, depending on the time of the journey. Because of icy seas the opening stage of the journey in the winter months went by way of St.Petersburg and Libau, while in the summer one would travel by ship from Hanko to Lübeck. From Hamburg onward the price of the ticket included meals. In addition, emigrants received remuneration for railroad tickets bought for the trip between Vaasa (or Turku) and Hanko.[4] Also from 1888 comes the information that one could get to America for 145 marks, if he left from Hanko on May 8 on the steamship *Orion* to England. The price of the ticket included meals from Liverpool onward.[5] It is not clear from the advertisement which shipping line emigrants travelling on the *Orion* would make connections with. On the basis of newspaper information, we still have for this stage no knowledge on how much a voyage to America by way of Sweden cost Finnish emigrants.

When Norddeutscher Lloyd began its conquest of the trade in transporting Finnish emigrants in the fall of 1889, its agents advertised that they

[2] K e r o 1969 II, p. 84.
[3] *Waasan Lehti*, September 7, 1887.
[4] For example, *Wasa Tidning*, April 6, 15, 1888; *Wasabladet*, May 12, 1888.
[5] *Wasa Tidning*, May 4, 1888.

would sell tickets to America at a price of 120 marks.[6] The cost of the trip by way of Sweden was 135—174 marks in the fall of 1889.[7] It is evident, however, that Norddeutscher Lloyd soon increased their prices, since the lower price of tickets was no longer used as a sales attraction in advertisements for 1890.[8] In 1890—91, the price of the trip by way of Sweden was probably about 130 marks.[9] Since these very years were the »golden years» of Norddeutscher Lloyd in Finland, this German company's prices certainly could not have been much higher. It is most likely that they were in the same range as other shipping companies.

The draft of an agreement drawn up between the Finland Steamship Company and certain English companies in the fall of 1891 shows that they intended to set the price of a ticket — apparently between Hanko and New York — at 150 marks, and that it was their purpose to maintain prices competitive with those of Norddeutscher Lloyd.[10] This price apparently did not remain in force, however, at least not for very long, since in the spring of 1892 the price of a ticket on the Cunard line from Hanko to New York was only 140 marks.[11]

As stated above, we can verify the cost of the trip from Hanko to America during the periods 1892—96 and 1899—1914, in those cases when the opening stage of the journey was made on ships of the Finland Steamship Company. In some years, several different prices seem to have been in use at the same time.[12] But these differences were so small that they do not make an examination of price fluctuations mentionably more difficult. Table 24 lists the prices that were most commonly in force in July of each year for Cunard Line passengers from Hanko to New York and for Allan Line passengers from Hanko to Quebec.

There appear to be three periods when the price of tickets was rather low: first, around 1890, then in 1895 and finally in 1904. Both 1895 and 1904, however, were years marked with economic depression in North America, when emigration was scarce. For this reason, the number of emigrants who

---

[6] For example, *Waasan Lehti,* November 16, 1889.

[7] For example, *Waasan Lehti,* November 9, 20, 1889; *Wasa Tidning,* September 27, 1889.

[8] For example, *Waasan Lehti,* January 25, 1890; *Wasa Tidning,* January 3, 1890.

[9] For example, *Waasan Lehti,* May 3, 27, 1891.

[10] Means of arrangement between Finnish Steam Navigation Co. of Helsingfors, the Cunard, Guion, Inman and White Star Lines. TYYH:s:m:7:18.

[11] The passenger lists of the Finland Steamship Company for 1892. TYYH:s:m:7:6.

[12] For example in 1914 the price of tickets on the Cunard Line between Hanko and New York was normally 274 marks. In the summer of 1914 the prices of some tickets on the same line between Hanko and New York were, however, 248, 253, 263 or 269 marks (TYYH:s:m:7:13). The reasons for the differences are not revealed in the available material.

Table 24. The prices of tickets on the Cunard Line between Hanko and New York and on the Allan Line between Hanko and Quebec, 1892—96, 1899—1914 (according to information contained in the passenger lists of the Finland Steamship Company).[13]

	Cunard Line Hanko—New York	Allan Line Hanko—Quebec
1892	140 marks	..
1893	170 »	170 marks
1894	..	130 »
1895	..	95 »
1896	179 »	161 »
1897	..	..
1898	..	..
1899	181 »	155 »
1900	181 »	155 »
1901	195 »	169 »
1902	195 »	169 »
1903	202 »	176 »
1904	86 »	86 »
1905	185 »	185 »
1906	216 »	192 »
1907	230 »	206 »
1908	246 »	211 »
1909	253 »	197 »
1910	246 »	204 »
1911	249 »	211 »
1912	274 »	225 »
1913	274 »	218 »
1914	274 »	232 »

took advantage of the cheap trip was rather small. The low prices around 1890, on the other hand, occurred at a time when »fat years» prevailed in the United States, for which reason, the importance of the low prices was relatively great.

As shown above the price of tickets dropped from 270 marks at the beginning of the 1870's to about 130 marks at the beginning of the 1890's. By the 1910's the price again increased to about 270 marks. How did this effect the possibilities of the potential emigrant in leaving? In any case, it is clear that the purchasing of tickets extended into broader segments of the population around 1890 than it did at the beginning of the 1870's. The effects of the raise in ticket prices occurring from around 1890 to the First World War are, on the other hand, more difficult to calculate. It would be very difficult to get an exact picture of the evolution of real incomes among the population interested in emigration. But it is known that a raise in real

13 TYYH:s:m:7:1—7, 10—13.

income did occur to some degree,[14] so we may say that an increase in income compensated in part for the increase in the price of tickets. However, at the end of the 1880's as well as on the eve of the First World War, the price of tickets was certainly too high for emigrants to pay for them with their own money, except on rare occasions. Thus according to information compiled by T o i v o n e n from interviews with persons emigrating from Southern Ostrobothnia during 1890—1930, 69.4 % received the money for the trip from a bank or an individual, or received a ticket from overseas.[15]

The trip to Hanko from, for example, Ostrobothnia cost something, but its proportion of the total expenses of an emigrant was very small. Sometimes it seemed to be free: the profits included in the prices from Hanko to the destination in America were so great that ticket sellers were able, for advertising purposes, to compensate the emigrant the travel expenses between his home and Hanko. New York, Boston, or Quebec was the destination of only few emigrants, so that the prices between Hanko and these harbors given above made up only a part of the expenses of the trip. The destination of many more was some mid-western mining town or logging center, and for some it was even the Pacific coast. If the destination chanced to be far from the harbor of arrival, a railroad ticket there cost more than the steamship ticket. Thus in 1893, when the trip on the White Star Line between Hanko and New York generally cost 170 marks, an emigrant would have to pay 493:30 marks to travel from Hanko to San Francisco, while the voyage from Kokkola through Hanko and New York to Astoria, Ore., cost 481:25 marks. The prices on North American railroads do not seem, however, to have increased as rapidly as those of steamship tickets, since in 1913 the trip between Hanko and San Francisco cost 607 marks and that between Hanko and Astoria, 547:25 marks.[16] Thus in the same period that the price of the trip between Hanko and New York increased 61 %, the price of that between Hanko and San Francisco increased only around 23 %.

The prices of tickets to Australia, New Zealand, and South Africa were noticeably higher than those to North America. Thus, in 1902, when the trip from Hanko to New York cost 195 marks, a ticket to Cape Town, South Africa cost 340 marks. In the same year a ticket to Australia cost 505 marks. Information about ticket prices to New Zealand is not available for 1902, but in the previous year the trip cost 550 marks,[17] so travelling to New Zea-

14 For further information on the development of incomes among agricultural population see B j ö r k q v i s t 1958, pp. 99—108; G r o u n d s t r o e m 1909, pp. 32 —41.

15 T o i v o n e n 1963, p. 57.

16 The passenger lists of the Finland Steamship Company for 1893 and 1913. TYYH:s:m:7:6,9.

17 The passenger lists of the Finland Steamship Company for 1901—02. TYYH: s:m:7:1—2.

land was apparently more expensive for the emigrants than travelling to any other country. The high price of tickets may have been one reason why relatively few Finnish emigrants moved to South Africa, Australia, and New Zealand. Another reason was probably the fact that the prepaid ticket system was not widely established in these countries.[18]

Table 24 shows that in some of the trough years of emigration, such as 1908, the price of a ticket could be as high or higher than in the preceding peak year. This perhaps indicates that shipping companies did not believe it paid to try to attract new customers by lowering ticket prices, even when their ships were nearly empty. Only the competition between shipping lines was able to send the price of tickets downward. But the important thing is that there existed a system of transportation that was able to convey rapidly millions of emigrants from Europe to countries overseas and that the prices of tickets on this system were always low enough that millions of those desiring to emigrate were able in one manner or another to obtain the money for the trip.

6. Prepaid tickets

The relationship between the number of customers on different shipping lines and the number of prepaid tickets received by these customers has been examined above. It appeared that one distinguishing feature of those shipping lines important to Finnish emigrants was a relatively large portion of passengers using prepaid tickets.

Since the majority of emigrants were »common people» and since the price of a ticket to America was, except for the trough years, 1895 and 1904, regularly over 100 Finn marks, the procuring of a ticket was not always a simple matter. Money needed for the purchase of tickets could be obtained from either Finland or America. T o i v o n e n in her dissertation explained the former quite thoroughly. According to her examination, which was based primarily on interviews, 36.5 % of the emigrants from Southern Ostrobothnia travelled with the aid of loans obtained either from private individuals or from banks, 30.6 % either received their travel money from home or used their own savings — or inherited money, while 32.9 % received their tickets from overseas. According to T o i v o n e n, »the trade or social class of the borrower does not seem to have determined the source from which the travel funds were obtained.» The current interest generally paid on loans was 6 %.[1]

---

[18] Before the First World War the passenger lists of the Finland Steamship Company contain no entries of prepaid tickets sent from Australia, New Zealand, or South Africa to Finland.

[1] T o i v o n e n 1963, pp. 56—58.

Since T o i v o n e n in her dissertation explained the procuring of money from Finland thoroughly, the following will center on an examination of the circumstances connected with the use of prepaid tickets coming from America. T o i v o n e n has treated this but briefly, showing only how great a percentage of Finnish emigrants used prepaid tickets during the period 1894—1921.[2] The research of emigration historians outside of Finland has also dealt quite sparingly with the problems connected with prepaid tickets. The first study shedding some degree of light on this question — the Dane K r i s t i a n H v i d t's report before a congress of Nordic historians — was published only in 1971.[3] H v i d t has also treated the significance of prepaid tickets in his dissertation, which was published in 1971.[4] To a certain extent the question has also attracted attention in Norway[5] and Sweden.[6] Research on this point has illustrated primarily the manner in which the number of prepaid tickets has fluctuated during different years and periods.

From the year 1892 on materials[7] concerning the use of prepaid tickets by Finnish emigrants are abundant, if indeed they are also extremely difficult to deal with. Information about the receivers of prepaid tickets has been preserved in the Finland Steamship Company's passenger lists, most of which are available. If this material is augmented by information from passport lists on each emigrant's home commune, occupation, etc., statistics can be prepared which show, for example, how great a role prepaid tickets played in various parts of Finland and how much the members of different social classes were forced to rely on prepaid tickets. To our knowledge, these kinds of questions have not attracted much attention in studies done outside of Finland.

Suomen Tilastollinen Vuosikirja (Statistical Yearbook of Finland) contains information on how large a proportion of the emigrants carried by shipping companies in 1894—1914 bought their tickets in Finland and how large a proportion made the journey with tickets sent from America.[8] For the years 1891—93 corresponding information is available in various sta-

[2] T o i v o n e n 1963, pp. 58—59.
[3] H v i d t 1971 I pp. 132—134.
[4] H v i d t 1971, pp. 347—352, 478—480.
[5] S e m m i n g s e n 1950, pp. 54—57.
[6] B e r i t B r a t t n e has treated the question of prepaid tickets shortly in her dissertation (pp. 100—105) published in 1973. Her material covers only the years 1883—89.
[7] The passenger lists of the Swedish police departments reveal only in exceptional cases whether a person travelled with a prepaid ticket or with a ticket purchased by the person in question in Finland or Sweden. For this reason investigations on the use of prepaid tickets by Finnish emigrants cannot extend back beyond 1891, if they are to be based on statistics concerning their use.
[8] STV 1915, Table 63 (pp. 114—115).

Table 25. The numbers of emigrants travelling with tickets bought in Finland and prepaid tickets, 1891—1914.

	Bought in Finland		Prepaid		Total
1891	7	50.0 %	7	50.0 %	14
1892	2,599	81.8 %	578	18.2 %	3,177
1893	3,536	67.6 %	1,695	32.4 %	5,231
1894	608	56.6 %	467	43.4 %	1,075
1895	2,157	72.4 %	824	27.6 %	2,981
1896	3,766	76.2 %	1,176	23.8 %	4,942
1897	1,833	71.7 %	724	28.3 %	2,557
1898	2,763	75.3 %	904	24.7 %	3,667
1899	9,026	73.0 %	3,331	27.0 %	12,357
1900	6,533	61.4 %	4,109	38.6 %	10,642
1901	8,983	71.0 %	3,676	29.0 %	12,659
1902	15,364	70.6 %	6,389	29.4 %	21,753
1903	9,728	60.5 %	6,359	39.5 %	16,087
1904	7,108	68.7 %	3,243	31.3 %	10,351
1905	12,423	70.2 %	5,285	29.8 %	17,708 [9]
1906	10,912	66.3 %	5,554	33.7 %	16,466
1907	11,074	69.0 %	4,982	31.0 %	16,056
1908	4,736	75.8 %	1,512	24.2 %	6,248
1909	15,397	75.9 %	4,886	24.1 %	20,283
1910	13,943	71.2 %	5,628	28.8 %	19,571 [10]
1911	6,568	66.0 %	3,377	34.0 %	9,945
1912	7,911	69.1 %	3,536	30.9 %	11,447
1913	15,637	73.2 %	5,733	26.8 %	21,370
1914	3,744	64.7 %	2,042	35.3 %	5,786
Total	176,356	69.9 %	76,017	30.1 %	252,373

[9] According to *Suomen Tilastollinen Vuosikirja* 18,341 emigrants left in 1905, 12,883 of these with tickets bought in Finland and 5,458 with prepaid tickets. The figures for 1905 emigrants in *Suomen Tilastollinen Vuosikirja* probably include 796 Russians. In one set of statistics preserved in the archives of the Finland Steamship Company the entry is made concerning emigration for 1905 that 12,423 of the travellers used tickets bought in Finland and 5,285 used prepaid tickets. TYYH:s:m: 7:17.

[10] For the years 1910, 1912, and 1913, the following numbers of emigrants are found in the archives of the Finland Steamship Company:

	Bought in Finland	Prepaid ticket
1910	13,943 (also 13,866)	5,628 (also 5,596)
1912	7,884	3,474
1913	15,574	5,796

Suomen Tilastollinen Vuosikirja mentions that it had received information from the Helsinki Steamship Company as well as from the Finland Steamship Company (STV 1915, pp. 114—115 note 1), which may explain why the figures in *Suomen Tilastollinen Vuosikirja* are a little larger for 1910 and 1912 than those found in the Finland Steamship Company's statistics. The difference for 1913 probably resulted from a mistake made in the Finland Steamship Company's computation, for in *Suomen*

tistical reports preserved in the archives of the Finland Steamship Company. Material available for 1891 is still so scarce, however, that it does not present the possibility of drawing any conclusions, but Table 25 gives a fairly reliable picture for the period 1892—1914.

According to the table 176,356 or 69.9 % of Finnish emigrants during the years 1891—1914 travelled with a ticket bought in Finland, while 76,017, or 30.1 % received tickets from North America.

The table shows that, in relative terms, the number of prepaid tickets neither rose nor declined in a straight line. On the other hand it seems to have been almost a rule that the percentage of prepaid tickets was smaller during peak years of emigration than in the years immediately following, but that, in absolute terms, the number of prepaid tickets was at its greatest just at the peak year of each cycle. The corresponding occurred also in Denmark, and here the rise in the percentage of prepaid tickets has been held to spring from the fact that, in the years following a great wave of emigration, a greater than usual number of emigrants newly arrived in America arranged a chance for their relatives to come to America.[11]This interpretation seems to be quite sound. Thus, it seems that, for example, the 1902 emigrants were already in the following year eager to subsidize the trip to America for relatives and friends who had remained in Finland, for in 1903 the number of prepaid tickets was, in both relative and absolute terms, exceptionally large. On the other hand, in the case of Finnish emigration it seems that the more difficult economic crises in the United States and Canada caused emigrants to consider whether or not it paid to send tickets to relatives and friends in Finland. The low number of prepaid tickets sent in 1904 and 1908 point to this fact. But, then, it may also be true that there were not many requests from Finland for prepaid tickets in these years, for the rather widespread return of emigrants back to Finland in 1903 and 1907,[12] doubtlessly brought information about worsening economic opportunities in America to the areas from which emigrants would be leaving.

As mentioned above, 30.1 % of Finnish emigrants in the years 1891—1914 travelled with prepaid tickets. Not enough material is available from other countries to make detailed comparisons in this matter. It is known that in Sweden over 50 % of all emigrants in the middle of the 1880's used prepaid tickets. In the period 1872—74, around 40 % of all Norwegian emi-

---

Tilastollinen Vuosikirja the number of those travelling with tickets paid in Finland is somewhat smaller and the number of those travelling with prepaid tickets somewhat larger than in a table found in the archives of the Finland Steamship Company.

11 H v i d t 1971, pp. 348—351.

12 K e r o 1972, p. 15; STV 1910, Table 49 (p. 81).

grants received prepaid tickets.[13] In Denmark, prepaid ticket users composed in 1877—95, 12.9—32.3 % of all emigrants migrating overseas.[14] But these statistics are from such a variety of periods, that comparisons can be made only with the greatest reservation. However, we can perhaps conjecture that Swedes and Norwegians received relatively a little more prepaid tickets than Finns did, and that Danes received relatively somewhat less. But on the basis of merely this conjecture, it is not profitable to begin deliberating whence these differences arose.

As mentioned above, a body of statistics dealing with emigrants who left Finland in 1905 has been prepared at the IGHUT. This material makes it possible to answer to a certain degree the following questions: How large a percentage of emigrants leaving in different months used prepaid tickets?[15] How great a percentage of members of each social class travelled with tickets received from America? What kinds of differences can be discovered by examining emigration from different provinces? How great a percentage of men and how great a percentage of women received their tickets from America? How great a role did tickets sent from America play among those of different marital statuses? How were prepaid tickets divided among the age groups? Were there differences between emigration by families and emigration of individuals? Are there differences discoverable between emigration from urban and that from rural areas? Was the role of prepaid tickets different in Finnish-speaking areas than in Swedish-speaking areas? To what extent did immigrants to different parts of America receive prepaid tickets?

The following table contains figures on how great a percentage of emigrants leaving in each month of 1905 travelled with tickets received from America,[16] how great a percentage bought tickets in Finland, and how great a percentage travelled by way of Sweden. It is not known which of these last possessed tickets sent from America and which did not.

The number of tickets sent from America fluctuated greatly during the year. It was proportionally at its smallest in January when only 14.7 % of the emigrants used tickets coming from America. After this the percentage of those using tickets sent from America grew almost continuously until July when it reached 41.0 % of all emigrants. From August to December the proportion of tickets received from America relative to all travel tickets

---

[13] H v i d t 1971 I, p. 133.

[14] H v i d t 1971, p. 348.

[15] The times of departure were determined on the basis of the ships' departure from Hanko or Gothenburg.

[16] Perhaps a small portion of those travelling with prepaid tickets were Finnish Americans visiting Finland, whose prepaid ticket was in fact the second half of a round-trip ticket bought in America.

Table 26. Monthly use of various kinds of tickets, 1905.

	Bought in Finland		Prepaid ticket		Via Sweden	
January	1,445	84.8 %	250	14.7 %	9	0.5 %
February	1,094	74.0 %	379	25.6 %	5	0.3 %
March	1,396	71.1 %	528	26.9 %	40	2.0 %
April	1,206	71.4 %	439	26.0 %	44	2.6 %
May	1,369	67.2 %	605	29.7 %	62	3.0 %
June	722	57.2 %	500	39.6 %	41	3.2 %
July	552	57.6 %	393	41.0 %	13	1.4 %
August	643	63.7 %	353	35.0 %	14	1.4 %
September	652	60.5 %	389	36.1 %	36	3.3 %
October	625	67.2 %	292	31.4 %	13	1.4 %
November	605	62.6 %	356	36.8 %	6	0.6 %
December	497	65.3 %	249	32.7 %	15	2.0 %
Total	10,806	68.2 %	4,733	29.9 %	298	1.9 %

remained approximately the same as before; fluctuating between 31.4 % and 36.8 %. In the latter part of the year, therefore, about every third emigrant used a prepaid ticket.

Since emigration from Finland to America was quite scanty in early fall, 1904 and intensified only in November and December,[17] it can be seen as having just revived in January, 1905, from the slump it had been in during an economic depression in America. The fact that the proportion of prepaid tickets was so low in January, 1905 indicates that the increase of emigration was not in the beginning due to a growth in the number of prepaid tickets. Information from America doubtlessly formed the basis for the growth of emigration, but the initiative was with those intending to emigrate who bought tickets when the proper occasion arose. Only after a period of economic boom had prevailed in America for a few months and after emigration had been going in strength for several months did tickets sent from America begin to play a more important part.

As mentioned above, the economic depressions of 1904 and 1908 in America were reflected in the low number of prepaid tickets for those years. The continued growth of the proportion of prepaid tickets in the first part of 1905 might also have reflected this. It seems only natural that after a depression at the end of 1904 and the beginning of 1905 immigrants would have scarcely had the money to send prepaid tickets to Finland. But once the economic situation had improved for several months, circumstances would have been totally different: the sending of prepaid tickets to Finland would no longer cause hardships.

---

[17] SVT XXVIII:2, p. 21. About 30 % of emigrants leaving Finland in 1904 left during the last two months of the year.

As indicated above, emigrants were almost without exception »common people».[18] Since the emigrant group consisted partly of farmers, partly of crofters, farmers' and crofters' children, landless rural laborers and various kinds of workers, the existence of differences in financial means can be assumed. When departure for America was in question, how important a role did prepaid tickets play among the most well-to-do emigrant group, the farmers, and among the other groups »below» them? In the following table, emigrants are divided into the same seven groups as they were earlier when the occupational and social composition of emigration was examined. The table shows how large a percentage of the members of each group bought tickets in Finland, how large a percentage received prepaid tickets and how great a percentage travelled by way of Sweden.

Table 27. *Financing of the trip to America among emigrants from various social classes, 1905.*

	Bought in Finland		Prepaid ticket		Via Sweden	
Farmers	565	82.2 %	104	15.1 %	18	2.6 %/
Children of farmers	3,161	79.4 %	731	18.4 %	91	2.3 %
Crofters	388	77.4 %	109	21.8 %	4	0.8 %
Children of crofters	1,271	66.5 %	622	32.6 %	17	0.9 %
Cottagers	2,583	61.3 %	1,603	38.0 %	29	0.7 %
Workers	1,731	61.8 %	1,023	36.5 %	48	1.7 %
Others	1,107	63.7 %	541	31.1 %	91	5.2 %
Total	10,806	68.2 %	4,733	29.9 %	298	1.9 %

The significance of tickets sent from America appears to have been smallest with farmers. Then follow, in order of increasing importance; farmers' children, crofters, »others», crofters' children, workers, and cottagers. The table clearly demonstrates that the poorer the social group to which the emigrant belonged the more his leaving depended on his receiving a ticket from relatives or friends already in America. Thus while of the most well-to-do emigrant group, farmers, 15.1 % used tickets received from America, 38.0 % of the poorest group, cottagers, depended on this means. It is probable that in the 1870's and 1880's only a very small percentage of Finnish emigrants received prepaid tickets,[19] and this is probably one reason why there were so many farmers among the emigrants in the opening phases

---

18 For more information on the social and occupational structure of emigration see above pp. 81—90.

19 By then there was already an abundance of prepaid ticket sellers in America, but otherwise the system of transporting Finnish emigrants was still undeveloped.

of emigration, and why the members of the poorer social classes were so few: farmers and their children simply had the best opportunity to procure the expensive tickets for the trip to America.

Did tickets arriving from America compose an equally important factor in all areas of Finland? The following table shows by province how great a proportion of each province's emigrants went with a ticket purchased in Finland and how great a proportion received their tickets from America.

Table 28. *Financing of the trip to America, by province, 1905.*

	Bought in Finland		Prepaid ticket		Via Sweden	
Uusimaa	410	60.9 %	259	38.5 %	4	0.6 %
Turku and						
Pori	2,169	71.1 %	666	21.8 %	217	7.1 %
Häme	387	73.7 %	134	25.5 %	4	0.8 %
Viipuri	600	73.3 %	216	26.4 %	2	0.2 %
Mikkeli	209	72.6 %	76	26.4 %	3	1.0 %
Kuopio	365	61.4 %	228	38.4 %	1	0.2 %
Vaasa	5,411	72.6 %	1,997	26.8 %	44	0.6 %
Oulu	1,255	51.5 %	1,157	47.5 %	23	0.9 %
Total	10,806	68.2 %	4,733	29.9 %	298	1.9 %

On the basis of the table it appears that Oulu Province diverged clearly from the rest of Finland, for while 29.9 % of the whole country's emigrants travelled with prepaid tickets, 47.5 % of the emigrants from Oulu Province did. Then came Uusimaa, Kuopio, Vaasa, Viipuri, Mikkeli, and Häme. Emigrants from Turku and Pori Province used according to the table tickets arriving from America the least; only 21.8 % of these had received tickets from beyond the Atlantic. It should be noted, however, that a larger percentage travelled by way of Sweden from Turku and Pori Province than from the rest of the country. Some of those travelling through Sweden had doubtlessly received their tickets from America, so the use of prepaid tickets among emigrants from Turku and Pori Province was probably in fact just as common as among those from e.g. Häme Province.

It is rather difficult to explain why 47.5 % of the emigrants from Oulu Province travelled with prepaid tickets, while the corresponding figure for some of the other provinces was only about 25 %. One reason may have been differences in wealth standard. Oulu and Kuopio might be considered to be the country's poorest provinces. On the other hand, Uusimaa, in which prepaid tickets also played an important role, was one of the wealthiest areas of the country. As far as degree of wealth standard is concerned, however, it is possible, that Uusimaa Province's emigrants, of which a larger than average percentage left from towns, might have been closer to the population of the northern provinces than to that of Uusimaa's rural areas. Besides, the degree of wealth standard of the area of departure, other factors such as the occupational and sex composition of emigration, and the place of settlement and occupation in America may also have been of influence here. In addition, it is possible that in certain areas those intending to go to America received money from America in place of a prepaid ticket, in which case the number of prepaid tickets would no longer give a correct picture of how dependent emigration from that area was on aid from relatives and friends in America.

Did men and women receive relatively the same amount of travel tickets from America? The following table shows how many men, women, and persons whose sex cannot be determined [20] received tickets from America, and how many bought them in Finland.

Table 29. The division of different kinds of tickets among men and women, 1905.

	Bought in Finland		Prepaid ticket		Via Sweden	
Men	8,318	75.7 %	2,462	22.4 %	203	1.8 %
Women	2,465	51.1 %	2,263	47.0 %	91	1.9 %
Unknown	23	65.7 %	8	22.9 %	4	11.4 %
Total	10,806	68.2 %	4,733	29.9 %	298	1.9 %

The table indicates that women received noticeably more tickets from America than men: nearly a half of women emigrants travelled to America with tickets received from America, while only a little more than every fifth male emigrant depended on aid from America. This was doubtlessly due in part to the fact that when a family moved to America, often the husband went there first, usually with resources gathered in Finland. The wife and children then followed in a few months' or years' time, when the husband had earned the sum of money required for prepaid tickets.

The extensive use of prepaid tickets by women might also be due to the fact that »a severe lack of women» dominated among the Finnish Americans, for which reason the procuring of wives from Finland was probably quite common. Tickets for the trip were offered to acquaintances, or perhaps at times to unknown women, if they would agree to marry the sender of the ticket. The fact that unmarried women received more tickets from America than married ones also points to this kind of »match-making emigration». Of the 4,819 female emigrants in 1905, 1,148 were married and 3,413 were not. Of the former, 497 or 43.3 % received tickets from America;

---

[20] Unknowns have come into the group because now and then an entry such as so and so »with two children» appears in the passenger lists.

of the latter 1,633 or 47.8 % used prepaid tickets.[21] This explanation is weakened, however, by the fact that unmarried men also received more tickets from America than married men did. The number of men known to emigrate in 1905 was 10,983 of which 7,869 were unmarried and 2,522 were married. Of the former 1,828 or 23.2 % used prepaid tickets; of the latter 485 or 19.2 % did. There is yet another factor besides those producing the differences between married and unmarried women, that may have caused the differences among men: farmers, who used prepaid tickets relatively the least, belonged for the most part to the married group and thus lowered the percentage of this group's use of prepaid tickets.

How great a role did prepaid tickets play in financing the trip to America among different age groups? In the following table emigrants have been divided into nine age groups and »unknown», on the basis of information in the passport lists concerning the year of birth.

Table 30. *Financing of the trip to America among different age groups, 1905.*

	Bought in Finland		Prepaid ticket		Via Sweden	
Under 16	299	49.4 %	299	49.4 %	7	1.2 %
16—20	2,663	62.9 %	1,486	35.1 %	84	2.0 %
21—25	3,125	72.7 %	1,093	25.4 %	83	1.9 %
26—30	2,003	73.2 %	689	25.2 %	46	1.7 %
31—35	1,141	76.0 %	334	22.3 %	26	1.7 %
36—40	456	75.0 %	137	22.5 %	15	2.5 %
41—45	295	74.3 %	91	22.9 %	11	2.8 %
46—50	153	75.4 %	42	20.7 %	8	3.9 %
Over 50	406	52.1 %	360	46.2 %	14	1.8 %
Unknown	265	56.3 %	202	42.9 %	4	0.8 %
Total	10,806	68.2 %	4,733	29.9 %	298	1.9 %

According to the table, the largest proportion of prepaid ticket users is found in the »under 16» group: almost half of this group travelled with prepaid tickets in 1905.[22] Among the 16—20-year olds, about 35 %, clearly

21 Widows and divorcees totalled 79. Of these, 22 or 27.8 % used prepaid tickets. There were 179 women whose marital status is unknown, and of these 111 or 62.0 % had received prepaid tickets. The last-mentioned group contained primarily young girls, about whom nothing is entered in the lists regarding marital status, but who doubtlessly were unmarried.

22 This was perhaps the most important, although not the only, reason, why unmarried persons received more prepaid tickets than married persons did. For if under 16-year olds are excluded from the unmarried group, 68.4 % of the remainder used tickets bought in Finland and 29.6 % prepaid tickets, while 2.0 % went by way of Sweden. Of all married persons 71.7 % used tickets bought in Finland, 26.8 % used prepaid tickets, and 1.5 % travelled by way of Sweden.

a smaller percentage, travelled with prepaid tickets. In the age groups 21—25 years, 26—30 years, 31—35 years, 36—41 years and 46—50 years the relative number of those using prepaid tickets was rather small, since of the members of these groups only 20.7 % — 25.4 % travelled with tickets received from America. 42.9 % of the »age unknown» group, of which the majority were probably children, travelled with prepaid tickets.

Thus, according to the table, prepaid tickets played the largest relative role among the youngest and the oldest age groups. The extensive use of prepaid tickets by members of the youngest age group was undoubtedly due to the fact that a relatively large number of them had fathers in America, who sent them tickets. The relatively large number of prepaid tickets received by members of the oldest group probably resulted from the fact that children of a family, once they had one after the other moved to America, sent prepaid tickets to parents left alone in Finland. In addition it is likely that the »over 50» age group included a larger than average number of people who had already been living in America for a long period of time and who had bought a round-trip ticket for their trip to Finland.

It was probably much easier for those of prime working age to raise the money for a ticket, either by saving or by borrowing: those giving and endorsing loans could have more faith in their ability to repay the loan than in others'. Moreover, if a ticket had to be procured from America, those between the ages of 20 and 50 generally had to request it from brothers, sisters, more distant relatives, or even friends, in which cases the procuring of the ticket was probably more difficult than in those cases where relations between children and parents were in question. The low proportion of prepaid tickets among these age groups resulted primarily from factors such as these.

The following table reveals how often men travelling alone, women travelling alone, men and wives travelling together, families with children travelling together, mothers travelling with children (and these children), fathers travelling with children (and these children) used prepaid tickets. Besides these, the group, children travelling with other than parents, is included in the table.

The table shows that prepaid tickets played somewhat different roles among the members from the different categories. The group consisting of mothers with their children used prepaid tickets relatively the most. This was undoubtedly due to the fact that the father of the family had already earlier immigrated to America and then sent prepaid tickets for his family. Also more than half of the men going to America with their children used prepaid tickets (or round-trip tickets bought in America). In the cases of children travelling to America unaccompanied by their parents, again over half went with prepaid tickets. In this last case, it was undoubtedly usually

Table 31. Financing of the trip to America by single emigrants and emigrants with families, 1905.

	Bought in Finland		Prepaid ticket		Via Sweden	
Men alone	7,698	77.2 %	2,084	20.9 %	190	1.9 %
Women alone	1,611	50.5 %	1,503	47.1 %	75	2.4 %
Men and wives together	281	81.9 %	56	16.3 %	6	1.7 %
Families with children	393	81.4 %	73	15.1 %	17	3.5 %
Mothers with children	731	44.4 %	906	55.1 %	8	0.5 %
Fathers with children	20	47.6 %	22	52.4 %	—	—
Children with others than parents	72	44.2 %	89	54.6 %	2	1.2 %
Total	10,806	68.2 %	4,733	29.9 %	298	1.9 %

a question of parents (or one of them) who had earlier immigrated to America and sent prepaid tickets to Finland when they learned of a relative or a friend coming to America who could bring the children left in Finland along with him when he came.

Of the 3,189 women travelling alone, 1,503 or 47.1 % used prepaid tickets. The »match-making emigration» referred to above may in part explain the greater than average use of prepaid tickets by this group. But other factors may also have been of influence here. It is possible that Finnish-American boarding-houses and families sought young women from Finland as servants, and sent prepaid tickets to those seen as suited for the position. In addition, part of the women travelling alone were already married, and were going to join their husbands. Whatever the reasons, there was a vast difference between women travelling alone and men travelling alone, for, of 9,972 of the latter, only 2,084 or 20.9 % had received prepaid tickets.

If a man and wife travelled to America together, they rarely financed their trip with prepaid tickets. Of the 343 persons belonging in this category only 56 or 16.3 % had received tickets from America. If they had children accompanying them, the proportion using prepaid tickets was even smaller. In fact, only 15.1 % of those belonging to the group of entire families travelling together had received prepaid tickets. There are at least two reasons for the small number of prepaid tickets used by families. On the other hand, it is possible that when an entire family migrated to America they would have sold their property in Finland and bought tickets with the money thus raised. On the other hand, it is possible that it was difficult for an entire family to get tickets from America. It was probably rather easy to find in America a relative or friend who, against some kind of security would agree to send one ticket, but it was probably difficult to find a person who was willing (or who had the funds) to send several tickets.

It has already been mentioned that emigration leaving urban areas was in some ways different from that leaving rural areas. Differences can also be discovered in the use of prepaid tickets. Of the 14,241 emigrants leaving from rural areas, 4,153 or 29.2 % used tickets received from America, 9,811 or 68.9 % used tickets bought in Finland, and 277 or 1.9 % travelled by way of Sweden. At the same time, of 1,596 urban emigrants, 580 or 36.3 % used prepaid tickets, 995 or 62.3 % bought tickets in Finland, while 21 or 1.3 % travelled through Sweden. Therefore, use of prepaid tickets was somewhat more common among those leaving from towns than among emigrants from rural areas. This difference was probably due to the fact that a rather large proportion of emigrants from towns were women, and, as has been shown, a greater percentage of women than men received prepaid tickets. It could also be argued that it was more difficult to find endorsers for a loan in towns than in rural districts where people knew one another over broad areas.

If a comparison between Finnish-speaking and Swedish-speaking areas is desired, this can be made primarily in the southern part of Turku and Pori Province and in Vaasa Province. In Turku and Pori Province this question may be studied in Vehmaa, Mynämäki and Åland sheriff listricts, the communes of which have been categorized as Finnish- and Swedish-speaking.[23] 583 emigrants left from these communes in 1905, of which 237 were from Finnish-speaking and 346 from Swedish-speaking communes. Of the Finnish-speaking emigrants 38 or 16.0 % used prepaid tickets, and 199 or 84.0 % travelled with tickets bought in Finland. Of the Swedish-speaking group, 62 or 17.9 % used prepaid tickets, 94 or 27.2 % bought tickets in Finland, and 190 or 54.9 % travelled by way of Sweden. Since it is not possible to estimate which of those travelling through Sweden used prepaid tickets, it is much a matter of conjecture whether the two language groups in Turku and Pori Province differed from each other as users of prepaid tickets. As far as emigrants travelling by way of Hanko are concerned, however, Swedish speakers seem to have made more general use of prepaid tickets. Thus, 39.7 % of Swedish-speaking emigrants going by way of Hanko used prepaid tickets, while only 16.0 % of Finnish-speaking emigrants did.

In this study, the communes of Vaasa Province have also been divided into Finnish- and Swedish-speaking.[24] In 1905, 5,383 emigrants left Finnish-

---

[23] The distribution is made on the basis of the situation in 1900. At this time Eckerö, Hammarland, Jomala, Finström, Geta, Saltvik, Sund, Vordö, Lumparland, Lemland, Föglö, Kökar, Sottunga, Kumlinge, Brändö, Iniö, Houtskär, Korpo and Nagu were Swedish-speaking. Velkua, Taivassalo, Kivimaa (Kustavi), Lokalahti, Vehmaa, Uusikirkko, Uusikaupunki rural commune, Pyhämaa, Pyhämaan luoto, Laitila, Karjala, Mynämäki, Mietoinen, Lemu, Askainen, Merimasku and Rymättylä were Finnish-speaking.

[24] The distribution is made on the basis of the situation in 1900. Besides the rural, Swedish-speaking communes mentioned above (p. 101) the towns Kaskinen, Pietarsaari, Kokkola, Kristiinankaupunki and Uusikaarlepyy have been included in

speaking communes and 1,877 left Swedish-speaking communes. In 192 cases, the language cannot have been determined because of dual-language communes. Of the Finnish-speaking emigrants, 1,736 or 32.2 % travelled with prepaid tickets, 3,641 or 67.6 % bought their tickets in Finland, while 6 or 0.1 % travelled by way of Sweden. Of the Swedish-speaking group, 184 or 9.8 % were users of prepaid tickets, 1,657 or 88.3 % travelled with tickets bought in Finland, while 36 or 1.9 % travelled by way of Sweden. The use of prepaid tickets thus seems to have been much more common among the Finnish-speaking than the Swedish-speaking population of Ostro-bothnia, exactly the opposite of what occurred in Turku and Pori Province. We cannot be certain as to the differences between Turku and Pori Province and Vaasa Province, however, since such a large part of the Swedish-speak-ing emigrants from Turku and Pori Province travelled by way of Sweden.

If we start with the assumption that the extent of the use of prepaid tickets depended fundamentally on the standard of wealth in the area of departure, we can argue that, since the standard of living was higher in Swedish-speaking Ostrobothnia than Finnish-speaking Ostrobothnia, Swed-ish speakers departing as emigrants did not need financial support from American cousins as often as did Finnish speakers. This, however, cannot be proved convincingly. In Swedish-speaking areas, where the pioneering of new land had ended earlier than in the Finnish-speaking areas, the aver-age size of farms was probably, by the end of the 19th century declining more rapidly than in Finnish-speaking areas.[25] On a small farm, the procu-ring of the means necessary to buy a ticket was scarcely a simple procedure.

It can also be argued that the number of prepaid tickets might depend on which area in the United States emigrants from a given area in Finland settled. The following table divides the areas of destination into eight groups and shows how many Finnish- and Swedish-speaking emigrants settling in each group of states had prepaid tickets, how many had tickets bought in Finland and how many travelled by way of Sweden.

If the difference resulted primarily from the area of destination, a some-what similar proportion (high or low) of emigrants going to the same group

---

the Swedish-speaking group. The definition is not applied to Vaasa, since both language groups were of almost equal size in this town. The cases, in which the emigrant is known to be from Vaasa Province, but in which his home commune is not known are included in this same group. The population of the rest of the com-munes is considered Finnish-speaking. There were small Finnish-speaking minorities in Swedish-speaking communes and likewise Swedish-speaking minorities in Finnish-speaking communes. However, with the exception of Vaasa, the division of the com-munes into language groups appears so clear-cut that emigrants belonging to the language minority do not decisively lessen the reliability of the figures.

[25] On the economic difficulties of Swedish-speaking Ostrobothnia see J u t i k-k a l a 1958, pp. 355—356.

Table 32. *Financing of the trip to different parts of North America by Finnish- and Swedish-speaking emigrants from Vaasa Province.*

	Finnish-speaking			Swedish-speaking		
Destination [26]	Bought in Finland	Prepaid ticket	Via Sweden	Bought in Finland	Prepaid ticket	Vi Swe
1	1,230 61.3 %	774 38.6 %	3 0.1 %	462 79.9 %	99 17.1 %	17 2
2	348 68.5 %	160 31.5 %	— —	31 70.5 %	10 22.7 %	3 6
3	1,360 81.9 %	301 18.1 %	— —	507 92.0 %	35 6.4 %	9 1
4	167 75.6 %	53 24.0 %	1 0.5 %	246 98.0 %	3 1.2 %	2 0
5	85 78.0 %	23 21.1 %	1 0.9 %	309 93.9 %	16 4.9 %	4 1
6	419 50.8 %	405 49.1 %	1 0.1 %	49 71.0 %	19 27.5 %	1 1
7	19 90.5 %	2 9.5 %	— —	6 100.0 %	— —	— -
8	13 41.9 %	18 58.1 %	— —	47 95.9 %	2 4.1 %	— -
Total	3,641 67.6 %	1,736 32.2 %	6 0.1 %	1,657 88.3 %	184 9.8 %	36 1

of states, be they Finnish- or Swedish-speaking, should have used prepaid tickets. However, although great differences appeared in the numbers of prepaid tickets used by immigrants to the different groups of states, from group to group, a greater proportion of Finnish-speaking than Swedish-speaking immigrants used prepaid tickets. This indicates that the differences in the numbers of prepaid tickets used by the two language groups did not result, at least not mainly, from the wealth of the area of destination, from the network of emigration agents, or from any other such factors.

Thus it appears that factors connected both to the area of departure and to the area of destination serve as an equally poor explanation why a larger proportion of Ostrobothnian Finnish-speaking emigrants used prepaid tickets than the Swedish speakers. On the basis of material available, the question must remain a mystery. There is, however, still another possibility worth mentioning. It is within the realm of possibility that Swedish-speaking emigrants received a proportionately small number of prepaid tickets because the Ostrobothnian Swedish-speaking population in America had the habit of sending those desiring to leave for America money in the place of a ticket, the ticket thus being bought in Finland. If such a custom existed, it probably extended to the emigrants only from a given area, Swedish-speaking Ostrobothnia, and not to Finland's entire body of Swedish-speaking immi-

---

[26] The areas of destination in the table are as follows:

1) Massachusetts, New York, Connecticut, New Hampshire, New Jersey, Rhode Island, Maine, Pennsylvania, and Vermont. 2) Ohio, Illinois, and Indiana. 3) Minnesota, Michigan, and Wisconsin. 4) North and South Dakota, Nebraska, Montana, Wyoming, Idaho, Colorado, Nevada, New Mexico, and Utah. 5) California, Oregon, Washington, and Alaska. 6) Canadian provinces. 7) Southern states of the USA in this case Texas, Alabama, Florida, Louisiana, South Carolina, North Carolina. 8) The destination unknown, Australia, and South Africa.

Language unknown			Total		
Bought in Finland	Prepaid ticket	Via Sweden	Bought in Finland	Prepaid ticket	Via Sweden
59 61.5 %	37 38.5 %	— —	1,751 65.3 %	910 33.9 %	20 0.7 %
5 31.3 %	9 56.3 %	2 12.5 %	384 67.6 %	179 31.5 %	5 0.9 %
34 75.6 %	11 24.4 %	— —	1,901 84.2 %	347 15.4 %	9 0.4 %
5 100.0 %	— —	— —	418 87.6 %	56 11.7 %	3 0.6 %
8 100.0 %	— —	— —	402 90.1 %	39 8.7 %	5 1.1 %
2 9.5 %	19 90.5 %	— —	470 51.4 %	443 48.4 %	2 0.2 %
— —	— —	— —	25 92.6 %	2 7.4 %	— —
— —	1 100.0 %	— —	60 74.1 %	21 25.9 %	— —
113 58.9 %	77 40.1 %	2 1.0 %	5,411 72.6 %	1,997 26.8 %	44 0.6 %

grants to America. It appears, for example, that, in Finland Proper, the Swedish-speaking population used prepaid tickets proportionally more frequently than the Finnish-speaking population.

As mentioned above, the number of prepaid tickets used by those going to some groups of states was somewhat greater than that used by those going to other groups. A basic assumption made here is that the destination marked on the ticket and in the passenger list was the destination to which the immigrant actually went.[27] In the following examination of the proportion of prepaid tickets among tickets bought for travel to different states, it is again assumed that, with the exception of a few harbor towns, the place

---

[27] It is the purpose of the author in a continuation of this study to examine more extensively the distribution of Finnish immigrants among various areas of North America. Then the question of whether the destination marked on the ticket and the passenger list was actually the destination of the emigrant will be a most essential one. In the present connection, the question cannot be dealt with very broadly, but it can be stated that a comparison of information gathered from interviews with information in the passenger lists indicates that, at least at the beginning of the twentieth century, the entries concerning destinations in the passenger lists are extremely useful in determining the area to which emigrants leaving Finland were making their way. It is necessary, however, to take into account the following circumstances: if the destination was listed in the passenger lists as Boston, Mass., or Portland, Maine, the actual destination was located somewhere in the New England region, though not necessarily in Boston or Portland. If the destination in the passenger lists was New York, the actual destination in most cases was New York, but it was also in some cases a locality near New York in either New Jersey or Connecticut. But if the destination in the passenger lists was Quebec or Halifax, the actual destination was almost without exception located somewhere in Minnesota, Michigan, or Ontario. And it should be stated again that what is presented above concerning the reliability of the entries in the passenger lists describes the situation only for the beginning of the twentieth century. There is reason to suspect that the

Table 33. *The financing of tickets by Finnish immigrants to the most important states and provinces of the United States and Canada, 1905.*

State or province	Bought in Finland		Prepaid ticket		Via Sweden		Total
Massachusetts	1,869	56.6 %	1,385	41.9 %	51	1.5 %	3,305
Michigan	2,463	79.3 %	609	19.6 %	32	1.0 %	3,104
New York	1,474	67.5 %	609	27.9 %	102	4.7 %	2,185
Minnesota	1,288	88.7 %	141	9.7 %	23	1.6 %	1,452
Quebec	135	14.4 %	798	85.3 %	3	0.3 %	936
Ontario	669	79.9 %	164	19.6 %	4	0.5 %	837
Ohio	405	69.5 %	174	29.8 %	4	0.7 %	583
Pennsylvania	383	73.4 %	130	24.9 %	9	1.7 %	522
Wisconsin	261	83.1 %	40	12.7 %	13	4.1 %	314
Illinois	206	66.9 %	90	29.2 %	12	3.9 %	308
Washington	251	86.9 %	33	11.4 %	5	1.7 %	289
California	205	83.3 %	31	12.6 %	10	4.1 %	246
Oregon	141	65.3 %	61	28.2 %	14	6.5 %	216
Montana	129	79.1 %	33	20.2 %	1	0.6 %	163
Maine	56	35.4 %	102	64.6 %	—		158
New Hampshire	83	64.8 %	45	35.2 %	—		128
Utah	121	94.5 %	6	4.7 %	1	0.8 %	128
Colorado	106	92.2 %	8	7.0 %	1	0.9 %	115
Others and unknown	561	66.2 %	274	32.3 %	13	1.5 %	848
Total	10,806	68.2 %	4,733	29.9 %	298	1.9 %	15,837

of destination found in the passenger lists is precisely the place to which the immigrant travelled. The following table shows how great a percentage of immigrants to the North American states and provinces most important from the standpoint of Finnish immigration received their tickets from America, and how great a percentage travelled with tickets bought in Finland.

The largest percentage of travellers with prepaid tickets arrived in Quebec, where of a total of 936 immigrants, 798 or 85.3 % had received prepaid tickets. Those arriving in Maine had the second largest proportion of prepaid tickets: of 158 immigrants to this state, 102 or 64.6 % had received prepaid tickets. After these, prepaid tickets played the next most important role in financing immigration to Massachusetts and New Hampshire. Immigrants to Utah, Colorado, and Minnesota possessed the least number of prepaid tickets. Thus, of 128 immigrants to Utah, only 6 or 4.7 % had received prepaid tickets; of 115 immigrants to Colorado, 8 or 7.0 % had prepaid tick-

---

entries in the nineteenth century are not quite so reliable, although these, too, can doubtlessly be used to benefit in studying the distribution of immigration into different areas of destination.

ets; and of 1,452 immigrants to Minnesota, only 141 or 9.7 % arrived with prepaid tickets. To what are such large differences as these due?

The small percentage of prepaid tickets among immigrants to Utah, Colorado, Washington, California, and to a certain extent Wisconsin, probably resulted basically from the fact that a noticeably great number of the immigrants to these states came from Swedish-speaking communes in Ostrobothnia,[28] emigrants from which used, for one reason or another, prepaid tickets rather rarely. But the low numbers of prepaid tickets in Minnesota was certainly due to another cause.[29] The table shows that the proportion of prepaid tickets among tickets bought for Quebec was extremely high. But evidently, possessors of prepaid tickets to Quebec normally travelled onward to Minnesota, Michigan, Wisconsin or Ontario with new tickets bought in Quebec.[30] Thus, it is difficult to examine these states and provinces individually, and we must be content basically to determine how great a proportion of immigrants to all five as a unit were users of prepaid tickets. In 1905 a total of 6,643 people immigrated to these five states. Of these, 1,752 or 26.4 % had prepaid tickets, 4,816 or 72.5 % had purchased tickets in Finland, and 75 or 1.1 % came by way of Sweden. Since an average of 29.9 % of Finnish immigrants travelled with prepaid tickets in 1905,

---

[28] According to the compilations made at the IGHUT the following numbers of Swedish- and Finnish-speaking immigrants arrived in 1905 from Vaasa Province in Utah, Colorado, Washington, California, and Wisconsin:

	Swedish-speaking	Finnish-speaking
Utah	100	13
Colorado	65	23
Washington	160	45
California	119	21
Wisconsin	72	87

On the destinations of the Swedish-speaking Finns see also N ä s e 1922, pp. 256 —261; B a c k m a n 1945, pp. 12—16; S h e p p e r s o n 1970, p. 4; M y h r m a n 1972, pp. 271—377.

[29] According to the compilations mentioned above the following numbers of Swedish- and Finnish-speaking immigrants arrived in 1905 in Minnesota and Ontario:

	Swedish-speaking	Finnish-speaking
Minnesota	173	424
Ontario	36	380

[30] Almost every year in the beginning of the twentieth century hundreds of Finns had a ticket to the city of Quebec. This city is not, however, included by I l m o n e n in the list of cities in the Province of Quebec, where Finns were living (I l m o n e n 1926, p. 302). This indicates that the Finns who had a ticket to Quebec must have travelled with a new ticket to some other place where Finns have been living.

192

immigrants to the mid-western states and provinces used prepaid tickets only slightly less frequently than did other immigrants.

Table 33 shows that there was a difference of about ten percentage points between the amount of prepaid tickets used by immigrants to the two mid-western states most important for Finnish immigration: of immigrants going to Minnesota, only 9.7 % used prepaid tickets that entitled them to travel to that state, while 19.6 % of immigrants to Michigan possessed such a ticket. Because of large numbers travelling to Quebec with prepaid tickets, it cannot be stated with any certainty whether this difference was real or only apparent. Since Michigan, however, is much closer to Quebec than Minnesota is, it would seem rather strange if more of those coming to Quebec by prepaid ticket would have procured tickets to Minnesota than to Michigan: the ticket which the immigrant himself would have to buy would cost more to Minnesota than to Michigan. On the basis of the above, it seems evident that a smaller proportion of the immigrants going to Minnesota in 1905 used prepaid tickets than of those going to Michigan. If this difference between Minnesota and Michigan is real, it explains why Minnesota's proportion of Finnish immigration was so surprising small [31] in 1905. It was because Minnesota's »attraction», the strength of which depended, among others, on the number of prepaid tickets, was weaker than normal in 1905.

In the eastern United States, 64.6 % of Maine's Finnish immigration occurred with the aid of prepaid tickets: of the 158 immigrants going to Maine, 102 had prepaid tickets. A larger than average percentage of immigrants also to Massachusetts and New Hampshire possessed prepaid tickets: 41.9 % of the former's Finnish immigrants used them and 35.2 % of the latter's. On the other hand, only 27.0 % of Finnish immigration to New York and 24.9 % of immigration to Pennsylvania occurred with the aid of prepaid tickets. Thus, a smaller than average percentage of immigrants to these two states used prepaid tickets. Since there were important harbor towns where Finnish immigrants landed in three of the above-mentioned states, we must consider whether these differences were only apparent as they were to a certain extent in the mid-western states.

A part of those with tickets paid to New York undoubtedly travelled onward to, for example, Connecticut or New Jersey, but since the percentage of immigrants arriving in New York who had prepaid tickets was smaller than average, we can at least be sure that New York cannot be ranked in the same category as Quebec as a port of arrival, but that the destinations

---

[31] In 1910 there were 31,144 Finns (born in Finland) in Michigan, 26,637 in Minnesota, and 10,744 in Massachusetts (W a r g e l i n 1924, p. 61). On the basis of this one could wait that Finnish immigration to Minnesota would have been stronger in 1905 than it was. On the distribution of Finns in America see also van C l e e f 1918, pp. 1—7.

of prepaid ticket users and other immigrants going to New York were to a large extent the same.

In addition to New York City, Boston was also an important port of arrival for immigrants. Of the 3,305 Finns who had tickets to Massachusetts, 1,489 travelled with tickets paid to Boston. Of these latter, 631 or 42.4 % travelled with prepaid tickets and 815 or 54.7 % with tickets bought in Finland. 43 or 2.9 % of these travelled by way of Sweden. Those with tickets to other parts of Massachusetts numbered 1,816, of which 754 or 41.5 % used prepaid tickets, 1,054 or 58.0 % purchased tickets in Finland, while 8 or 0.4 % went by way of Sweden. Thus there does not seem to be much of a difference between Boston and the rest of Massachusetts in the use of prepaid tickets, which probably means that Boston was not a locality parallel to Quebec, although those with tickets to Boston rather often immigrated in actuality to some Finnish settlement near Boston.

Portland, Maine, was not so important a port of arrival for immigration as were New York City and Boston, nor was Maine so important an area of Finnish settlement as New York and Massachusetts. In 1905 a total of 158 Finns bought tickets to Maine. Of these, 18 tickets were to Portland and 140 to other localities. Of the former 15 or 83.3 %, and of the latter 87 or 62.1 %, were prepaid tickets. A larger proportion of the small group of immigrants with tickets to Portland travelled with prepaid tickets than of those going to other areas in Maine, but Maine as a whole was a state to which an exceptionally large proportion of immigrants travelled with prepaid tickets.

As stated above, about 26 % of immigrants to the Mid-West came with prepaid tickets. However, over 35 % of the immigrants to Maine, Massachusetts and New Hampshire sought aid from overseas in obtaining a ticket. The difference is indeed great. If we assume that prepaid tickets are factors with which we can measure the strength of the »attraction» of different areas in the United States, it seems that in 1905 the »attraction» of eastern states was much greater than that of the mid-western states. The number of prepaid tickets received by the Finnish-speaking population of Vaasa Province indicates that the »attraction» of the western states was still weaker than that of the Mid-West.[32] But this comparison must be made with great re-

---

[32] The emigrants from Finnish-speaking areas of Vaasa Province to the groups of states mentioned above used prepaid tickets and others in 1905 as follows:

The group of states	Bought in Finland		Prepaid ticket		By way of Sweden	
1	1,230	61.3 %	774	38.6 %	3	0.1 %
2	348	68.5 %	160	31.5 %	—	
3	1,360	81.9 %	301	18.1 %	—	
4	167	75.6 %	53	24.0 %	1	0.5 %

194

serve, for, to some degree, different areas in North America drew immigrants from different areas within Finland, for which reason the living conditions in the area of departure may also have affected the percentage of immigrants going to a given area in North America who used prepaid tickets. Thus proportionately few users of prepaid tickets went to the western United States undoubtedly because a very large percentage of the immigrants to that area came from Swedish-speaking Ostrobothnia, while immigrants to Maine used prepaid tickets more frequently than average because an exceptionally large proportion of immigration came from Oulu Province.[33]

The use of prepaid tickets in 1905 was near the average use for the period 1891—1914: in that period 30.1 % of the emigrants used prepaid tickets, while the proportion of prepaid ticket users for 1905 was 29.8 % according to the Finland Steamship Company's information, and 29.9 % according to a compilation made at the IGHUT. It is possible that the distribution of prepaid tickets at, for example, the beginning of the 1890's diverged greatly from the situation existing in 1905, or that use of prepaid tickets was fundamentally different in those years when travel by means of such tickets was exceptionally common or exceptionally rare. The role of prepaid tickets in the emigration process cannot therefore be completely explained on the basis of statistics for only one year. The material for 1905 examined here raises three questions in particular for future study. In the first place, it would be desirable to explain with a firmer foundation than is presented here the actual role of prepaid tickets in the shaping of emigration cycles. Secondly, there is cause to study in depth how decisively the growth of emigration in different areas depended on the development of the prepaid ticket system. Thirdly, it would be appropriate to explain

5	85	78.0 %	23	21.1 %	1	0.9 %
6	419	50.8 %	405	49.1 %	1	0.1 %
7	19	90.5 %	2	9.5 %	—	
8	13	41.9 %	18	58.1 %	—	
Total	3,641	67.6 %	1,736	32.2 %	6	0.1 %

The figures for group three are too low and those for group six too high, because Quebec has been included in group six. Of the immigrants to the Minnesota—Michigan area, about 26 % apparently received prepaid tickets (see above pp. 190—191). The number of immigrants to Canada who used prepaid tickets is difficult to estimate, likewise on account of Quebec. In 1905, the number of prepaid tickets bought for Ontario was 164, while the total number of tickets bought to Ontario was 837. Prepaid ticket users thus made up 19.6 % of the total emigrant group, that is exactly the same proportion as in Michigan. This indicates that the Finnish centers of Ontario did not noticeably differ in the use of prepaid tickets from the Finnish centers on the United States' side in the same area.

[33] According to compilations made at the IGHUT 56 (35.4 %) of the 158 Finnish immigrants to Maine in 1905 came from Oulu Province.

what kind of effect the generalization of the use of prepaid tickets had on the composition of a given area's emigration. The new statistical material in emigration history to be completed in the near future at the IGHUT will illuminate these questions at least to a certain degree.

7. The trip from Finland to countries overseas

The stream of emigrants flowing from Europe to countries overseas was composed of numerous different branches, which originated both in the interior and coastal regions of Europe and merged together at a few port towns on the shores of the Atlantic. From these port towns one great stream flowed to North America and several smaller ones to other parts of the globe. In the 1870's and 1880's the emigrant stream originating in Finland went almost entirely by way of Sweden; only a small branch flowed through Norway and joined the main current coming from Sweden in England.[1]

Those travelling through Sweden generally first left for Stockholm from some Finnish coastal town, most frequently perhaps from Vaasa. Those leaving from Oulu Province apparently also used Swedish coastal vessels that carried the traveller from the ports of northern Sweden to Stockholm.[2]

In exceptional cases travel by ship from Finland to England made its appearence already at the end of the 1880's.[3] The most common route, however, still went by way of Stockholm. The establishment of winter traffic between Stockholm and Hanko and the opening of railroad connections from Ostrobothnia to Hanko had already changed, however, the course of the stream of emigrants by the end of the 1880's: in winter and early spring the main branch of emigrants to Stockholm began flowing through Hanko. And when winter traffic was difficult one could in an emergency resort to the route that went from Hyvinkää to St. Petersburg and from there to Libau, from which ships were able to leave more regularly in the winter than from Hanko.[4]

The forceful thrust of Norddeutscher Lloyd into the market of Finnish emigrants at the end of the 1880's did not at first change the initial stage

---

[1] The majority of those travelling through Norway are listed in the passenger lists of the Trondheim Police Department. The number of these emigrants is shown in the tables 1—4 on pp. 26, 28 and 36. It should be noted, however, that some of the Finns listed in the Trondheim Police Department passenger lists had been working in Norway for some time. Some of these were apparently listed as Norwegians.

[2] The routes of the trips are revealed in e.g., certain travel accounts. See, for example, *Sankarin Maine*, October 8, 1880; *Työmies*, July 29, 1891.

[3] See above p. 33.

[4] See above p. 34.

of the route travelled by Finnish emigrants, for this German company, too, in the beginning carried emigrants by way of Stockholm.[5] In 1890, however, Norddeutscher Lloyd began transporting emigrants during the winter season from Hanko to Copenhagen. In the summertime, on the other hand, emigrants were still transported with some regularity from the coastal towns of the Gulf of Bothnia to Stockholm.[6]

When the Finland Steamship Company began its regular transport of emigrants between Hanko and Hull in the fall of 1891, the situation changed completely within a few years. The number journeying through Sweden tumbled; the relatively few Finnish emigrants arriving in Stockholm after 1891 had left from probably either the Åland Islands or Oulu Province.[7] Within a couple of years, travel by way of Denmark and Germany also declined appreciably. The main current of emigration began to flow from Hanko to Hull, and this remained the situation at least up to the First World War.

When the main current of emigration still flowed through Sweden, Stockholm was thus the first depot for Finnish emigrants. From here the journey continued by either train or boat to Gothenburg, whence one sailed to Hull. The German companies however carried their customers from Stockholm to either Copenhagen or Lübeck. If the destination was first Copenhagen, the trip was continued from there by ship to Lübeck. One went across Germany by train to Bremerhaven where he boarded an ocean-going liner. Emigrants arriving in Hull travelled by train across England, usually to Liverpool, where the transatlantic voyage began. On the other hand, the relatively few emigrants who used the Thingvalla (Scandinavian—American) Line boarded the transatlantic vessel already in Copenhagen. Emigrants arriving in Trondheim were sometimes able to board a transatlantic liner already in Norway, but normally they went from Trondheim to England, and there boarded a transatlantic liner.

The trip from Finland to the harbors from which transatlantic lines

---

5 The passenger lists of the Stockholm Police Department still for 1889 included the names of a large number of Finnish emigrants for whom the Swedish agent of Norddeutscher Lloyd, Borin, was responsible.

6 See above p. 29.

7 When corresponding names for the Finns appearing in the passenger lists of the Gothenburg Police Department for 1905 were sought in the passport lists, they were found primarily in the lists of the passport authorities of the Åland Islands, and these emigrants were generally also from the Åland Island. The passenger lists of the Gothenburg Police Department also contain the names of many Finns for which no corresponding name was found in the passport lists. Quite frequently these had some typically northern-Ostrobothnian name such as Lassinantti, which indicates that a large portion of emigrants travelling without a passport came from Oulu Province.

embarked took, under the best circumstances, only a few days. But in the worse cases emigrants might be forced to wait for transport at Hanko or in Sweden according to travel accounts for weeks, and the trip dragged on for long periods. Stopovers lasting several days might also occur in Germany and England.[8] The length of the transatlantic crossing depended largely on the ships, which were of very unequal quality. In most cases, however, it was made in ten days or so. Through the whole period of their migration, Finnish emigrants travelled from their homes to a North American port city in about two weeks.[9] The trip to Australia and New Zealand, of course, lasted much longer.

If the destination of the emigrant was in the interior or western part of North America, a trip of several days still remained after arriving in New York, Boston, Quebec, Portland, or Philadelphia. Thus Oskari Tokoi says that when he travelled from New York to Carbon, Wyom., in 1891, the trip lasted a whole week.[10] By the time Tokoi came to America in 1891, transportation by train had almost completely replaced boat travel into the interior. When Finnish emigration was in its opening stages, however, the trip to Michigan, for example, still occurred in part by boat through the lakes and canals and only in part by train.[11]

The first problem facing one on emigration was the procuring of money needed to buy a ticket.[12] Then followed the preparations necessary for obtaining a passport. A clergyman's certificate had to be obtained from the local parish and a travel permit from the bailiff (or city authorities). Then he could request a passport from some passport official, in most cases from the government of his own province.[13]

Usually not much equipment was taken along on the trip. Most took along only a small amount of extra clothing and some food. Thus, Nestori Kuusisto who left Siikainen for America in 1902 took along only underwear, cured mutton, bread, and tobacco.[14] Another villager from Siikainen, Frans

[8] *Yhdyswaltain Sanomat,* July 19, 1889; *Hangö,* February 16, 1893; *New Yorkin Lehti,* June 1, 1893; Tokoi 1947, pp. 23—29. In the beginning, delays occurred primarily because obstructions of ice slowed down the voyage of a ship or made navigation completely impossible for short periods of time. Later, delays were caused largely by the fact that so many emigrants accumulated at Hanko that the transport capacity was not sufficiently large.

[9] Compare Engelberg 1944, p. 31.

[10] Tokoi 1947, pp. 28—29.

[11] For example, *Sankarin Maine,* October 8, 1880.

[12] For further information on the procuring of money needed to buy the ticket see Toivonen 1963, pp. 56—59.

[13] Toivonen 1963, p. 56.

[14] Interview with Nestori Kuusisto in 1966. Notes of the author.

Gröndal, who left for America in 1907, took with him two good suits, boots, and rye-meal bread and butter as provisions.[15]

A large majority of the emigrants experienced their leaving as a rather festive occasion, for which reason departing emigrants called on relatives and friends to say goodbye and organized farewell parties. An account preserved from 1891 could well have described the departure of a great number of emigrants:

> »Because of it we walked around in our Sunday clothes for a week, and didn't do the daily chores. 'What need have we to work when we will soon be going to America', so we thought and walked around with cigarettes in our teeth saying goodbye to friends, who wished us a good trip and shook our hands warmly. And finally the awaited day came when we had to say goodbye to the home folks, but that was hardest of all. It wouldn't have been otherwise, but they were weeping the whole morning because 'he was leaving and would probably never be seen again'... From the churchyard hill we turned around and looked at the village and a strange feeling arose in the breast, which finally burst into a sigh, but we continued our journey...».[16]

A relative or friend often went along on the first stage of the trip which was made by horse. Usually the first destination was some railroad station from which the journey would continue by train. When emigration was at its liveliest, there might be dozens and perhaps sometimes hundreds of emigrants on the same train. And quite certainly the ten- or a hundredfold group of emigrants raised a vigorous clamor. Often they even sang. The author of the travel account quoted above says that when he travelled by train from Kokkola to Vaasa, the journey progressed as follows:

> »When we were all inside the train, the conductor's shrill whistle sounded and we left... we sang with all our strength, so that the conductor asked us to sing a little quieter, so we would not cause a disturbance on the train, then we settled down a bit, but again after we had left the station some one started a song and then the others joined in right away...».[17]

With a little home-packed lunch and some clothes as equipment, the emigrants left as if marching joyfully off to war. In the 1870's and the beginning of the 1880's the ticket was usually purchased at either Stockholm or Gothenburg. Later it would be bought from some ticket seller active in the home commune, from some »ticket office» of a near-by town, or from such centers as Oulu, Vaasa, Seinäjoki, Tampere, Pori, or Hanko. When the competition between shipping lines was at its keenest, the emigrant did not

---

[15] Interview with Frans Gröndal in 1966. Notes of the author.
[16] *Työmies,* July 29, 1891.
[17] *Työmies,* July 29, 1891.

have to search out a place to buy his ticket, for tickets were sold even in the trains, and the ticket agents at Seinäjoki, for example, even fought among themselves to fetch customers from the station to their »ticket offices».[18]

There were »emigrant hotels» where travellers to overseas lands lodged at least in Vaasa, Seinäjoki, Hyvinkää, and Hanko.[19] Conditions in these hotels were doubtlessly anything but pleasant. However, the festive atmosphere seems very often to have lasted up to the very departure of the ship. Thus a description written in 1891 probably fits a good number of departures of emigrant ships: »When the ship began to move away from the dock ... then the air was filled with hurrahs.»[20]

For some the festive spirit ended already with the doctor's examination made at the harbor: a small portion of those intending to emigrate were turned back home because of some illness such as trachoma.[21] The majority of those attempting to emigrate, however, made it on board the ship, and after the hurrahs had been shouted, the situation doubtlessly often developed as follows:

»The evening began to grow dusk, everyone watched, did the coast of our dear Finland still wax blue on the horizen; night fell and with the night came a storm, everyone had to go down into the hold. Each sought out a sleeping berth, but in vain. They had to sleep on the floor of the hold, since there was no other place. Several had already begun to throw up and there was vomit all over the place. Many were not able to get up, what filth there was there, in Finland not even pigs lived in that kind of smell, and what was still worse it was so tight that we had to lay one top of each other, since we were somewhere around 200 and it was one small »hold» where we were.»[22]

The above description from 1892 was about the trip on the steamship *Nidaros,* and it was perhaps written in order to cause difficulties for the operations of Norddeutscher Lloyd. Apparently, however, it is quite factual

---

[18] See above p. 144.

[19] For example, Norddeutscher Lloyd had emigrant hotels in Seinäjoki, Vaasa and Hanko (*Työmies,* August 6, 1890).

[20] *Työmies,* July 29, 1891. K. A. Järvi's article, »*Siirtolaisten lähtö*» (the Departure of Emigrants) appearing in the *Waasan Lehti,* February 22, and February 25, 1893, is also a good description of the departure of emigrants from their homeland. On the departure and travel of emigrants see also K o l e h m a i n e n — H i l l 1951, pp. 3—6.

[21] For example, Lempi Tuomisto from Parkano says that when she left for America in 1906 with two other girls from Parkano, both of her companions were turned back home at Hanko on account of trachoma. Interview with Lempi Tuomisto in 1967. TYYH:s:ä:tape 93.

[22] *Työmies,* June 24, 1892.

and pictures rather well the journeys also of customers of shipping lines other than Norddeutscher Lloyd around the beginning of the 1890's.

If the trip went by way of Sweden as was common in the opening phases of emigration, the first sea voyage for the emigrant was generally from some coastal town on the Gulf of Bothnia to Stockholm. On the basis of travel accounts, this voyage does not seem to have been any great adventure. The arrival at Stockholm, however, was already a more bewildering experience. Employees of emigration agents were waiting at the harbor and quickly laid seige to arriving emigrants. In a travel account from 1880, the arrival in Stockholm is described as follows:

> »But then a great tumult arose, when the gangplanks of the ship were lowered; so many people rushed from the dock onto the ship that there was no room to move. They asked and pumped us about tickets ... and we heard one and another selling their favors in both Swedish and Finnish ...».[23]

Then from the harbor the Finnish emigrants marched to their lodgings, »as if a battalion of Russians were on the move.»[24]

The trip from Stockholm to Gothenburg — if it was made by train — progressed rather painlessly. The journey from Gothenburg to Hull, however, is described, at least at the beginning of the 1870's, in the same terms as the above-quoted passage about the trip of the steamship *Nidaros* from Hanko to Copenhagen. According to one travel account, on the ship leaving Gothenburg,

> »Each shipping line [has] its own section, the boundaries of which were, however, no more than chalk marks, and thus travellers would wade in each other's vomit, which is abundant on the North Sea; and for this reason this is the worst section of the trip to America.»[25]

By the eve of the First World War, travelling from Finland to England was probably somewhat more pleasant, but persons emigrating around this time also remember the trip as anything but pleasing. Thus Julia Salmentausta from Parkano said that when she travelled from Hanko to Hull in 1909, there was a storm. During it some people prayed and sang hymns, while other played cards. Some became sea-sick and the awful smell of vomit filled the ship. For food there was only potatoes and herring.[26]

When the ship left Finland there were generally only Finns aboard; only exceptionally were there a few Russians among them. The Finns usually came into a certain amount of contact with emigrants from Sweden, Norway,

[23] *Sankarin Maine,* October 8, 1880.
[24] *Työmies,* July 29, 1891.
[25] *Sankarin Maine,* April 18, 1879.
[26] Interview with Julia Salmentausta in 1967. TYYH:s:ä:tape 93.

and Denmark in the ports of these countries, if the trip went by that route. As the trip continued from Germany or England, Finnish emigrants joined the stream of emigrants coming from all parts of Europe. Then Finns seem to have classed their travelling companions as either eastern Europeans or others. Toward the former, they felt their own superiority. And this prejudice of the Finns was also taken into account in the advertising of shipping companies. That is to say, one shipping company tried to attract Finnish emigrants with the fact that it transported only Norwegian, Danish, Swedish, and Finnish emigrants.[27] The following travel account from 1892 generally describes the attitude of the Finns toward eastern Europeans. After leaving Bremerhaven,

> »The flock of Poles, or the so-called »Polacks» was many times larger than our own. And when I remember the »Polacks» I also remember the sin of those »*Darmstadt*»[28] directors or of the Bremen Line, that they did not separate us into different holds from the »Polacks», but ordered us all together like sprats into salt . . .»[29]

This quotation reveals very well the desire to remain separate from other emigrant groups. It appears that the attitude of Finns toward emigrants coming from eastern Europe in particular has generally been such. They may not have felt the same prejudice toward those coming from western Europe but, with the possible exception of the Swedish-speaking Finns, we cannot speak of their forming any contacts. It seems more likely that the withdrawal into their own life style, that was so typical of Finnish immigrants, began already on the boat trip overseas.

In the opening phases of emigration the choice of a transatlantic line probably depended completely on chance, only a few had perhaps received instructions from America for the trip. One travel account from the beginning of the 1870's describes the procuring of a ticket and the choice of route to be travelled in the following manner:

> »On my trip to Stockholm, I met a Swede, who was also going to America, Boston. Since I didn't have any other goal than America, I figured it was all the same which line I went on and to which coastal town. I knew that New York was the largest city, and that there would have been a lot of new things to see there, but since I knew that that city was a highway for the whole world, I figured that some side road would be more peaceful for a greenhorn, and for that reason I decided to leave for Boston along with the Swede.»[30]

---

[27] See above p. 152.

[28] A ship owned by Norddeutscher Lloyd.

[29] *Työmies,* May 27, 1892. See also E n g e l b e r g 1944, p. 44.

[30] *Sankarin Maine,* April 18, 1879.

As the phenomenon of emigration developed, the choice of route and transatlantic line gradually came to be based more and more on rather exact information concerning conditions of travel.[31]

The transatlantic crossing in the 1870's, 1880's and 1890's was also a harsh experience for the emigrants. Numerous travel accounts contain complaints about such things as poor food, cramped conditions, filth, and the fact that the voyage took much longer than had been promised. As an example of the accounts of the transatlantic crossing at this time, let us take a description of a trip made at the beginning of the 1870's:

>The agent took all Scandinavians, Finns, and Germans together to a dark and stinking coop in the forward hold of the ship. This disgusted us all for which reason we resisted going into the hold. The steerage deck was completely empty and we stowed our junk in a couple of sections, but at the same time the agent came with other officials and drove us out of there. All brought their stuff below, except I didn't hurry with my suitcase, which was my only luggage. I told the agent that I had a steerage ticket and I wouldn't go into that coop which wasn't fit for a man who murdered his own father. The agent said that it was the steerage advertised... But the agent turned elsewhere and another official locked up the rooms from which the baggage had been removed, except for my suitcase, which remained under lock... The trip went commendably well and the Finns, who were 8, were commendably good at sea, for none of them threw up...»[32]

One travel account preserved from the beginning of the 1890's describes travelling on a Norddeutscher Lloyd ship in especially gloomy terms. One purpose of the description was perhaps to blacken Norddeutscher Lloyd. But since Norddeutscher Lloyd's Finnish agents had attacked English—American shipping lines in exactly the same manner, this travel account probably gives a good description of what travel on the transatlantic lines was like at its worst:

>After we put out to sea, hungry, sorrowful and crushed in spirit, in the hope that the service would improve, but we were greatly disappointed in this hope, for the service got still worse. There was never enough food served on board ship and that small amount of bad food could not be had except by crowding, vexation and fighting.»[33]

There were many ports of arrival in North America, but fewer in the other countries toward which emigration was directed. At the port of arrival immigration officials examined those newly arriving in the country. A few

---

[31] See above pp. 131—159.
[32] *Sankarin Maine,* April 18, 1879.
[33] *Työmies,* June 24, 1892.

unlucky ones were forced even at this stage to return home. Most frequently this forced return was due to an illness of the immigrant, such as trachoma. But the cause could also sometimes have been that the immigrant did not have the so-called disembarkment money, or that he was thought to have entered the country as a recruit of some American company. Thus, according to newspaper reports a group of nine Finnish immigrants was returned home from New York in 1892, the reason being that one member of the group possessed a letter from America, in which a Finnish contractor living in Michigan urged the receiver of the letter to gather men in Finland to chop firewood in Michigan. On the basis of this, immigration authorities held that the group of Finns were in violation of the law which stated that American corporations could not recruit a work force for themselves overseas.[34] — The majority of emigrants, however, passed through examinations and were free to seek their fortunes in the promised land.

By 1890 there apparently were some interpreters at the ports of arrival, who were able to ask the immigration official's questions of Finns unskilled in English.[35] At times shipping companies also had Finnish speaking representatives at the ports of arrival (and departure) who brought customers of their own line to their offices and when necessary accompanied them to the train by which they could continue their journey inland.[36]

If the ocean voyage presented problems, so did the train trip. After immigrants separated in numerous different directions from the port of arrival, many had to travel alone for days.[37] This was without a doubt a rather frightening experience for those unskilled in English, even though railroad employees doubtlessly saw their passengers to their destinations with care, knowing full well that most immigrants had no way of knowing at which stations they must get off. Letters sent to Finland sometimes demonstrated in a striking manner how travellers were cared for, so that they would not get lost:

»The whole trip from Hanko on was led and shepherded so that you could not escape except into the sea; if on land someone left the herd by mistake then surely he was guided back; they feared that he would get lost in a strange place, interpreters always met us where ever we touched land and commanded us as a warring host from the ship to the train and the train to the ship and 'telekafi' or telegrams flowed

---

34 *Hufvudstadsbladet,* June 15, 1892; *Työmies,* July 8, 1892. The importation of contract labor was forbidden by the Foran Act in 1885. For further information on the Foran Act see E r i c k s o n 1957, pp. 148—166.

35 For example, *New Yorkin Lehti,* June 30, July 21, 1892.

36 For example, *New Yorkin Lehti,* June 30, July 21, 1892.

37 On the travelling of emigrants unskilled in foreign languages see, for example, Nylander 1950, pp. 10—11.

on ahead so that a shepherd would be waiting to meet us at the station. So that no matter how much of a dunce you are you will surely be brought to the place shown on your ticket...»[38]

A relative or friend usually met the immigrant when he arrived at his destination. It was doubtlessly a great relief to join the company of familiar people after a long and fearful trip. But if the trip was fearful, it was also an experience that the immigrant would never forget. There were probably a great number of people among the immigrants who had not been to a single city before their departure, who saw trains and ships for the first time when they emigrated,[39] or who for the first time in their life had contact with people other than the inhabitants of their own village. At that, the trip overseas was but the first phase in the long process of adjusting oneself to a new environment.

---

[38] Frans Lendén and Kustaa Grönfors, April 11, 1903, to Frans Uusikartano. TYYH:s:m:Satakunta:HON:III:1. For further information on this letter see N i i t e- m a a 1966 (*Turun Sanomat*, May 22, 1966).

[39] For example, one travel account from 1880 tells of how several Finnish emigrants saw such an amazing contrivance as a train for the first time in their lives. *Sankarin Maine*, October 8, 1880.

Summary

Migration from Finland to America, as it did also from other European countries, began as a migration of sailors. The moment that this migration began cannot be precisely defined. It can be said, however, that, while in the first decades of the nineteenth century Finnish sailors now and then deserted ships sailing in American coastal waters and remained in America thus becoming immigrants, an appreciable increase in the number of sailors migrating occurred at the time of the gold discoveries in California.

The emigration of sailors probably continued to be relatively common from the time of the California Gold Rush to the First World War. It is perhaps typical of such emigration that a very great portion of the emigrants left from towns — from such seafaring centers as Oulu, Raahe, Kokkola, and Turku.

After the end of the Civil War in the United States the migration to America received a new tone; in addition to sailors, the normal population of rural districts began to become interested in emigrating. The year 1866 seems to mark rather clearly a turning point; at that time the first fairly large groups of emigrants left from the Tornio River Valley and from the vicinity of Kokkola. By the beginning of the 1870's emigration was already fairly extensive from these two areas and also from the vicinity of Kristiinankaupunki. Emigration from the interior parts of Oulu and Vaasa Provinces also began to occur at the beginning of the 1870's.

At the beginning of the 1880's emigration spread beyond Oulu and Vaasa Provinces to the northern portion of Turku and Pori Province and to the Åland Islands. By the end of the decade, it began to appear in the coastal area between Turku and Pori, although emigration from this region was still comparatively slight in the 1890's.

It can be said that by the beginning of the 1890's migration to America was occurring from all the provinces of Finland. However, with the exception of that from Vaasa and Oulu Provinces, that from the northern portion of Turku and Pori Province, and that from the Åland Islands, this emigration was rather slight, so that there were communes in Häme and Mikkeli Provinces, for example, where migration to America was still an almost unknown phenomenon at the end of the 1890's. Around the turn of the century the phenomenon of emigration spread to all parts of Finland, but it remained rather weak in the areas that it »conquered» last.

Finns received examples in emigration from their relatives living in northern Norway; those living in the Tornio River Valley doubtlessly also, from Finns living on the Swedish side of the river. In Swedish-speaking Ostrobothnia trips seeking work in Sweden were undoubtedly also of significance, in addition to which sailors who had emigrated spread to the coastal regions information about the opportunities offered in America. There was also perhaps some significance in the fact that, at the middle of the nineteenth century, America had become in the eyes of the educated classes an ideal land where all things were better than they were in old Europe.

Finnish official emigration statistics begin for Oulu and Vaasa Provinces already at the beginning of the 1880's, but include the entire country only from 1893. For this reason there have been extremely varying concepts of emigration occurring before 1893. Earlier estimates on the number of emigrants have been examined in this study in the light of the passenger lists of shipping companies and of information about emigration preserved in newspapers. The result of this procedure indicates that before 1870, perhaps several hundred persons intending to emigrate took out passports, in addition to which, already at this early stage, a rather large group of Finnish sailors had deserted their ships when they were sailing in American waters, and thus emigrated. In the 1870's there were probably about 3,000 emigrants, in the period 1880—86, about 18,000 and in 1887—92, about 40,000. All in all, perhaps about 61,000 emigrants left before 1893. The number of those leaving during 1893—1914 was about 270,000, so the number of emigrants leaving before the First World War was something over 330,000. However, 7—8 % of the persons included in this calculation, that is based on names appearing in the passenger lists, travelled to America more than once. Thus, the number of persons taking part in this emigration was smaller than 330,000: quite likely it was a little over 300,000. If Finnish emigration is compared to emigration from other European countries, we can see that from the end of the 1890's Finland was one of those European countries where emigration had a very great effect on population trends. In the 1870's, the 1880's and the beginning of the 1890's, on the other hand, Finnish emigration was rather meagre according to the European yardstick.

Finnish emigration has commonly been viewed as a particularly Ostrobothnian phenomenon. This generalization can to a large extent be accepted. However, it should be kept in mind when examining the geographical distribution of Finnish emigration that the boundaries between areas of strong and weak emigration did not go along provincial or regional borders. Thus, beyond the borders of Vaasa Province, emigration was also quite strong from northern Satakunta, from the vicinity of Rauma, from the Åland Islands, and from several communes along the coast and archipelago of Finland Proper.

Emigration from Finnish towns and their neighboring communes was generally stronger than from the surrounding countryside. However, an extremely large portion of the emigrants leaving from towns, perhaps as much as 70—80 %, were people who had moved to these towns from the countryside and for whom the town in the homeland was only a temporary stop-over on the trip to America.

Looking at the great migration from the whole of Europe, we may say that an economic situation existed where a labor shortage, caused by America's rapid economic growth, prevailed on the American side of the North Atlantic economic area, while on the European side where economic growth was slower there existed an over-abundant work force. During this migration, labor reserves in Europe moved to the American side. Finnish emigration was a part of this phenomenon.

Several Finnish studies of emigration history discuss the question of why Finnish emigration was concentrated in Ostrobothnia. This study has attempted to answer the question of how the situation arose in which emigration occurred much more frequently from a given area of Finland, broader than just Ostrobothnia, than it did from the rest of the country. Here I have come to stress the following factors, all of which are rather well presented in studies concerned with the problem of Ostrobothnian emigration. First, it must be noted that an extremely rapid growth in population occurred in Emigration Finland at the end of the nineteenth century. Second, not one important industrial center sprang up in Emigration Finland at the end of the nineteenth century. Third, a sort of division of labor seems to have developed between internal migration and emigration: people from Emigration Finland went to America, while those from the rest of Finland went to such industrial centres as Helsinki, Turku, Tampere, Viipuri, and St. Petersburg.

An important background factor of emigration, which affected the rest of Finland as well as just Emigration Finland, is that at the end of the nineteenth and beginning of the twentieth centuries, the mobility of the Finnish people was clearly increasing. Thus, emigration was the form that the increased mobility of the people from certain areas took, while in other areas this increased mobility appeared as an acceleration of internal migration. Of the motives for emigrating, it can be said that in the main they were economic, but that in less ordinary cases, emigrants might base their leaving on almost any cause whatsoever.

Emigration was not evenly distributed between one month and another, one year and another, or decade and another, but fluctuated greatly in its strength. At least three kinds of regular fluctuations can be distinguished: 1) seasonal changes, 2), changes depending on short-term economic cycles, and 3) changes occurring in longer cycles of about twenty years.

In the 1870's and 1880's, Finnish emigration was generally at its strongest in the early summer, but later the peak of emigration during each year occurred already in April. In very exceptional cases in the twentieth century the peak of emigration occurred in December. In part conditions of travel determined the monthly distribution of emigration: in the 1870's and 1880's winter navigation was still in its beginning stages, which forced emigrants to time their departures in the early summer. Later, the development of winter navigation made a more balanced distribution of emigration throughout the year possible. To some extent seasonal work in America and Finland probably also had an effect on the distribution of emigration.

The movement of short-term cycles discernible in America shows up very clearly in Finnish emigration: when a period of boom occurred in America, Finnish migration to America increased immediately, while during American periods of bust, the Finnish migration became weaker. The rare exceptions to this pattern might have been due to the results of presidential elections, for example, or to labor strikes occurring in America.

Two long-term cycles can be distinguished in Finnish emigration: one extended from 1874 to 1893 and the other, from 1894 to 1914. Contrary to that of other Nordic countries, Finnish emigration was appreciably more extensive in the latter than in the former of these cycles. This doubtlessly resulted in part from the rather late start of emigration from Finland, but its most important cause was probably the stagnation of population growth in Finland in the 1860's. Because of this, there were comparatively few people in Finland suitable for emigration in the 1880's, the greatest decade of emigration from Scandinavia.

Almost 90 % of Finnish emigrants left from rural districts. A large portion of those leaving from towns were probably etape emigrants, who had first moved from the countryside to the towns, and then continued their journey to countries overseas. Over half of the emigrants in the 1870's were farmers and their children. As the phenomenon of emigration developed, the proportions especially of farmers, but also clearly of their children, declined. Correspondingly, the proportions of cottagers and of workers increased. This change in structure was probably due in the first place to the fact that in the early stages only farmers had sufficient means to purchase tickets for the trip. In the second place it possibly resulted from the fact that emigration spread from Oulu and Vaasa Provinces to the rest of Finland, which meant that the population base for emigration was different at the beginning of the twentieth century than it was in the 1880's. Perhaps also of influence was the fact that as industrialism occurred the occupational structure of Finland as a whole changed from a purely agricultural system to one which included to a certain degree also industrial trades.

The streams of emigrants originating in different parts of Finland differed to some extent from each other. Farmers appeared relatively frequently among emigrants from Oulu, Mikkeli, and Viipuri Provinces; crofters, particularly among emigrants from Turku and Pori Province; cottagers, among those from Kuopio and Vaasa Provinces; and workers and people in other occupational categories, among emigrants from Uusimaa Province.

Almost 65 % of the emigrants leaving Finland during 1869—1914 were men. Compared to that of other Nordic countries, Finnish emigration was quite male-dominated. Especially in the opening phases of emigration the proportion of men among the emigrants was greater than that of women. The largest proportion of women occurred among emigrants leaving from Oulu Province, the smallest, among those emigrating from Mikkeli Province. There were almost as many women as men among emigrants from towns. There were several rural areas, however, the emigration from which was pretty well balanced among the sexes. In particular, the coast and archipelago of Finland Proper should be mentioned as such an area. The sex composition of a given area's emigration was affected by that area's population structure, by its job opportunities, by the attitudes toward emigration, by internal migration, and possibly also by the opportunities for work in the locality toward which the area's migration was directed. On the other hand, the composition of emigration leaving a given area might have determined the locality in America to which these people migrated.

The immigrant population in the area of its settlement was not so male-dominated as the immigrant stream was, for it was more common among men than among women to return to the homeland. The structures of the societies formed by Finnish immigrants in different parts of the United States probably varied greatly due to the differences existing in work opportunities. — While, on the one hand, men formed a definite majority of Finnish immigrants in the United States and Canada, on the other hand, the migration from Finland to South Africa and Australia was still much more male-dominated.

Finnish emigrants, as emigrants in general came from relatively young age groups from the beginning of emigration up to the First World War. However, it can be observed that, as the phenomenon of emigration developed, the average age of those leaving became lower. In particular, the proportions of 0—4-year olds and 15—19-year olds among all emigrants grew as emigration became older. Emigration of the very young was typical especially in Vaasa Province, while emigration from Uusimaa and Viipuri Provinces was to a certain extent composed of older age groups. Women

14

who emigrated were on the average younger than men. Urban emigration differed from rural emigration in that those under 16-years and over 25-years composed a larger proportion of emigrants from towns than from the countryside. Emigration itself fundamentally affected the distribution of emigrants' ages: in an area where emigration had been occurring for some time, emigrants would in time be composed principally of those just arriving at working age. Changes in the birth and death rates also undoubtedly had some influence. Thus the effect of the famine years of the 1860's was distinctly evident in the age distribution of Finnish emigrants still in 1905.

When researchers have studied how great a proportion of emigration from Nordic countries was at different times composed of the movement of entire families, and how great a proportion was composed of the movement of individuals, they discovered that as the phenomenon of emigration developed a definite shift occurred from family emigration to individual emigration. On the basis of available material, it seems probable that the same shift occurred in Finland.

Looking at the different areas of Finland, we discover that emigration from Oulu and Viipuri Provinces was distinctly an emigration of families, while that from Turku and Pori, Häme, Kuopio and Mikkeli Provinces was definitely an emigration of individuals. Family emigration composed a larger proportion of urban than of rural emigration. Also family emigration was more common from the Finnish-speaking districts of Ostrobothnia than it was from the Swedish-speaking districts.

The opening phase of Finnish emigration, from the beginning of the 1870's to the middle of the 1880's, can be called the golden age of Swedish emigration agents. At this time Finnish emigrants travelled almost exclusively by way of Sweden and they bought their tickets in either Stockholm or Gothenburg. Already in the 1870's some Finns travelled with so-called prepaid tickets, which immigrants in America sent to their relatives in Europe. In the beginning the prepaid tickets received by Finns entitled them to a free trip only from Stockholm onward. Finnish-American small businessmen, who acted as agents for shipping companies apparently sold a major portion of the prepaid tickets. Advertisements by them and by the shipping companies appeared primarily in the *Amerikan Suomalainen Lehti,* which each spring published guides for immigrants arriving from Finland. These guides were probably of rather great importance, for the *Amerikan Suomalainen Lehti* had quite a large circle of readers in Finland, particularly in Oulu and Vaasa Provinces.

From 1886 emigrants were able to buy their tickets in Finland, for in that year a Vaasa merchant began to act as representative for the Swedish agent for the Inman Line. Rather shortly thereafter more emigration agencies that were subordinate to agents in Sweden emerged. In 1889, the situation changed fundamentally. In that year The Scandinavian & Finlanders Emigrant Co. of New York began a collaboration with Norddeutscher Lloyd of Germany in a conquest of the market in transporting Finnish emigrants. The Scandinavian & Finlanders Emigrant Co. was owned by a Finnish Jew named G. A. Grönlund who had moved to America.

In the fall of 1889 and in 1890, The Scandinavian & Finlanders Emigrant Co. organized a fierce offensive against its competitors. It made use of newspaper advertising in both Finnish-American and Finnish newspapers. In addition, in the fall of 1889 it sent a man named V. K. Hultin from New York to Vaasa, where he established the main base for The Scandinavian & Finlanders Emigrant Company's operations in Finland. The company procured so many agents in other localities in Finland, particularly in Ostrobothnia, that The Scandinavian & Finlanders Emigrant Company's network of agents at the beginning of the 1890's was much more dense than those of its competitors. At the beginning of its operations it also dropped the price of tickets so low that it was able to compete energetically with other companies.

Norddeutscher Lloyd and The Scandinavian & Finlanders Emigrant Co. succeeded so well in their conquest of the trade of Finnish emigrants that in 1890 Norddeutscher Lloyd carried more Finnish emigrants than any other company and a year later, perhaps more than all other companies combined. Although its competitors tried to use the same advertising devices as Norddeutscher Lloyd and its associates, they did not at first succeed. Already in 1891, however, The Scandinavian & Finlanders Emigrant Company and Norddeutscher Lloyd began to run into difficulties. Grönlund gradually provoked the opposition of the Finnish-American press and with it that of Finnish-Americans. Although he procured his own newspaper as a counterweight to this, he was no longer able to salvage his affairs. Finnish-Americans gradually lost confidence in Grönlund. In the fall of 1891 the Finland Steamship Company started a regular transport of emigrants to England and began to collaborate with the companies that carried emigrants to countries overseas. By the following year, the Finland Steamship Company had already won for itself a very large share of the transport trade. Cholera, for which reason the transport of emigrants going by way of Germany in particular ran into difficulties, apparently fostered the company's breakthrough.

Norddeutscher Lloyd and The Scandinavian & Finlanders Emigrant Co. still transported a rather large number of Finnish emigrants in 1893, but they were clearly going downhill and had already lost the lion's share of the trade to the Finland Steamship Company and the shipping lines it represented. In 1894 the story ended when The Scandinavian & Finlanders Emigrant Co. went bankrupt and its Finnish agents were forced to halt their operations. After this the trade of Finnish emigrants was practically speaking completely in the hands of the Finland Steamship Company and the shipping lines it represented. In the latter part of the 1890's competition came primarily from the Scandinavian-American Line, while at the beginning of the twentieth century the Steamship Company Nord that had been established in Finland was for a short time a competitor. During the period of operations of the last-mentioned company, the German lines also again received a brief opportunity to compete for Finnish emigrants.

The most important companies carrying Finnish emigrants during the period of the Finland Steamship Company's monopoly were the Allan, White Star, Cunard, American, Canadian Pacific Railroad, and Scandinavian-American lines. The central position of these companies was perhaps due to the fact that they had large numbers of agents selling prepaid tickets in America. In part, however, it could be that the popularity of the Allan Line, for example, resulted from the fact that Finns had been accustomed to trust certain shipping companies that had been continually carrying Finns since the 1870's.

Plenty of information is available on the prices of tickets from the end of the 1880's. At that time a trip between Finland and New York cost between 120 and 180 marks. During this period the ticket price was at its lowest at the end of 1889 when Norddeutscher Lloyd dropped its prices to 120 marks. At the beginning of the 1890's the prices of tickets seem to have been between 130 and 140 marks, from which they rose for a time, then dropped in 1895 to under a hundred marks. After this, ticket prices gradually rose until 1903—04 when a price war between the Finland Steamship Company and the Steamship Company Nord occurred. During this price war, the price of a ticket from Hanko to New York dropped to 79 marks. Thereafter increases again occurred until on the eve of the First World War, a ticket from Hanko to New York cost 270 marks. The price of the trip between Hanko and Quebec was generally lower than that between Hanko and New York. The trip from Finland to the port of arrival in America was generally only part of the journey. Particularly if the destination was in the western United States, the trip from Hanko to the port of arrival might involve less than half of the travel expenses. The trips to Australia, New Zealand and South Africa cost much more than those to the United States and Canada.

About one-third of Finnish emigrants used the so-called prepaid tickets received from America. Finns received these most frequently in just those years when emigration was at its greatest. Thus the arrival of prepaid tickets was one of the factors fostering a growth in emigration. However it appears that when emigration began to increase after a trough year, the users of prepaid tickets were relatively few. The significance of prepaid tickets became appreciable only after emigration had continued in force for some time.

The poorest segments of the population wanting to emigrate, such as cottagers, relied the most on prepaid tickets. Among the farm-owning class, on the other hand, prepaid tickets played a much smaller role. Emigrants from Oulu Province in particular seem to have relied frequently on prepaid tickets, while those leaving from Häme, Viipuri, Turku and Pori and Vaasa Provinces used prepaid tickets relatively rarely. In relative terms, women received prepaid tickets more than men did, while of the different age groups, those under 16-years and over 50-years relied on prepaid tickets more frequently than the average. In regards to family emigration, the use of prepaid tickets was very common in so far as it was a question of the mother and children going to join the father in America. On the other hand, when the whole family travelled together, they rarely used prepaid tickets. In the Swedish-speaking areas of Ostrobothnia the use of prepaid tickets was much less frequent than in the Finnish-speaking areas. Those going to the eastern United States received prepaid tickets more frequently than those going to the Mid-West or to the western states. It can be argued that the differences appearing in the frequency of the use of prepaid tickets resulted in part from the standard of living of the area of departure, from the wealth of immigrants at the place of destination, and from the amount of work offered to immigrants in various parts of the United States during a given time. However, it can also be argued that money was sent to some areas in the place of a ticket, in which case the significance of American financing in covering the cost of the journey is not fully apparent in the available sources.

The recruiting of immigrants is discussed in, for example, nineteenth-century newspapers as if it played an important role in the migration process. When one examines the attempts that are claimed to be recruiting, however, it appears that the number of those actually recruited was very small. The earliest recruiting attempts were from the 1860's and 1870's. These may have had a significance to the extent that the few emigrants then recruited served as pathfinders for the people from northern Finland who later immigrated to northern Michigan. In addition to the United States, Canada, Australia, and Brazil have also shown interest in Finnish immigrants, but recruiting done on their behalf apparently produced very meagre results.

During the opening phases of emigration, the departure occurred from some Ostrobothnian coastal town, whence the trip proceeded first to Stockholm, then to Gothenburg and Hull. At the beginning of the 1890's however, Hanko became the most common port of departure, from which the trip continued to either Stockholm, Copenhagen, Lübeck or Hull. When the Finland Steamship Company gained its monopoly as the transporter of emi-

214

grants, the Hanko—Hull course became almost the only route used by
Finns. From England and Germany the trip proceeded by ocean liner to
New York, Boston, Quebec, or some other port town. From these the journey
generally continued by train.

The trip from the home village to America was an overwhelming experience for the emigrant; frequently there may have been persons along on the
trip who had never even visited a city before. During the opening phases
in particular travelling was anything but pleasant: crowded conditions, poor
food, and sea-sickness were the lot of almost everyone. During the trip to
America, Finns came into contact with emigrants coming from other countries. But here Finnish emigrants generally separated themselves from
emigrants from other countries.

Appendices

Appendices

Appendix A. The strength of emigration by the communes of Finland in 1870—1914.

Towns	Number of emigrants	Uusimaa [1] Average emigration	Average population	Annual mean emigration per 1,000 mean population
Helsinki/Helsingfors [2]	8,797	195.5	74,835	3.6
Lovisa/Loviisa	100	2.2	2,409	0.9
Borgå/Porvoo	196	4.4	4,414	1.0
Ekenäs/Tammisaari	67	1.5	2,125	0.7
Hangö/Hanko	339	7.5	3,599 [3]	2.1
Total	9,499	211.1	86,661 [4]	2.4
Rural communes				
Hangö rural commune	—	—	2,719 [5]	—
Bromarv	67	1.5	2,742 [6]	0.5
Tenala	30	0.7	3,828	0.2
Ekenäs rural commune	3	0.1	1,789	0.1
Pojo/Pohja	90	2.0	4,377	0.5
Karis and Svartö Iron Works [7]	56	1.2	3,277	0.4
Snappertuna	12	0.3	2,490	0.1
Ingå and Fagervik	27	0.6	3,632	0.2
Degerby	6	0.1	1,421	0.1
Karjalohja	13	0.3	2,027 [8]	0.1
Sammatti	3	0.1	952 [8]	0.1
Nummi	26	0.6	3,097	0.2
Pusula	31	0.7	3,221	0.2
Pyhäjärvi	187	4.2	3,430	1.2
Vihti	42	0.9	6,876	0.1
Lohja/Lojo	134	3.0	5,293 [9]	0.6
Sjundeå	22	0.5	3,933	0.1
Kyrkslätt	25	0.6	5,756	0.1
Esbo/Espoo	81	1.8	5,547	0.3
Helsinge/Helsinki rural	207	4.6	9,155	0.5

[1] The number of emigrants from Uusimaa and Viipuri Provinces has been counted on the basis of official emigrant statistics for 1893—1914. In the other provinces the number of emigrants also includes the emigrants found in the passport lists for 1870—92.

[2] Suomenlinna/Sveaborg is included with Helsinki. The Swedish and Finnish names of the rural localities are included in the list, if both Swedish and Finnish languages were used in the beginning of the 20th century in the locality and if the lingual minority was at least 20 % of the total population. The Finnish names of towns whose Finnish-speaking minority was smaller than 20 % of total population have also been included.

[3] The average population of the years 1880, 1890, 1900, and 1910.

[4] Hanko is included with the average population only for the years 1880, 1890, 1900, and 1910.

[5] The population of the year 1910.

[6] The average population of the years 1870, 1880, 1890, and 1900.

[7] A small parish inside Karis commune.

[8] The average population of the years 1890, 1900, and 1910.

[9] Nummi parish, which belonged in 1870 to the province of Turku and Pori, but later to Lohja and Uusimaa, is included already in 1870 with Lohja.

	Number of emigrants	Average emigration	Average population	‰
Nurmijärvi	422	9.4	8,161	1.2
Tuusula/Tusby	217	4.8	5,598	0.9
Sibbo	50	1.1	6,123	0.2
Pornainen	26	0.6	2,173	0.3
Mäntsälä	111	2.5	7,346	0.3
Pukkila	17	0.4	2,052	0.2
Askola	2	0.0	2,861	0.0
Borgå/Porvoo rural	61	1.4	12,128	0.1
Pernå	136	3.0	6,291	0.5
Liljendal	28	0.6	1,599	0.4
Myrskylä/Mörskom	52	1.2	2,467	0.5
Orimattila	226	5.0	8,595 [10]	0.6
Iitti	339	7.5	10,772 [11]	0.7
Jaala	57	1.3	3,200 [11]	0.4
Artjärvi	52	1.2	2,639	0.5
Lappträsk/Lappträski (Lapinjärvi)	159	3.5	4,627	0.8
Elimäki	261	5.8	5,612	1.0
Anjala	152	3.4	2,416	1.4
Strömfors/Ruotsinpyhtää	250	5.6	3,488	1.6
T o t a l	3,680	81.8	171,301	0.5
T h e w h o l e p r o v i n c e	13,179	292.9	257,362	1.1

Turku and Pori [12]

T o w n s				
Turku/Åbo	2,715	60.3	32,068	1.9
Pori	2,403 [13]	53.4	11,512	4.6
Rauma	575	12.8	4,233	3.0
Uusikaupunki	286	6.4	3,984	1.6
Naantali	13	0.3	698	0.4
Mariehamn/Maarian- hamina	251	5.6	737	7.6
T o t a l	6,243	138.7	53,233	2.6

R u r a l c o m m u n e s				
Eckerö	396	8.8	1,231	7.1
Hammarland	769	17.1	1,834	9.3

[10] The part of Orimattila, which belonged in 1870 to Häme, is included already in 1870 with Orimattila and Uusimaa.
[11] The average population of the years 1880, 1890, 1900, and 1910.
[12] The number of emigrants contain the emigrants found in the passport lists for 1870—92 and in the official statistics for 1893—1914.
[13] In addition to the emigrants mentioned in the table the copies of Pori city administration's passport lists for 1885—87 contain 71 emigrants, most of whom were apparently from Pori town.

	Number of emigrants	Average emigration	Average population	‰
Jomala	1,126	25.0	2,733	9.1
Finström	789	17.5	2,237	7.8
Geta	436	9.7	1,053	9.2
Saltvik	732	16.3	2,338	7.0
Sund	557	12.4	1,781	7.0
Vårdö	268	6.0	1,109	5.4
Lumparland	147	3.3	574	5.7
Lemland	748	16.6	1,860	8.9
Föglö	467	10.4	1,695	6.1
Kökar	64	1.4	707	2.0
Sottunga	44	1.0	372	2.7
Kumlinge	133	3.0	918	3.3
Brändö	135	3.0	1,173	2.6
Iniö	176	3.9	672	5.8
Velkua	179	4.0	529	7.6
Taivassalo	464	10.3	2,708	3.8
Kivimaa (Kustavi)	451	10.0	2,319	4.3
Lokalahti	154	3.4	1,652	2.1
Vehmaa	186	4.1	3,239	1.3
Uusikirkko	194	4.3	4,536	0.9
Uusikaupunki rural commune	20	0.4	538	0.7
Pyhäranta and Pyhämaa	286	6.4	3,546	1.8
Laitila	1,125	25.0	7,337	3.4
Karjala	59	1.3	994	1.3
Mynämäki	95	2.1	4,135	0.5
Mietoinen	24	0.5	1,626	0.3
Lemu	8	0.2	783	0.3
Askainen	59	1.3	1,211	1.1
Merimasku	105	2.3	978	2.4
Rymättylä	285	6.3	2,403	2.6
Houtskär	480	10.7	1,848	5.8
Korpo	228	5.1	2,463	2.1
Nagu	124	2.8	3,243	0.9
Pargas/Parainen	191	4.2	6,513	0.6
Kakskerta	21	0.5	631	0.8
Kaarina	265	5.9	2,905	2.0
Piikkiö and Kuusisto	36	0.8	2,494	0.3
Paimio	39	0.8	3,976	0.2
Sauvo	24	0.5	2,936	0.2
Karuna	20	0.4	1,560	0.3
Kimito/Kemiö	155	3.4	5,363	0.6
Dragsfjärd/Dragsfjärdi	111	2.5	3,421	0.7
Vestanfjärd	32	0.7	1,490	0.5
Hitis	153	3.4	1,604	2.1
Finby/Finbyy (Särkisalo)	12	0.3	1,462	0.2

	Number of emigrants	Average emigration	Average population	‰
Perniö	67	1.5	6,570	0.2
Kisko	40	0.9	2,503	0.4
Suomusjärvi	14	0.3	1,654	0.2
Kiikala	53	1.2	2,625	0.5
Pertteli	13	0.3	2,397 [14]	0.1
Kuusjoki	76	1.7	2,014 [14]	0.8
Muurla	3	0.1	1,319	0.1
Uskela	58	1.3	3,264	0.4
Angelniemi	31	0.7	934	0.7
Halikko	48	1.1	5,038	0.2
Marttila and Karinainen	163	3.6	3,631	1.0
Koski	126	2.8	2,769	1.0
Eura subordinate parish (Tarvasjoki)	56	1.2	1,448	0.8
Prunkkala	39	0.9	1,222	0.7
Lieto	120	2.7	3,833	0.7
Räntämäki (Maaria)	302	6.7	4,109	1.6
Paattinen	25	0.6	929	0.6
Raisio	87	1.9	1,799	1.1
Naantali rural commune	21	0.5	849	0.6
Rusko	2	0.0	645	0.0
Masku	19	0.4	1,433	0.3
Vahto	22	0.5	761	0.7
Nousiainen	30	0.7	2,848	0.2
Pöytyä	216	4.8	4,414	1.1
Oripää	127	2.8	1,442	1.9
Yläne	57	1.3	2,623	0.5
Honkilahti	271	6.0	1,430	4.2
Hinnerjoki	433	9.6	1,542	6.2
Eura	201	4.5	2,762	1.6
Kiukainen	366	8.1	3,568	2.3
Lappi	503	11.2	3,086	3.6
Rauma rural commune	404	9.0	3,268	2.8
Eurajoki	584	13.0	5,170	2.5
Luvia	226	5.0	2,677	1.9
Pori rural commune	798	17.7	5,442	3.3
Ulvila	704	15.6	5,073	3.1
Nakkila	205	4.6	3,886	1.2
Kullaa	127	2.8	2,541	1.1
Noormarkku	706	15.7	3,627	4.3
Pomarkku	681	15.1	3,659	4.1
Ahlainen	271	6.0	3,859	1.6
Merikarvia	1,842	40.9	6,662	6,1
Siikainen	1,434	31.9	3,983	8.0
Kankaanpää	2,063	45.8	6,995	6.5

[14] The average population of the years 1890, 1900, and 1910.

	Number of emigrants	Average emigration	Average population	‰
Honkajoki	621	13.8	2,569	5.4
Karvia	947	21.0	3,093	6.8
Parkano	1,618	36.0	5,552	6.5
Jämijärvi	756	16.8	2,731	6.2
Ikaalinen	2,134	47.4	9,410	5.0
Viljakkala	101	2.2	2,316	0.9
Hämeenkyrö	546	12.1	7,150	1.7
Lavia	342	7.6	4,524	1.7
Suodenniemi	188	4.2	2,368	1.8
Mouhijärvi	98	2.2	3,759	0.6
Suoniemi	49	1.1	1,619	0.7
Karkku	201	4.5	3,054	1.5
Tyrvää	455	10.1	7,598	1.3
Kiikka	275	6.1	3,357	1.8
Kiikoinen	230	5.1	2,081	2.5
Kauvatsa	85	1.9	2,359	0.8
Harjavalta	111	2.5	1,621	1.5
Kokemäki	358	8.0	6,712	1.2
Huittinen	279	6.2	8,553	0.7
Köyliö	273	6.1	3,061	2.0
Säkylä	288	6.4	2,130	3.0
Vampula	138	3.1	2,641	1.2
Punkalaidun	96	2.1	5,259	0.4
Alastaro	269	6.0	3,862	1.6
Metsämaa	71	1.6	1,368	1.2
Loimaa	765	17.0	8,815 [15]	1.9
Loimaa's part of Ypäjä	10	0.2	1,266 [15]	0.2
T o t a l	37,510	833.6	342,943	2.4
The whole province	43,753	972.3	396,176	2.5

Häme

Towns				
Hämeenlinna	104	2.3	4,673	0.5
Tampere	2,961	65.8	24,510	2.7
T o t a l	3,065	68.1	29,183	2.3

Rural communes				
Somero	183	4.1	6,988	0.6
Somerniemi	20	0.4	1,624	0.2
Tammela	481	10.7	12,144	0.9
Jokioinen	45	1.0	3,464	0.3
Ypäjä	28	0.6	1,728	0.3

[15] The average population of the years 1880, 1890, 1900, and 1910.

	Number of emigrants	Average emigration	Average population	‰
Humppila	18	0.4	2,243	0.2
Urjala	172	3.8	8,773	0.4
Kylmäkoski	35	0.8	1,564	0.5
Akaa	80	1.8	2,974	0.6
Kalvola	27	0.6	3,396	0.2
Sääksmäki	37	0.8	5,577	0.1
Pälkäne	80	1.8	4,031	0.4
Lempäälä	176	3.9	4,330	0.9
Vesilahti	92	2.0	5,985	0.3
Tottijärvi	8	0.2	1,299	0.2
Pirkkala	357	7.9	4,891	1.6
Ylöjärvi	127	2.8	2,784	1.0
Messukylä	123	2.7	3,227 [16]	0.8
Kangasala	157	3.5	5,645	0.6
Sahalahti	22	0.5	2,101	0.2
Orivesi and Juupajoki	395	8.8	7,043	1.2
Teisko	75	1.7	3,928	0.4
Kuru	301	6.7	3,905	1.7
Ruovesi and a part of Vilppula	808	18.0	11,244	1.6
Kuorevesi	134	3.0	2,430	1.2
Korpilahti	96	2.1	9,493	0.2
Jämsä	80	1.8	11,098	0.2
Längelmäki	87	1.9	3,816	0.5
Eräjärvi	42	0.9	1,615	0.6
Kuhmoinen	49	1.1	6,131	0.2
Kuhmalahti	28	0.6	1,735	0.3
Luopioinen	5	0.1	3,664	0.0
Tuulos	10	0.2	1,872	0.1
Hauho	50	1.1	4,908	0.2
Tyrväntö	18	0.4	1,576	0.3
Hattula	60	1.3	3,863	0.3
Hämeenlinna rural commune	13	0.3	1,372	0.2
Vanaja	15	0.3	2,669	0.1
Renko	28	0.6	2,616	0.2
Janakkala	86	1.9	6,236	0.3
Loppi	79	1.8	6,053	0.3
Hausjärvi	216	4.8	8,085	0.6
Kärkölä	55	1.2	3,837	0.3
Nastola	51	1.1	4,630	0.2
Hollola and Lahti [17]	393	8.7	10,456	0.8
Koski	13	0.3	2,815	0.1

[16] The average population of the years 1880, 1890, 1900, and 1910.

[17] Lahti has been included with Hollola for the whole research period, although since 1906 the emigrants from Lahti are separated in the official statistics from the emigrants from Hollola. In 1906—14 64 emigrants left Lahti.

	Number of emigrants	Average emigration	Average population	‰
Lammi	28	0.6	6,612	0.1
Asikkala	187	4.2	8,562	0.5
Padasjoki	60	1.3	4,875	0.3
T o t a l	5,730	127.3	232,066	0.5
The whole province	8,795	195.4	261,249	0.7

Viipuri [18]

T o w n s				
Viipuri	1,004	22.3	20,855	1.1
Sortavala	87	1.9	1,597	1.2
Käkisalmi	42	0.9	1,399	0.6
Lappeenranta	88	2.0	1,897	1.1
Hamina	65	1.4	2,863	0.5
Kotka	782	17.4	6,767 [19]	2.6
T o t a l	2,068	46.0	42,755 [19]	1.1

Rural communes				
Pyhtää	314	7.0	3,478	2.0
Kymi	1,564	34.8	9,959 [19]	3.5
Haapasaari	—	—	334 [20]	0.0
Sippola	589	13.1	5,946	2.2
Vehkalahti	259	5.8	8,931	0.6
Miehikkälä	79	1.8	3,913 [19]	0.5
Virolahti	295	6.6	8,216 [19]	0.8
Säkkijärvi	2,054	45.6	11,158	4.1
Suursaari and Tytärsaari	19	0.4	1,180	0.3
Lapvesi	612	13.6	9,558	1.4
Lemi	32	0.7	4,179	0.2
Luumäki	54	1.2	5,971	0.2
Valkeala	851	18.9	11,208	1.7
Suomenniemi	38	0.8	2,091	0.4
Savitaipale	234	5.2	6,771	0.8
Taipalsaari	27	0.6	3,659	0.2
Joutseno	66	1.5	3,700	0.4
Ruokolahti	513	11.4	8,221	1.4
Rautjärvi	79	1.8	3,717	0.5
Kirvu	242	5.4	6,933	0.8
Jääski	729	16.2	6,543	2.5

[18] As mentioned above the numbers of emigrants from the communes of Viipuri Province include only the emigrants taken from the official statistics for 1893—1914.

[19] The average population of the years 1890, 1900, and 1910.

[20] The population of 1910.

	Number of emigrants	Average emigration	Average population	‰
Antrea	237	5.3	9,075	0.6
Viipuri rural commune and Nuijamaa	1,529	34.0	20,688	1.6
Johannes	100	2.2	5,522	0.4
Koivisto	91	2.0	7,813	0.3
Seiskari	—	—	767 [21]	—
Lavansaari	—	—	1,066 [21]	—
Kuolemajärvi	19	0.4	4,028	0.1
Uusikirkko	65	1.4	11,901	0.1
Kivennapa and Terijoki	218	4.8	11,500	0.4
Muolaa	356	7.9	12,298	0.6
Heinjoki	64	1.4	2,820	0.5
Valkjärvi	66	1.5	6,590	0.2
Rautu	36	0.8	4,833	0.2
Sakkola and Metsäpirtti	112	2.5	8,698	0.3
Pyhäjärvi	264	5.9	5,521	1.1
Räisälä	79	1.8	5,404	0.3
Käkisalmi rural commune	35	0.8	2,334	0.3
Kaukola	60	1.3	3,366	0.4
Hiitola	201	4.5	6,682	0.7
Kurkijoki	446	9.9	7,066	1.4
Parikkala	239	5.3	11,767	0.5
Jaakkima	719	16.0	10,948	1.5
Sortavala rural commune	210	4.7	15,264	0.3
Uukuniemi	70	1.6	4,802	0.3
Ruskeala	47	1.0	4,639	0.2
Soanlahti	17	0.4	1,230 [21]	0.3
Suistamo	12	0.3	6,432	0.0
Korpiselkä	5	0.1	2,083	0.0
Suojärvi	—	—	4,461	0.0
Salmi, Orusjärvi, Salmi subordinate parish and Manssila	9	0.2	8,265 [22]	0.0
Mantsinsaari	—	—	1,406	—
Kitelä	—	—	3,704	—
Impilahti	17	0.4	6,136	0.1
Total	13,973	310.5	334,559	0.9
The whole province	16,041	356.5	367,261	1.0

[21] The average population of the years 1900, and 1910.
[22] The average population of the years 1890, 1900, and 1910.

Mikkeli

Towns	Number of emigrants	Average emigration	Average population	‰
Mikkeli	252	5.6	2,637	2.1
Heinola	71	1.6	1,358	1.2
Savonlinna	54	1.2	2,128	0.6
Total	377	8.4	6,123	1.4

Rural communes				
Heinola rural commune	59	1.3	5,855	0.2
Sysmä	81	1.8	8,854	0.2
Hartola	26	0.6	7,614	0.1
Luhanka	8	0.2	2,256	0.1
Leivonmäki	127	2.8	1,939	1.4
Joutsa	163	3.6	5,946	0.6
Mäntyharju	95	2.1	12,672	0.2
Ristiina	71	1.6	6,544	0.2
Anttola	33	0.7	2,470 [23]	0.3
Mikkeli rural commune	603	13.4	12,394 [23]	1.1
Hirvensalmi	70	1.6	6,430	0.2
Kangasniemi	1,001	22.2	10,554	2.1
Haukivuori	237	5.3	3,639	1.5
Pieksämäki and Virtasalmi	1,064	23.6	12,356 [23]	1.9
Jäppilä	124	2.8	1,904 [23]	1.5
Joroinen	97	2.2	7,963	0.3
Juva	261	5.8	11,654	0.5
Puumala	70	1.6	5,730	0.3
Sulkava	83	1.8	5,581	0.3
Sääminki	100	2.2	8,435	0.3
Kerimäki	107	2.4	10,950 [24]	0.2
Enonkoski	32	0.7	1,690 [24]	0.4
Savonranta	6	0.1	2,304	0.0
Heinävesi	56	1.2	7,701	0.2
Kangaslampi	6	0.1	1,873 [25]	0.1
Rantasalmi	96	2.1	9,160 [25]	0.2
Total	4,676	104.0	172,209	0.6

The whole province	5,053	112.3	178,332	0.6

[23] The average population of the years 1880, 1890, 1900, and 1910.
[24] The average population of the years 1890, 1900, and 1910.
[25] The average population of the years 1880, 1890, 1900, and 1910.

Kuopio

	Number of emigrants	Average emigration	Average population	‰
Towns				
Kuopio	811	18.0	9,807	1.8
Joensuu	148	3.3	2,802	1.2
Iisalmi	257	5.7	2,021 [26]	2.8
Total	1,216	27.0	13,417 [27]	2.0
Rural communes				
Leppävirta and				
Varkaus Iron Works	232	5.2	14,892	0.3
Suonenjoki	250	5.6	6,797	0.8
Hankasalmi	464	10.3	6,431 [25]	1.6
Rautalampi	229	5.1	11,928	0.4
Vesanto	153	3.4	3,311	1.0
Karttula	162	3.6	9,299 [24]	0.4
Kuopio rural commune	407	9.0	16,341	0.6
Tuusniemi	162	3.6	7,037	0.5
Maaninka	166	3.7	5,674	0.7
Pielavesi	621	13.8	10,818 [24]	1.3
Keitele	193	4.3	3,962 [24]	1.1
Kiuruvesi	1,170	26.0	8,285	3.1
Iisalmi rural commune	1,085	24.1	21,437 [26]	1.1
Rutakko	3	0.1	1,040	0.1
Lapinlahti	430	9.6	6,966	1.4
Varpaisjärvi, Nilsiä				
and Muuruvesi	467	10.4	16,947 [28]	0.6
Parish of Juvan-				
koski mill	5	0.1	729 [28]	0.1
Kaavi	199	4.4	8,280	0.5
Polvijärvi	183	4.1	4,215 [28]	1.0
Kuusjärvi	46	1.0	3,060 [28]	0.3
Liperi	90	2.0	12,079 [28]	0.2
Kontiolahti	328	7.3	8,034	0.9
Rääkkylä	62	1.4	6,036	0.2
Kitee	72	1.6	11,681	0.1
Kesälahti	47	1.0	3,339	0.3
Pälkjärvi	25	0.6	2,461	0.2
Tohmajärvi and				
Värtsilä	228	5.1	8,342	0.6
Kiihtelysvaara	175	3.9	7,000	0.6
Ilomantsi and Kovero	38	0.8	13,529 [28]	0.1
Eno	32	0.7	5,118	0.1

[26] The average population of the years 1900, and 1910.
[27] The population of Iisalmi is included only from the years 1900, and 1910.
[28] The average population of the years 1880, 1890, 1900, and 1910.

	Number of emigrants	Average emigration	Average population	‰
Pielisjärvi	137	3.0	11,144	0.3
Juuka	330	7,3	8,482	0.9
Rautavaara	26	0.6	1,961	0.3
Nurmes and				
Valtimo	457	10.2	10,490	0.9
Kuhmoniemi (part)	6	0.1	103 29	1.0
T o t a l	8,680	192.9	270,820	0.7
T h e w h o l e p r o v i n c e	9,896	219.9	282,540	0.8

Vaasa

T o w n s				
Nikolainkaupunki (Vasa/ Vaasa	4,904	109.0	11,642	9.4
Kaskö/Kaskinen	243	5.4	909	5.9
Kristinestad/Kristiinan- kaupunki	947	21.0	2,791	7.5
Nykarleby/Uusikaarlepyy	883	19.6	1,176	16.7
Jakobstad/Pietarsaari	1,563	34.7	3,140	11.1
Gamlakarleby/Kokkola	1,092 30	24.3	2,562	9.5
Jyväskylä	401	8.9	2,537	3.5
T o t a l	10,033	222.9	25,458	8.8

R u r a l c o m m u n e s				
Sideby	1,369	30.4	2,737	11.1
Isojoki	2,002	44.5	4,625	9.6
Lappfjärd/ Lapväärtti	3,334	74.1	5,961	12.4
Kristinestad rural commune (Tjöck)	134	3.0	1,408	2.1
Karijoki	1,202	26.7	2,452	10.9
Närpes and Övermark	6,783 31	150.7	13,873	10.7

[29] The average population of the years 1880, 1890, and 1900.

[30] According to the passport lists 382 emigrants left Kokkola town in 1870—92. According to the register of Kokkola parish the number of emigrants was only 151. On the basis of the available materials it is very difficult to say, if the passport lists or the register of the parish is more reliable.

[31] In addition to these 6,783 emigrants the passport lists of Kaskinen city administration contain in 1885—89 440 emigrants whose destination was America. The home commune in Finland is not however mentioned in the lists. In 1876—81 these lists do not make difference between those who took a passport to America and those who travelled elsewhere. On the basis of the passport lists of the years 1882—84, and 1890—92 one can suppose that most of the emigrants in 1885—89 were from Närpes and Övermark and that a part of the emigrants in 1876—81 went to America. The real number of emigrants from Närpes and Övermark could thus be about 7,300. In counting the number of emigrants to countries overseas it is also important to know that a part of the emigrants whose destination in the passport lists is Sweden in fact migrated to America. Thus it has been revealed

	Number of emigrants	Average emigration	Average population	‰
Korsnäs	2,416	53.7	4,467	12.0
Teuva	2,271	50.5	5,912	8.5
Kauhajoki	3,608	80.2	9,621	8.3
Kurikka	2,231	49.6	7,018	7.1
Jalasjärvi	3,793	84.3	9,849	8.6
Peräseinäjoki	1,438	32.0	3,971	8.1
Ilmajoki	2,892	64.3	9,969	6.4
Seinäjoki	838	18.6	2,905	6.4
Ylistaro	4,622	102.7	8,922	11.5
Isokyrö	4,495	99.9	7,528	13.3
Vähäkyrö	2,010	44.7	4,719	9.5
Laihia	3,295	73.2	6,612	11.1
Jurva	1,676	37.2	4,667	8.0
Pörtom	1,375	30.6	3,119	9.8
Petolax	1,102	24.5	2,248	10.9
Bergö	190	4.2	693	6.1
Malax	1,724	38.3	4,419	8.7
Solf	1,143	25.4	3,279	7.7
Korsholm	3,968	88.2	8,505	10.4
Replot	748	16.6	2,636	6.3
Kvevlax	1,618	36.0	3,699	9.7
Maxmo	790	17.6	1,921	9.2
Vörå	3,921	87.1	8,226	10.6
Nurmo	1,577	35.0	3,651	9.6
Lapua	4,716	104.8	10,399	10.1
Kauhava	3,832	85.2	7,325	11.6
Ylihärmä	1,402	31.2	3,156	9.9
Alahärmä	2,844	63.2	5,310	11.9
Oravais	1,695	37.7	3,754	10.0
Munsala	2,826	62.8	4,836	13.0
Nykarleby rural commune	1,497	33.3	3,597 [32]	9.3
Jeppo	1,298	28.8	2,365 [32]	12.2

at the IGHUT that in 1873 there were 60 emigrants (11.4 % of the emigrants who can be revealed both in the passport and passenger lists) whose destination in the passport list is Sweden but who can be found in the passenger lists of the Gothenburg Police Department. In the passenger lists their destination is America. In 1882 there were 207 (12.2 %) emigrants of same kind. Most of them were from Swedish-speaking communes.

[32] The average population of the years 1880, 1890, 1900, and 1910.

[33] In 1904—14 the official statistics contain only 25 emigrants from Esse. This is due to the mistake of the Central Bureau of Statistics which mixed the emigrants from Ähtäri and Esse (in Finnish Ähtävä, see above p. 40). It is probable that the real strength of emigration from Esse was about 10 ‰.

[34] The register of Kokkola rural parish contain in 1870—1914 2,306 emigrants. On the basis of this material the strength of emigration from Kokkola rural commune is 10.0 ‰.

	Number of emigrants	Average emigration	Average population	‰
Jakobstad rural commune (Pedersöre)	2,526	56.1	6,257	9.0
Purmo	1,196	26.6	2,566	10.4
Esse	744 33	16.5	2,509	6.6
Terjärv	1,467	32.6	3,062	10.6
Kronoby	1,514	33.6	3,264	10.3
Larsmo	560	12.4	2,210	5.6
Gamlakarleby rural commune (Karleby)	1,932 34	42.9	5,127	8.4
Nedervetil	939	20.9	2,083	10.0
Kälviä	1,595	35.4	3,371	10.5
Lohtaja	1,881 35	41.8	3,255	12.8
Himanka	990	22.0	2,641	8.3
Kannus	1,558	34.6	3,773	9.2
Toholampi	2,346	52.1	3,279	15.9
Ullava	552	12.3	1,155	10.6
Kaustinen	1,611	35.8	2,997	11.9
Veteli	1,797	39.9	3,269	12.2
Lestijärvi	369	8.2	857	9.6
Halsua	534	11.9	1,189	10.0
Perho	824	18.3	1,709	10.7
Soini	679	15.1	2,802	5.4
Lehtimäki	564	12.5	1,832	6.8
Alajärvi	3,423	76.1	5,601	13.6
Vimpeli	1,295	28.8	2,693	10.7
Evijärvi	2,193	48.7	3,986	12.2
Kortesjärvi	1,971	43.8	3,451	12.7
Lappajärvi	2,417	53.7	4,944	10.9
Kuortane	1,822	40.5	4,409	9.2
Töysä	902	20.0	2,843	7.0
Alavus	3,596	79.9	7,402	10.8
Virrat	1,376	30.6	7,239	4.2
Ähtäri	1,275	28.3	4,969	5.7
Pihlajavesi	237	5.3	1,763	3,0
Multia	307	6.8	3,376	2.0
Keuruu and a part of Vilppula	827	18.4	8,422	2.2
Petäjävesi	266	5.9	4,198	1.4
Jyväskylä rural commune and Toivakka	765	17.0	8,769	1.9
Uurainen	466	10.4	2,666	3.9
Saarijärvi and Pylkönmäki	2,165	48.1	10,070	4.8

35 The register of Lohtaja parish contain in 1870—1914 2,091 emigrants. (V i r-
t a n e n 1972, pp. 25—26). On the basis of this material the strength of emigration
from Lohtaja is 14.3 ‰.

	Number of emigrants	Average emigration	Average population	‰
Karstula	3,593	79.8	7,489	10.7
Kivijärvi and				
Kinnula	1,581	35.1	4,684	7.5
Pihtipudas	859	19.1	4,184	4.6
Viitasaari	1,216	27.0	8,907 [36]	3.0
Konginkangas	220	4.9	2,046 [37]	2.4
Sumiainen	55	1.2	1,939	0.6
Laukaa and				
Äänekoski	695	15.4	10,150	1.5
T o t a l	148,375	3,297.2	384,873	8.6
The whole province	158,408 [38]	3,520.2	409,630	8.6

Oulu

T o w n s				
Oulu	3,570	79.3	13,287	6.0
Raahe	767	17.0	3,284	5.2
Kemi	270	6.0	1,129 [37]	5.3
Tornio	99	2.2	1,250	1.8
Kajaani	140	3.1	1,376	2.3
T o t a l	4,846	107.7	20,100 [39]	5.4

R u r a l c o m m u n e s				
Sievi	1,359	30.2	3,859	7.8
Rautio	395	8.8	1,290	6.8
Ylivieska	1,254	27.9	5,567	5.0
Alavieska	777	17.3	2,780	6.2
Kalajoki	2,636	58.6	4,981	11.8
Merijärvi	533	11.8	1,633	7.2
Oulainen	1,511	33.6	4,297	7.8
Pyhäjoki	1,626	36.1	4,160	8.7
Salo subordinate				
parish	191	4.2	1,457 [37]	2.9
Salo	916	20.4	2,408 [37]	8.5
Vihanti	539	12.0	2,915 [37]	4.1

[36] The average population of the years 1880, 1890, 1900, and 1910.
[37] The average population of the years 1880, 1890, 1900, and 1910.
[38] As mentioned above the passport lists of Kaskinen city administration contain in 1885—89 440 emigrants whose home commune is not mentioned in the list. The passport lists of the bailiff of Kokkola bailiff district also contain in the 1880's 12 emigrants of this kind. The emigrants mentioned in the passport lists of Kaskinen city administration were from the neighbourhood of Kaskinen and those mentioned in the passport lists of Kokkola bailiff from the neighbourhood of Kokkola.
[39] Kemi is included with the average population only for the years 1880, 1890, 1900, and 1910.

	Number of emigrants	Average emigration	Average population	‰
Rantsila	821	18.2	3,239 [37]	5.6
Paavola	889	19.8	4,257 [40]	4.7
Revonlahti	307	6.8	1,354 [40]	5.0
Siikajoki	721	16.0	1,883 [40]	8.5
Hailuoto	742	16.5	2,118	7.8
Pyhäjärvi	1,471	32.7	5,131	6.4
Reisjärvi	1,015	22.6	2,863	7.9
Haapajärvi	1,739	38.6	4,934	7.8
Nivala	1,365	30.3	6,482	4.7
Kärsämäki	784	17.4	2,426	7.2
Haapavesi	1,253	27.8	5,397	5.2
Pulkkila	739	16.4	2,372 [40]	6.9
Piippola and Pyhäntä	587	13.0	3,062 [40]	4.2
Kestilä	584	13.0	2,527 [40]	5.1
Säräisniemi and Vuolijoki	359	8.0	3,521	2.3
Paltamo	494	11.0	3,996	2.8
Kajaani rural commune	43	1.0	2,773	0.4
Sotkamo	731	16.2	8,203	2.0
Kuhmoniemi	1,086	24.1	6,706	3.6
Ristijärvi	184	4.1	2,042	2.0
Hyrynsalmi	325	7.2	1,954	3.7
Suomussalmi	873	19.4	6,046	3.2
Puolanka	944 (1,401) [41]	21.0 (31.1) [41]	4,449	4.7 (7.0) [41]
Utajärvi	545	12.1	4,015	3.0
Muhos	709	15.8	4,009	3.9
Tyrnävä	502	11.2	2,999	3.7
Temmes	122	2.7	1,065	2.5
Lumijoki	423	9.4	2,199	4.3
Liminka	636	14.1	3,163	4.6
Kempele	138	3.1	1,113	2.8
Oulunsalo	133	3.0	1,120	2.7
Oulujoki	769	17.1	3,900	4.4
Ylikiiminki	359	8.0	2,096	3.8
Kiiminki	228	5.1	1,577	3.1
Haukipudas	625	13.9	3,818	3.6
Ii	945	21.0	5,693	3.7
Kuivaniemi	235	5.2	1,676	3.1
Pudasjärvi	1,447 (1,913) [41]	32.2 (42.5) [41]	8,634 [40]	3.7 (4.9) [41]
Taivalkoski	866	19.2	2,978 [40]	6.4
Kuusamo	1,078 (1,934) [43]	24.0 (43.0) [43]	8,576	2.8 (5.0) [43]

[40] The average population of the years 1880, 1890, 1900, and 1910.
[41] The number of emigrants within parentheses according to the registers of the parish.

	Number of emigrants		Average emigration		Average population	‰	
Kuolajärvi (Salla)	197	(307) [42]	4.4	(6.8) [42]	2,890	1.5	(2.4) [42]
Kemijärvi	256	(1,005) [42]	5.7	(22.3) [42]	4,042	1.4	(5.5) [42]
Rovaniemi	311		6.9		7,011	1.0	
Tervola	278	(371) [42]	6.2	(8.2) [42]	2,802	2.2	(2.9) [42]
Simo	604		13.4		2,702	4.9	
Kemi rural commune	642		14.3		4,803	3.0	
Alatornio	358	(1,227) [42]	8.0	(27.3) [42]	5,913	1.4	(4.6) [42]
Karunki	46	(448) [42]	1.0	(10.0) [42]	1,884	0.5	(5.3) [42]
Ylitornio	168	(877) [42]	3.7	(19.5) [42]	3,942	0.9	(4.9) [42]
Turtola	35	(193) [42]	0.8	(4.3) [42]	1,584	0.5	(2.7) [42]
Kolari	17	(56) [42]	0.4	(1.2) [42]	1,474	0.3	(0.8) [42]
Muonionniska	19	(91) [42]	0.4	(2.0) [42]	1,068	0.4	(1.9) [42]
Enontekiö	—	(37) [42]	—	(0.8) [42]	791	—	(1.0) [42]
Kittilä	126	(261) [42]	2.8	(5.8) [42]	2,751	1.0	(2.1) [42]
Sodankylä	191	(381) [42]	4.2	(8.5) [42]	3,569	1.2	(2.4) [42]
Inari	10	(30) [42]	0.2	(0.7) [42]	1,222	0.2	(0.6) [42]
Utsjoki	—	(8) [42]	—	(0.2) [42]	443	—	(0.5) [42]
Total	42,811		951.4		228,655	4.2	
The whole province	47,657		1,059.0		248,629	4.3	

The whole country

Towns	37,347	829.9	266,050	3.1
Rural communes	265,435	5,898.6	2,137,471	2.8
Total	302,782	6,728.5	2,403,521	2.8

[42] The number of emigrants within parentheses according to the registers of parishes.

[43] The numbers within parentheses are from Jorma Pätynen's pro gradu thesis (Pätynen 1972, p. 27).

Appendix B. The age structure of emigration according to passenger lists in 1873 and according to both passenger and passport lists in 1882 and 1905.

| | 1873 | | 1882 | | | | 1905 | | | |
| | Passenger lists | | Passport lists | | Passenger lists | | Passport lists | | Passenger lists | |
Age	Number of emigrants	% of the 1873 emigrants	Number of emigrants	% of the 1882 emigrants	Number of emigrants	% of the 1882 emigrants	Number of emigrants	% of the 1905 emigrants	Number of emigrants	% of the 1905 emigrants
Under 1	1	0.2	—	—	12	0.7	34	0.2	215	1.4
1	3	0.6	7	0.4	15	0.9	107	0.7	76	0.5
2	—	—	16	0.9	13	0.8	91	0.6	132	0.8
3	3	0.6	5	0.3	10	0.6	127	0.8	156	1.0
4	2	0.4	9	0.5	16	0.9	120	0.8	242	1.5
0—4	9	1.7	37	2.2	66	3.9	479	3.0	821	5.2
5	—	—	8	0.5	7	0.4	108	0.7	53	0.3
6	2	0.4	2	0.1	5	0.3	94	0.6	61	0.4
7	1	0.2	5	0.3	7	0.4	72	0.5	77	0.5
8	3	0.6	5	0.3	10	0.6	78	0.5	58	0.4
9	1	0.2	7	0.4	5	0.3	54	0.3	66	0.4
5—9	7	1.3	27	1.6	34	2.0	406	2.6	315	2.0
10	1	0.2	8	0.5	8	0.5	54	0.3	60	0.4
11	2	0.4	4	0.2	15	0.9	44	0.3	111	0.7
12	—	—	7	0.4	2	0.1	44	0.3	6	0.0
13	—	—	4	0.2	—	—	40	0.3	14	0.1
14	—	—	7	0.4	7	0.4	46	0.3	40	0.3
10—14	3	0.6	30	1.8	32	1.9	228	1.4	231	1.5
15	—	—	5	0.3	2	0.1	79	0.5	65	0.4
16	—	—	18	1.1	7	0.4	188	1.2	186	1.2
17	4	0.8	33	1.9	38	2.2	530	3.3	581	3.7
18	13	2.5	72	4.2	65	3.8	974	6.2	1,019	6.4
19	23	4.4	51	3.0	80	4.7	1,317	8.3	1,214	7.7
15—19	40	7.6	179	10.6	192	11.3	3,088	19.5	3,065	19.4
20	18	3.4	58	3.4	82	4.8	1,224	7.7	1,013	6.4
21	35	6.6	48	2.8	84	5.0	1,045	6.6	700	4.4
22	44	8.3	29	1.7	61	3.6	851	5.4	962	6.1
23	34	6.4	40	2.4	64	3.8	1,036	6.5	730	4.6
24	37	7.0	89	5.2	101	6.0	736	4.6	626	4.0
20—24	168	31.8	264	15.6	392	23.1	4,892	30.9	4,031	25.5
25	41	7.8	72	4.2	114	6.7	633	4.0	621	3.9
26	22	4.2	73	4.3	89	5.2	666	4.2	527	3.3
27	22	4.2	80	4.7	76	4.5	632	4.0	501	3.2
28	22	4.2	66	3.9	73	4.3	523	3.3	463	2.9
29	12	2.3	55	3.2	46	2.7	504	3.2	336	2.1

| | 1873 | | 1882 | | | | 1905 | | | |
| | Passenger lists | | Passport lists | | Passenger lists | | Passport lists | | Passenger lists | |
Age	Number of emigrants	% of the 1873 emigrants	Number of emigrants	% of the 1882 emigrants	Number of emigrants	% of the 1882 emigrants	Number of emigrants	% of the 1905 emigrants	Number of emigrants	% of the 1905 emigrants
25—29	119	22.5	346	20.4	398	23.5	2,958	18.7	2,448	15.5
30	29	5.5	58	3.4	74	4.4	413	2.6	468	3.0
31	6	1.1	39	2.3	47	2.8	408	2.6	253	1.6
32	17	3.2	45	2.7	33	1.9	311	2.0	223	1.4
33	16	3.0	43	2.5	32	1.9	273	1.7	204	1.3
34	12	2.3	25	1.5	30	1.8	267	1.7	238	1.5
30—34	80	15.2	210	12.4	216	12.7	1,672	10.6	1,386	8.8
35	16	3.0	25	1.5	36	2.1	242	1.5	216	1.4
36	9	1.7	32	1.9	35	2.1	207	1.3	117	0.7
37	13	2.5	30	1.8	28	1.7	83	0.5	89	0.6
38	5	0.9	16	0.9	32	1.9	115	0.7	89	0.6
39	7	1.3	20	1.2	19	1.1	102	0.6	85	0.5
35—39	50	9.5	123	7.3	150	8.8	749	4.7	596	3.8
40	14	2.7	28	1.7	39	2.3	101	0.6	122	0.8
41	7	1.3	13	0.8	14	0.8	114	0.7	69	0.4
42	4	0.8	22	1.3	16	0.9	90	0.6	75	0.5
43	3	0.6	26	1.5	10	0.6	65	0.4	50	0.3
44	1	0.2	11	0.6	12	0.7	65	0.4	60	0.4
40—44	29	5.5	100	5.9	91	5.4	435	2.7	376	2.4
45	5	0.9	8	0.5	24	1.4	63	0.4	61	0.4
46	2	0.4	11	0.6	8	0.5	50	0.3	34	0.2
47	4	0.8	10	0.6	9	0.5	46	0.3	32	0.2
48	3	0.6	8	0.5	6	0.4	41	0.3	31	0.2
49	1	0.2	6	0.4	7	0.4	37	0.2	29	0.2
45—49	15	2.8	43	2.5	54	3.2	237	1.5	187	1.2
50	1	0.2	4	0.2	9	0.5	29	0.2	38	0.2
51	2	0.4	2	0.1	6	0.4	30	0.2	17	0.1
52	1	0.2	6	0.4	5	0.3	18	0.1	18	0.1
53	2	0.4	3	0.2	3	0.2	22	0.1	10	0.1
54	—	—	3	0.2	4	0.2	15	0.1	9	0.1
50—54	6	1.1	18	1.1	27	1.6	114	0.7	92	0.6
55	1	0.2	1	0.1	5	0.3	10	0.1	9	0.1
56	—	—	—	—	5	0.3	9	0.1	16	0.1
57	—	—	4	0.2	2	0.1	7	0.0	3	0.0
58	—	—	4	0.2	2	0.1	15	0.1	9	0.1
59	—	—	1	0.1	1	0.1	14	0.1	4	0.0

| | 1873 | | 1882 | | | | 1905 | | | |
| | Passenger lists | | Passport lists | | Passenger lists | | Passport lists | | Passenger lists | |
Age	Number of emigrants	% of the 1873 emigrants	Number of emigrants	% of the 1882 emigrants	Number of emigrants	% of the 1882 emigrants	Number of emigrants	% of the 1905 emigrants	Number of emigrants	% of the 1905 emigrants
55—59	1	0.2	10	0.6	15	0.9	55	0.3	41	0.3
60	—	—	—	—	1	0.1	15	0.1	2	0.0
61	—	—	1	0.1	—	—	8	0.1	2	0.0
62	—	—	1	0.1	1	0.1	6	0.0	5	0.0
63	—	—	—	—	—	—	3	0.0	2	0.0
64	—	—	—	—	—	—	5	0.0	2	0.0
60—64	—	—	2	0.1	2	0.1	37	0.2	13	0.1
65	—	—	—	—	—	—	2	0.0	1	0.0
66	—	—	—	—	—	—	3	0.0	2	0.0
67	—	—	1	0.1	1	0.1	2	0.0	3	0.0
68	—	—	—	—	—	—	1	0.0	—	—
69	—	—	—	—	—	—	2	0.0	—	—
65—69	—	—	1	0.1	1	0.1	10	0.1	6	0.0
70	—	—	—	—	—	—	1	0.0	3	0.0
71	—	—	—	—	—	—	—	—	—	—
72	—	—	—	—	—	—	—	—	—	—
73	—	—	—	—	—	—	3	0.0	1	0.0
74	—	—	—	—	—	—	1	0.0	—	—
70—74	—	—	—	—	—	—	5	0.0	4	0.0
Over 74	—	—	1	0.1	—	—	1	0.0	—	—
Unknown	1	0.2	305	18.0	26	1.5	471	3.0	2,225	14.0
Total	528		1,696		1,696		15,837		15,837	

Appendix C. The age structure of male and female emigration according to official emigration statistics.[1]

	Under 16				16—20				21—25			
	Men		Women		Men		Women		Men		Women	
1893	845	13.5	657	23.1	1,612	25.7	792	27.9	—	—	—	—
1894	149	23.4	152	20.5	153	24.0	141	19.0	—	—	—	—
1895	287	13.9	298	15.2	575	27.9	506	25.9	—	—	—	—
1896	250	8.1	284	13.5	916	29.8	526	25.0	—	—	—	—
1897	95	11.0	100	9.5	265	30.6	309	29.4	—	—	—	—
1898	198	9.9	217	14.8	677	33.8	412	28.1	—	—	—	—
1899	743	9.8	726	16.2	2,297	30.2	1,221	27.3	—	—	—	—
1900	730	11.7	703	17.0	1,529	24.4	1,053	25.5	1,474	23.5	1,102	26.7
1901	678	8.2	706	16.3	1,944	23.6	1,033	23.9	2,120	25.7	1,147	26.5
1902	1,233	7.7	1,267	17.9	4,294	26.7	1,705	24.1	4,325	26.9	1,777	25.1
1903	1,018	9.7	1,050	16.1	2,857	27.3	1,716	26.3	2,126	20.3	1,715	26.3
1904	814	13.2	888	18.5	1,610	26.1	1,236	25.8	1,277	20.7	1,096	22.9
1905	820	6.8	813	15.0	3,067	25.6	1,533	28.3	3,388	28.2	1,390	25.6
1906	710	6.0	691	12.3	3,331	27.9	1,700	30.4	3,823	32.1	1,520	27.2
1907	632	6.0	666	11.4	2,691	25.7	1,780	30.6	3,475	33.2	1,683	28.9
1908	397	12.0	406	16.3	644	19.4	601	24.1	1,025	31.0	601	24.1
1909	967	7.7	952	14.3	2,498	20.0	1,716	25.9	4,088	32.7	1,853	27.9
1910	970	7.8	967	14.7	2,910	23.4	1,704	26.0	3,978	32.0	1,810	27.6
1911	611	12.7	622	13.7	1,058	21.9	1,237	27.2	1,384	28.7	1,146	25.2
1912	695	12.3	676	13.3	1,251	22.1	1,474	29.1	1,708	30.2	1,317	26.0
1913	827	6.4	869	12.2	2,858	22.1	2,092	29.3	4,416	34.2	1,880	26.3
1914	403	11.0	368	13.0	710	19.4	711	25.2	1,058	29.0	688	24.4
Total	14,072	8.8	14,078	15.0	39,747	24.9	25,198	26.9	39,665	29.0	20,725	26.2

	26—30				31—35				36—40			
	Men		Women		Men		Women		Men		Women	
1893—1899	—	—	—	—	—	—	—	—	—	—	—	—
1900	1,230	19.6	551	13.3	481	7.7	230	5.6	366	5.8	183	4.4
1901	1,614	19.6	684	15.8	714	8.7	262	6.1	553	6.7	167	3.9

Year												
1904	1,262	20.5	715	14.9	591	9.6	351	7.3	260	4.2	159	3.3
1905	2,171	18.1	819	15.1	1,258	10.5	384	7.1	543	4.5	155	2.9
1906	1,903	16.0	830	14.8	1,031	8.6	380	6.8	493	4.1	143	2.6
1907	1,701	16.3	817	14.0	921	8.8	385	6.6	459	4.4	160	2.8
1908	567	17.1	373	14.9	332	10.0	230	9.2	146	4.4	96	3.8
1909	2,297	18.4	1,062	16.0	1,322	10.6	515	7.8	692	5.5	221	3.3
1910	2,081	16.7	985	15.0	1,208	9.7	497	7.6	677	5.5	255	3.9
1911	756	15.7	730	16.0	456	9.4	373	8.2	260	5.4	197	4.3
1912	934	16.5	765	15.1	462	8.2	381	7.5	286	5.1	204	4.0
1913	2,401	18.6	1,179	16.5	1,202	9.3	531	7.4	614	4.8	264	3.7
1914	661	18.1	481	17.0	400	11.0	258	9.1	195	5.3	138	4.9
Total	24,748	18.1	12,045	15.3	12,847	9.4	5,700	7.2	6,877	5.0	2,793	3.5

Year	41—45				Over 45				Unknown			
1893—1899	—	—	—	—	—	—	—	—	—	—	—	—
1900	200	3.2	92	2.2	229	3.7	175	4.4	26	0.4	43	1.0
1901	312	3.8	100	2.3	260	3.2	156	3.6	42	0.5	69	1.6
1902	497	3.1	185	2.6	441	2.7	259	3.7	71	0.4	66	0.9
1903	336	3.2	165	2.5	307	2.9	207	3.2	47	0.5	52	0.8
1904	166	2.7	86	1.8	152	2.5	166	3.5	26	0.4	97	2.0
1905	356	3.0	97	1.8	350	2.9	146	2.7	48	0.4	89	1.6
1906	315	2.6	82	1.5	249	2.1	145	2.6	66	0.6	105	1.9
1907	259	2.5	82	1.4	245	2.3	150	2.6	87	0.8	103	1.8
1908	82	2.5	42	1.7	77	2.3	84	3.7	43	1.3	66	2.6
1909	257	2.1	91	1.4	301	2.4	142	2.1	87	0.7	83	1.3
1910	276	2.2	91	1.4	292	4.4	181	2.8	52	0.4	73	1.1
1911	123	2.6	64	1.4	130	2.7	136	3.0	43	0.9	46	1.0
1912	139	2.5	76	1.5	150	2.7	169	3.3	27	0.5	17	0.3
1913	324	2.5	113	1.6	246	1.9	172	2.4	31	0.2	38	0.5
1914	111	3.0	75	2.7	92	2.5	84	3.0	21	0.6	20	0.7
Total	3,753	2.7	1,441	1.8	3,521	2.6	2,365	3.0	717	0.5	967	1.2

1 SVT XXVIII: 1—11.

Appendix D. The age structure of male and female emigration in 1882 and 1905 according to passport and passenger lists.

Age	1882 Passport lists Men	%	Women	%	1882 Passenger lists Men	%	Women	%	1905 Passport lists Men	%	Women	%	1905 Passenger lists Men	%	Women	%
Under 1	—	—	—	—	6	0.4	6	1.9	24	0.2	10	0.2	112	1.0	96	2.0
1	3	0.2	4	1.2	8	0.6	7	2.2	61	0.6	46	1.0	37	0.3	37	0.8
2	10	0.7	6	1.9	8	0.6	5	1.6	41	0.4	49	1.0	68	0.6	59	1.2
3	2	0.1	3	0.9	4	0.3	6	1.9	65	0.6	62	1.3	85	0.8	68	1.4
4	3	0.2	6	1.9	9	0.7	7	2.2	63	0.6	56	1.2	122	1.1	113	2.3
5	5	0.4	3	0.9	4	0.3	3	0.9	60	0.5	48	1.0	31	0.3	21	0.4
6	1	0.1	1	0.3	2	0.1	3	0.9	52	0.5	41	0.9	35	0.3	23	0.5
7	1	0.1	4	1.2	2	0.1	5	1.6	38	0.3	33	0.7	41	0.4	35	0.7
8	3	0.2	2	0.6	5	0.4	5	1.6	41	0.4	37	0.8	31	0.3	26	0.5
9	3	0.2	4	1.2	3	0.2	2	0.6	31	0.3	23	0.5	24	0.2	40	0.8
10	5	0.4	3	0.9	5	0.4	3	0.9	22	0.2	32	0.7	29	0.3	30	0.6
11	3	0.2	1	0.3	11	0.8	4	1.2	20	0.2	24	0.5	51	0.5	58	1.2
12	5	0.4	2	0.6	1	0.1	1	0.3	18	0.2	26	0.5	3	0.0	3	0.1
13	3	0.2	1	0.3	—	—	—	—	22	0.2	18	0.4	5	0.0	9	0.2
14	5	0.4	2	0.6	4	0.3	3	0.9	22	0.2	24	0.5	17	0.2	23	0.5
15	2	0.1	3	0.9	1	0.1	1	0.3	34	0.3	45	0.9	32	0.3	33	0.7
16	14	1.0	4	1.2	5	0.4	2	0.6	78	0.7	110	2.3	87	0.8	99	2.1
17	28	2.0	5	1.6	34	2.5	4	1.2	275	2.5	255	5.3	359	3.3	222	4.6
18	64	4.7	8	2.5	53	3.9	12	3.7	625	5.7	349	7.2	704	6.4	315	6.5
19	47	3.4	4	1.2	61	4.5	19	5.9	936	8.5	381	7.9	917	8.3	297	6.2
20	49	3.6	9	2.8	66	4.8	16	5.0	884	8.0	340	7.1	728	6.6	285	5.9
21	44	3.2	4	1.2	69	5.0	15	4.7	741	6.7	304	6.3	484	4.4	216	4.5
22	20	1.5	9	2.8	45	3.3	16	5.0	582	5.3	269	5.6	733	6.7	229	4.8
23	29	2.1	11	3.4	48	3.5	16	5.0	782	7.1	254	5.3	567	5.2	163	3.4
24	80	5.8	9	2.8	90	6.6	11	3.4	533	4.9	203	4.2	467	4.3	159	3.3
25	61	4.5	11	3.4	89	6.5	25	7.8	457	4.2	176	3.7	474	4.3	147	3.1
26	65	4.7	8	2.5	77	5.6	12	3.7	472	4.3	194	4.0	384	3.5	143	3.0
27	72	5.3	8	2.5	70	5.1	6	1.9	463	4.2	169	3.5	383	3.5	118	2.4
28	62	4.5	4	1.2	61	4.5	12	3.7	391	3.6	132	2.7	357	3.3	106	2.2
29	49	3.6	6	1.9	40	2.9	6	1.9	368	3.4	136	2.8	266	2.4	70	1.5

33	37	2.7	6	1.9	28	2.0	4	1.2	219	2.0	54	1.1	169	1.5	35	0.7
34	24	1.8	1	0.3	27	2.0	3	0.9	210	1.9	57	1.2	189	1.7	49	1.0
35	23	1.7	2	0.6	32	2.3	4	1.2	188	1.7	54	1.1	178	1.6	38	0.8
36	30	2.2	2	0.6	33	2.4	2	0.6	170	1.5	37	0.8	98	0.9	19	0.4
37	29	2.1	1	0.3	27	2.0	1	0.3	66	0.6	17	0.4	75	0.7	14	0.3
38	15	1.1	1	0.3	28	2.0	4	1.2	90	0.8	25	0.5	70	0.6	19	0.4
39	19	1.4	1	0.3	17	1.2	2	0.6	78	0.7	24	0.5	68	0.6	17	0.4
40	25	1.8	3	0.9	31	2.3	8	2.5	86	0.8	15	0.3	102	0.9	20	0.4
41	12	0.9	1	0.3	11	0.8	3	0.9	92	0.8	22	0.5	60	0.5	9	0.2
42	16	1.2	6	1.9	16	1.2	—	—	71	0.6	19	0.4	57	0.5	18	0.4
43	26	1.9	—	—	10	0.7	—	—	54	0.5	11	0.2	41	0.4	9	0.2
44	10	0.7	1	0.3	11	0.8	1	0.3	52	0.5	13	0.3	45	0.4	15	0.3
45	8	0.6	—	—	19	1.4	5	1.6	49	0.4	14	0.3	49	0.4	12	0.2
46	11	0.8	—	—	7	0.5	1	0.3	47	0.4	3	0.1	28	0.3	6	0.1
47	10	0.7	—	—	8	0.6	1	0.3	36	0.3	10	0.2	26	0.2	6	0.1
48	7	0.5	1	0.3	5	0.4	1	0.3	30	0.3	11	0.2	23	0.2	8	0.2
49	5	0.4	1	0.3	5	0.4	2	0.6	29	0.3	8	0.2	22	0.2	7	0.1
50	4	0.3	—	—	7	0.5	2	0.6	24	0.2	5	0.1	26	0.2	12	0.2
Over 50	22	1.6	6	1.9	24	1.8	12	3.7	116	1.1	77	1.6	73	0.7	45	0.9
Un-known	168[1]	12.3	132	41.0	101[1]	0.7	11	3.4	192	1.7	248	5.1	1,209	11.0	1,016	21.1

[1] In addition, the statistics prepared at the IGHUT, that appear in the appendix, contain five persons whose ages and sexes are unknown.

240

Appendix E. The number of advertisements aimed at emigrants by shipping companies, their agents and »immigrant recruiters» published in the Waasan Lehti, the Wasa Tidning and the Wasabladet from 1887 to 1897, calculated half-yearly.

	Waasan Lehti	Wasa Tidning	Wasa-bladet	Total
Jan. 1 — June 30, 1887	—	—	14	14
July 1 — Dec. 31, 1887	4	—	3	7
Jan. 1 — June 30, 1888	48	72	43	163
July 1 — Dec. 31, 1888	41	48	17	106
Jan. 1 — June 30, 1889	60	97	26	183
July 1 — Dec. 31, 1889	128	197	23	348
Jan. 1 — June 30, 1890	91	139	53	283
July 1 — Dec. 31, 1890	34	49	12	95
Jan. 1 — June 30, 1891	33	61	19	113
July 1 — Dec. 31, 1891	35	39	6	80
Jan. 1 — June 30, 1892	6	63	64	133
July 1 — Dec. 31, 1892	35	63	51	149
Jan. 1 — June 30, 1893	52	149	90	291
July 1 — Dec. 31, 1893	65	63	42	170
Jan. 1 — June 30, 1894	—	72	38	110
July 1 — Dec. 31, 1894	—	108	31	139
Jan. 1 — June 30, 1895	—	146	113	259
July 1 — Dec. 31, 1895	—	60	79	139
Jan. 1 — June 30, 1896	—	76	70	146
July 1 — Dec. 31, 1896	—	52	37	89
Jan. 1 — June 30, 1897	—	31	32	63
July 1 — Dec. 31, 1897	—	27	26	53

Appendix F. The number of Finnish emigrants to South Africa, New Zealand and Australia, by month, 1883—1914 (according to the passenger lists of the Gothenburg and Stockholm police departments, and the passenger lists of the Finland Steamship Company).

	South Africa		Australia and New Zealand	
January	16	2.1 %	21	7.0 %
February	58	7.6 %	15	5.0 %
March	69	9.0 %	4	1.3 %
April	59	7.7 %	17	5.7 %
May	37	4.8 %	26	8.7 %
June	19	2.5 %	27	9.0 %
July	45	5.9 %	42	14.0 %
August	78	10.2 %	30	10.0 %
September	115	15.1 %	42	14.0 %
October	135	17.7 %	46	15.4 %
November	97	12.7 %	12	4.0 %
December	35	4.6 %	17	5.7 %
Total	**763**		299	

Appendix G. The number of emigrants, by month, 1869—1914.

	1869—79		1880—91		1892—1902		1904—14	
January	—	—	640	1.5 %	3,063	5.0 %	10,884	7.1 %
February	—	—	1,105	2.6 %	4,039	5.6 %	9,577	6.3 %
March	3	0.1 %	1,628	3.9 %	6,545	9.0 %	15,869	10.4 %
April	18	0.6 %	3,434	8.2 %	10,232	14.6 %	19,211	12.6 %
May	229	8.2 %	7,619	18.1 %	9,151	12.6 %	17,526	11.5 %
June	887	31.9 %	10,646	25.4 %	7,749	10.7 %	13,062	8.6 %
July	560	20.1 %	6,303	15.0 %	5,890	8.1 %	11,121	7.3 %
August	331	11.9 %	2,407	5.7 %	5,070	7.0 %	12,435	8.2 %
September	365	13.1 %	3,314	7.9 %	5,864	8.1 %	13,209	8.7 %
October	267	9.6 %	2,808	6.7 %	5,170	7.1 %	10,864	7.1 %
November	107	3.9 %	1,427	3.4 %	5,674	7.8 %	11,091	7.3 %
December	12	0.4 %	649	1.5 %	3,746	5.1 %	7,250	4.8 %

Appendix H. The shares of different shipping companies of the emigrants transported by the Finland Steamship Company, 1892, 1895, 1900, 1905, and 1910.

	1892		1895		1900		1905		1910	
Allan	795	25.0 %	236	7.9 %	2,044	19.2 %	3,430	18.7 %	4,008	20.6 %
American	31	1.0 %	752	25.2 %	2,552	24.0 %	1,797	9.8 %	965	5.0 %
Anchor	8	0.3 %	120	4.0 %	350	3.3 %	888	4.8 %	739	3.8 %
Beaver	13	0.4 %	3	0.1 %	431	4.0 %	2	0.0 %	—	—
Cunard	725	22.8 %	960	32.2 %	2,468	23.2 %	5,399	29.5 %	4,196	21.6 %
Dominion	219	6.9 %	173	5.8 %	1,516	14.2 %	939	5.1 %	—	—
Guion	411	12.9 %	—		—		—		—	
Inman	471	14.8 %	—		—		—		—	
State	2	0.1 %	34	1.1 %	97	0.9 %	341	1.9 %	—	—
White Star	502	15.8 %	478	16.0 %	1,173	11.0 %	4,804	26.2 %	5,392	27.7 %
	3,177									
Castle	—		104	3.5 %	—	0.0 %	—		—	0.0 %
Orient	—		7	0.2 %	3	0.0 %	—		2	0.0 %
Union	—		114	3.8 %	8	0.1 %	—		—	
			2,981		10,642					
C.P.R.	—		—		—		486	2.7 %	2,411	12.4 %
Scandinavian-American	—		—		—		185	1.0 %	581	3.0 %
Union-Castle	—		—		—		61	0.3 %	37	0.2 %
							18,332			
Donaldson	—		—		—		—		227	1.2 %
Holland Lloyd	—		—		—		—		1	0.0 %
Pacific	—		—		—		—		17	0.1 %
Royal Line	—		—		—		—		60	0.3 %
Thomson	—		—		—		—		3	0.0 %
White Star — Dominion	—		—		—		—		823	4.2 %
									19,462	

Appendix I. The percentage of tickets bought in Finland and in America of the emigrants transported by the Finland Steamship Company 1895, 1900, 1905 and 1910.

	1895 Bought in Finland	1895 Prepaid-ticket	1900 Bought in Finland	1900 Prepaid-ticket	1905 Bought in Finland	1905 Prepaid-ticket	1910 Bought in Finland	1910 Prepaid-ticket
Allan	137 58.1 %	99 41.9 %	1,199 58.7 %	845 41.3 %	2,279 66.4 %	1,151 33.6 %	3,036 75.7 %	972 24.3 %
American	523 69.5 %	229 30.5 %	1,688 66.1 %	864 33.9 %	1,465 81.5 %	332 18.5 %	813 84.2 %	152 15.8 %
Anchor	110 91.7 %	10 8.3 %	323 92.3 %	27 7.7 %	877 98.8 %	11 1.2 %	656 88.8 %	83 11.2 %
Beaver	3 100.0 %	— —	377 87.5 %	54 12.5 %	2 100.0 %	— —	— —	— —
Castle	104 100.0 %	— —	— —	— —	— —	— —	— —	— —
Cunard	656 68.3 %	304 31.7 %	1,471 59.6 %	997 40.4 %	3,461 64.1 %	1,938 35.9 %	3,069 73.1 %	1,127 26.9 %
Dominion	136 78.6 %	37 21.4 %	881 58.1 %	635 41.9 %	516 55.0 %	423 45.0 %	— —	— —
Orient	7 100.0 %	— —	3 100.0 %	— —	— —	— —	2 100.0 %	— —
State	29 85.3 %	5 14.7 %	72 74.2 %	25 25.8 %	330 96.8 %	11 3.2 %	— —	— —
Union	114 100.0 %	— —	8 100.0 %	— —	— —	— —	— —	— —
White Star	338 70.7 %	140 29.3 %	611 52.1 %	562 47.9 %	3,331 69.3 %	1,473 30.7 %	3,887 72.1 %	1,505 27.9 %
C.P.R.					415 85.4 %	71 14.6 %	1,128 46.8 %	1,283 53.2 %
Scand. Amer.					146 78.9 %	39 21.1 %	371 63.9 %	210 36.1 %
Union-Castle					61 100.0 %	— —	37 100.0 %	— —
Donaldson							215 94.7 %	12 5.3 %
Holland Lloyd							1 100.0 %	— —
Pacific							17 100.0 %	— —
Royal Line							49 81.7 %	11 18.3 %
Thomson							— —	3 100.0 %
White Star— Dominion							585 71.1 %	238 28.9 %
Total	2,157 72.4 %	824 27.6 %	6,633 62.3 %	4,009 37.7 %	12,883 70.3 %	5,449 29.7 %	13,866 71.2 %	5,596 28.8 %

Appendix J. *The number of emigrants from each Finnish province carried by transatlantic shipping-lines, 1905.*

	Uusimaa		Turku and Pori		Häme		Viipuri		Mikkeli		Kuopio		Vaasa		Oulu		Total	
Cunard	178	26.4 %	980	32.1 %	179	34.1 %	238	29.1 %	123	42.7 %	170	28.6 %	2,430	32.6 %	820	33.7 %	5,118	32.3 %
White Star	230	34.2 %	835	27.4 %	183	34.9 %	200	24.4 %	64	22.2 %	156	26.3 %	1,953	26.2 %	616	25.3 %	4,237	26.8 %
Allan	87	12.9 %	488	16,0 %	54	10.3 %	121	14.8 %	37	12.8 %	167	28.1 %	1,501	20.1 %	552	22.7 %	3,007	19.0 %
American	76	11.3 %	239	7.8 %	49	9.3 %	97	11.9 %	28	9.7 %	44	7.4 %	714	9.6 %	159	6.5 %	1,406	8.9 %
Dominion	23	3.4 %	69	2.3 %	9	1.7 %	47	5.7 %	20	6.9 %	23	3.9 %	353	4.7 %	131	5.4 %	675	4.3 %
Anchor	29	4.3 %	130	4.3 %	15	2.9 %	25	3.1 %	6	2.1 %	11	1.9 %	125	1.7 %	40	1.6 %	381	2.4 %
C.P.R. Scand.	11	1.6 %	37	1.2 %	20	3.8 %	64	7.8 %	3	1.0 %	15	2.5 %	169	2.3 %	56	2.3 %	375	2.4 %
American	23	3.4 %	23	0.8 %	8	1.5 %	16	2.0 %	3	1.0 %	2	0.3 %	62	0.8 %	23	0.9 %	160	1.0 %
State	5	0.7 %	33	1.1 %	4	0.8 %	6	0.7 %	1	0.3 %	2	0.3 %	43	0.6 %	11	0.5 %	105	0.7 %
Union-Castle	2	0.3 %	—		—		—		—		—		48	0.6 %	2	0.1 %	52	0.3 %
F.A.A.[1]	5	0.7 %	1	0.0 %	—		2	0.2 %	—		3	0.5 %	8	0.1 %	2	0.1 %	21	0.1 %
Orient	—		—		—		—		—		—		2	0.0 %	—		2	0.0 %
By way of Sweden	4	0.6 %	217	7.1 %	4	0.8 %	2	0.2 %	3	1.0 %	1	0.2 %	44	0.6 %	23	0.9 %	298	1.9 %
	673		3,052		525		818		288		594		7,452		2,435		15,837	

1 These passengers had a ticket only to England. It is probable, however, that they travelled to countries overseas.

Abbreviations

STV   = Suomen Tilastollinen Vuosikirja (Finland's Statistical Yearbook)

SVT   = Suomen Virallinen Tilasto (Official Statistics for Finland)

SVA   = Suomen Valtionarkisto (National Archives of Finland)

TMA   = Turun Maakunta-arkisto (Turku and Pori Provincial Archives)

TYYH (IGHUT) = Turun Yliopiston yleisen historian laitos (Institute of General History at the University of Turku)

Bibliography

I Unpublished material

1. S u o m e n   V a l t i o n a r k i s t o (Finnish National Archives)
   a. The archives of the Central Bureau of Statistics
      — Copies of the passport lists for 1883—1914.
      — Letters sent by passport authorities to the Central Bureau of Statistics.
      — Lists of emigrants sent by parishes to the Central Bureau of Statistics.
   b. The archives of the Uusimaa provincial government
      — Passport lists of the Uusimaa provincial government for 1850—1914.
      — Copies of the Hanko city administration's passport lists for 1877—78, 1880—92.

2. H ä m e e n   M a a k u n t a - a r k i s t o (Häme Provincial Archives)
   a. The archives of the Häme provincial government
      — Passport lists of the Häme provincial government for 1850—82, 1886—1914.

3. O u l u n   M a a k u n t a - a r k i s t o (Oulu Provincial Archives)
   a. The archives of the Oulu provincial government
      — Passport lists of the Oulu provincial government for 1850—1914.
   b. The archives of the Raahe city administration
      — Passport lists of the Raahe city administration for 1865—1892.

4. S a v o - K a r j a l a n   M a a k u n t a - a r k i s t o (Savo-Karjala Provincial Archives)
   a. The archives of the Kuopio provincial government
      — Passport lists of the Kuopio provincial government for 1865—1914.
   b. The archives of the Mikkeli provincial government
      — Passport lists of the Mikkeli provincial government for 1883—1914.
   c. The archives of the Viipuri provincial government
      — Passport lists of the Viipuri provincial government for 1865—85.

5. T u r u n   M a a k u n t a - a r k i s t o (Turku and Pori Provincial Archives)
   a. The archives of the Turku and Pori provicial government
      — Passport lists of the Turku and Pori provincial government for 1849—1914.
      — Copies of the Pori city administration's passport lists for 1885—87.
   b. The archives of the Pori city administration
      — Passport lists of the Pori city administration for 1890—1903.
   c. The archives of the Rauma city administration
      — Passport lists of the Rauma city administration for 1865—77, 1879.

d. The archives of the Uusikaupunki city administration
— Passport lists of the Uusikaupunki city administration for 1865—81, 1888—92.
e. The archives of the Åland sheriff
— Passport lists of the Åland sheriff for 1865—1914.
f. The archives of the Kankaanpää bailiff
— Lists of work permits for 1890, 1893, 1895, 1900 and 1905.

6. Vaasan Maakunta-arkisto (Vaasa Provincial Archives)
   a. The archives of the Vaasa provincial government
   — Passport lists of the Vaasa provincial government for 1849—1914.
   — Copies of the Kokkola city administration's passport lists for 1874—92.
   — Copies of the Pietarsaari city administration's passport lists for 1865—92.
   — Copies of the Kaskinen city administration's passport lists for 1874—92.
   — Copies of the Kristiinankaupunki city administration's passport lists for 1865—70, 1880—92.
   — Copies of the Uusikaarlepyy city administration's passport lists for 1871—74, 1878—92.

7. Mariehamns Stadsarkiv (Mariehamn City Archives)
   — Passport lists of the Mariehamn city administration for 1882—1914.

8. Turun Yliopiston yleisen historian laitoksen siirtolais-historian tutkimusarkisto (The Research Archives on Finnish Emigration, Institute of General History, University of Turku)
   — Passenger lists of the Gothenburg Police Department (microfilm) for 1869—1914.
   — Passenger lists of the Malmö Police Department (microfilm) for 1869—1888.
   — Passenger lists of the Stockholm Police Department (microfilm) for 1869—1902.
   — Passenger lists of the Trondheim Police Department (microfilm) for 1869—1900.
   — Passenger lists of the Finland Steamship Company (microfilm) for 1892—1914.
   — Statistical material in the archives of the Finland Steamship Company (microfilm) for 1891—1914.
   — Membership lists of the Finnish church in Harlem, New York, (microfilm) for about 1900—10.
   — Letters from America to northern Satakunta (microfilm) in the years 1888—1914.

9. Registers of the following parishes:
   — Kokkola rural parish for 1840—1895
   — Kokkola town parish » 1860—1900
   — Alatornio » 1860—1914
   — Enontekiö » 1860—1914
   — Inari » 1860—1914
   — Karunki » 1860—1914
   — Kemijärvi » 1860—1914
   — Kittilä » 1860—1914
   — Kolari » 1860—1914
   — Kuolajärvi (Salla) » 1860—1914
   — Kuusamo » 1860—1914
   — Lohtaja » 1860—1914

248

— Muonionniska (Muonio) for 1860—1914
— Pudasjärvi » 1860—1914
— Puolanka » 1860—1914
— Sodankylä » 1860—1914
— Tervola » 1860—1914
— Turtola » 1860—1914
— Utsjoki » 1860—1914
— Ylitornio » 1860—1914

10. Manuscripts

Blomfelt, Frank, Emigrationen från ett skärgårdslandskap (Emigrationen från Åland 1856—1918 med särskild hänsyn till Finström och Föglö socknar). Phil. Lic. thesis at the University of Uppsala in 1968. (Blomfelt 1968).

Kallio, Bruno, Elämäni-tarina. Manuscript at the IGHUT.

Kero, Reino, Satakuntalainen amerikansiirtolaisuus ennen ensimmäistä maailmansotaa. Lähtö ja muuttoliikkeet. Phil. Lic. thesis at the University of Turku in 1970. (Kero 1970).

Pätynen, Jorma, Siirtolaisuus Kuusamosta ennen ensimmäistä maailmansotaa (1864—1914). Pro gradu thesis at the University of Turku in 1972. (Pätynen 1972).

Skaug, Arne, Fluctuations in Migration from Norway since 1900, Compared with Other Countries, and Causes of These Fluctuations (Development in Trade, Social Conditions etc). Memorandum for General Study Conference on Peaceful Change. Paris, June 28 — July 3, 1937. (Skaug 1937).

Vainio, Esa, Vuosien 1865—1892 ulkomaanpassiluetteloiden arvo valtamertentakaisen siirtolaisuuden tutkimuksessa. Unpublished manuscript at the IGHUT.

Vainio, Esa and Tuominen, Taru-Terhikki, Emigrants from Finland in 1865—1892 according to passport lists. Unpublished manuscript at the IGHUT.

Virtanen, Keijo, Palaava suomalainen kaukosiirtolaisuus. Pro gradu thesis at the University of Turku in 1972. (Virtanen 1972).

II Interviews with Immigrants and Returned Emigrants

Name	Place of birth	Year of birth	Place where interviewed	Year of interview
Aalto, Alina	Ikaalinen	1885	Virginia, Minn.	1966
Aalto, Wilhelm	Merikarvia	1883	Merikarvia	1967
Aaltonen, Aleksi	Parkano	1879	Covington, Mich.	1967
Aho, Alina	Pomarkku	1893	Eveleth, Minn.	1967
Ahola, Edla	Honkajoki	1888	Lantana, Fla.	1967
Airola, John	Nakkila [1]	1889	Fitchburg, Mass.	1967

[1] Left from Pori.

Airola, Saima	Kannus [2]	1888	Fitchburg, Mass.	1967
Aittoniemi, Juha	Parkano	1888	Kihniö	1966
Anttila, Elma	Ikaalinen	1893	Chicago, Ill.	1967
Anttila, Hilda	Merikarvia	1883	Crystal Falls, Mich.	1967
Anttila, Iivari	Kankaanpää	1891	Karvia	1964
Anttila, Johannes	Kankaanpää	1881	Siikainen	1967
Anttila, John	Pori rural	1895	Astoria, Ore.	1967
Aronen, Anselm	Karvia	1889	Karvia	1967
Autio, Arne	Pomarkku	1894	Butte, Mont.	1967
Beldon, Hilma	Ahlainen	1893	San Pedro, Calif.	1967
Berden, Julius	Parkano	1888	Parkano	1964
Berg, Herman	Merikarvia	1899	Crystal Falls, Mich.	1967
Falke, Lyyli	Parkano	1896	Lantana, Fla.	1967
Forsman, Charles	Ulvila	1882	Lake Worth, Fla.	1967
Friberg, Wilhelmiina	Merikarvia	1877	Fitchburg, Mass.	1967
Friman, Herman	Merikarvia	1886	Nashwauk, Minn.	1967
Gadell, Anselm	Karvia	1878	Aura, Mich.	1967
Gröndahl, Frans	Siikainen	1886	Siikainen	1966
Hakala, Emil	Ikaalinen	1889	Amasa, Mich.	1967
Hakala, Fanny	Nakkila [3]	1894	Fitchburg, Mass.	1967
Hakamäki, Fredrik	Parkano	1894	Parkano	1966
Halme, Josef	Jämijärvi	1890	Duluth, Minn.	1967
Halme, Juho	Siikainen	1890	Siikainen	1967
Halme, Lyydi	Jämijärvi	1893	Siikainen	1967
Halminen, Frans	Siikainen	1882	Siikainen	1967
Hautaluoma, Frans	Pomarkku	1888	Karvia	1967
Hautaluoma, Leander	Pomarkku	1886	Karvia	1967
Havunen, Juho	Parkano	1879	Kihniö	1966
Heikkilä, Matti	Kankaanpää	1895	Kankaanpää	1967
Heikkilä, Rikhard	Kankaanpää	1887	Ishpeming, Mich.	1967
Heino, August	Ikaalinen	1891	Maple, Wisc.	1967
Heino, Ida	Pori rural	1895	Hibbing, Minn.	1966
Heino, John	Pori rural	1897	Aberdeen, Wash.	1967
Hiedanpää, Ville	Karvia	1886	Karvia	1964
Hietala, Tyyne	Parkano	1890	Cloquet, Minn.	1966
Hietanen, Anselm	Parkano	1893	Keewatin, Minn.	1967
Huhtala, Karl	Pöytyä [4]	1892	Lake Worth, Fla.	1967
Hytönen, Hilda	Kankaanpää	1886	Eveleth, Minn.	1967
Hällfors, Lauri	Ulvila	1891	Fitchburg, Mass.	1967
Ibbotson, Lydia	Eurajoki [5]	1894	Eveleth, Minn.	1966
Johnson, Helmi	Lempäälä [6]	1902	Lake Worth, Fla.	1967
Joki, Otto	Parkano	1887	Duluth, Minn.	1967
Joki, Salomon	Ikaalinen	1884	Negaunee, Mich.	1967
Jokinen, Isaac	Parkano	1891	Keewatin, Minn.	1967

[2] Left from Pori.
[3] Left from Pori.
[4] Left from Pori.
[5] Left from Pori rural.
[6] Left from Noormarkku.

Joutsen, Aino	Siikainen	1894	Grayland, Wash.	1967
Juhola, Emil	Kankaanpää	1894	Duluth, Minn.	1967
Järvi, Frank	Jämijärvi	1883	Negaunee, Mich.	1967
Kaleton, Arne	Pomarkku	1893	Los Angeles, Calif.	1967
Kallio, Bruno	Noormarkku	1893	Lantana, Fla.	1967
Kallio, Nikolai	Pomarkku	1884	Pomarkku	1967
Kallio, Väinö	Merikarvia	1892	Crystal Falls, Mich.	1967
Kallioniemi, Jaakko	Karvia	1894	Karvia	1967
Kangas, Väinö	Honkajoki	1891	Lantana, Fla.	1967
Kari, Olga	Parkano	1892	Kihniö	1967
Kivelä, Iivari	Ikaalinen	1884	Ikaalinen	1964
Kivimäki, Juha	Jämijärvi	1877	Jämijärvi	1967
Kivimäki, Rikhard	Kankaanpää	1887	Kankaanpää	1967
Kivineva, Juha	Parkano	1890	Kihniö	1966
Kiviniemi, Edvard	Ikaalinen	1885	Kihniö	1966
Kivistö, Alfred	Pori rural	1887	Minneapolis, Minn.	1966
Kivistö, Eli	Ikaalinen	1881	Los Angeles, Calif.	1967
Kivistö, Svante	Karvia	1893	Karvia	1967
Koivisto, Oskari	Siikainen	1889	Kankaanpää	1967
Koriansalo, Aleksi	Parkano	1883	Parkano	1967
Korpela, Hugo	Kankaanpää	1891	Kankaanpää	1964
Korpela, Svante	Jämijärvi	1888	Lantana, Fla.	1967
Korpijärvi, Mari	Parkano	1891	Kihniö	1967
Korpunen, Iisakki	Merikarvia	1886	Merikarvia	1967
Koskela, Frans	Kankaanpää	1887	Kankaanpää	1964
Koski, John	Kankaanpää	1894	Negaunee, Mich.	1967
Koski, Lempi	Ikaalinen	1893	Lantana, Fla.	1967
Koskimaa, Aleksandra	Parkano	?	Kihniö	1967
Koskimaa, Samuel	Jalasjärvi [7]	1887	Kihniö	1967
Kuivila, Alexandra	Kankaanpää	1885	Negaunee, Mich.	1967
Kujala, Aleksi	Parkano	1890	Kihniö	1967
Kukkola, Olga	Merikarvia	1893	Conneaut, Ohio	1967
Kuoppasalmi, Johan	Parkano	1886	Parkano	1967
Kuuri, Eino	Ikaalinen	1889	Duluth, Minn.	1967
Kuusisto, Nestori	Siikainen	1884	Siikainen	1966
Kyyny, Toivo	Ikaalinen	1894	Ikaalinen	1967
Kärysoja, Frans	Jämijärvi	1895	Jämijärvi	1966
Laakso, Lauri	Pori rural	1900	Nashwauk, Minn.	1967
Lack, Ida	Siikainen	1889	Lake Worth, Fla.	1967
Lahti, Helga	Pori	1888	Virginia, Minn.	1967
Lahti, Jooseppi	Parkano	1887	Kihniö	1967
Lahti, Lydia	Siikainen	1873	San Pedro, Calif.	1967
Lahti, Maria	Merikarvia	1891	Amasa, Mich.	1967
Lahti, Markku	Honkajoki	1878	Honkajoki	1964
Lahti, Toivo	Parkano	1891	Virginia, Minn.	1966
Laiho, Hilja	Kiikoinen [8]	1890	Duluth, Minn.	1967

---

[7] Left from Parkano.
[8] Left from Pori rural.

Laine, Emil	Karvia [9]	1891	Butte, Mont.	1967
Laine, Frank	Ahlainen	1880	Cloquet, Minn.	1966
Laitinen, Hilma	Merikarvia	1890	Negaunee, Mich.	1967
Lalli, Alina	Parkano	1886	Astoria, Ore.	1967
Lamminen, Emmi	Siikainen	1886	Lake Worth, Fla.	1967
Lamminen, Selim	Pori	1896	Cloquet, Minn.	1966
Lampi, Ed	Ikaalinen	1893	Esko, Minn.	1966
Lampi, Lyyti	Ikaalinen	1893	Esko, Minn.	1966
Lehti, Kalle	Ahlainen	1885	Merikarvia	1964
Lehtinen, Helmi	Pori	1893	Aberdeen, Wash.	1967
Lehtinen, Walfrid	Noormarkku	1889	Negaunee, Mich.	1967
Lehtonen, Ellen	Kankaanpää	1895	St. Paul, Minn.	1967
Lehtonen, Frank	Jämijärvi	1887	Negaunee, Mich.	1967
Lehtonen, Väinö	Kankaanpää	1891	Kankaanpää	1967
Lemberg, Sigrid	Pori rural	1897	Duluth, Minn.	1967
Lepistö, Wilhelmiina	Noormarkku	1887	Virginia, Minn.	1967
Leppänen, Toivo	Ikaalinen	1890	Ikaalinen	1964
Levänpää, Frank	Jämijärvi	1891	Superior, Wisc.	1967
Lindberg, Juho	Noormarkku	1888	Kankaanpää	1967
Lindberg, Tyyne	Ikaalinen	1887	San Pedro, Calif.	1967
Lindström, Tekla	Kankaanpää	1887	San Pedro, Calif.	1967
Lähdetluoma, Akseli	Karvia	1885	Karvia	1967
Lähteenmäki, Frans	Siikainen	1885	Siikainen	1966
Malm, Victor	Pori rural	1897	Nashwauk, Minn.	1967
Mannila, Jalmari	Pori rural [10]	1892	Lake Worth, Fla.	1967
Marjamäki, Kalle	Parkano	1889	Parkano	1967
Matthews, Fanny	Merikarvia	1889	Crystal Falls, Mich.	1967
Mattila, Akseli	Honkajoki	1886	Honkajoki	1964
Mattila, Väinö	Merikarvia	1893	Merikarvia	1967
Metsälä, Jenny	Noormarkku	1890	Lantana, Fla.	1967
Mikkola, Oskar	Noormarkku	1879	Duluth, Minn.	1967
Mustapää, Fanni	Merikarvia	1895	Merikarvia	1967
Myllykoski, Anselmi	Isojoki [11]	1887	Siikainen	1966
Myllyviita, Vilhelm	Karvia	1889	Karvia	1967
Mäkelä, Edla	Parkano	1890	Fitchburg, Mass.	1967
Mäkelä, Konsta	Ikaalinen	1888	Maple, Wisc.	1967
Mäki, Artur	Ikaalinen	1892	Lake Worth, Fla.	1967
Mäki, Emil	Parkano	1893	Lantana, Fla.	1967
Mäki, Frank	Merikarvia	1889	Crystal Falls, Mich.	1967
Mäki, Frans	Noormarkku	1894	Kullaa	1964
Mäki, Hilda	Jämijärvi	1888	Jämijärvi	1967
Mäki, Hilja	Jämijärvi	1889	Waukegan, Ill.	1967
Mäki, Iver	Ikaalinen	1886	Crystal Falls, Mich.	1967
Mäki, Jalmar	Pomarkku	1888	Keewatin, Minn.	1967
Mäki, Jalmari	Merikarvia	1894	Crystal Falls, Mich.	1967
Mäki, John	Karvia	1891	Trout Creek, Mich.	1967

[9] Left from Parkano.
[10] Left from Pori.
[11] Left from Siikainen.

Mäki, Lempi	Suoniemi [12]	1897	Saginaw, Minn.	1966
Mäki, Nestor	Ikaalinen	1888	Duluth, Minn.	1967
Mäki, Oscar	Ahlainen	1895	Fitchburg, Mass.	1967
Mäki, Selim	Siikainen	1891	Lake Worth, Fla.	1967
Mäki, William	Honkajoki	1886	Duluth, Minn.	1967
Nelson, Aini	Merikarvia	1896	Virginia, Minn.	1966
Niemelä, Herman	Parkano	1887	Kihniö	1967
Niemelä, Wilhelm	Parkano	1881	Kihniö	1967
Niemi, Emma	Ikaalinen	1884	Lantana, Fla.	1967
Niemi, Frans	Siikainen	1892	Siikainen	1966
Niemi, Jaakko	Pomarkku	1879	Pomarkku	1967
Niemi, Josefiina	Siikainen	1893	Marquette, Mich.	1967
Niemi, William	Parkano	1889	Duluth, Minn.	1967
Nikula, Alfina	Honkajoki	1885	Hibbing, Minn.	1966
Norrgard, Henry	Siikainen	1887	Lake Worth, Fla.	1967
Norrgard, Josefina	Siikainen	1892	Lake Worth, Fla.	1967
Nummelin, Jenny	Merikarvia	1883	Virginia, Minn.	1967
Nurmi, Sam	Karvia	1885	Negaunee, Mich.	1967
Oja, Eino	Parkano	1899	Keewatin, Minn.	1967
Ojala, Vilho	Ikaalinen	1891	Duluth, Minn.	1967
Ollila, Henry	Merikarvia	1890	Crystal Falls, Mich.	1967
Ollila, Hilma	Merikarvia	1891	Crystal Falls, Mich.	1967
Otava, Hulda	Karvia	1890	Mt. Iron, Minn.	1966
Otava, John	Karvia	1890	Mt. Iron, Minn.	1966
Pakkanen, John	Ikaalinen	1888	Lake Worth, Fla.	1967
Pakkanen, Matilda	Ikaalinen	1894	Lake Worth, Fla.	1967
Palmqvist, Anton	Pomarkku	1887	Brandwood, Wisc.	1967
Papunen, Jaakko	Karvia	1887	Karvia	1964
Papunen, Lempi	Parkano	1887	Parkano	1967
Pelto, Josefina	Merikarvia	1898	Marquette, Mich.	1967
Pelto, Nestori	Merikarvia	1882	Duluth, Minn.	1967
Pentti, Julius	Parkano	1888	Parkano	1966
Polvi, Josef	Ikaalinen	1892	Negaunee, Mich.	1967
Polvi, Oskari	Kankaanpää	1890	Kankaanpää	1964
Puolamäki, Jooseppi	Parkano	1887	Parkano	1964
Pursi, Selma	Jämijärvi	1891	Lake Worth, Fla.	1967
Pääsky, Gerhard	Parkano	1885	Parkano	1966
Rajala, Kalle	Ikaalinen	1878	Parkano	1967
Rajalahti, Arvid	Jämijärvi	1885	Jämijärvi	1967
Ranta, Anselm	Karvia	1884	Karvia	1967
Ranta, Ida	Honkajoki	1889	Hibbing, Minn.	1966
Ranta, Vilho	Kankaanpää	1888	Negaunee, Mich.	1967
Rapell, Saima	Pori	1894	Lake Worth, Fla.	1967
Raukola, Frans	Kankaanpää	1881	Kankaanpää	1967
Rinnet, Olga	Kankaanpää	1879	Siikainen	1967
Rintala, Viktor	Virrat [13]	1884	Parkano	1967
Rintamäki, Edvard	Parkano	1878	Parkano	1967

---

[12] Left from Pori.
[13] Left from Parkano.

Riuttanen, Matti	Parkano	1889	Hibbing, Minn.	1967
Ruoho, Kia	Parkano	1892	Hibbing, Minn.	1967
Rusko, Emil	Karvia	1888	Lake Worth, Fla.	1967
Saarela, Julia	Parkano	1888	Parkano	1967
Saari, Alma	Karvia	1895	Eveleth, Minn.	1966
Saari, Elviira	Jämijärvi	1890	Winlock, Wash.	1967
Saarinen, Milia	Merikarvia	1896	Ashtabula Harbor, Ohio	1967
Salo, Artturi	Honkajoki	1885	Honkajoki	1967
Salo, Hilja	Kankaanpää	1890	Fitchburg, Mass.	1967
Salo, Matti	Kankaanpää	1890	Fitchburg, Mass.	1967
Salo, Senia	Parkano	1896	Cloquet, Minn.	1966
Salo, Väinö	Merikarvia	1894	Hibbing, Minn.	1966
Samuelson, Milka	Pori rural	1887	Grayland, Wash.	1967
Sandberg, Elina	Merikarvia	1889	Townsend, Mass.	1967
Satola, Hilja	Honkajoki	1890	Long Beach, Calif.	1967
Seppi, Antti	Kankaanpää	?	Watton, Mich.	1967
Seppälä, Alfred	Honkajoki	1888	Honkajoki	1967
Seppälä, Anni	Nakkila 14	1897	Fitchburg, Mass.	1967
Seppälä, Hilda	Kankaanpää	1885	Honkajoki	1967
Seppälä, John	Parkano	1880	Duluth, Minn.	1967
Sikala, Toivo	Kankaanpää	1892	Kankaanpää	1964
Sillanpää, Lempi	Ahlainen	1893	Cloquet, Minn.	1966
Sillanpää, Nestori	Tammela 15	1891	Cloquet, Minn.	1966
Silta, Oiva	Ikaalinen	1893	Long Beach, Calif.	1967
Sippola, Verner	Ikaalinen	1889	Lake Worth, Fla.	1967
Siro, Verner	Ikaalinen	1889	Lake Worth, Fla.	1967
Sjöroos, Uno	Pori rural	1892	Astoria, Ore.	1967
Soisenniemi, Minna	Parkano	1888	Kihniö	1967
Stenback, Frank	Noormarkku	1884	Duluth, Minn.	1967
Stone, Artur	Ikaalinen	1893	Lakewood, Minn.	1967
Stonewall, Jalmar	Kokemäki 16	1882	Duluth, Minn.	1967
Suominen, Sigrid	Pori rural	1907	Cloquet, Minn.	1966
Suurimaa, Juho	Jämijärvi	1885	Jämijärvi	1966
Särkelä, Aleksandra	Siikainen	1899	Negaunee, Mich.	1967
Tammelin, Hilma	Siikainen	1892	Siikainen	1967
Toivola, Taavetti	Ikaalinen	1892	Ikaalinen	1964
Tuomela, Frank	Ahlainen	1893	Nashwauk, Minn.	1966
Tuomiluoma, Frans	Siikainen	1883	Siikainen	1966
Tuominen, Jalmari	Merikarvia	1890	Merikarvia	1967
Tuorila, Artturi	Siikainen	1883	Siikainen	1966
Törmä, Frank	Karvia	1891	Watton, Mich.	1967
Törmä, Fred	Parkano	1888	Nashwauk, Minn.	1967
Törmä, Kalle	Ikaalinen	1888	Esko, Minn.	1966
Uusitalo, Artturi	Siikainen	1882	Crystal Falls, Mich.	1967
Vainionpää, Heikki	Kankaanpää	1878	Kankaanpää	1967
Watunen, Edward	Parkano	1891	South Range, Wisc.	1967

14 Left from Pori.
15 Left from Ahlainen.
16 Left from Pori.

Wesslin, Vihtori	Noormarkku	1885	Noormarkku	1966
Westerviik, Herman	Ahlainen	1885	Cloquet, Minn.	1966
Westerviik, Hilja	Parkano	?	Cloquet, Minn.	1966
Wienola, Frank	Ikaalinen	1886	Crystal Falls, Mich.	1967
Viherlaakso, Jalmari	Hämeenkyrö [17]	1887	Ikaalinen	1966
Viiriäinen, Hilja	Pomarkku	1900	Hibbing, Minn.	1966
Viita, John	Parkano	1889	Covington, Mich.	1967
Viita, Nick	Kankaanpää	1902	Lake Worth, Fla.	1967
Viitala, Vihtori	Merikarvia	1881	Merikarvia	1967
Viitanen, Lempi	Ikaalinen	1885	Ikaalinen	1966
Wirta, Andrew	Pori rural [18]	1893	Aberdeen, Wash.	1967
Vuorisalo, Artturi	Siikainen	1893	Siikainen	1966
Vähätalo, Kalle	Ikaalinen	1891	Kankaanpää	1967
Vähätalo, Väinö	Ikaalinen	1895	Ikaalinen	1966
Yli-Karhula, Selmi	Karvia	1893	Karvia	1967
Ylinen, Johannes	Kankaanpää	1892	Kankaanpää	1967
Ylitalo, Oskari	Honkajoki	1886	Honkajoki	1964
Åkerlund, Vihtori	Ahlainen	1884	Ahlainen	1964
Österlund, Viktor	Merikarvia	1888	Merikarvia	1967

Other persons interviewed

Lähteenmäki, Olavi, M. A.		Turku	1973
Vainio, Esa, B. A.		Turku	1972

III Published material

1. Secondary works and memoirs

Alanen, Yrjö, Siirtolaisemme ja kotimaa. Siirtolaisuuden vaikutuksesta kansamme oloihin ja luonteeseen. Kansanvalistusseuran toimituksia 154. Helsinki 1910. (Alanen 1910).

B a c k m a n, W o l d., Emigrationen från Munsala socken. En enquête av Samfundet Folkhälsan i Svenska Finland. Bidrag till kännedom af Finlands natur och folk 88: 7. Helsingfors 1945. (B a c k m a n 1945).

B j ö r k q v i s t, H e i m e r, Prisrörelsen och penningvärde i Finland under guldmyntfotsperioden 1878—1913. En struktur- och konjunkturanalys. Publikationer utgivna av Finlands Banks institut för ekonomisk forskning. Serie B: 19. Helsingfors 1958. (B j ö r k q v i s t 1958).

B r a t t n e, B e r i t, Bröderna Larsson. En studie i svensk emigrantagentverksamhet under 1880-talet. Studia Historica Upsaliensia L. Uppsala 1973. (B r a t t n e 1973).

C a r l s s o n, S t e n, Emigrationen från Småland och Öland 1861—1930. Social och regional fördelning. Historielärarnas förenings årsskrift 1966—1967. (C a r l s s o n 1966—67).

---

[17] Left from Ikaalinen.
[19] Left from Pori.

— Frikyrklighet och emigration. Ett bidrag. Kyrka, folk, stat. Till Sven Kjöllerström. Lund 1967. (C a r l s s o n 1967).

— Från familjeutvandring till ensamutvandring. En utvecklingslinje i den svenska emigrationens historia. Emigrationer. En bok till Wilhelm Moberg 20. 8. 1968. Stockholm 1968. (C a r l s s o n 1968).

C a s t r é n, J a l m a r, Rautateittemme kehitysvaiheista. Valtionrautatiet. Toimittanut Einari Kaskimies. Porvoo 1935. (C a s t r é n 1935).

van C l e e f, E u g e n e, The Finn in America. The Geographical Review VI (1918). (van C l e e f 1918).

D a v i e, M a u r i c e R., World Immigration with Special Reference to the United States. New York 1936. (D a v i e 1936).

D u r c h m a n, W. K., Muistelmia ja mietelmiä Amerikan suomalaisten siirtolaisten oloista ja sielunhoidosta. Tampere 1901 (D u r c h m a n 1901).

E i s e m a n, A l b e r t a, From Many Lands. Forge Village, Mass., 1970. (E i s e m a n 1970).

E n g e l b e r g, R a f a e l, Suomi ja Amerikan suomalaiset. Keskinäinen yhteys ja sen rakentaminen. Helsinki 1944. (E n g e l b e r g 1944).

E r i c k s o n, C h a r l o t t e, American Industry and the European Immigrant 1860— 1885. Studies in Economic History. Published in coöperation with the Committee on Research in Economic History. Cambridge, Mass., 1957. (E r i c k s o n 1957).

F a i r c h i l d, H e n r y P r a t t, Immigration. A World Movement and its American Significance. New York 1914. (F a i r c h i l d 1914).

F o e r s t e r, R o b e r t F., The Italian Emigration of our Times. Reprint 1969. New York 1969. (F o e r s t e r 1924).[1]

F o x, Paul, The Poles in America. Reprint. New York 1970. (F o x 1922).

G e b h a r d, H a n n e s, Maanviljelysväestö, sen suhde muihin elinkeinoryhmiin ja sen yhteiskunnallinen kokoonpano Suomen maalaiskunnissa v. 1901. Tilattoman Väestön Alakomitea. Tilastollinen tutkimus yhteiskuntataloudellisista oloista Suomen maalaiskunnissa v. 1901 I. Maanviljelysväestö. Helsinki 1913. (G e b h a r d 1913).

G i b b s, C. R. V e r n o n, Passenger Liners of the Western Ocean. A Record of the North Atlantic Steam and Motor Passenger Vessels from 1838 to the Present Day. Second edition. Sl. 1957. (G i b b s 1952).

G r e e n l e a f, B a r b a r a K a y e, America Fever. The Story of American Immigration. New York 1970. (G r e e n l e a f 1970).

G r o u n d s t r o e m, O., Maanviljelystyöväen palkat Suomessa vuosina 1890 ja 1907. Yhteiskuntataloudellinen Aikakauskirja 1909. (G r o u n d s t r o e m 1909).

— Om emigrationen från Finland. Ekonomiska Samfundet i Finland. Föredrag och förhandlingar Band II, häfte 3. Helsingfors 1901. (G r o u n d s t r o e m 1901).

G u i l l e t, E d w i n C., The Great Migration. The Atlantic Crossing by Sailingship since 1770. Second edition. Toronto 1963. (G u i l l e t 1937).

G y l l i n g, E d v a r d, Eräitä uusia tilastotietoja Suomen siirtolaisuudesta. Yhteiskuntataloudellinen Aikakauskirja 1910. (G y l l i n g 1910).

— Siirtolaisuutemme ja tilaton väestö. Sosialistinen Aikakauslehti näytenumero 3/1906. (G y l l i n g 1906).

H e d g e s, J a m e s B., The Colonization Work of the Northern Pacific Railroad. The Mississippi Valley Historical Review 3/1926. (H e d g e s 1926).

---

[1] In the case of reprints the year of the first edition within parentheses.

Hedman, E. A., Amerikan muistoja. Näkemiäni ja kokemiani neljänkymmenen vuoden täällä oloni ajalla. Helsinki 1926. (Hedman 1926).

Hjelt, Aug., Suomen siirtolaisuusliikkeestä. Yhteiskuntataloudellinen Aikakauskirja 1905. (Hjelt 1905).

Hoglund, A. William, Finnish Immigrants in America 1880—1920. Binghamton, N. Y., 1960. (Hoglund 1960).

Holmio, Armas K. E., Michiganin Suomalaisten Historia. Hancock, Mich., 1967. (Holmio 1967).

Hrdlicka, Ales, The Old Americans. A Physiological Profile. Reprint 1970. New York 1970. (Hrdlicka 1925).

Hvidt, Kristian, Flugten til Amerika eller drivkræfter i masseudvandringen fra Danmark 1868—1914. Skrifter udgivet af Jysk Selskab for Historie 22. Odense 1971. (Hvidt 1971).

— Informationsspredning og emigration med særligt henblik på det atlantiske transportsystem. Emigrationen fra Norden indtil 1. Verdenskrig. Rapporter til det Nordiske Historikermøde i København 1971, 9—12 august. København 1971. (Hvidt 1971 I).

Ilmonen, S., Amerikan suomalaisen raittiusliikkeen historia. Edellinen osa. Ishpeming, Mich., 1912. (Ilmonen 1912).

— Amerikan Suomalaisten historiaa I—III. I Hancock, Mich., 1919, II Jyväskylä 1923, III Hancock, Mich., 1926. (Ilmonen 1919, 1923, 1926).

— Amerikan suomalaisten sivistyshistoria I—II. Johtavia aatteita, harrastuksia, yhteispyrintöjä ja tapahtumia siirtokansan keskuudessa. Hancock, Mich., 1930 and 1931. (Ilmonen 1930, 1931).

International Migrations I—II. Edited by Walter F. Willcox. New York 1929 and 1931. (International Migrations).

Jerome, Harry, Migration and Business Cycles. Publications of the National Bureau of Economic Research, Incorporated, No. 9. New York 1926. (Jerome 1926).

Jones, Maldwyn Allen, American Immigration. Second Impression. Chicago, Ill., 1961. (Jones 1960).

Jutikkala, Eino, Geographical Distribution of Emigration in Finland. A Comparative Study of Factors Affecting Overseas Emigration from Finland. International Population Conference, Vienna 1959. Vienna 1959. (Jutikkala 1959).

— Etelä-Pohjanmaa ja siirtolaisuus. Historiallinen Aikakauskirja 1963. (Jutikkala 1963).

— Suomen talonpojan historia. Toinen uudistettu ja lisätty laitos. Suomalaisen Kirjallisuuden Seuran toimituksia 257. Turku 1958. (Jutikkala 1958).

— Väestö ja asutus 1500-luvulta 1800-luvun puoliväliin. Suomen Kulttuurihistoria II. Jyväskylä 1934. (Jutikkala 1934).

Järnefelt [Rauanheimo], Akseli, Suomalaiset Amerikassa. Helsinki 1899. (Järnefelt 1899).

Kelley, Allen C., International Migration and Economic Growth: Australia, 1865—1935. The Journal of Economic History 3/1965. (Kelley 1965).

Kero, Reino, Charles Linn. Amerikansuomalainen self-made-man 1800-luvulta. Suomen Silta 4/1971. (Kero 1971 II).

— Ekonomiska faktorer som förklaringsgrund i emigrationsforskningen. Emigrationen fra Norden indtil I. Verdenskrig. Rapporter til det Nordiske historikermøde i København 1971, 9—12 august. København 1971. (Kero 1971 III).

257

— James Fiskin perintötarinoiden tausta. Turun Historiallisen Yhdistyksen Julkaisuja XXV. Vammala 1971 (K e r o 1971 I).

— The Return of Emigrants from America to Finland. Publications of the Institute of General History. University of Turku, Finland. Nr 4. Turku 1972. (K e r o 1972).

— Siirtolaisuus Suomesta Amerikkaan vuosien 1849—1865 välisenä aikana. Oulun Historiaseuran Julkaisuja II. Oulu 1969. (K e r o 1969 I).

— Suomen kuvernöörien siirtolaisraportit vuosina 1873—1874. Turun Historiallisen Yhdistyksen Julkaisuja XXI. Forssa 1969. (K e r o 1969 II).

— Yhdysvaltojen kuva Suomen sanomalehdissä 1800-luvun puolivälin jälkeen (noin vuosina 1850—1875). Turun Historiallisen Yhdistyksen Julkaisuja XX. Turku 1967. (K e r o 1967).

K i l p i, O. K., Suomen siirtolaisuudesta. Oma Maa V. Tietokirja Suomen kodeille. Porvoo 1910. (K i l p i 1910).

— Suomen siirtolaisuus ja 19. vuosisadan kansantalous. Taloustieteellisiä tutkimuksia XXII. Helsinki 1917. (K i l p i 1917).

K o i v u k a n g a s, O l a v i, An Attempted Finnish Utopian Settlement in Queensland. Journal of the Royal Australian Historical Society 1/1972. (K o i v u k a n g a s 1972 II).

— Finnish Migration to Australia before World War II. Area of Origin and Migration Characteristics. Publications of the Institute of General History. University of Turku, Finland. Nr 4. Turku 1972. (K o i v u k a n g a s 1972 I).

K o l e h m a i n e n, J o h n I., The Finns in America. A Bibliographical Guide to their History. Hancock, Mich., 1947. (K o l e h m a i n e n 1947).

— Sow the Golden Seed. A History of the Fitchburg (Massachusetts) Finnish-American Newspaper. Raivaaja (the Pioneer) 1905—1955. Fitchburg, Mass., 1955. (K o l e h m a i n e n 1955).

— Suomalaisten siirtolaisuus Norjasta Amerikkaan. Fitchburg, Mass., Sa. (K o l e h m a i n e n 1946).

K o l e h m a i n e n, J o h n I. & H i l l, G e o r g e W., Haven in the Woods. The Story of the Finns in Wisconsin. Second Printing. Madison, Wisc., 1965. (K o l e h m a i n e n — H i l l 1951).

K ä l v e m a r k, A n n - S o f i e, Reaktionen mot utvandringen. Emigrationsfrågan i svensk debatt och politik 1901—1904. Studia Historica Upsaliensia XLI. Uppsala 1972. (K ä l v e m a r k 1972).

Laurén, L. L., Waroitus, muuttamisesta pois isänmaasta. Rahwaankirjoja kristillissiweellisestä sisällöstä I. Nikolainkaupunki [Vaasa] 1872. (Laurén 1872).

L e i n o n e n, A l e x, Suomalaiset Amerikassa. Oulun Wiikko-Sanomia, May 27, June 3, 17, 23, July 8, August 12 and 19, 1876. (L e i n o n e n 1876).

L e n t o, R e i n o, Maassamuutto ja siihen vaikuttaneet tekijät Suomessa vuosina 1878—1939. Väestöpoliittisen tutkimuslaitoksen julkaisuja A: 5. Helsinki 1951. (L e n t o 1951).

L j u n g m a r k, L a r s, For Sale — Minnesota. Organized Promotion of Scandinavian Immigration 1866—1873. Studia Historica Gothoburgensia XIII. Stockholm 1971. (L j u n g m a r k 1971).

L o p r e a t o, J o s e p h, Italian Americans. Brattleboro, Vt., 1970. (L o p r e a t o 1970).

Mattson, H., Minnen af öfverste H. Mattson. Lund 1890. (Mattson 1890).

M y h r m a n, A n d e r s, Finlandssvenskar i Amerika. Skrifter utgivna av Svenska Litteratursällskapet i Finland Nr 453. Folklivsstudier IX. Helsingfors 1972. (M y h r m a n 1972).

N i i t e m a a, V i l h o, Australiansuomalainen Erakko-seura vv. 1902—1904. Turun Historiallisen Yhdistyksen Julkaisuja XXV. Vammala 1971 (N i i t e m a a 1971).
— Mitä siirtolaiskirjeet voivat historiantutkimukselle antaa. Turun Sanomat 22. 5. 1966. (N i i t e m a a 1966).

N i l s s o n, F r e d, Emigrationen från Stockholm till Nordamerika 1880—1893. En studie i urban utvandring. Monografier utgivna av Stockholms Kommunalförvaltning 31. Stockholm 1970. (N i l s s o n 1970).

N o r m a n, H a n s, Amerika eller Örebro? En undersökning av utvandringens lokala variationer från Örebro län. Utvandring. Den svenska emigrationen till Amerika i historiskt perspektiv. En antologi redigerad av Ann-Sofie Kälvemark. Malmö 1973. (N o r m a n 1973).

Nylander, Lydia, Punapuiden varjossa. Kertomus amerikansuomalaisen siirtolaisperheen elämästä. Helsinki 1950. (Nylander 1950).

N ä s e, J o h a n n e s, Finlandssvenskarna i Amerika. Bidrag till utredning av emigrationsfrågan. Arkiv för Svenska Österbotten. Band I, häfte 3—4. Vasa 1922. (N ä s e 1922).

O d é n, B i r g i t t a, Emigrationen från Norden till Nordamerika under 1800-talet. Aktuella forskningsuppgifter. Historisk Tidskrift 1963. (O d é n 1963).

P r p i c, G e o r g e J., The Croatian Immigrants in America. New York 1971. (P r p i c 1971).

R a s i l a, V i l j o, Suomen torpparikysymys vuoteen 1909. Yhteiskuntahistoriallinen tutkimus. Kajaani 1961. (R a s i l a 1961).

R o b e r t s, P e t e r, The New Immigration. A Study of the Industrial and Social Life of Southeastern Europeans in America. Reprint 1970. New York 1970. (R o b e r t s 1912).

R o n d a h l, B j ö r n, Emigration, folkomflyttning och säsongarbete i ett sågverksdistrikt i södra Hälsingland 1865—1910. Söderala kommun med särskild hänsyn till Ljusne industrisamhälle. Studia Historica Upsaliensia XL. Uppsala 1972. (R o n d a h l 1972).

R o s e n b e r g, A n t t i, Muuttoliike Uudenmaan läänissä esi-industrialistisen kauden lopulla (1821—1880). Historiallisia Tutkimuksia LXX. Lahti 1966. (R o s e n b e r g 1966).

S e m m i n g s e n, I n g r i d, Veien mot vest. Annen del. Utvandringen fra Norge 1865—1915. Oslo 1950. (S e m m i n g s e n 1950).

S h e p p e r s o n, W i l b u r S., Restless Strangers. Nevada's Immigrants and their Interpreters. Reno, Nevada, 1970. (S h e p p e r s o n 1970).

S i l f v e r s t e n, C a r l J., Finlandssvenskarna i Amerika. Deras materiella och andliga strävanden. Duluth, Minn., 1931. (S i l f v e r s t e n 1931).

S u l k a n e n, E l i s, Amerikan suomalaisen työväenliikkeen historia. Fitchburg, Mass., 1951. (S u l k a n e n 1951).

Suomen Höyrylaiva Osakeyhtiö 1883—1933. Helsinki 1933. (*Suomen Höyrylaiva Osakeyhtiö 1833—1933*).

Suomen Tilastollinen Vuosikirja 1885, 1895, 1905, 1910, 1914, 1915. (STV).

Suomen Virallinen Tilasto VI. Väkiluvun-tilastoa 5. Helsinki 1880. (SVT).

Suomen Virallinen Tilasto XXVIII. Siirtolaisuustilasto 1—11. Helsinki 1905—1915. (SVT).

S v a l e s t u e n, A n d r e s A., Nordisk emigrasjon. En komparativ oversikt. Emigrationen fra Norden indtil I. Verdenskrig. Rapporter til det Nordiske historikermøde i København 1971, 9—12 august. København 1971. (S v a l e s t u e n 1971).

Syrjälä, F. J., Historia-aiheita Amerikan suomalaisesta työväenliikkeestä. Fitchburg, Mass., Sa. (Syrjälä 1925).

Tarkkanen, Matti, Siirtolaisuudesta. Helsinki 1896. (Tarkkanen 1896).

Tedebrand, Lars-Göran, Västernorrland och Nordamerika 1875—1913. Utvandring och återinvandring. Studia Historica Upsaliensia XLII. Uppsala 1972. (Tedebrand 1972).

Teijula, Ilmari, Suomen siirtolaisuusolot. Katsaus siirtolaisuustiedustelun tuloksiin. Sosialinen Aikakauskirja 12/1921. Helsinki 1921. (Teijula 1921).

Thomas, Brinley, Migration and Economic Growth. A Study of Great Britain and the Atlantic Economy. Cambridge 1954. (Brinley 1954).

Thomas, Dorothy S., Social and Economic Aspects of Swedish Population Movements 1750—1933. New York 1941. (Thomas 1941).

Toivonen, Anna-Leena, Etelä-Pohjanmaan valtamerentakainen siirtolaisuus 1867—1930. Historiallisia tutkimuksia LXVI. Seinäjoki 1963. (Toivonen 1963).

Tokoi, Oskari, Maanpakolaisen muistelmia. Isänsä muistiinpanojen perusteella kirjoittanut Irene Tokoi. Lahti 1947. (Tokoi 1947).

Tolonen, F., Muutamia historiatietoja Amerikan suomalaisista sanomalehdistä. Silmäys nykyisen suomalaisen siirtolaisuuden alkuun. Amerikan Suometar 1899—1919. Muistojulkaisu. Hancock, Mich., 1919. (Tolonen 1919).

Ward, David, Cities and Immigrants. A Geography of Change in Nineteenth-century America. Second Printing. New York 1972. (Ward 1971).

Wargelin, John, The Americanization of the Finns. Hancock, Mich., 1924. (Wargelin 1924).

Waris, Heikki, Työläisyhteiskunnan syntyminen Helsingin Pitkänsillan pohjoispuolella I. Historiallisia tutkimuksia XVI, 1. Helsinki 1932. (Waris 1932).

Wasastjerna, Hans R., Minnesotan Suomalaisten Historia. Superior, Wisc., 1957. (Wasastjerna 1957).

Wittke, Carl, We Who Built America. The Saga of the Immigrant. Revised edition. Second Printing. Cleveland, Ohio, 1967. (Wittke 1967).

Åkerman, Sune, Migrationen — ett tvärvetenskapligt forskningsområde. Utvandring. Den svenska emigrationen till Amerika i historiskt perspektiv. En antologi redigerad av Ann-Sofie Kälvemark. Malmö 1973. (Åkerman 1973).

2. Newspapers and periodicals

Aamulehti (Finland) 1890
Amerikan Suomalainen (USA) 1894
Amerikan Suomalainen Lehti (USA) 1880—93
Amerikan Suometar (New York Mills, Minn., USA) 1889
Amerikan Suometar (Hancock, Mich., USA) 1901—03
Amerikan Uutiset (USA) 1894
Folkvännen (Finland) 1890
Hangö (Finland) 1890—1904
Hufvudstadsbladet (Finland) 1869, 1889—90, 1892
Litteraturblad för allmän medborgerlig bildning (Finland) 1853
Mikkelin Sanomat (Finland) 1888
New Yorkin Lehti (USA) 1891—93
Nya Pressen (Finland) 1892
Oulun Wiikko-Sanomia (Finland) 1876
Päivälehti (Finland) 1891—92

Rauman Lehti (Finland) 1890
Sankarin Maine (USA) 1879—80
Sanomia Turusta (Finland) 1874, 1890
Satakunta (Finland) 1882—1904
Siirtolainen (USA) 1894—96, 1900—01
Swen Tuuwa (USA) 1878—79
Tietokäsikirja Amerikan Suomalaisille (USA) 1912
Työmies (Ishpeming, Mich., USA) 1889—1893
Uusi Kotimaa (USA) 1887
Uusi Suometar (Finland) 1874, 1893, 1899
Waasa (Finland) 1904
Waasan Lehti (Finland) 1887—93
Wasabladet (Finland) 1888—99
Wasa Tidning (Finland) 1888—97
Vestra Nyland (Finland) 1889—90
Yhdyswaltain Sanomat (USA) 1885, 1887, 1889